City
Schools

LESSONS FROM NEW YORK

City
Schools

EDITED BY
DIANE RAVITCH AND
JOSEPH P. VITERITTI

THE JOHNS HOPKINS UNIVERSITY PRESS   BALTIMORE AND LONDON

KH

© 2000 The Johns Hopkins University Press
All rights reserved. Published 2000
Printed in the United States of America on acid-free paper
9 8 7 6 5 4 3 2 1

The Johns Hopkins University Press
2715 North Charles Street
Baltimore, Maryland 21218-4363
www.press.jhu.edu

Library of Congress Cataloging-in-Publication Data will be found
at the end of this book.
A catalog record for this book is available from the British Library.

ISBN 0-8018-6341-4
ISBN 0-8018-6342-2 (pbk.)

10/19/06

Contents

Contributors

Diane Ravitch (Editor) is a research professor in the School of Education at New York University. She also holds the Brown Chair in Education Policy at the Brookings Institution. She served as assistant secretary in the U.S. Department of Education between 1991 and 1993. She was chair of the Chancellor's Commission on Educational Standards and Accountability in New York. Her publications include *The Great School Wars: New York City, 1805–1973*, *The Troubled Crusade: American Education, 1945–1980*, and *Left Back: A Century of Failed School Reforms* (forthcoming).

Joseph P. Viteritti (Editor) is a research professor of public administration at New York University's Robert F. Wagner School of Public Service. He has served as special assistant to the chancellor of the New York City public school system, and as a senior advisor to the school superintendents in San Francisco and Boston. His publications include *Choosing Equality: School Choice, the Constitution, and Civil Society* and *Across the River: Politics and Education in the City*.

Professors Ravitch and Viteritti edited *New Schools for a New Century: The Redesign of Urban Education* (1997).

Dale Ballou is a professor in the department of economics at the University of Massachusetts, Amherst, and co-author of *Teacher Pay and Teacher Quality*. He writes frequently on labor issues in education.

Stephan F. Brumberg is a professor of education at Brooklyn College, where he is director of the Advanced Certificate Program in Educational Administration and Supervision. He has served as a senior assistant to the chancellor of schools in New York, and was executive director of the Chancellor's Commission on Educational Standards and Accountability.

Gail Foster is founder and president of the Toussaint Institute, where she serves as editor of the Directory of Historically Black Independent Schools. She is the co-author of *High Schools with Character*.

Michael Heise is a professor of law at Case Western University School of Law. He has previously served as deputy chief of staff and senior legal advisor to the U.S. secretary of education, and has written widely on school finance.

Clara Hemphill is the author of *The Parents' Guide to New York City's Best Public Elementary Schools* and *The Best Public Middle Schools in New York City*. She wrote this chapter while she was a senior research fellow at the Public Education Association.

Paul T. Hill is a research professor of public affairs and director of the Center on Reinventing Education at the University of Washington. He is co-author of *Reinventing Public Education* and *High Schools with Character*. **Mary Beth Celio** is a research assistant at the Center on Reinventing Education at the University of Washington.

Pearl Rock Kane is an associate professor of organization and leadership at Teachers College, Columbia University, where she is director of the Klingenstein Center for Independent School Education. She recently conducted a study of charter schools in New Jersey.

Frank J. Macchiarola is president of Saint Francis College in Brooklyn. From 1978 through 1983 he served as chancellor of schools in New York City. He has previously served as dean of the Benjamin Cardozo School of Law at Yeshiva University, professor in the School of Business at Columbia University, and president of the Academy of Political Science.

Thomas Nechyba is an associate professor of economics at Duke University. He is a faculty research fellow at the National Bureau of Economic Research in Cambridge, Massachusetts, and presently serves as the associate editor of the *Journal of Public Economic Theory*.

Paul E. Peterson is Henry Lee Shattuck Professor of Government at Harvard University, where he is director of the Program on Education Policy and Governance. He has evaluated school choice programs in

Milwaukee, Cleveland, Denver, Washington, D.C., and San Antonio. His most recent books are *Earning and Learning: Why Schools Matter* and *Learning from School Choice.* **William G. Howell** is a program associate at Harvard's Program on Education Policy and Governance.

Christine H. Rossell is a professor of political science at Boston University. Her most recent books are *Bilingual Reform in Massachusetts* and *The Carrot and the Stick for School Desegregation.*

Marvin Schick is a consultant for the Avi Chai Foundation, and has twenty-five years of voluntary service as president of the Rabbi Jacob Joseph School, the oldest Jewish parochial school in the country. He writes frequently on Jewish affairs.

Lee Stuart is the lead organizer of South Bronx Churches. She was instrumental in founding the Bronx Leadership Academy High School and remains active in education. An ecologist by training and an organizer by vocation, she was one of the co-founders of SHARE, a nationwide community building and food assistance program that she helped to create while pursuing doctoral and postdoctoral studies in California.

Paul Teske is an associate professor of political science at the State University of New York at Stony Brook. **Mark Schneider** is a professor of political science at the same institution. **Christine Roch** is an assistant professor in the department of public administration and urban studies at Georgia State University. **Melissa Marschall** is assistant professor in the department of government at the University of South Carolina. Schneider, Teske, and Marschall are the co-authors of *Choosing Schools: Consumer Choice and the Quality of Schools.*

Emanuel Tobier is a professor emeritus of economics and planning in the Robert F. Wagner Graduate School of Public Service at New York University, where he served as chair of the program in urban planning. He was formerly chief economist for the Regional Plan Association of New York and has written extensively on education and demography in the New York metropolitan region.

Joanna P. Williams is a professor of psychology and education at Teachers College, Columbia University. She is the author of more than one hundred scholarly articles. She is a fellow of the American Psychological Association and the National Conference on Research in English, and was recently a member of the National Reading Panel.

Acknowledgments

This volume was prepared under the auspices of the Program on Education and Civil Society at New York University, a collaboration undertaken by the Robert F. Wagner Graduate School of Public Service and the School of Education. General funding for the program is provided by the John M.Olin Foundatin; specific support for this project was obtained from the Achelis and Bodman Foundations. Opinions expressed in each of the chapters are solely attributable to their authors.

Among the many individuals who helped bring this project to fruition, we would especially like to acknowledge Kevin Kosar, Joyce Kong, and Patrick Jameson. Jacqueline Wehmueller, our editor at Johns Hopkins University Press, was a source of ideas and support from beginning to end. Maria Blanchard did an excellent job as copy editor, and Carol Zimmerman helped us through the final stages of production. Our thanks to all.

City
Schools

Introduction

DIANE RAVITCH AND JOSEPH P. VITERITTI

Throughout its history New York City has served as a major port of entry for those who have come to America in search of a better life. They came to escape poverty and political oppression, seeking to enjoy the full benefits of living in a free and prosperous society. Many also came with the hope of acquiring a decent education for themselves or their children. Gaining access to a good education has always been an essential part of the American dream. For the better half of the twentieth century New York City public schools have helped fulfill that dream by educating the many children who showed up at their doors, thus offering to newcomers the real threshold to a new life. Until the mid-1960s, the city boasted one of the most highly regarded public school systems in the nation. Its instructional materials and curriculum guides were used widely by school districts around the country. Many of the system's graduates, the sons and daughters of poor immigrant families, went on to assume leading roles in the professions, the arts, business, science, communications, and technology—all contributing to New York's position as a world-class city.

Today, New York City's population includes more than 1.3 million school-age children. About 80 percent of them attend the city's 1,100 public schools. Nearly 270,000 children are enrolled in approximately 900 private or parochial schools. Because New York is so very large, enrollments fluctuate, as do the number of schools in the public and private sectors. In the early part of the twentieth century, the city's schools helped to prepare immigrant children for American life, readying most for jobs in commerce and industry and a favored few for higher education. Today, students' expectations are far higher than they were in the early twentieth century and, indeed, the economy requires higher levels of education; college has become a necessity for most students, not just for the talented elite. A high school diploma has become a minimal requirement for today's youth, and a good education—that is, a firm command of literacy, numeracy, technological skills, and the ability to work on one's own and with others—is a necessity both for entry to postsecondary education and for the modern workplace.

While the wave of immigrants that reached New York's shores during the early part of the twentieth century came from southern and eastern Europe, today's new arrivals are more likely to have begun their journey in Asia, the Caribbean, or Latin America. Unlike the bulk of European immigrants, who were uneducated, many of those who now come from Asia and the Caribbean have had the benefit of a respectable education, bringing with them even more demanding expectations for the school system than did their European predecessors.

Is the city's school system up to the task of delivering high-quality universal education? Designed in the industrial age as a hierarchical, centralized bureaucracy, the system has struggled, with mixed results, to prepare young people for the heightened demands of the new economy. This struggle becomes even more challenging, and the outcome even more doubtful, when this large impersonal bureaucratic system of education is expected to meet the extraordinary needs of the many thousands of children who live in extreme poverty, often with a single parent, and limited social or educational resources.

Why study New York City? Are its problems so unusual, so specific to a giant bureaucratic system that it has no relevance to other city school systems? The assumption of the contributors to this volume is that New York City is, if anything, "super-typical" of American urban education. It is unique only because of its size, but in every other respect the problems of New York City are the problems of urban education in America writ large. And because they are writ large, they contain lessons for other cities. Like other cities, New York has seen large demographic changes in the past generation; its schools enroll huge numbers of children with very poor levels of education achievement; it has a serious teacher shortage, made even worse by a peculiar combination of inaction and overregulation by its state education department; it has well-intentioned programs in bilingual and special education that benefit adults employed in them more than the children enrolled in them. And like other urban school systems, New York is in search of strategies to solve these problems and others as well. Like other cities, New York is beginning to experiment with charter schools and other forms of educational choice. Like other cities, New York has seen a steady stream of "reforms" that change nothing, that are long on rhetoric and regulation, but short on results for children. Ultimately, whether the city under consideration is New York, Washington, D.C., Detroit, Los Angeles, or

Chicago, the only educational change that matters is student performance, that is, whether children are learning and getting a better education.

Assessing Performance

Between 1976 and 2000, the operating budget for the New York City school system grew from $2.549 billion ($7.541 billion in constant dollars) to $10.075 billion. During this same period, enrollments declined from 1,099,004 to 1,047,187. Controlling for both inflation and enrollment, per-pupil spending rose from $6,862 to $9,621, or 40 percent. A large part of the spending growth is attributable to burgeoning special education enrollments that began in the early 1980s.[1] Significant losses that occurred during the fiscal crisis of the 1970s have been recouped. While substantial reductions were recorded in per-pupil spending for 1992 and 1996, the 6.5 percent increase in 1998 was the largest single-year change recorded since 1980. Approximately eighty cents on every dollar spent on public education in New York City actually finds its way to a school in some form or another; less than fifty cents on every dollar is spent on direct instructional services,[2] a figure that is not unusual in American education. According to reports from the Organization for Economic Cooperation and Development, a majority of education staff in the United States are noninstructional personnel, which is not the case in the leading nations of Europe and Asia.[3]

As in other cities, there is a wide range of achievement among school districts that is closely correlated with race and class. At one extreme are District 26 in Queens, and District 2 in Manhattan, where in 1998 the percentage of students reading at grade level on the standardized city tests were 80.2 percent and 72.5 percent respectively. At the other extreme are District 9 in the southeast Bronx and District 5 in Harlem, where only a third of the children read at grade level.[4] There are many outstanding schools in the New York City public school system. And there are many that have been identified by the state education department as chronically low-performing. Without exception, the latter are found in low-income communities where the children are disproportionately African American and Hispanic.

Since 1989, the state education department has issued a list of low-performing public schools that are supposedly targeted for corrective intervention and run the risk of being closed if significant improvements are not made. During the first eight years of monitoring (1989–97), 125 of the 139 schools on the state's SURR list (Schools under Registration Review) were located in New York City. Half of the other fourteen schools were schools in urban areas such as Buffalo, Rochester, and Utica.[5] Over the years, some schools got promoted off the list, and some others got added, and the criteria for getting on the list were redefined. As of January 2000,

TABLE I.1 Education Budget and K–12 Enrollment, 1976–2000

Year	Enrollment	Current $ (billions)	Constant 1999 $ (billions)	Spending per Student	% Change
1976	1,099,004	2.549	7.541	6,862	—
1977	1,077,097	2.791	7.856	7,293	6.3
1978	1,036,243	2.601	6.932	6,690	−8.3
1979	998,969	2.257	5.534	5,539	−17.2
1980	963,048	2.583	5.685	5,903	6.6
1981	943,805	2.717	5.449	5,774	−2.2
1982	942,215	2.969	6.667	6,132	6.2
1983	918,384	3.231	5.850	6,370	3.9
1984	924,842	3.625	6.250	6,758	6.1
1985	931,145	4.005	6.658	7,150	5.8
1986	935,993	4.891	7.065	7,549	5.6
1987	932,341	4.802	7.354	7,887	4.5
1988	933,206	5.258	7.681	8,231	4.4
1989	925,246	5.749	7.954	8,597	4.5
1990	918,011	6.365	8.304	9,046	5.2
1991	931,910	6.694	8.354	8,964	−0.9
1992	950,452	6.626	7.982	8,398	−6.3
1993	971,690	7.213	8.436	8,682	3.4
1994	996,262	7.561	8.636	8,669	−0.2
1995	1,009,593	7.863	8.760	8,677	0.1
1996	1,035,850	7.835	8.483	8,189	−5.6
1997	1,049,873	8.085	8.554	8,147	−0.5
1998	1,057,608	8.812	9.178	8,678	6.5
1999	1,056,697	9.478	9.665	9,147	5.4
2000	1,047,187	10.075	10.075	9,621	5.2

Source: Emanuel Tobier, based on data from City of New York, Comprehensive Annual Financial Report of the Comptroller, year 2000 data based on estimates prepared by Citizens Budget Commission, enrollment data from 1976 to 1999 from New York State Department of Education, year 2000 enrollment estimate prepared by Emanuel Tobier.

97 of the 105 schools on the state SURR list were located in New York City. A recent study found that SURR schools have a disproportionate number of teachers who are not fully licensed, who have less than five years of classroom experience, and who lack an advanced degree.[6] A similar staffing pattern is found at other low-performing schools that are not on the SURR list. It is one of the gravest inequities in American urban education that public schools serving the children with the greatest educational and social needs are likeliest to have the least experienced teachers and the greatest turnover of staff.

A report published by *Education Week* in 1998 indicated that New York has the fourth highest dropout rate among the ten largest urban school districts in the nation.[7] The Board of Education has reported that only 45 percent of its youngsters graduate from high school in four years.[8] The disparities among racial groups are large. Among whites and Asians the four-year graduation rates are 70 percent and 66 percent respectively; for blacks and Hispanics, the averages are 42 percent and 38 percent. Many years ago, young men and women could find jobs adequate to support a family even if they did not have a high school diploma. Such jobs are increasingly scarce in the modern economy. Today, failing to graduate high school places one at the margins of the economic and social life of the city, with little prospect for finding a desirable job, making a good wage, or advancing into a career.

Employers are not happy with the skills, knowledge, and work habits of the school system's graduates. In a survey of 450 employers conducted in 1998 for the New York City Partnership and Chamber of Commerce, only 7 percent of those polled said they believed that students coming from the city public schools have the skills to succeed in the world of work. Eighty-six percent expressed the belief that a high school diploma is no guarantee that the typical city student has mastered the basics, and some 95 percent said that the school system is in need of fundamental change.[9]

Demography, we suggest, is not necessarily destiny. One can identify schools, public and private, in which children have compiled impressive records of educational achievement in the very neighborhoods in which other schools are on the state's SURR list. The responsibility of policy makers and research analysts goes beyond describing the causes of educational failure to identifying the sources of educational success for the full range of children. The search for answers requires close study of the successful schools in unpromising circumstances, but also attention to pedagogical strategies and issues of governance, social policy, and the politics of urban education.

Enabling Schools to Succeed

In the past, New York State and New York City were distinguished for their high educational standards. The state offered rigorous Regents examinations at the end of high school, and students who passed their Regents exams earned a sense of high accomplishment as well as recognition by their school. What gave the Regents examinations their unusual influence was that they were a "curriculum based" examination: the state published its curriculum, and the exams tested whether students had learned it well. The exams functioned as an external audit, or what Cornell economist John H. Bishop has called "a curriculum-based external exit examination."[10]

Bishop has argued that such exams help to produce high achievement because students know what they are expected to learn and teachers know what to teach and how to prepare students for the exams. In the mid-1990s, the New York State Board of Regents decided that all students should be required to pass five Regents examinations in order to graduate from high school. The first such exam in English language arts was administered to high school juniors in 1999, and exams in American history, mathematics, science, and global history will be phased in by 2003.

The Regents intend that all students should be well-educated when they finish school, and this is certainly commendable. To reach this goal, however, two things must happen: First, the state standards that describe what is to be taught and learned must be clarified; and second, dramatic steps must be taken to improve instruction. If the latter does not happen, large numbers of students will not pass the exams or there will be political pressure to lower their rigor. In New York City, only 22 percent of high school graduates obtained a Regents diploma in 1997 (compared to 51 percent in the rest of the state); in some New York City high schools, not more than 5 percent of graduates earned a Regents diploma.[11]

For standards to function well they must offer a clear signal to students, teachers, and parents about what will be tested. Educators have an inordinate fear of "teaching to the test," but the best tests gauge whether students learned what they were taught. If standards are not specific and clear, teachers do not know how to help students get ready for the exams. If the exams do not test what was taught in the classrooms, they are likely to be gauges of students' social class background, or whether their parents were educated and had books in the home. "If tests do not have real consequences, students do not know (as Albert Shanker used to say) whether 'it counts.'" An examination system is a valuable way of providing students incentives to study and work hard in school, but only if they are given a fair opportunity to learn what will be assessed.

At present in New York City (as in other school districts), there is much confusion about standards and curricula. Some schools oppose any external standards, believing that teachers should be on their own; some follow guidelines that were issued many years ago; others align their curriculum with one or another national program. The Board of Education, which is committed to centralized control of almost all school functions, such as maintenance, supplies, personnel, and lunches, has essentially left districts, schools, and teachers free to devise their own standards and curriculums. This causes serious problems for children who move from one school to another, and it causes equally serious problems for teachers who are unsure about what is expected of them. Under these circumstances, the tests given by state and city authorities become the de facto standards, though there are no clear documents that describe what will be tested and what students are expected to know.

Regulation Instead of Innovation

At a time when education reform across the nation has been characterized by a devolution of decision making away from central headquarters to school-based professionals,[12] the city and state of New York continue to rely on regulation as the fulcrum of education reform. Perhaps the largest exception to this statement is the state's new achievement standards, which seek to promote higher achievement by establishing stakes and accountability. To help students reach the new, higher standards, the state must ensure that students have equal opportunity to learn the material that will be tested. Yet in New York City, there is a severe shortage of qualified teaching personnel, especially in mathematics and science.[13] The Board of Regents responded to this critical problem by adopting regulations that impose new certification requirements on individuals who want to enter the teaching profession and requiring teachers to take more courses in pedagogy.[14] These regulations have the effect of making it more difficult to become a teacher, thus shrinking the pool of prospective teachers, but they do not ensure that teachers will be better educated and more qualified for teaching.

The Regents changed teacher certification to reflect children's developmental levels (e.g., "early childhood educator," "childhood educator," "adolescence educator") instead of subject matter expertise, at the same time that they are requiring all students to pass subject-matter examinations to graduate from high school. In the absence of any research to demonstrate the validity of this change, and in the light of a pressing need for teachers who have mastered the teaching of subject-matter, this is a strange policy indeed. Teachers will continue to take examinations that have little relation to the subject matter that they teach, and will be required to complete teacher education programs that bear little or no relation to substantive expertise in academic subjects like history, math, or science.

The Board of Regents has also set new accreditation requirements for schools of education. If 80 percent of a college's graduates do not pass an examination for a teacher's license, then it could lose its accreditation after three years. Two dozen of the state's 113 teacher education programs were immediately placed on the danger list.[15] But even in programs that pass muster, there is nothing to ensure that teachers will be properly trained to provide effective reading instruction, or better prepared to work with at-risk students so that they do not end up in special education; or to help Hispanic children succeed in the regular English-language curriculum (as well as full participation in society). In the meantime, the major factors that contribute to the severe teacher crisis continue to prevail: poor working conditions, noncompetitive salaries, and a heavy-handed, bureaucratic management style that discourages those with a commitment and a zeal for teaching.

The heavy hand of regulation also has imposed unnecessary burdens on principals. It is virtually impossible to have an effective school without a strong academic leader in the principal's office. New York City has a principal crisis. Until a new contract was agreed upon in late 1999, the city paid principals substantially less than their peers in the neighboring suburbs, less even than senior teachers in their own schools. In the main, however, the principal crisis results from the constant erosion of their authority to run their schools and the system's refusal to allow principals to control either their staffs or their budgets. In effect, they are to be held accountable but not given the authority that goes with accountability. Because of the Board of Education's hostile treatment of its principals, there was a substantial exodus of experienced school leaders during the late 1990s—a loss that will be harmful for many years to come.

In the city school system there has been much discussion of school-based management and school-based decision making, but the reality is that the system is more centralized now than it has been in at least three decades. The New York State legislature passed a governance law in 1996 that amended the city's decentralization statute. The 1969 law created thirty-two community districts, some of which were notoriously corrupt. The new law granted the chancellor authority to approve and remove district superintendents appointed by local school boards, and to transfer principals from their schools for "persistent educational failure." An advocacy group in the Bronx, the Industrial Areas Foundation, has contested that this power has been used too sparingly for the removal of principals with poor records of performance.[16]

The net effect of the 1996 law was to recentralize power in the hands of the chancellor, while leaving in place the community school boards, stripped of power but nonetheless a costly and cumbersome administrative structure. Because of this legislation, the school system's chancellor holds a remarkable degree of power over the city's 1,100 schools and the system's massive central machinery. His singular authority to fire personnel at will is unprecedented in the history of the city. Centralizing this much control in the hands of a single public official is unlikely to be the last word on governance in public education. No private-sector organization, no matter how large, functions without significant delegation of authority to operating units. In the case of public education, this means individual schools, not local school boards. Those who are on the front lines of education, and most especially school leaders, must have both authority and responsibility over the organizations that they manage.

Charter Schools

In an effort to strengthen leadership and managerial autonomy at the school level in exchange for accountability, thirty-six states and the District of Columbia adopted charter school laws in the 1990s. Charter schools are public schools that are independent of any local school district and that agree to meet performance standards. They accept accountability for student performance in exchange for autonomy from regulation. Under most state laws, charter schools can come about in one of two ways. Regular public schools can convert to charter status if the professionals and parents at an existing public school vote to opt out of the administrative structure of the local school district or new schools are created when a group of parents and / or educators, a nonprofit group, or a for-profit group submits a proposal to a public authority to acquire a charter. The chartering authority might be a state education department, a public university, a local school board, or a special state agency set up for the purpose of reviewing proposals and granting charters—all depending upon the provisions of the legislation in a particular jurisdiction.

A charter entitles a school to a portion of the per-pupil state and local funding, and releases the school from certain regulatory restrictions that govern regular public schools. In return for autonomy and funding, the charter establishes specific performance standards and financial reporting requirements. If the school fails to meet these expectations, it may lose its charter and be closed. A charter school would also close if students did not want to go there. Strong charter school laws tend to allow for the widest range of managerial autonomy, full per-capita funding, and the largest number of schools. States that limit chartering authority to local school boards tend to have fewer charter schools, since most local school boards do not welcome competition. Arizona, with the most far-reaching statute in the nation, has more than 270 charter schools; and the competition they stimulate has already begun to motivate public school districts throughout the state to initiate their own innovations.[17]

National surveys of charter schools have found high levels of satisfaction among parents, students, and teachers associated with them.[18] Charter schools have been especially well received by poor and minority families eager to find alternatives to the failing institutions that are often available in their communities. These same surveys indicate, however, that it is not unusual for charter schools to be constrained by inadequate capital funding or political opposition from local school district authorities and teachers' unions.[19]

New York State adopted charter school legislation in December 1998. The New York law allows one hundred new charter schools to be created: fifty authorized by the state Board of Regents and fifty by the trustees of the state university. An unlimited number of conversions are allowed, but public schools in New York City cannot be converted without the approval of the chancellor, a requirement which serves as an effective cap on the number of conversions that are realized. The law sets the per-pupil allocation of funds for charter schools at $6,023, while the average per-pupil expenditure for regular schools exceeds $8,700. Unless the financial provisions are changed in the future, the city is unlikely to have many new charter schools.

One hundred or so new charter schools are unlikely to create a great deal of competitive pressure for the remaining six thousand public schools throughout the state, especially if the charters do not enjoy financial parity with other public schools. Typically, most new charter schools around the country are small by design, averaging about two hundred students. By guaranteeing a limited supply of new institutions, the law is more likely to stimulate competition among parents than schools, especially in the city, where there is a shortage of high-quality institutions with space to accommodate students in search of meaningful alternatives.

As charter laws go, New York's statute creates a good measure of managerial autonomy at the school level. It releases principals and other school personnel from a host of regulatory burdens, and allows them discretion to utilize resources as they see fit. Schools with fewer than two hundred students are exempt from collective bargaining arrangements that govern the managerial prerogatives of principals.[20] Nonetheless, even with the passage of a relatively strong charter school law, nearly all of the 1,100 public schools in New York City will continue to operate under the same rules of governance as they always have.

Private and Parochial Schools

New York City has 270,000 students in some nine hundred nonpublic schools, as table I.2 indicates. The largest sector is that of the Catholic schools, followed by the Jewish day schools. In addition to the nondenominational independent schools, there are a variety of Christian schools as well as a small number of Islamic schools. Parents send their children to these institutions for a variety of reasons. Some do so because they want their children educated in a setting that reflects their own religious upbringing. Others are attracted by a particular philosophical approach or orientation that they believe meets the specific needs of their children. Thus there are Montessori schools and Walldorf schools, and a growing number of black independent schools that are not affiliated with faith-based communities.

A large number of parents seek out nonpublic schools to provide their children with a better education. This was the motivation for many parents who participated in the city's first lottery for private scholarships. When the School Choice Scholarship Foundation (SCSF) was established by philanthropists in 1997 to provide private scholarships for poor children to attend nonpublic schools, more than 26,000 families applied to fill 1,300 seats.

TABLE I.2   New York City Nonpublic School Enrollments

Type	Number of Students	As % of NYC Enrollment
Catholic	142,829	10.69
Jewish		
Nonaffiliated	6,983	0.52
Conservative	716	.05
Orthodox	64,636	4.84
Lutheran	4,577	0.34
Seventh Day Adventists	2,111	0.16
Episcopal	3,462	0.26
Quakers	1,088	0.08
Islamic	1,304	0.16
Greek Orthodox	2,201	0.16
Russian Orthodox	95	0.01
Presbyterian	50	0.00
Christian Fundamentalists	4,199	0.31
Nondenominational	33,020	2.47
Total	267,271	20.05

Source: This data was acquired from the New York State Education Department, Division of Nonpublic Schools.

In 1999, after the Children's Scholarship fund set up by Ted Forstmann and John Walton announced a similar program for low-income families, one-third of those eligible applied for an opportunity to attend private or parochial schools. A large number of poor children who leave public education end up in Catholic schools. Parochial schools have always played an important role in educating the urban poor, and over the last several decades, an increasing number of their students have not been Catholic. Research from New York, as well as a variety of scholarship programs in other cities, indicates that some poor parents are attracted by the religious aspect of the curriculum, but they are motivated even more by the high academic standards and sense of physical security that many of these schools offer.[21] Evidence from various public and private experiments implemented thus far suggests that poor parents are capable of being intelligent shoppers when they have the opportunity to choose the schools their children attend.[22] They want the same things for their children as the middle class wants for theirs: safe and sound learning environments that place a high value on the education and well-being of students.

The overwhelming majority of children in New York attend the regular public schools. In order to provide an education of value for every child who lives in the city, it is necessary to restructure public education, to close the salary gaps that favor suburban school districts, to allow good leadership to flourish in the schools, to recruit excellent teachers, to establish meaningful standards and accountability for students and teachers, to reduce the power of bureaucracy, and to adopt research-based, effective pedagogical practices. The status quo has many defenders, but it is not good for children.

In assembling this collection of essays, we have called upon a diverse group of contributors: political scientists, economists, a legal scholar, a psychologist, a journalist, activists, practitioners, and even a former chancellor. While not necessarily agreeing with one another, all are concerned about the future of urban schools and the children who depend on them.

The chapters are organized into five parts. The first part includes chapters by Emanuel Tobier and Clara Hemphill. Tobier, an economist by training, draws also on his considerable expertise as a demographer to trace the changing profile of the school-age population over the past three decades, and evaluates how well the school system has prepared its clientele for the current job market in the metropolitan region. Hemphill, a journalist who has written two books on the best public schools in New York City, describes what distinguishes these institutions from others, and discusses the impediments they face in trying to remain effective.

Part two is about governance. Pearl Kane of Teachers College writes about the New Visions initiative, a highly acclaimed coalition of schools that have often been called "charterlike schools," and she explains how the operation of these institutions might change if they were permitted to convert to charter status. Labor economist Dale Ballou provides us with an overview of how the union contract limits the discretion of school principals over their staffs and budgets. Lee Stuart, an environmental scientist turned activist, offers a firsthand account of the difficulties she and her associates at South Bronx Churches encountered in creating the Bronx Leadership Academy, an innovative public high school located in one of New York's most economically depressed neighborhoods.

Part three addresses pedagogical issues. Stephan Brumberg of Brooklyn College describes the severe teacher crisis in New York City and considers how the policies of the state Board of Regents will exacerbate the existing shortage of qualified personnel. Joanna Williams, an educational psychologist from Teachers College and a member of a congressionally appointed panel on reading, evaluates the school system's lack of a consistent approach to reading. Former chancellor Frank Macchiarola assesses how a federal court decision handed down in 1980 during his tenure continues to affect the organization, effectiveness, and cost of services provided for students classified as handicapped, as well as the persistent overidentification of students for special education. Christine Rossell of Boston University paints a detailed picture of the policies and procedures associated with programs for students who are limited English proficient (LEP).

Part four introduces us to three distinct sectors of nonpublic schools. Paul Hill and Mary Beth Celio of the University of Washington discuss the complex role of inner-city Catholic schools, religious institutions with a clientele that extends well beyond church membership. Marvin Schick, who has served for twenty-five years as president of the Rabbi Jacob Joseph School, tells us about the mission, operation, and diversity of Jewish day schools. Gail Foster of the Toussaint Institute describes the background and operation of black independent schools.

Part five deals with the issue of school choice. Paul Teske and Mark Schneider focus on how public school choice has enhanced the education of under-served populations in New York. Paul Peterson, who has evaluated school choice programs in six American cities, collaborates with his Harvard colleague William Howell to assess the School Choice Scholarship initiative in New York. The last chapter is a collaboration between economist Thomas Nechyba and law professor Michael Heise, integrating the issue of school finance reform with that of school choice.

That there are lessons for other cities in the New York City experience seems clear. One theme that emerges again and again from the varied contributors to this volume is that schools work best when they function as "a family." This happens when the adults in the school community know the students well as individuals. Large, anonymous schools are ineffective for the overwhelming majority of youngsters who are enrolled in urban schools. Children who come from socially stressed communities need to attend schools where they are known, where adults have a personal stake in their success, and where their presence, absence, and participation are carefully attended to by teachers and administrators. Small does not necessarily mean better, but large (i.e., two to five thousand students in a single school) often means anonymous and chaotic. In the best of the smaller schools (i.e., with an enrollment of not more than eight hundred youngsters), the emphasis is on instruction and helping children get the education they need to succeed in life. Like some other big cities, New York has to figure out what to do with the behemoths left over from an earlier age, the huge high schools that in all but a few cases are little more than warehouses for confused and alienated teenagers. Some have been divided into thematic minischools; others, like big public housing projects, are shunned by parents who have choices and should probably be closed.

Another theme is that urban children, like all children, need schools with excellent teachers and principals. The numbers of such people are currently inadequate to the needs of today's schools, and piling on regulations from the state capitol and the system's central bureaucracy is not likely to increase their numbers. Better salaries, better working conditions, and greater autonomy at the school level are critical for professional educators to act like professionals. We must find more effective ways to identify the most capable people and improve the quality of professional development available to them.

Another lesson is that the educational system of the city must draw upon all of the larger community's resources to create good schools for the city's children. The huge, creaking, inefficient bureaucratic structure created more than a century ago is straining to maintain its iron grip as education grows in new directions and struggles to break free of the stranglehold of one-size-fits-all, top-down management. With the beginning of the new century, urban education stands at a threshold, seeking better ways to educate the city's children, better means to prepare all for full participation in the life of the great city.

If there is much to be learned from studying New York, New York also has much to learn from the sweeping range of reforms invigorating urban school districts across the rest of the country. Chicago, once described as the "worst public school system in the nation," has figured out how to end social promotion in a way that raises educational standards while providing the curricular and remedial supports needed for students to meet those standards.[23] Houston has managed to out-source a large portion of its non-instructional functions—such as school lunches, building maintenance and personnel services—to private operators so that the resources and energy of the school system can be focused on the important business of instruction.[24] Los Angeles recently became a beneficiary of an ambitious charter school provision that allows California to create 100 new schools a year, adding to the 156 charter schools that existed prior to 1999. Milwaukee has overcome enormous political, legal, and bureaucratic obstacles to enact a choice program that offers alternatives to low-income families whose children are not adequately served by the public schools.[25]

What is most encouraging about the current national scene is the wide variety of innovative approaches being tried in different places. Astute educators realize that no single plan can replace the existing bureaucratic system. They understand that different children have different needs. New York is one of the last and perhaps the most conspicuous remnant of factory model schooling left from the previous century. As stubborn as it might be, New York is destined for change. It must change in order to maintain its position as a world class city; it will because the city can no longer tolerate a dysfunctional command structure that saps initiative from educators; it should because right thinking people cannot justify a system that educates only some of its children well.

We remain hopeful for the future. We envision an educational system that rejects conformity and mediocrity in favor of creativity, quality, flexibility, and accountability. We envision an educational system that is as diverse as the imaginations of its best professionals and responsive to the changing needs of its student population.[26] We envision a system in which the function of central authorities would be reconfigured from a regulatory role to one that is concerned with setting standards and monitoring for performance. Under this plan the chancellor's office would be expected to promulgate a core curriculum that helps students meet standards and tells teachers, as well as students, what is expected of them and what they will be held accountable for. Schools with a long record of academic failure would be forced to close. For too long the school system has imposed a rigid, uniform approach to education, and allowed far too many students to perform poorly. We must now reverse that, allowing innovative educators to unleash their creativity, while setting high levels of performance for all schools.

NOTES

1. See chapter 9.
2. Bruce S. Cooper, "Bringing Money to the Classroom: A Systemic Resource Allocation Model Applied to the New York City Public Schools," November 16, 1998, unpublished paper.
3. "Education at a Glance: OECD Indicators on Education" (Paris: Organization of Economic and Cultural Development, 1992).
4. Somini Sengupta, "For the 2d Year, Pupil Reading Scores Gain," *New York Times,* June 3, 1998.
5. Carol Ascher, Ken Ikeda, and Norm Fruchter, "Schools on Notice: New York State Education Department's 1996–1997 Schools under Registration Review Process," Institute for Education and Social Policy, New York University, January, 1998, p. iii.
6. Ibid., pp. 24–25.
7. "Quality Counts: The Urban Challenge—Public Education in 50 States," *Education Week,* January 8, 1998.
8. Graduation and high school performance data reported in the next three paragraphs are derived from "The State of City Schools, '98" (New York: Public Education Association, 1998), pp. 3–8.
9. "Some Gains, But No Guarantees: How New York City's Employers Rate the Public Schools," an Opinion Research Report from Public Agenda Conducted for the New York City Partnership and Chamber of Commerce, July 1998.
10. John H. Bishop, "Signalling, Incentives, and School Organization in France, Britain, and the United States," in *Improving America's Schools: The Role of Incentives,* ed. Eric A. Hanushek and Dale W. Jorgenson (Washington, D.C.: National Academy Press, 1996).
11. "State of the City Schools, '98" (New York: Public Education Association, 1998).
12. See Diane Ravitch and Joseph P. Viteritti, eds., *New Schools for a New Century: The Redesign of Urban Education* (New Haven: Yale University Press, 1997).

13. See chapter 6.

14. "Teaching to Higher Standards: New York's Commitment," Regent's Task Force on Teaching, University of the State of New York and the State Education Department.

15. See Randal C. Archibald, "Getting Tough on Teachers," *New York Times Education Life,* November 1, 1998; Jessica L. Sandham, "N.Y. to Require Accreditation for Ed. Schools," *Education Week,* August 5, 1998.

16. Industrial Areas Foundation, "Metro IAF Parents Charge Chancellor Crew with Delinquency in Educational Dead Zones," October 29, 1997.

17. See Robert Maranto et al., "Do Charter Schools Improve District Schools? Three Approaches to the Question," in *The Frontiers of Public Education: Lessons from Arizona Charter Schools,* ed. Robert Maranto et al. (Boulder, Colo.: Westview Press, forthcoming).

18. See RPP International, "A National Study of Charter Schools" (Washington, D.C.: Office of Educational Research and Improvement, U.S. Department of Education, 1998); RPP International and University of Minnesota, "A Study of Charter Schools: First Year Report" (Washington, D.C.: Office of Research and Improvement, U.S. Department of Education, 1997); Gregg Vanourek, Bruno V. Manno, Chester E. Finn, and Louann A. Bierlien, "Charter Schools as Seen by Those Who Know Them Best" (Washington, D.C.: Hudson Institute, 1997).

19. See also Tom Loveless and Claudia Jasin, "Starting from Scratch: Political and Organizational Challenges Facing Charter Schools," *Education Administration Quarterly* 34 (1998); Eric Rofes, "How Are School Districts Responding to Charter Laws and Charter Schools?" (Berkeley, Calif.: Policy Analysis for California Education, University of California, 1998).

20. See chapter 4.

21. Paul Peterson and Brian Hassel, eds., *Learning from School Choice* (Washington, D.C.: Brookings Institution Press, 1998), esp. chaps. 11–14.

22. See Mark Schneider et al., "Shopping for Schools: In the Land of the Blind, the One-Eyed Parent May Be Enough," *American Journal of Political Science* 42 (1998); Mark Schneider et al., "School Choice and Culture Wars in the Classroom: What Different Parents Seek from Education," *Social Science Quarterly* 79 (1998). In addition see chapters 13 and 14 in this volume.

23. See Paul G. Vallas, "Saving Public Schools," presentation at the Manhattan Institute, New York, December 9, 1998; and G. Alfred Hess, "Understanding Achievement (and Other) Changes under Chicago School Reform," *Educational Evaluation and Policy Analysis* 21 (1999).

24. See Donald R. McAdams, "Lessons from Houston," in Diane Ravitch, ed., *Brookings Papers on Education Policy* (Washington, D.C.: Brookings Institution Press, 1999).

25. Joseph P. Viteritti, *Choosing Equality: School Choice, the Constitution, and Civil Society* (Washington, D.C.: Brookings Institution Press, 1999), pp. 98–108.

26. For contrasting visions of the present and the future, see Diane Ravitch and Joseph P. Viteritti, "New York: The Obsolete Factory," in Ravitch and Viteritti, eds., *New Schools for a New Century* (New Haven: Yale University Press, 1997); and Diane Ravitch and Joseph P. Viteritti, "A New Vision for City Schools," *Public Interest* 122 (1996).

PART I

Education in the City

1 Schooling in New York City: The Socioeconomic Context

EMANUEL TOBIER

Long-run economic and social trends unfailingly shape and constrain the performance of and resources available to any locality's public school system. It would be difficult to sort out the reasons behind the visibly declining reputation of New York City's public schools over the past thirty years or so without an understanding of the changing circumstances and backgrounds of its students. Nor would it make much sense to prescribe for their future without some idea of who the prescription is for. New York City's public school "problem" is, of course, a widely shared one. Much the same can and has been said of inner-city schools throughout the United States. Indeed, since the early 1980s, performance anxiety has spread to mainstream suburban school districts as their students' test scores have been shown to compare unfavorably with those of their counterparts (and potential competitors) in other advanced industrial countries.

Since the 1960s, big city public school systems like New York's have been the target of criticism from virtually all points of the political and social compass. The severity and sweep of the criticism is in its way a backhanded tribute to the overwhelming importance attached to schools and schooling. It seems as if schools and school people have become, not altogether happily for them, the main if not the exclusive instruments for transmitting what are regarded as society's core values and for realizing the economic and human potential of young people. It is a tall order indeed for what many have come to regard as a highly dysfunctional enterprise.

Today's inner-city schools are faced with what may be a unique situation for which there is really no comparable historical precedent. True, a century ago America's big city schools found themselves responsible for educating large numbers of children who were "foreign" (most of them actually being the native-born children of immigrant parents). They, along with their parents, were viewed by many within the public education system of that era as possessing a set of values, abilities, and aspirations that were inferior to those held by "American" parents and their progeny. Nevertheless, it is widely believed that the public schools of that long ago time came through with flying colors despite the heavy criticism of their efforts by school reformers of the period.[1] Success may indeed have been theirs, a not unwarranted conclusion in view of the upward economic and social mobility experienced by the descendants of these earlier cohorts of newcomers to the city and country.

But times have changed. The heightened pressures on today's big city public schools arise from two principal transformations in the wider society in which they function. One reflects the changes that have taken place in the character of families and communities. The other flows from major transformations in the economy. Parents in particular and families in general cannot help but have a significant influence on the kinds of adults children become. If the existence of stable and supportive families and intimately involved grassroots civic associations serve to improve school outcomes, then these long-ago schools must have had an easier time of it. For intact families and a dense array of such organizations then dominated the urban landscape to an extent that is now scarcely possible to believe. For a variety of reasons, families, nuclear or extended, have become less dependable as sources of support, guidance, and discipline. So have a whole range of neighborhood-based intermediary institutions. The resulting vacuum has been filled, with unsettling consequences, by peers, the electronic mass media, and bureaucratic providers of social services.

This seems to be a universal phenomenon. But in the American context, lower income black and Latino children living in the nation's cities have seemingly been placed most at risk by these developments. As a result, and virtually by default, big city public school systems have been put into the position of being in loco parentis. But public schools as institutions, and most teachers as individuals, are all too aware of their limited abilities to overcome educational difficulties attributable to parental inadequacy or of those that arise from the atrophy of other socializing agencies.

But schools then had an easier time of it for another reason. Less was riding on what they could—or could not—impart to their students. The economic environment in which they operated simply did not place that high a value on extensive formal education. The economies of big cities, New York included, were then dominated by industrial activities, in which success, much less subsistence, was not advanced by school-taught skills beyond the basic ones of reading, writing, and simple arithmetic. As a result, the relationship between the worlds of work and school was then tenuous for the vast majority of people.[2]

This is a world we have lost. The economies of major cities, New York in the vanguard, have undergone a tremendous transformation within the relatively recent past. As a result, their "natural" industries are those that create, use, and disseminate ideas, information, knowledge, images. Entry by individuals into this virtuous circle of well-being is predicated on their possessing at a minimum what must by past standards be regarded as extremely high levels of formal education. Whoever lacks such qualifications, barring their possession of exceptional or unique talents—star athletes, pop stars, and so forth—is likely to be permanently relegated to the ranks of the city's rapidly shrinking and low-wage goods-producing-and-handling sector or to the ampler reaches of the low-paying and local service economy. That's why the public schools are now seen as make-or-break institutions.

Counting Students

Statistically speaking, long-term trends in overall public school enrollment in New York City, summarized in table 1.1, can be said to be the result of three factors: (1) changes in the size of the city's school-age population; (2) the degree to which this population is actually enrolled in school; and (3) the extent to which enrollment is divided between public and nonpublic schools.

For much of the period under review, trends in the school-age population could adequately be represented by changes in the number of 5- to 17-year-olds, a span which in the normal course of events should take a child from kindergarten through the completion of high school. More recently, because of the expansion in pre-kindergarten education, a rise in the proportion of "over-age" high school students, and the increasing provision of some form of post–high school education, there has been a significant broadening in the age groups which the public education system must take into account. But even under a more inclusive definition of the target group—say, 3- to 21-year-olds—5- to 17-year-olds would still constitute four-fifths of the total; and, in any case, the core group's changes over time closely track those taking place in the broader age category.

As table 1.2 shows, the city's 5- to 17-year-old population fell steadily between 1930 and 1950, from 1.5 to 1.3 million, an overall decline of 17 percent. It then reversed course and increased by 32 percent between 1950 and 1970. By the latter year, it attained what will very likely prove to be its all-time high of just over 1.6 million. Between 1970 and 1990, it relinquished all of these gains and then some as its school-age population fell to under 1.2 million, an eighty-year low. However, in the 1990s, the city's school-age population ascended once again, increasing by 13 percent to reach just over 1.3 million by 1997.

TABLE 1.1 Trends in Enrollment in New York's Schools by Race/Ethnicity, 1970–1971 to 1997–1998

	Total	Black	Asian/ Native American	Hispanic	White
Actual data, in thousands:					
1970–71					
Public	1,132.0	389.2	17.5	289.9	435.4
Nonpublic	407.3	32.0	2.9	46.5	325.9
Total	1,539.3	421.2	20.4	335.4	761.3
1980–81					
Public	941.3	363.4	38.6	286.3	253.0
Nonpublic	313.2	49.7	9.2	50.0	204.3
Total	1,254.5	413.1	47.8	336.3	457.2
1990–91					
Public	932.0	354.3	74.6	325.7	177.4
Nonpublic	267.8	51.6	12.1	47.9	156.2
Total	1,199.8	405.9	86.7	373.6	333.6
1997–98					
Public	1,057.5	378.5	116.1	395.6	167.3
Nonpublic	268.9	53.3	13.5	46.4	155.7
Total	1,326.4	431.8	129.6	442.0	323.0
	Total	Black	Asian/ Native American	Hispanic	White
Percentage change:					
1971–81					
Public	−16.8	−6.6	120.6	−1.2	−41.9
Nonpublic	−23.1	55.3	217.2	7.5	−37.3
Total	−18.5	−1.9	134.3	0.0	−39.9
1981–91					
Public	−1.0	−2.5	93.3	13.8	−29.9
Nonpublic	−14.5	3.8	31.5	−4.2	−23.5
Total	−4.4	−1.7	81.4	11.1	−27.1
1991–98					
Public	13.5	6.8	55.6	21.5	−5.7
Nonpublic	0.4	3.3	11.6	−3.1	−0.3
Total	10.6	6.4	49.5	18.3	−3.2

TABLE 1.2 Total Population and School-age Population (Aged 5 to 17), by Race/Ethnicity, New York City, 1930–1996

	1930	1940	1950	1960	1970	1980	1990	1996
All ages			(in thousands)					
White	6,548	6,921	6,890	6,053	4,967	3,687	3,165	2,787
Black	324	453	729	1,060	1,548	1,702	1,863	1,886
Hispanic	45	62	246	613	1,202	1,429	1,725	1,906
Asian	13	19	27	56	178	275	527	649
Total	6,930	7,455	7,892	7,782	7,895	7,093	7,280	7,228
			(as a percent of total population)					
White	94.5	92.8	87.3	77.8	62.9	52.0	43.5	38.6
Black	4.7	6.1	9.2	13.6	19.6	24.0	25.6	26.1
Hispanic	0.6	0.8	3.1	7.9	15.2	20.1	23.7	26.4
Asian	0.2	0.3	0.3	0.7	2.3	3.9	7.2	9.0
Total	100.0	100.0	100.0	100.0	100.0	100.0	100.0	100.0
5–17			(in thousands)					
White	1,434	1,281	1,064	1,094	814	477	339	338
Black	53	88	125	220	422	416	372	449
Hispanic	10	14	57	153	398	374	369	413
Asian	1	2	3	10	13	49	80	111
Total	1,497	1,385	1,249	1,477	1,647	1,316	1,160	1,311
			(as a percent of 5–17 yr. olds)					
White	95.8	92.5	85.2	74.1	49.4	36.2	29.2	25.8
Black	3.5	6.4	10.0	14.9	25.6	31.6	32.1	34.2
Hispanic	0.7	1.0	4.6	10.4	24.2	28.4	31.8	31.5
Asian	0.0	0.1	0.2	0.7	0.8	3.7	6.9	8.5
Total	100.0	100.0	100.0	100.0	100.0	100.0	100.0	100.0
5–17			(as a percent of total population)					
White	21.9	18.5	15.4	18.1	16.4	12.9	10.7	12.1
Black	16.4	19.4	17.1	20.8	27.3	24.4	20.0	23.8
Hispanic	22.2	22.6	23.2	25.0	33.1	26.2	21.4	21.7
Asian	7.7	10.5	11.1	17.9	7.3	17.8	15.2	17.1
Total	21.6	18.6	15.8	19.0	20.9	18.6	15.9	18.1

Source: 1930–1990 data from U.S. Census of Population; 1996 data from Housing and Vacancy Survey.

In the period before World War II, enrollment in the city's schools, taking both public and nonpublic sectors into account, expanded at a more rapid pace than the underlying school-age population. This was due to the increasing rate of enrollment in high school of 16- and 17-year-olds. By the 1920s, the proportion of 6- to 15-year-olds who were in school was approaching levels not greatly different from those which prevail today. However, at the time only a little more than half of 16- and 17-year-olds remained on in what would have been the final two years of high school. Indeed, in the 1920s, only about a quarter of those who began high school actually graduated.[3]

Using today's terminology, three quarters of that era's young people were high school dropouts, although the consequences of being a dropout then bear hardly any comparison to those which today's laggards incur. But in the 1930s, against a background of prolonged mass unemployment and prodded by the imposition of a higher minimum legal working age, high school attendance rates rose sharply, as did the number of high school graduates. Attendance rates would continue to inch up for a couple of decades after World War II before stabilizing at their present levels in the period between 1960 and 1980. While higher attendance rates were at first accompanied by higher graduation rates, improvement on this score soon petered out. Thus a not inconsequential fraction of students still fail to complete regular high school.

Historically, nonpublic school enrollment over the past half century or so has played a much larger role in New York City's school picture than it has nationally. In 1930, there was virtually no difference with respect to the public schools' share of total enrollment between the nation and New York City: 90 percent in New York, 91 percent nationally. But over the next three decades, these differences widened considerably. By 1960, the nonpublic schools' share in New York City had risen to 30 percent. Nationally, the comparable figure was only 14 percent.

In the nonpublic schools, typically known as private or independent schools, students are drawn overwhelmingly from wealthy or upper middle-income families and are charged high tuition fees. Schools of this kind have never accounted for more than a tiny fraction of the city's overall school enrollment. The heavy infantry, so to speak, of New York's nonpublic school sector has always been found in religiously affiliated institutions. In their 1950s heyday, they were overwhelmingly run out of the parishes of the city's two Catholic dioceses.

Between 1930 and 1960, ignoring intervening fluctuations, public school enrollment in New York fell by over 100,000, while enrollment in nonpublic schools rose by more than 300,000. Over four-fifths of this huge increase was accounted for by Catholic schools. By 1960, Catholic schools were enrolling one out of four of the city's elementary and secondary school students. The lion's share of the expansion in the Catholic school system in New York takes place prior to the 1950s.

Nationally, the Catholic school system was expanding as well but hardly at the same pace. At the peak of its relative importance in the early 1960s, Catholic schools only accounted for 13 percent of the nation's elementary and secondary school enrollment, or only half of its New York City share.

Catholic schools, though, were private schools with a difference. They were heavily subsidized so that the direct cost to the student's family, who were largely of working-class or lower middle-class background, proved to be anywhere from modest to trivial. The principal source of this subsidy was the mainly unpaid (or, more accurately, poorly paid) labor of the nuns and priests who taught in and administered the schools. In the 1960s, however, enrollment in the Catholic school system began its long decline which, three decades or so later, has still not run its course. Since 1960, Catholic school enrollment in New York City has fallen by 60 percent. Inner-city Catholic schools have faced, to simplify greatly, two kinds of problems. One is that their market has suburbanized. The second is that they have become too expensive to keep going for those who have remained behind. Unlike the nuns and priests of a bygone day, most of the teachers are now lay people who can't or won't get by without what they consider to be a living wage.

The decline of New York's once robust Catholic school sector is part of a national trend. Catholic school enrollment for the United States as a whole fell by over 50 percent between 1960 and 1990, as suburbanizing Catholics sent more of their children to the public schools. Catholic schools still matter in New York. They currently enroll one out of ten, compared with one out of twenty nationally. But obviously they count for much less than they did three or so decades ago.[4]

The Impact of Racial and Ethnic Change

More consequential than the changes that have taken place in aggregate enrollment trends are the changes in the racial and ethnic backgrounds of New York's public school students. As the racial composition of the city's adult population shifted from white to black and Latino, the transformation has been even more extensive in the racial and ethnic composition of the city's school-age population. Between 1930 and 1996, as table 1.2 shows, New York City's white school-age population, which by definition excludes Hispanics, fell twice as fast as that of whites 18 years of age and over. Contrastingly, the combined black and Latino school-age population expanded thirteen-fold, nearly twice as fast as that of its adult component. Close to the end of the twentieth century, only one out of ten of the city's whites fall into the 5-to-17-year-old age group, while for blacks and Hispanics the comparable rate is better than one out of five.

Whites accounted for 96 percent of all 5- to 17-year-olds in New York City in 1930. Since then, their share has fallen persistently and dramatically. By 1996 it was down to 26 percent of the total. Between 1930 and 1950, white decline was the joint result of a Depression-induced drop in the birth rate—an earlier baby bust—and the passage of restrictionist immigration legislation in the mid-1920s. Immigration—then as now—had a disproportionate effect on the size of the city's school-age population because of New York's magnetic pull for immigrants. The political decision made to sharply curtail immigration from southern and eastern Europe had a disproportionately negative impact on enrollment in New York's public schools.

Immigration's resurgence half a century later, set in motion by a now revised set of political priorities, has, expectably, had the opposite effect. While the earlier period of mass immigration was dominated by whites (overwhelmingly from Europe) today's mass immigration is much more differentiated; in New York's case, it involves Latinos, blacks, Asians, and whites more or less in that order of significance.

Suburbanization and All That

The nature of population change in New York City during the quarter of a century or so after World War II was one in which suburbanizing white households were being replaced in roughly equal numbers by incoming black and Latino ones. From an economic point of view, better-off whites, with brighter earning prospects, were being succeeded by less advantaged black and Latino families. The black migrants were largely the products of the rural American South, and Latinos at this point in time were overwhelmingly from Puerto Rico, then still a predominantly agricultural society.

It was not that the newcomers fared badly in this period. On the whole, the city's economy performed well between the end of the 1930s and the latter part of the 1960s. While the city's blue-collar industries, where blacks and Latinos were most likely to find employment, were contracting, their rate of decline was still quite gradual. And there were still a great many jobs that had been vacated by whites who were retiring or moving out of the city. As a result, the unemployment rate fell for New York's blacks and Latinos through the 1960s and their family incomes, adjusted for inflation, rose sharply as well. Blacks and Latinos, moving north, generally improved their economic situations.[5]

True, there were clouds gathering on the horizon. In the 1960s, welfare rolls exploded and out-of-wedlock births began to climb among the city's minority families despite their generally improving economic circumstances. Between 1960 and 1970, reflecting these trends, the percentage of the city's under-18 population in female-headed families rose from 11 percent of the total to 19 percent. Such disturbing phenomena were hardly unique to New York City, but were fast becoming commonplaces in central cities throughout America.

Prior to World War II, the city's rapidly growing black and Puerto Rican populations were confined, by both discrimination and choice, to earlier established black and Puerto Rican neighborhoods. But by the 1960s, it was no longer possible, because of the enormous scale of the white exodus, to hold the line with respect to racial change. The number of school-age whites residing in the city fell by 24 percent between 1950 and 1970, from just under 1.1 million to a little over 800,000. Their place was taken, with a good deal to spare, by the offspring of black and Latino migrants to the city. In this period, New York's black school-age population more than trebled, going from 125,000 to 422,000. Their Latino counterparts experience a sixfold increase, from 57,000 at the period's outset to just under 400,000 at its conclusion. Between 1950 and 1970, while overall school enrollment (public and nonpublic) rose by a thumping 14 percent, white enrollments fell by 45 percent and the minority student count soared by 75 percent. As would be expected, the shift in the racial composition of enrollment was greatest in the public schools. Between 1950 and 1970, the minority share, overwhelmingly black and Latino, increased from 17 percent to 62 percent of the total.

At first, the neighborhood public school was viewed as just another setting in which the issue of racial integration (or segregation) needed to be addressed. For obvious historical reasons, this issue played out mainly as a black and white affair. For New York's civil rights advocates, black or white, the heart of the matter was no longer de jure segregation but de facto segregation brought about by the operation of market forces. Their goal was racial integration, and their preferred instruments were some combination of racially targeted busing across school district lines and the extensive construction of subsidized housing for minority families in what were at the time white neighborhoods. Whites in general and white parents with children in the public schools in particular objected strenuously to both of these possibilities. For the most part, New York's white families with school-age children resolved this dilemma by voting with their feet (and dollars), by moving to virtually all-white suburbs where busing and racial integration were only remote possibilities.[6]

The City's Economy Buckles

Stable in the 1950s and robust in the 1960s, New York's economy went headlong into a deep funk in the 1970s. Between 1969 and 1977, employment in New York City dropped in each year, shedding 700,000 jobs—or 17 percent—in the process. It declined through thick and thin, irrespective of what was happening in and to the national economy. New York's precipitous economic decline must, of course, be viewed in the context of a much broader set of developments. Although this was not apparent at the time, the early 1970s marked a turning point in the U.S. economy. Henceforth, output, earnings, and income growth would increase at a much slower pace than they had during the preceding quarter of a century. The golden age of post–World War II economic growth had ended. Worst hit by the ensuing protracted period of economic stagnation were the older cities—New York among them—of the Northeast and Midwest regions, the newly christened Rustbelt.[7]

Though all sectors of the city's economy felt the pinch of adversity, its minority-employing blue-collar industries suffered most of all and would continue to do so long after the white-collar portions of the local economy achieved a robust recovery. These difficulties were greatly exacerbated and prolonged as the economic crisis escalated into a fiscal crisis as well, in the course of which New York City's municipal government came close to bankruptcy. Not only were there many fewer jobs for the city's residents, but public services such as education also sustained sharp cutbacks.

Reacting to these developments on the economic front, and for the first time in its recorded history, the city's population fell in the 1970s, dropping by close to a million persons. Out-migration from the city, already substantial in the 1960s, increased significantly as mobile—that is, employable—and, in the circumstances, overwhelmingly white New Yorkers headed for the exits. The city's inflation-adjusted median household income, which had risen by 30 percent in the preceding decade, fell by 10 percent in the 1970s. For black and Latino households the slippage was worse, 13 percent and 17 percent, respectively.

The city's school-age population dropped by 20 percent between 1970 and 1980, leading to a 16 percent decline in public school enrollments and an even sharper drop, 23 percent, in those of nonpublic schools (with Catholic schools down by 35 percent). In racial terms, white enrollments, reflecting the very sharp drop in the white school-age population, decreased 40 percent, declining by 42 percent and 37 percent in public and nonpublic schools respectively. Black enrollments declined by 2 percent in the 1970s, falling by 7 percent in the public schools and increasing by 56 percent in the nonpublic ones. Latino enrollments barely changed, with a 50 percent pickup in nonpublic school enrollments offsetting a 2 percent public school drop-off. The minority share of overall public school enrollment advanced from just over three-fifths to not quite three-quarters of the total. Whites continued to predominate in the nonpublic sector, but there too their share was dwindling. At the end of the 1970s, minority children accounted for just a bit less than 40 percent of nonpublic school enrollment, compared with 22 percent a decade earlier.

There are a number of explanations for the sharp turndown in school enrollments during this period. One of them was the end of the baby boom in the mid-1960s and the ensuing baby bust. Baby boomers—otherwise known as persons born in the two decades or so after World War II—were having many fewer children than their parents did. This meant that by and by there was bound to be a commensurately large drop in overall school enrollments. Thus, at the national level, overall school enrollment dropped by 9 percent in the 1970s, after having gained 29 percent over the preceding ten-year period. The trend in school enrollment in New York City itself during this nationwide transition from baby boom to baby bust was affected by other factors as well.

Those middle-class baby boomers—white, black, brown, whatever—who were having children, albeit at a diminished rate, were also leaving the city at an accelerating pace. The mere fact of their departure represented nothing new. The first quarter of a century or so after World War II had already seen a substantial exodus of middle-class families with children from New York. Middle-class families moved out of the city in the early part of this period primarily because they could afford a higher standard of living, the suburbs had what they wanted, and the price was right. By the 1960s, racial change, rising crime rates, and the tense state of race relations in general and in the city's public schools in particular provided additional incentives to move. In the 1970s, the rate of middle-class outmigration intensified as the city's declining economy added another powerful reason, to an already considerable list, to leave. And now, reflecting the continued growth in their respective middle classes and the lessening role of discriminatory practices in real estate markets, there were now more black and Latino families moving out of the city in this period as well.

Without question, the 1970s proved to be the worst of times for New York City's public schools. The city's fiscal crisis and falling enrollments led to deep cuts in school budgets. Extensive and, as proved to be the case, ill-advised school closings were carried out. The system's ability to accomplish its objectives, even to define them, already damaged by the racial controversies of the previous decade, was now still more gravely impaired. During this period the performance of students took a dramatic downward turn.

A combination of a rapidly deteriorating local economy and a seemingly unending flight of middle-class families reversed what had been a long-term improvement in the economic well-being of the city's school-age population. By 1970, the poverty rate among the city's children had fallen to the point where it was a little more than a third of what it had been in 1940 (using today's standards for defining states of poverty and nonpoverty). However, between 1970 and 1980, the poverty rate for this age group increased from 22 percent to 31 percent. Close to four out of ten of the city's black children fell below the poverty line. For Latinos it was more like one out of two. And poverty now was unlike the poverty of earlier times in (at least) one vital respect. Then the great majority of poor children were raised in intact families. No longer. An extensive swath of the city's school districts were now faced with the considerable task of educating large numbers of children being raised in very marginal circumstances by unmarried and—worse still—never-married mothers.[8]

While the lion's share of the city's poor and near poor children were enrolled in its public schools, nonpublic schools as a group could not by any means be looked upon as privileged strongholds. In the 1970s, over a third of the students enrolled in the city's nonpublic middle schools were either poor or near poor (with the near poor category defined as twice the poverty level). Most of them were black and Latino, and as it happens they did considerably better than their public school counterparts at least as regards such indicia as rates of graduation.

People and Jobs in the New Economy

By the mid-1970s, an overwhelming consensus had formed, which was that New York's economy along with its population would continue to contract for the foreseeable future. Pessimism was rife. However, true to form, the doomsayers were proven dead wrong. Attesting to its underlying resilience, New York's economy revived in the latter part of the decade and then went from strength to strength—propelled almost exclusively by its Manhattan-based knowledge and information intensive industries—through most of the 1980s.

As its employment briskly rose, the city's population began to expand again, however modestly. Its racial mix continued to alter along much the same lines as it had in previous decades. But the extent and nature of the city's improving economic prospects brought some changes from the earlier pattern. The city's white (and overwhelmingly middle- and upper-income) population continued to fall in absolute terms. But, highly responsive to the glittering prospects presented by the city's increasingly high-pay white-collar economy, its rate of out-movement dropped sharply.

The city's black population continued to expand but its rate of growth was only a fifth of what it was in earlier decades. In-migration of southern-born blacks dried up as the contraction in the city's blue-collar job base intensified (and as economic opportunity widened for blacks in the South). Paralleling trends in the city's black population, and for many of the same reasons, there was a dramatic slowdown in the growth of the city's Puerto Rican population as the New York City-bound migration from the Island slackened. While the city's black and Puerto Rican populations continued to be dominated by low and moderate income families, restored prosperity brought with it a quickening rate of growth in the size of their respective middle classes.[9] While the movement of middle income blacks and Latinos from the city to its suburbs picked up in the 1980s, for the most part such families remained within the city forming new and quite substantial enclaves of their own.

Something new was added to the mix, however. There were now more and more non-Puerto Rican Latinos, as well as Asians from everywhere and blacks from the Caribbean. The dramatically elevated presence of these groups beginning in the 1980s reflected the impact of increasing levels of immigration into the country and the fact that New York City's once again vibrant economy, after the doldrums of the 1970s, had rekindled the city's attractiveness for larger and larger numbers of the country's newcomers. In fact, within each of the city's racial and ethnic groups—white, black, Latino, or Asian—the share of the foreign-born population rose sharply. Most of them were not highly educated but had relatively little trouble in finding work. They represented what was in effect a new working class.

Though the city's overall population rose by 3 percent in the 1980s, its school-age population continued to fall, dropping by another 12 percent (on top of its decade-earlier 20 percent decline). Part of the difference in the these growth rates reflected the fact that a major change was under way in the nature of the city's childbearing population. It was shifting from one that was mainly native born toward one increasingly dominated by foreign-born parents; it would take a few years more before the latter group made its full presence felt in the city's public schools. Despite the continuing sharp drop in the city's school-age population, public school enrollments—after falling by 200,000 or so between the early 1970s and the early 1980s—stabilized at around 930,000 for the better part of the next decade.

In absolute terms, the number of white students in the city's public schools declined by another 30 percent in the 1980s, but this was offset by a 25 percent rise in the ranks of minority students. There were considerable differences, though, as far as the growth rates of different minority groups were concerned. The number of Asian students, still small in relative terms, skyrocketed. Latino students, many fewer of whom are of Puerto Rican background, increased by 14 percent in the 1980s, drawing close to parity with blacks in the process. Black public school enrollment continued to fall in the 1980s, but more slowly than in the previous decade.

As overall public school enrollments barely budged in the 1980s, nonpublic school enrollment tumbled by another 15 percent. This was on top of its decade-earlier 23 percent drop. The bulk of this was due to declining Catholic school enrollment, although parochial schools continued to account for nearly two-thirds of overall enrollments in the nonpublic sector. Other kinds of nonpublic schools, mainly those with Jewish affiliations, added students. In absolute terms, black nonpublic school enrollment eked out a 3 percent gain in the 1980s, a far cry from its 56 percent advance in the 1970s. Latino enrollment in the nonpublic school sector fell by 4 percent. The racial composition of the shrinking nonpublic sector continued to alter as the share of whites fell from 65 percent to 58 percent during the 1980s and the minority share moved up from 35 percent to 42 percent.

One reason why public school enrollments held up well in the 1980s is that an increasing proportion of the city's 5- to 17-year olds seemed to be forsaking its nonpublic schools. *Forsaking*, though, may not be quite the right word to use in this connection since it implies an element of volition. Another factor was at work. There were simply fewer and fewer school-age children being born or raised in New York City whose parents could afford to or wished to make the economic sacrifice required to send them to nonpublic schools. In a similar fashion, there were fewer and fewer children born in New York City whose parents will ever be financially able to move to the city's suburbs and their schools.

Through the 1970s, suburbanization was a realistic option for a sizable number of New York City families with school- or preschool-age children, either because their incomes were rising or because suburban housing prices were still relatively modest. Except for the very top of the income distribution, family income growth has slowed a great deal since then, while suburban housing prices have soared. A similar kind of income-price squeeze has impaired the ability of New York City parents to send their children to nonpublic schools. The result is that fewer and fewer families with children who live in the city have much of a choice as to where their children attend school. Under present circumstances, they are effectively optionless. As far as they and their children are concerned, it is literally and increasingly a New York City public school or nothing.

There is no gainsaying the fact that the city's economy recorded substantial gains in the 1980s. The city's median household income rose by 20 percent in inflation-adjusted terms during this decade, which is double the national rate of growth. As part of this process, most families in each of its major racial or ethnic groups experienced significant increases in their incomes. Black median household income in fact advanced by 25 percent, and that of Hispanics increased by 17 percent, in both instances far outstripping their respective performances at the national level. But this picture of rising prosperity hardly tells the full story, for rising income levels were accompanied by widening inequality in the income distribution. Most tellingly, the overall poverty rate in New York City remained at 20 percent and the poverty rate among the children enrolled in its schools continued to hover at around 30 percent (35 percent for those in public schools, and a "mere" 20 percent for nonpublic school students).

Two factors can be said to account for the persistence of this degree of poverty in the face of the impressive gains recorded in income and employment during this period. One was the increase in the proportion of children being raised by single and poorly educated women. The second was the fall in real earnings of less-skilled, low-paid workers. In past times, the kind of economic growth experienced in New York in the 1980s could have been counted upon to benefit nearly everyone. However, this proved not to be the case during this particular expansion both locally and nationally.

Income inequality is a particularly striking aspect of life in New York. For it is preeminently one of those places in which a really massive number of the victors in the "winner take all" economy congregate. This niche has always been an important part of the city's economic structure. But the enormous expansion experienced by the global economy during the last couple of decades—and by the prizes it bestows—and Manhattan's magnetic pull for those who operate within its dramatically widening realm has come to dominate the city's economic life to an unprecedented extent. Manhattan is where its movers and shakers work, live, and play.[10]

Unfortunately, the city is also, at least for the foreseeable future, one of those places where a very substantial portion of the population is poor and where the expectations, voiced and unvoiced, are that succeeding generations of the children of the poor will continue to live in roughly comparable circumstances. Today, the occupants of this niche—a sort of modern-day *Beggar's Opera*—for the most part reside in upper Manhattan, in most of the Bronx, and in extensive stretches of Brooklyn.

Bust Follows Boom Once Again

Starting in the late 1980s, the city's economy, after more than a decade of growth—and hopeful that it had put its bad old boom-and-bust days behind it—embarked on a veritable roller coaster ride. Its job count plunged by 300,000 or so, or 10 percent, between 1989 and 1993. The lion's share of this decline was experienced by its white-collar businesses. While the city's dwindling blue-collar industries continued to wither away at their long accustomed pace, they had become too unimportant to make much of a difference in the overall scheme of things.

What happened in and to the city's economy during this period was tied, though not very closely, to developments in the national economy. The decline in the city's economy led on the way down, was deeper, and lagged on the way up. At the national level, the relatively mild 1990–1991 recession was followed by a recovery which, though quite sluggish at first, soon gathered speed and is still going strong. By now it represents the American economy's longest and strongest peacetime expansion. New York's economy began its recovery in 1994, but it really only hit its full stride in 1996, when the city's bellwether financial services industry, taking off in the slipstream created by the great bull market's second wind, began to expand as if the sky were the limit.

By the end of 1998, the city was close to once again having the same number of private sector jobs it had at its peak in the late 1980s. And in terms of average earnings, the quality of the jobs that have been added at such a furious pace in the last few years were far superior to those that were shed so abundantly earlier in the decade. That's the good news, no question about it. The bad news is that this high value-added economic growth is still not sufficient, if you define success on that score as that which is capable of significantly improving the economic and social circumstances of a really substantial number of the parents of children in the city's public schools. There seems to be a profound disconnect at the present time and possibly for the foreseeable future between the kinds and amounts of private sector jobs that can realistically be expected to locate within New York City and the skills and inclinations possessed by a great many of the parents who have children in its public schools. Even more chillingly, this disconnect extends to their children as they "age" out of the school system and into what looks like may be a distinctly bleak labor market for them.

Between 1989 and 1993, as the city's economy went into a tailspin, the citywide poverty rate rose from 21 percent to 27 percent. But, as of 1997, several years into the current recovery, it had fallen back only to 24 percent, which was not only well above its pre-recession level but higher than it was in 1977 at the tail end of that decade's long economic collapse. The story is pretty much the same as far as the economic status of the city's children are concerned. The poverty rate among those under 18, already at a third of the total in 1989, rose as high as 45 percent in 1993 and by 1997 had fallen only to the 40 percent level.

Any way you look at it, the recent trends in the economic situation of the children in the city's public school population have simply been dismal. Between the 1989–90 and 1997–98 school years, a period in which the number of students registered in the city's public elementary and middle schools rose by 12 percent, the number on public assistance increased by 22 percent, or twice as fast.[11] At the beginning of this period, public assistance rolls amounted to 42 percent of the elementary and middle school registers. By the period's end, the comparable figure was 46 percent. Only seven of the thirty-two school districts experienced a decline during this period in the number on welfare. And the degree of serious poverty has spread. At the beginning of this period, seven districts had welfare utilization rates which were above 30 percent. By the period's end, thirteen were in this position.

Not only has the poverty rate risen, but the number of poor children has been rising along with the increase in the city's school-age population. The city's school-age population, after two decades of substantial decline, turned up sharply in the 1990s. Between 1990 and 1997 it rose by

13 percent. This was wholly due to the rapid growth taking place in the number of children who are part of families headed by foreign-born parents. As recently as 1970, less than 20 percent of the city's children were in such families. By 1996, the comparable figure had risen to 46 percent. Between 1980 and 1996, the number of school-age children in households headed by native-born persons dropped by 25 percent, from 935,000 to 706,000. In the same period, the ranks of school-age children in foreign-born headed households advanced from 466,000 to 605,000. Seven-tenths of the children in these families were born in the United States. The percentage share of children with immigrant parents has risen sharply over the recent past within each of the city's major racial or ethnic groups. In each case, whites included, it has come to account for a substantial portion of all children.

Public School Enrollments Rebound

Virtually all of this increase in the children of recent immigrants now flows into the city's public schools. Enrollment for grades K through 12 in the public schools increased by 13 percent between the 1990–91 and the 1997–98 school years. The fastest growing of these groups are Asians and Latinos, up by 56 percent and 20 percent, respectively. Latinos, with 37 percent of the total, have become the dominant group, with blacks, at 36 percent, still a very close second. One out of ten public schoolers are Asians, a jump from their less than 2 percent share a quarter of a century earlier. Whites are now down to a scant 16 percent share, a far cry from their 96 percent share a half century ago.

Enrollment in the nonpublic schools, on the other hand, seems to have stabilized, at least for the time being, with continuing Catholic school losses being offset by increases in other kinds of (mainly Jewish) nonpublic schools. The white share has stabilized at 58 percent of the total. Half of the city's whites are in nonpublic schools and half in public schools. For the other groups, the nonpublic share is more like one out of ten.

As best one can tell, from such partial clues as births and migration statistics, it seems reasonable to assume that enrollment in the city's public and nonpublic schools will peak in the early part of the twenty-first century. By then public school enrollment might have inched ahead another 25–50,000 above its present level, and enrollment in the nonpublic sector should remain at or close to its present amount. Whatever the exact numbers are, one thing seems certain: An increasing portion of the students, particularly in the public schools, will have foreign-born parents. Between 1990 and 1997, the number of births in New York City to parents born in the United States fell by 24 percent while the number born to foreign-born parents remained virtually unchanged.

How Am I Doing?

A high proportion of the students enrolled in New York City's public schools perform poorly on a great variety of standardized tests. This is a problem of long standing, and as best one can tell the degree of underperformance shown hasn't changed by much over the past twenty years or so. Attempts to interpret the longer-term implications of year-to-year variations in test scores are almost impossible because the tests are often changed in ways that are hard to evaluate, or their results are renormed or otherwise highly qualified.

But some important facts relating to performance are unambiguously clear. One is that a very large percentage of those entering New York City's public high schools do not graduate. Another is that the lion's share of those who do graduate are able to get by without learning very much in the process. What the available data show is that the dropout rate, calculated by a variety of means, rose sharply from the early 1970s to the mid-1980s and has only begun to show a modest degree of improvement in the last few years.[12] For most of this period, there was a widening gap between the city's dropout rate and that of the state's suburban and small-town districts. The only districts in the state that New York City has kept up with, in a manner of speaking, are the other equally poor performing big-city school districts (Buffalo, Rochester, Syracuse, Yonkers). At the present time, the city's dropout rate is approximately twice that in the balance of the state.[13]

By the time the class of 1996 was ready to graduate from the city's public high schools, 14 percent of those who had started four years earlier had already dropped out of school altogether. Latinos have the highest dropout rate (18 percent); Asians, at 7 percent, the lowest. Relatively few graduate within a four-year time span. Among males, a little better than four out of ten graduate "on time," that is, within four years. Females do better on this score, with a 53 percent completion rate. Among males, whites and Asians, the least numerous groups, do best with on-time rates of 65 percent and 58 percent respectively. Blacks and Latinos, by far the most numerous members of the graduating class, do worst, blacks with a 37 percent on-time completion rate and Latinos clocking in at 33 percent. Women of all races best their own-group male rate, but white and Asian women substantially outperform their black and Latino counterparts. Just over 40 percent of all males who were part of the entering class that was scheduled to graduate in 1996 were still registered, officially at least, when the fall 1997 term began. So were a little over a third of its female members.[14]

Anyone reviewing these doleful statistics has to bear in mind that things are really worse than they seem. For graduating from a New York City public high school requires little more than persistence. Basically, the successful candidate needs to demonstrate the competence of an eighth grader, whatever that means, to get passing results in a series of examinations which are known as Regents Competency Tests. Very few of those who take these tests fail them. Approximately 80 percent of New York's on-time public high school graduates take this route of least resistance and for their pains acquire what is called a general diploma. Of the close to 40 percent of the class of 1996 who have not either fallen by the wayside or graduated on time, approximately a third ultimately succeed in acquiring a diploma, most of them apparently in the form of a General Equivalency Degree (GED). These, not to keep you in suspense, are even less highly regarded as an indicator of educational achievement than the General Diploma.[15] In fact, a surprisingly high proportion of on-time graduates— 10 percent overall, 20 percent for Latino males—end their high school careers with a GED.

About one-fifth—give or take a few points—of the on-time graduates receive a Regents-endorsed diploma, which demonstrates a considerably greater degree of academic achievement. This reflects the satisfactory completion of a course of study by those who intend to enter a four-year college. While males and females are awarded Regents diplomas at the same rate, there are very sharp differences among racial and ethnic groups. The lowest rates are among blacks and Latinos, 10 percent and 12 percent respectively. Asians, at 43 percent, achieved the highest rate, with whites next at 37 percent. The Asian performance is even more remarkable in view of the fact that two-thirds of these entering members are recent immigrants (defined for this purpose as anyone who entered the U.S. after 1988). Astoundingly—and depressingly—recent Asian immigrants received Regents-endorsed diplomas at better than twice the rate of nonimmigrant black and Latino graduates.

Among New York City's public high school graduates, these proportions—80 percent or so with general diplomas, 20 percent or so with Regents-endorsed ones—have remained pretty much unchanged since the late 1980s, lower in some years, higher in others, with no clear trend either way. It is not that much different in this respect from New York State's other "big-city" school districts. However, over 50 percent of public high school graduates in suburban districts graduate with Regents-endorsed diplomas and this percentage has been rising. In rural and so-called "small city" districts, the Regents share among graduates is currently at 46 percent of the total and it too has been on the upswing.

For inner-city minority youth, the payoff from simply graduating high school is considerable. As of 1990, according to the U.S. Census, only 30 percent of New York City's native-born black males 18 to 24 years of age who were high school dropouts were employed. For native-born black females, the comparable figure was 23 percent. As for their counterparts who had graduated, employment rates in this age group were considerably higher, at 53 percent and 47 percent, respectively.

But many high school graduates aspire to better things. According to the New York State Department of Education, four-fifths of the city's public high school graduates report that they intend to enroll in college, even though only 20 percent of them have taken what could be thought of as college preparatory work. A significant proportion of the general diploma holders do carry through on their plans and enroll in a community college, an entitlement since the late 1960s available to all of the city's high school graduates.

Their eagerness to go on demonstrates like nothing else does that they know what the score is out there in the job market. However, because of their inadequate—more like nonexistent—high school preparation, they are required to pass a number of remedial courses before being allowed to matriculate. For a great many of them, this represents too high a hurdle. Of those who enter the community college system as general diploma or GED holders from the city's public high schools, only a handful trickle through to graduation of even a two-year college. That's a pity, because the job prospects of a person, minority or nonminority, with a community college degree are immeasurably brighter than they are for someone who has only graduated from high school. The employment rate among 18- to 24-year-old native-born black males with an Associate degree is 75 percent, a full 25 percentage points higher than for those whose highest level of educational attainment is a high school degree.[16]

But just pushing more unprepared students into some form of post–high school education—in effect, ratcheting the social promotion game one notch higher—won't do the trick. In an increasingly competitive labor market, employers who are looking to fill jobs that pay reasonably well and offer a future will look for people with real skills. Even in a tight labor market they know from experience how little a dumbed-down high school diploma means, and they'll soon tumble to the real value of dumbed-down two- and four-year degrees.

The Challenges Ahead

The major tasks that will be confronting New York's City's huge public school system during the foreseeable future would seem to be dictated by the need to resolve a hard to hide contradiction. Long in the making, this arises from the relentlessly increasing divergence between the limited skills and abilities of a large portion of the city's resident working-age population and the increasing demands by employers for creative and well-trained people.

It would of course be nice if the city's public schools could do something to ease the severe employment problems faced by many of the parents of children who are in its schools, no little problem now that the welfare system is being reformed. But the system's first order of business would seem to be to improve the education of the young people who flow through its classrooms, carried along as they now are by the currents of social promotion, so that more of them will be employable in the kind of economy that the city is likely to see. This of course is easier said than done.

The city, needless to say, has a great deal at stake in efforts made by the schools to get their act together. And so obviously have the students and their parents. More and more of the employers who operate in the new economy have come to feel through real-time experience that a rising tide of graduates from the city's famously underperforming public high schools and colleges are simply unable to meet the requirements called for in the workplace. As a result, a higher proportion of these jobs are being filled either by commuters or by people moving here from other parts of the country (or of the world). Employers, large ones especially, are disinclined to speak for the record on this topic, not wishing to bring out the pickets and the protesters. So when push comes to shove, they just quietly leave town.[17]

Of course not all of the city's public schools fail. New York, after all, is a very big and diverse city. Though shrinking, a large portion of its still extensive middle class continues to use the public school system. However, at a minimum, two-thirds of the students in the city's public schools are not part of the middle class, even using a generous definition of who should and who should not be included in this category. This very large group of students can be said to be made up of two clearly defined subgroups. One of them consists of children who are part of working-class families in which one, or more usually, both parents are foreign-born. The second group includes the large number of U.S.-born children in economically marginal and socially unstable families headed by U.S.-born and raised parents. These are overwhelmingly black or Latinos of Puerto Rican background.

The general view of working-class immigrant parents is that they are hardworking, family oriented, and concerned with and attentive to their children's educational progress or lack thereof. Though living well this side of what is considered the good life—as this would be viewed in material terms—and having limited formal educational backgrounds themselves, they are nevertheless optimistic about the future. In these respects, they are probably not unlike their turn-of-the-century counterparts, a first generation working hard under difficult conditions to allow the second and third generations, educated in the city's schools, to climb the economic and social ladder. On the other hand, the common, if unspoken, view of the children of the city's down-on-their-luck native-born population is that it will be nothing short of a miracle if a high proportion of them do not go on to emulate their parents. A significant portion of the city's children are in families headed by poorly educated, unmarried women whose sustenance is mainly furnished by the state.

This makes it sound as if there were a sharp dichotomy between the have-a-chance children of working-class immigrant families and the children of beaten down native-born families (or, as many would characterize them, underclass). But the reality is more complex. There is a good deal of overlap between the families in the two groups so far as their having the sorts of characteristics that will be useful in rearing children who can benefit from education. And in real life, the two groups share the same neighborhoods and the same public schools and contend for the same resources. At the danger of considerable oversimplification, this raises a number of hard questions for school people. How, for example, can the still largely unaddressed woes of the one group be remedied so that schools can get on with their basic mission of equipping the children involved with what they need to become self-supporting and socially responsible adults? Additionally, what if anything can be done to keep the underclass's malaise from overwhelming the buoyant spirits thought to reside in the homes and families headed by foreign-born parents?

How then do the circumstances of the public school children raised by foreign-born parents differ from those raised by native-born parents? Some answers to these questions can be drawn from the decennial census. But it is well to bear in mind that this source, while valuable and irreplaceable, has severe limitations for an inquiry of this kind. It can only skim the surface of the complex phenomena involved. And, in addition, the most recent census available is now a decade old, a long time indeed in a city such as New York whose population characteristics have been altering so dramatically in the most recent period. With these ample caveats in mind, let's take a brief look at some of the relevant census findings.[18]

In 1990, 34 percent of all children 5 to 17 years of age enrolled in the city's public schools were in families whose incomes were below the poverty line. As a group, children with foreign-born parents were a good deal less likely to be poor than their native-born counterparts; 37 percent for the former, 29 percent for the latter. However, there are considerable differences by race or ethnicity within each of these groups. Overall, at 54 percent, the highest rate of poverty was experienced by children of Puerto Rican background, virtually all of whom have parents born in the fifty states. Among children in families headed by immigrants, the highest poverty rate—42 percent—was among non-Puerto Rican Latinos; the lowest—18 percent—among Asians. Among native-born headed households, the runner-up to Puerto Ricans for this dubious prize were blacks (40 percent), with whites the lowest at 13 percent. By far the most striking difference in intragroup poverty rates was among the city's black 5- to 17-year-olds; black children in families headed by U.S.-born parents had twice the poverty rate of those whose parents were immigrants. In fact most of the earlier mentioned difference in the poverty rate between children with immigrant and U.S.-born parents is due to this black intragroup difference.

Children in immigrant and native-born headed families also differ significantly in the kinds of families they are being brought up in. By 1990, only a little more than half of the city's public school children were in two-parent families, with over 80 percent of the remainder in families headed by single mothers. Among immigrant-headed families, 63 percent of all children were in married-couple households and 31 percent were being brought up by single mothers. For children of U.S.-born parents, the comparable figures were very different, at 44 percent and 51 percent, respectively. Almost all Asian children (87 percent) were in intact families and virtually all of their parents were immigrants. However, only half of all non-Puerto Rican Latino children, virtually all of whose parents are also born abroad, were part of intact families. Only 32 percent of black children with U.S.-born parents were in intact families, the lowest rate among the major racial and ethnic groups. The comparable rate for black children of immigrant parents was 53 percent, by far the widest intragroup difference.

There was, then, as of 1990 a higher rate of intact families among the increasing number of public school children with immigrant parents than was the case among their counterparts with U.S. parents, whose numbers are falling. Obviously, this has to be seen as an advantage for the public school system in the sense that wives and husbands together do better by their children, for a variety of reasons, than women on their own. But rejoicing on this score might be premature. For the married couple rate among immigrant families fell in a pretty significant manner between 1980 and 1990, as it did among families with children headed by U.S.-born parents. Moreover, the available data indicate that this pattern is continuing unabated in the current decade.[19] This trend toward increased family instability is not one that can be easily ignored in terms of its implications for the education of children, and particularly those in low and moderate income families.

Many children of immigrant parents face another difficulty in their schooling, and this arises from the fact that their parents are not English speakers, the primary language of instruction and homework. Fully a quarter of all children in households headed by foreign-born parents live in what the Census Bureau categorizes as "linguistic isolation"; that is to say no adults in their families speak English—and many fewer write it—well. For Asian and Latino children of immigrant parents, this figure is 38 percent. Approximately 30 percent of the children with immigrant parents who are in the public school system were themselves born abroad. A great many of them, depending upon the age they were when they entered the city's school system, are going to have different needs than those born in the United States. These, 70 percent of the total, are as likely to be serving as translators for their parents. They obviously have different instructional needs.

Culture, economic circumstances, and family structure are obviously even more important than parental ability to speak English in affecting how well children of immigrant parents perform in school. For example, though Asian and Latino school-going children experience the same degree of linguistic isolation, their economic and family circumstances are far different and so, as we have seen, is their in-school performance. In any event, the enormous diversity of linguistic backgrounds involved in the current period of mass immigration to New York City and the rapidly growing importance in the city's public-school-going population of children of foreign-born parents means that it is critical that the result of this aspect of classroom instruction is carefully monitored and that it not be simply the capricious result of knee-jerk reactions which are subsequently hardened into meaningless bureaucratic routines.

The demographic and social trends that have shaped New York City's public school system over the past half century are similar to those that have operated in all of America's big cities throughout this period. Their common property has been racial change as lower income minority populations and their school-age children have taken the place of departing middle-class whites. And from an economic point of view, there has been an almost across-the-board deterioration in the state of big-city local economies, making it difficult, at the very least, for their local school systems to respond in an appropriate way to their new constituencies.

Viewed from this admittedly glum perspective, however, New York stands out in certain respects. One of these certainly has been the resilience of its economy, which has had the effect of trimming its population losses, including those of its school-age population, to much lower levels than have typically been experienced in other big U.S. cities. A half century ago, the ten biggest American cities, led by New York, were all, with the exception of Los Angeles, located in the Northeast and Midwest. They ranged in size from New York's 7.9 million to Boston's just over 800,000. At the century's end, nine of these aging industrial cities, Los Angeles excepted, had sustained substantial population losses. As a group they fell by 30 percent. By far the best performer was New York City, dropping only 6 percent.

New York's superior showing has been due almost wholly to its continuing attractiveness to the growing number of new immigrants who have been flocking to the United States since the mid-1960s. The impact on the city's schools of this attraction, a result of the magnetic draw of the city's economy upon new immigrants, has been considerable. Nationally, only one out of twenty of America's 5- to 17-year-olds is foreign-born and 10 to 15 percent of this age group have parents who are foreign-born. In New York City's case, the comparable figures are one out of five and 45 to 50 percent, respectively.

Clearly the public school system has its work cut out for it. The social and economic pressures facing its students and their families are great. What New York has going for it, though, is an incredibly vital and dynamic economy. But it's not just a subway ride away. It's like that old line about "How do you get to Carnegie Hall?" Well, the answer to that was and is: "It takes practice" (and probably in these days a good agent as well). But the idea is still the same. Opportunity is still there, but it takes education, practice, and hard work to tap into it.

NOTES

1. Diane Ravitch and Maris Vinoviskis, eds., *Learning from the Past: What History Teaches Us about School Reform* (Baltimore: Johns Hopkins University Press, 1995).

2. Emanuel Tobier, "Manhattan's Business District in the Industrial Age," in *Power, Culture, and Place: Essays on New York City*, ed. John Mollenkopf (New York: Russell Sage Foundation, 1988).

3. Claudia Goldin, "America's Graduation from High School: The Evolution and Spread of Secondary Schooling in the Twentieth Century," *Journal of Economic History* 58 (1998).

4. For U.S. data on trends in Catholic and nonpublic school enrollment see U.S. Department of Education, National Center for Education Statistics, *Digest of Education Statistics, 1997 Edition*.

5. Charles Brecher and Emanuel Tobier, *Economic and Demographic Trends in New York City* (New York: Temporary Commission on City Finances, 1977).

6. Tamar Jacoby, *Someone Else's House: America's Unfinished Struggle for Integration* (New York: Free Press, 1998).

7. R. D. Norton, "Industrial Policy and American Renewal," *Journal of Economic Literature* 24 (1986).

8. Robert Berne and Emanuel Tobier, "The Context for Education Policy," in *Setting Municipal Priorities, 1988*, ed. Charles Brecher and Raymond Horton (New York: New York University Press, 1988).

9. New York City Council, "Hollow in the Middle: The Rise and Fall of New York City's Middle Class, December 1997" and the follow-up study published in December 1998, "New York City's Middle Class: The Need for a New Urban Agenda."

10. United Way of New York City, *Low Income Populations in New York City: Economic Trends and Social Welfare Programs, 1997;* for discussion of national trends in inequality, see Frank Levy, *American Incomes and Economic Change* (New York: Russell Sage Foundation, 1998).

11. Based on unpublished data provided by the Office of the Chancellor, New York City Board of Education, for purposes of its designating Chapter 1 schools.

12. Emanuel Tobier, "Population and Income," in *Setting Municipal Priorities, 1986,* ed. Charles Brecher and Raymond Horton (New York: New York University Press, 1985).

13. New York State Education Department, Statewide Profile of the Educational System, April 1998.

14. Division of Assessment and Accountability, Board of Education of the City of New York, *The Class of 1996: Four Year Longitudinal Report and 1995–96 Event Dropout Rates.*

15. Public Education Association, *State of the City's Schools, '98: A Performance Report on New York City's High Schools.*

16. Employment rates for 18- to 24-year-olds are calculated from PUMS microdata file, U.S. Census, 1990.

17. Heather MacDonald, "Gotham"s Labor Market Woes," *City Journal* 8 (1998).

18. PUMs microdata file, U.S. Census, 1980 and 1990.

19. Based on an analysis of data from the 1996 Housing and Vacancy Survey carried out for New York City by the U.S. Census Bureau.

2   Public Schools That Work

CLARA HEMPHILL

There is a common perception that the New York City public school system is a vast wasteland where a handful of schools serving mostly wealthy neighborhoods are adequate and all others are beyond repair. The truth is more complicated. New York City has scores of excellent public schools—not just in high-income neighborhoods but in poor and working-class neighborhoods as well. Some are small alternative schools, where kids call teachers by their first names and everyone sits on rugs on the floor. Some are larger, traditional neighborhood schools, where everyone wears uniforms and kids sit at desks in rows.

The good schools are as varied as the city itself. In one school in Brooklyn's Bedford-Stuyvesant, everyone—even the teachers—wears gray and burgundy plaid uniforms. The children learn grammar and spelling as they might in an old-fashioned parochial school, with plenty of drills and worksheets. In one Bronx school, teachers use Montessori methods to engage Spanish-speaking special education pupils. The school combines a highly structured environment—where routines are predictable and even the crayons are sorted by color—with classrooms that allow fidgety pupils to move freely from one activity to another. At one Queens school with many new immigrants, progressive Bank Street methods prevail: lessons in history, English, geography, and even math are woven into a particular theme, such as a semester-long study of China.

The presence of good and even excellent schools in some of the poorest neighborhoods of the city—the central Bronx, East Harlem, and Bushwick—is a testament to the extraordinary efforts of teachers and principals who have refused to accept the notion that good schools are possible only where the students are well-off. Even among the middle schools—long the weakest link in the chain of New York City public schools—there has been a remarkable level of innovation and reform in the past decade. The excellent schools, unfortunately, represent a small percentage of the system as a whole—perhaps 10 to 15 percent of the city's 1,100 schools. But in a system as vast as New York City's, a small percentage still yields a large number of schools where the education is inspiring and the prospects for graduates are good. Most important, these schools offer clues of what is needed to create even more good schools.

The development of scores of excellent public schools over the past decade is the product of efforts made by reformers both inside and outside the Board of Education. Their successes have been achieved in part by recognizing that there is no simple formula for improving schools that can be imposed from above. Each school must adapt to its neighborhood and to its pupils. Still, good schools—even those with very different philosophies and personalities—do have certain characteristics in common. These include effective principals, an emphasis on staff development, the ability to adapt to changing circumstances, high expectations for pupils, and a willingness to teach moral values and citizenship as well as basic skills. The size of a school makes a difference: the smaller the school, the less likely the principal will be overwhelmed by crowd control and the more likely he or she will be able to concentrate on teaching and learning. And autonomy counts: the best principals have managed to wrest authority from the central Board of Education to gain some control over hiring and budgets.

A Blueprint for Success: Ordinary Schools with Extraordinary Leaders

I visited one hundred elementary schools and fifty middle schools in New York City between 1995 and 1998 while researching my books, *The Parents' Guide to New York City's Best Public Elementary Schools* and *Public Middle Schools: New York City's Best*.[1] Some had superior test scores. Some had average scores—but had improved dramatically from previous years. Many of the schools I visited were alternative schools or programs for the "gifted"—good, even excellent schools, but ones whose success might be attributed to the fact that they are able to choose their own pupils. Some of the schools I admired the most, however, were ordinary neighborhood schools with extraordinary leaders. In some respects, these schools offer the most useful blueprint for replicating success throughout the system. Whatever the prospects of vouchers (which I oppose), "school choice," or charter schools, the vast majority of children in New York City will be attending their neighborhood schools for the foreseeable future. Understanding the dynamics of successful neighborhood schools—particularly those in very poor sections of the city—is key to improving the hundreds of inadequate schools in the system.

The single most important characteristic of a good school is a strong principal. It may seem obvious, but this simple fact is too often overlooked: the principal is the most important person in the building. A good principal can turn a school around against daunting odds. A good principal can inspire a staff, stretch scarce dollars while attracting extra grant money, and encourage parents to be involved. A bad principal can, just as surely, demoralize a staff, squander money, and alienate parents. As the late Ronald Edmonds wrote, "There are no good schools with bad principals."[2]

A good principal is an educational leader first—and an administrator second. A good principal breathes life into a school, gives it a culture and a personality. A good principal helps inexperienced teachers learn their craft and revives the spirits of burned-out teachers. A good principal creates a sense of community and fosters the feeling that everyone—from the teachers and parents to the crossing guard and the women serving lunch in the cafeteria—is working together for the sake of the children. Ask parents and teachers at a good school what they like about it and they're likely to say, "It feels like a family." Principals who are educational leaders rarely spend much time in the office. Rather, you'll find them in the halls, in the classrooms, chatting with students, offering advice to teachers. The best principals lead not by scolding or dictating orders but by identifying their teachers' strengths and helping them find ways to do better. They handle administrative tasks in a way that doesn't distract them from instruction. Dealing with mountains of paperwork or making sure a broken boiler gets fixed may be important for the smooth operation of a building, but it shouldn't keep a principal from the school's primary function of teaching and learning.

An effective school has a principal with a vision and a plan to make that vision a reality. Sandra Kase, for example, is the principal of P.S. 42, a beautiful school that's an oasis in a very poor and somewhat dangerous neighborhood in the central Bronx. In a decade, she transformed a grim, low-performing school into a cheerful, inviting place, where test scores are high and children discover and develop their talents in music and art, reading and mathematics.

Mrs. Kase remembers bursting into tears when she first arrived at P.S. 42 in 1987. The paint was peeling. Teachers were demoralized. The school was part of District 9, which had a history of corruption and nepotism, and she didn't expect moral support or ideas for reform from the district office. All of the six hundred children in her school had family incomes low enough to qualify for free lunch. Half were black. Half were Hispanic. Roughly 10 percent lived in homeless shelters, and more than 20 percent were classified as having limited proficiency in English. "I cried," Mrs.

Kase recalled. "I stood on those long stairs and said 'What am I getting my-self into?'" But she had a vision of a school where all children received the education generally reserved for the "gifted." And she went about her work.

One of the first things she did was fix up the building. Persistent phone calls to the central bureau of school facilities in Brooklyn eventually yielded results: the building was painted and plastered, even though it wasn't in line to be fixed up. She became a master grant writer, raising some $250,000 for books and furniture and money to send teachers to special conferences and continuing education courses. She bought cozy rugs, and round wooden tables and chairs, and mountains of blocks, and easels to paint on.

Most important, she changed the prevailing philosophy of the school. Instead of concentrating on what kids don't know, Mrs. Kase encouraged teachers to look at what kids *do* know. The teacher's job, she said, is to iden-tify and build on children's strengths. At P.S. 42, all children have the chance to study musical instruments, dance, and studio art—as well as ac-ademic subjects. Those who show particular talent in any area are invited to attend special Saturday classes outside the school—at the College of New Rochelle for music, for example, or at Lehman College in the Bronx for art.

Mrs. Kase's greatest achievement is building a cohesive, imaginative staff—even in a district with a chronic teacher shortage. She manages to combine extremely high standards for teachers with an understanding of how difficult their jobs can be. And, just as she admonishes her teachers to find the children's strengths, she also finds her teachers' strengths. She pairs an experienced teacher with a new one. They work together as a team, and the junior teacher picks up tips from the older one. The new teacher's loneliness and isolation are eased, and he or she picks up practical ideas on everything from how to manage an unruly class to how to teach reading.

The results of Mrs. Kase's efforts are remarkable. More than 66 percent of the children have reading scores above the national average—which puts P.S. 42 in the top 20 percent of schools citywide and some 30 percent-age points above what the Board of Education says is average for schools with similar demographics. P.S. 42 shows how an effective principal can make a difference, even under trying circumstances.

Staff Development: Teaching as a Performance Art

A principal—no matter how dedicated and dynamic—can't run a school alone, of course. Good teachers are key. And most good teachers are made—not born. They need to learn their craft over time. That's why ef-fective schools emphasize staff development. Anthony J. Alvarado, the charismatic superintendent of District 2 who transformed the schools of Manhattan's East Side under his tenure from 1987 to 1998, concentrated his efforts on teacher training. Educational researcher Richard Elmore, who studied the success of the District 2 schools, says teaching should be seen as a performance art. Even experienced teachers—like experienced musicians or actors—must practice continuously to improve their work, Elmore says.[3] In District 2, teachers seeking to upgrade their skills were paired with "master" teachers; substitutes took over their regular classes so the junior teachers could stay in the "master's" classroom for three solid weeks. The effort was expensive. Parents complained that class sizes ballooned because money was poured into staff development rather than reducing classes. But Alvarado maintained that a good teacher could handle a large class, while a mediocre teacher would be lost in even in a small class. Alvarado's results were impressive. District 2 schools, once avoided by anyone with a choice, became the most sought after in the city and even competed successfully against the most selective private schools for pupils.

Staff development is particularly important in neighborhoods undergoing change. P.S. 62 in the Richmond Hill section of Queens, for example, once had a stable, middle-class population of Irish and Italian American families and above average reading scores. Then, in the late 1980s, new immigrants began to move into the neighborhood. The school became extremely overcrowded. Classes of thirty-five were common. By 1995, there were more than one thousand children in a building designed for seven hundred. The proportion of children eligible for free lunch grew to 73 percent. About 18 percent of the school population had spent fewer than three years in the United States. Many of the newcomers, including Punjabi-speaking children and Sikhs from India, didn't speak a word of English. Several children from rural Guyana were ten or eleven years old and had never been in school before. Some didn't know how to hold a pencil. Test scores at P.S. 62 began to drop.

Principal Stephen Kramer sought the advice of the Leadership Center at Bank Street College of Education in Manhattan. They arranged for a staff developer to visit the school on a regular basis, and for teachers to visit successful schools such as P.S. 234—a high-achieving, progressive school in downtown Manhattan. Several of P.S. 62's reading teachers and assistant principals attended summer courses at Bank Street.

Teachers who had been used to front-of-classroom teaching, where the grown-up talks and the kids listen, began to experiment with ways of encouraging children to work independently. Senior teachers acted as mentors to new teachers, working together with them in their classrooms. Basal readers were supplemented with lots of good children's literature, and children began to read for pleasure. Teachers were encouraged to meet with one another and discuss which techniques seemed to work the best. High school students who spoke the various languages of the pupils were recruited to help out. The day I visited, a Punjabi-speaking high school girl was seated in the hall, helping four youngsters with their homework.

The school found that children were more engaged when their lessons were woven into a theme—such as China. Children read novels and folktales set in China, learned Chinese dances and songs, and made paper lions for Chinese New Year. They toured a Buddhist temple and ate at a restaurant in Manhattan's Chinatown. Even math was part of the theme: children learned to use abacuses and make pictures with "tangrams," Chinese geometric shapes that form a puzzle.

P.S. 62's readings scores gradually increased. By 1998, third and fourth graders were scoring just above the national average on standardized reading tests. There's a liveliness and excitement to the place that's contagious. Staff morale is high. Children love to come to school. However, the school still suffers from overcrowding. In 1998, the building was operating at 140 percent of its official capacity. But parents have resisted a redistricting plan that would send kids to other schools that are less crowded. In fact, parents fight to enroll their children at P.S. 62 and sometimes lie about their address to get them in.

Good Schools Focus on Instruction and Keep Expectations High

The day-to-day demands of running any school—particularly an overcrowded one like P.S. 62—are formidable. Every few minutes, it seems, someone interrupts the principal with a pressing problem that's not directly related to classroom instruction: a child has fallen sick; a deliveryman has refused to carry boxes up three flights of stairs; the boiler has broken down; the substitute teacher who promised to come never showed up. But one characteristic that good principals have in common is the ability to concentrate on instruction, despite such distractions.

Good principals also have high expectations for their pupils. They don't blame the children, or the neighborhood, or poverty for a school's poor performance. As a Brooklyn elementary school principal told me: "We don't say, 'Your mother is a drug addict so we don't expect anything of you.' Everybody learns to read." Good principals and good teachers have a deep respect for the children in their care. This seems so elementary that it's almost banal to repeat. But the sad truth is that there are many schools that don't have high expectations and many teachers who don't respect their children. An eighth grader in a redesigned middle school in Brooklyn, for example, told me the marked difference she saw in the attitude of teachers in her new minischool compared to those in her old, large junior high school. "Last year they'd say, 'If you're not interested in learning we don't really care. We're still getting paid whether we teach you or not,'" the girl told me. "This year, the teachers really pay attention to us. They take the time during their lunch periods to help us."

Some schools operate on the assumption that you can't teach children unless you address the social problems in their community. Many schools have an impressive array of social services: after school programs, summer camps, social workers to help kids with emotional problems, job training for parents, health clinics and dental care. These services may help children academically if, for example, a hearing problem is picked up at a health clinic. But a good principal recognizes that instruction—not social services—is the core of an effective school.

Dr. Renee Young is the principal of C.S. 21, a safe, orderly, and pleasant school with consistently good test scores in the Bedford-Stuyvesant section of Brooklyn. The school is in District 16, a low-performing district plagued by political infighting. The school is almost entirely black and Hispanic, and 85 percent of its 850 children qualify for free lunch. C.S. 21's test scores have never dropped below the national average, even though the "best" students in the district are skimmed off and sent to a special program for the "gifted." A traditionalist, Dr. Young says her philosophy comes from the parochial school education she received as a child in the same neighborhood. "The nuns made sure everyone learned," she says. "There were no learning-disabled kids. We were all poor and we all learned to read."

Children at C.S. 21 wear uniforms—burgundy plaid jumpers for girls, gray flannel trousers, white shirts, and burgundy plaid neckties for boys. Even the teachers wear clothes in the school colors: burgundy, gray, and white. The uniforms help create a sense of community in the school, a sense that everyone is working together.

At C.S. 21 the day starts with a "prep" period from 8:40 to 9:15, with children in the gym or the auditorium for various activities. The teachers plan their lessons together. Then, children have an uninterrupted block of time with their classroom teachers, from 9:15 to lunchtime. Recess and lunchtime, too, are for organized activities—playing a circle game or listening to a teacher read a story—not just running around. A special state grant allows the school to have classes until 4 p.m. and on Saturday morning. C.S. 21 combines high expectations with a focus on instruction.

Beyond Basic Skills: Lessons in Citizenship and Building a Community

Concentrating on instruction doesn't mean teaching skills in a vacuum. Good schools don't teach reading, writing, and arithmetic in isolation, but encourage children to see how what they learn in school relates to the world at large. Educators from John Dewey to Deborah Meier have emphasized the importance of schools as communities where children learn to be citizens in a democracy.[4] In a traditional school, that might mean old-fashioned civics lessons and reciting the pledge of allegiance. In a progressive school, that might mean encouraging activism by writing letters to city hall. Both teach children to be part of a larger community. Schools with a mix of children from different income brackets, cultures, religions, and ethnic groups are particularly well equipped to teach children to live together in a multiethnic democracy. Although public schools may not indoctrinate children in a religion, good schools instill moral values such as a respect for others. Including handicapped children in regular classrooms when appropriate, for example, is one way schools teach children to respect children who are different from themselves.

At good schools, lessons in citizenship are not tacked on as an extra but are an integral part of curriculum. At Manhattan New School on the Upper East Side, for example, kindergartners collected clothes, food, and money for hurricane victims in the Caribbean. The children studied arithmetic by counting the coins they collected. They studied geography and current events by finding the stricken islands on a map and clipping newspaper accounts of the disaster. They studied science when they learned about weather patterns. Schools that teach citizenship well build a sense of community among children and adults in a building and simultaneously link that community to the world outside.

At P.S. 102 in the Elmhurst section of Queens, Principal Harvey Sherer and his staff have built a cohesive school community allowing each ethnic group to enrich the lives of others. Some thirty-eight languages are represented at P.S. 102, including Korean, Chinese, Pashto, Punjabi, Tigre, and Twi. With the help of a Korean-speaking classmate, children videotape messages to send to video pen pals in Korea. They take trips to museums such as the Asia Society in Manhattan. They have an international lunch for which each child brings food from his country of origin. They sing Mexican folk songs and dance Russian folk dances—and also perform patriotic American songs. They even take a trip to McDonald's to introduce newcomers to American ways. This is multiculturalism at its best: not ethnic cheerleading, but cultural exchange; a place where each group influences and is influenced by others, where children feel proud of their origins and also proud to be Americans. The school, with 850 pupils, 60 percent of whom are eligible for free lunch, has almost twice as many children as the building was designed to serve. The playground has been turned over to portable classrooms. But the school has a sense of school spirit that's palpable, as well as test scores that are well above average.

Principals such as Harvey Sherer, Renee Young, Stephen Kramer, and Sandra Kase work under extraordinarily difficult circumstances. Spend a day with them and you come away impressed by their ability to overcome seemingly impossible obstacles. They must maneuver through a tangle of rules and regulations set by the central Board of Education. They aren't allowed to hire their own staff but must accept whoever is sent from the district office or the central board. They must go through a complicated and expensive centralized purchasing system to buy books and supplies. Many of them work in buildings that are terribly overcrowded and in a terrible state of disrepair. There is a conundrum in their success: the better their schools become, the more parents scramble to enroll their children, and the more crowded they become.

Schools Are Too Big—and Some Are Getting Bigger

While school reformers have touted the benefits of small schools for the past two decades,[5] and while dozens of new, small alternative schools have been created in recent years, other forces have conspired to increase the size of many neighborhood schools. Immigration in the 1980s and 1990s dramatically increased the number of children attending school in New York, and new construction failed to keep pace. A few new schools were built, but the School Construction Authority concentrated its efforts on building annexes to existing schools. The overall size of school buildings increased, sometimes quite dramatically. Some schools, with two or three annexes, have become so large they are unmanageable. The annexes put extra pressure on the rest of the building, because the cafeteria and auditorium are shared. Playgrounds have been turned over to portable classrooms. Principals have been put in charge of sprawling campuses with as many as four buildings, sometimes a mile or more apart from one another, with 1,500 or more elementary school pupils. In such a situation, it's a challenge for the principal to learn the names of each teacher—let alone a teacher's strengths and weaknesses. The logistics of crowd control become overwhelming. It becomes increasingly difficult to find the time to chat informally with children, to work individually with teachers, or to draw up strategies for improving instruction. Particularly at the middle school level, safety concerns increase as schools increase in size. Children are more likely to get into fights at large, anonymous schools where no one knows their names than in schools where kids have frequent, intimate contact with their teachers and principal. Some large schools are effective. But it takes a genius to run a large school—and the system doesn't have enough geniuses to staff all the giant schools we now have.

Political and fiscal realities are such that it's unlikely New York City will be able to build many new, small school buildings in the near future. But better use of the existing big buildings combined with creative use of unconventional spaces can make a difference. Creating semiautonomous "minischools" within a large school building is one way to make good use of less than ideal physical conditions. In the most successful of these experiments, the administrative functions remain with the building principal, but each "minischool" is assigned its own educational leader—called a "teacher-director," a "program director," or a "facilitator"—who works closely with teachers and concentrates on improving instruction. The Christa McAuliffe Middle School in the Bensonhurst section of Brooklyn, for example, is divided into three minischools, one on each floor, with about 350 pupils in each. Each floor has a "teacher-facilitator," who brings his own personality and flavor to the program. The reason Christa McAuliffe works, and other experiments in minischools do not, is that each "facilitator" has the autonomy, within certain limitations, to run his program as he sees fit. Each has the qualities of a good principal: a vision, a philosophy, a sense of where to take the school and ideas of how to get it there, the ability to bring out the best in the staff, and a genuine affection for the children in his care.

In my visits to schools, I found it was better to have a small school with an effective educational leader in an improvised space than a big school with, say, a nice gymnasium, a big library, and a principal bogged down in crowd control. I've seen schools in very odd spaces—a converted Civil War hospital, a nineteenth-century mansion, a former Macy's warehouse, a department store, and an office building—which worked well despite less than ideal physical conditions. Each had five hundred or fewer children—a size that most principals find manageable. This is not to say that resources aren't important. They are. The physical state of some public schools is so bad that some students' safety is in peril. Many schools are so gloomy that teachers and students feel defeated just entering the building each morning. But a small school with a strong leader and an adequate site is better than a large school with a weak leader and a spectacular physical plant.

The Obstacles That Principals Face

Even strong, effective leaders have difficulty exercising their authority under the tangle of Board of Education policies that limit strictly what principals may and may not do. Under the provisions of the contract with the United Federation of Teachers, for example, teachers with seniority may transfer to the school of their choice—over the objections of the principal. The more successful a school becomes, the more desirable it becomes as a place to teach—and the more teachers apply for transfers based on seniority. Some of these "UFT transfers" are good teachers any principal would be happy to have. But others are burned-out, alienated, and counting the days to retirement. The transfer plan has also held good teachers captive in bad schools. Until recently, teachers without sufficient seniority could not transfer to another school without the permission of their district superintendent—a rule one teacher described as a "plantation system." Defenders of the status quo say the contract agreement helps keep good teachers in the hard-to-staff schools without forcing them to stay indefinitely. But there are better ways to attract good teachers. Anthony Alvarado, for example, paid several excellent teachers $10,000 a year extra to work in a low-performing school. Their efforts helped increase the school's performance and got it off the state's list of worst schools, called Schools under Registration Review.

Some alternative schools and neighborhood schools with a particular philosophy have managed to bypass seniority rules under a special agreement between the Board of Education and the UFT. Under this agreement, schools that are designated as "school-based option" by a vote of 75 percent of the staff may hire their own teachers without regard to seniority. Unfortunately, most schools haven't agreed to this provision and the general hiring practices obtain.

In some districts, such as District 2 in Manhattan, principals are allowed to hire their own teachers, within the restrictions of the UFT contract. But in others, a district personnel board either hires the teachers, or assigns those who were recruited at the central Board of Education's hiring hall. These new teachers often show up the first week of school, never having met the principal. It's a toss-up which is worse: the patronage hire sent by the district office or the randomly assigned teacher, sent by central, who has no particular desire to work at the school in which he or she is placed.

Good principals come up with various schemes to get around the bureaucracy. For example, one middle school principal told me if he wants to hire a particular person to teach English, he advertises a position for a home economics teacher—knowing there are virtually no teachers certified to teach home economics in the city. Then, when no one applies for the home economics slot, he hires the English teacher he wants on the home economics line—and no one is the wiser.

Control over money is just as important as control over staffing. Unfortunately, principals have little control over their budgets. Capital projects, for example, are determined by central, sometimes without consultation with a principal. When I was interviewing one elementary school principal in Queens, an electrician from the School Construction Authority arrived and announced he was there to install a public address system. "But I don't want a public address system!" the principal protested. The electrician shrugged, and said orders were orders. He went ahead and put in the system. The principal sighed, shrugged, and continued her interview with me.

Ordering books can be a major chore. Board of Education regulations permit schools to purchase only from approved vendors and only items that appear on an approved list—an attempt to keep children from read-ing books that may contain, say, offensive racial stereotypes. But the rules are so complicated that schools usually wind up paying inflated prices, rather than the discount you'd expect for a large organization with the massive purchasing power of the Board of Education. If you want a book that's not on the approved list called "NYSTL" (New York State Textbook List), you're out of luck. It takes more than a year for a book to make the approved list, so if you want something that's new, or something from a small publisher who has no regular dealings with the Board of Education, you're also out of luck. An extraordinary number of teachers buy books for their pupils with their own money—a sign of their dedication, surely, but a haphazard way for a school system to purchase something as funda-mental as books.

Purchasing supplies can be tedious. One elementary school principal in the Bronx told me it took three years to get gym equipment for her special education children because the hand-operated go-carts, used to strengthen children's muscles, weren't on the approved list. She wanted white "write and wipe" boards on easels for her teachers. The approved list only had boards without easels. She wanted a camcorder; but, because of the com-plexity of vendor lists, she was required to buy three different components from three different vendors at a cost that was higher than if they had been purchased from a retail store.

These long-standing bureaucratic problems aren't impossible for a skillful principal to overcome. Good principals generally find a way to buy the books and equipment and to hire the people they need. Good princi-pals, if they have the backing of their district offices, can even get rid of in-competent teachers—although the process is enormously time-consum-ing. But the net effect of these and other Board of Education procedures and policies is to undermine principals' authority. The less authority prin-cipals have, the more difficult it is for them to lead their schools effectively.

Many principals complain that new Board of Education policies and initiatives under former Chancellor Rudolph Crew ignored their concerns and further restricted their authority. For example, a policy which goes by its bureaucratic number, "Circular 6," relieved teachers of lunchroom duty and so-called "administrative tasks" such as taking attendance in home-room. The policy, part of a contract agreement with the UFT, was an at-tempt to ease teachers' workload when the city failed to give them the salary increases the union had sought. However, it had the effect of in-creasing the principals' burden and undermining their ability to assign their staff as they saw fit. In one case, a principal couldn't install lockers in classrooms without negotiating with the UFT representative—because teachers were under no obligation to supervise children as they put their books in or removed them.[6] Similarly, the chancellor's requirement for "school leadership teams"—a committee of teachers, parents, and administrators charged with setting school policy—was seen by some as a further undermining of the principals' authority.

The Board of Education deserves praise for a few efforts to increase schools' autonomy. School-based budgeting, for example, began as a pilot program in several districts in the late 1990s. It gives principals some control over their budget. In one District 2 middle school, for example, the principal decided she could manage without an assistant principal for a year. With the money she saved on the salary, she purchased tables, desks, and chairs. The Board of Education under Chancellor Crew also eased principals' long-standing complaints about small repairs. Years ago, principals couldn't get a toilet repaired without going through one of the board's most backlogged bureaucracies, the division of school facilities. Under Crew, some money for repairs was allocated directly to the schools. Crew's administration also streamlined the process for purchasing some supplies. But these slight improvements haven't eased the bulk of principals' long-standing concerns: poor working conditions, and a lack of respect and appreciation for their work. Most say conditions deteriorated dramatically during the second half of the 1990s.

When you see firsthand what the principal's job is like, you become amazed that the system has retained as many good principals as it has. In fact, the system has been hemorrhaging talent for years. More than one hundred school administrators left in the summer of 1998—most for jobs in the suburbs, where typical salaries were $20,000 to $25,000 a year higher and schools are smaller, better equipped, and generally easier to run. Principals were particularly demoralized by an impasse in contract negotiations that left their salaries frozen from 1995 to 1999. With teachers' salaries creeping up, some principals actually earned less than the teachers they were supervising.

The number of applicants for jobs as principal has plummeted. Even in well-managed districts, such as District 2, some schools go without permanently assigned principals for years because virtually no one wants the job. One District 2 school had only an interim principal for more than three years. Only a handful of people applied for the job, and the superintendent, Alvarado, rejected all as unqualified.

Higher salaries, finally realized at the close of 1999, are imperative to retain good principals and to attract highly qualified candidates. But higher salaries alone will not keep people in jobs that a *New York Times* editorial described as "tenure in Hell."[7] Principals need to have autonomy and independence to run their schools without bureaucratic interference from the central Board of Education. They need to be able to hire their own staff and purchase the equipment they need. They need to have the leeway to experiment with new ideas without the pressure of producing better test scores overnight. They need to have schools of a reasonable size to allow them to be educational leaders—and not merely managers of giant factories.

In addition to a better contract, principals—like teachers—need a systematic way to hone their skills and to learn from others who are masters at their craft. As I visited schools, I found many principals who felt lonely and isolated. They'd ask me: "Have you met anyone who has problems similar to mine? Have you met anyone who's solved the crisis I'm struggling with now?" I was encouraged to see some districts had paired struggling principals with successful ones. For example, several principals from District 19, a low-performing district in the East New York section of Brooklyn, were assigned mentors in District 2 on Manhattan's East Side. The new principals spent three weeks shadowing their mentors, observing firsthand how they made decisions, worked with staff, and dealt with crises.

A promising program to prepare new principals is Bank Street College's Principals Institute, which offers an unusual eighteen-month training course, and recruits women and minorities in particular. Unlike traditional programs for school supervisors, the Principals Institute offers an internship that pairs a prospective principal with a mentor—a master principal—in a school for a full six months. But more needs to be done to train new principals and to give them the kind of continuing education that good schools now give teachers.

Despite the Many Difficulties, Reasons for Hope

The problems of the New York City school system are enormous. The obstacles to improvement are formidable. Teacher shortages are severe, and turnover is rapid. The physical condition of many buildings is appalling. Overcrowding is severe, and while experts disagree on the significance of class size, few defend the kindergarten classes of forty or more pupils that have become common in some schools. The departure of the city's most dynamic and admired educator, Anthony Alvarado, who accepted a job in California in 1998 after public squabbles with Chancellor Crew, was a serious loss to the city and its children.

Still, there is cause for hope. Alvarado left behind several dozen effective schools in his district—schools that promise to continue their recent history of excellence. He showed that systemic change is possible, that hiring effective principals and insisting on continuous staff development can transform education not just for a few schools but for a whole area of the city serving, in the case of District 2, some 22,000 pupils. Success stories in other districts show that even under current conditions (and even with unhelpful superintendents), good principals can create schools that teach children to love learning, schools that expand their opportunities and give them a glimpse of the possibilities that lie ahead. These principals, working under very difficult circumstances, have managed to achieve more than anyone imagined possible. If they can do so well under present conditions, imagine how well they could do if conditions were good.

Improving the quality of the principals is the single most important thing we can do to improve urban education. It's more important than recent initiatives to decrease class size or to provide universal pre-kindergarten, more important than the campaign to offer "school choice," and more important than increasing the length of the school year or the school day. It's even more pressing than repairing crumbling schools and buying new equipment such as computers. A good principal will make do in less than perfect conditions. But if the leadership of each building is uninspired, other efforts to improve education will fail.

The importance of strong principals has been well documented by scholars and policy analysts for decades. Scholars such as Thomas Sergiovanni have written exhaustively on the subject.[8] The 1991 Governors' Report on Education, issued under then-governor Bill Clinton, said that the key to a successful school is an effective principal.[9] Unfortunately, the Board of Education, while acknowledging the importance of school leadership, hasn't been successful in identifying and promoting its best teachers to become principals. While Chancellor Crew insisted he wanted to hold principals accountable for school performance, a number of his policies effectively weakened the principals' authority in the 1990s, discouraging some of the school system's best leaders and making a difficult job even more difficult.

Crew concentrated his efforts on abolishing tenure, which he maintained would allow him to fire hundreds of ineffective principals. Certainly, getting rid of deadwood is important. But the job of principal is so unattractive under current conditions that superintendents have trouble filling vacancies. The natural rate of attrition is so rapid—as principals leave for jobs in the suburbs, to district offices, or to early retirement under the board's generous buyouts—that great improvements in the system could be achieved simply by hiring good principals to fill vacancies. Indeed, Alvarado relied mostly on natural attrition to replace ineffective principals with good ones.

Unfortunately, principals—however hardworking and effective—have little political power. They are in the minority even within their own union, the Council of Supervisors and Administrators. Most of the CSA's membership of 4,500 is made up of assistant principals, district officials, and supervisors of special education programs; there are only about 1,100 principals in the system. Their union is dwarfed by the UFT, whose 70,000 members present a formidable political power in Albany.

Because principals have little political clout, support for improving their working conditions—as well as support for recruiting high-quality school leaders—must come from outside their ranks, from the leadership of the city: from the mayor and the chancellor. In his first term, Mayor Rudolph Giuliani made reducing crime his first priority. He poured money and expertise into the police department, and the effort paid off. Crime—one of the city's seemingly intractable problems for decades—declined dramatically. The number of murders decreased by 64.3 percent from 1992 to 1997. The number of crimes declined by 43.2 percent in the same period.[10] William Bratton, the police commissioner who presided over a decrease in the crime rate, credited the department's success to a reorganization that gave more power and responsibility to precinct commanders.[11] Now, the Board of Education and the police department aren't exactly analogous. Teaching children and locking up criminals clearly require different approaches and different skills. Measuring success in education isn't the same as measuring success in the war on crime. But it's interesting that a seemingly impossible goal—reducing the crime rate—was achieved by a city government committed to spending money and to organizing its staff in a way that gave middle managers leeway to make day-to-day decisions on their own without consulting their superiors. If the mayor and the Board of Education devoted the same passion, energy—and money—to improving education that Giuliani and Bratton devoted to the police department, then perhaps another seemingly impossible goal—quality schools for all New York City children—is also within our reach.

NOTES

1. *The Parents' Guide to New York City's Best Public Elementary Schools* (New York: Soho Press, 1997) and *Public Middle Schools: New York City's Best* (New York: Soho Press, 1999).

2. Ronald Edmonds, "Some Schools Work and More Can," *Social Policy* 7 (1979).

3. Richard F. Elmore, *Investing in Teacher Learning: Staff Development and Instructional Improvement in Community District #2, New York City* (New York: National Commission on Teaching and America's Future, 1997).

4. John Dewey, *Democracy and Education* (New York: Free Press, 1965); Deborah Meier, *The Power of Their Ideas: Lessons for America from a Small School in Harlem* (Boston: Beacon Press, 1965).

5. Leanna Stiefel, "The Effects of Size of Student Body on School Costs and Performance in New York City High Schools" (New York: Institute for Education and Social Policy, New York University, 1998); Middle School Task Force, Charles I. Schonhaut, chair, "Middle School Task Force Report" (Brooklyn: Board of Education, 1988); Carnegie Council on Adolescent Development, David Hornbeck, chair, "Turning Points: Preparing American Youth for the 21st Century" (New York: Carnegie Corporation, 1989). See also "Effects of School Size," a bibliography published by Diana Oxley for the Public Education Association, New York, 1987.

6. Lynette Holloway, "The Principal as Gulliver: Rule-Bound School Leaders Rely on Clever Diplomacy," New York *Times*, November 4, 1998, p. D1.

7. Editorial, New York *Times*, September 17, 1998.

8. Thomas J. Sergiovanni and David L. Elliott, *Educational and Organizational Leadership in Elementary Schools* (Englewood Cliffs, N.J.: Prentice-Hall, 1975), and *Moral Leadership: Getting to the Heart of School Improvement* (San Francisco: Jossey-Bass Publishers, 1992).

9. Task Force on Leadership and Management, Bill Clinton, chairman, "Time for Results: The Governors' 1991 Report on Education" (Washington, D.C.: National Governors' Association Center for Policy Research and Analysis, 1986).

10. Michael Massing, "The Blue Revolution," *New York Review of Books*, November 19, 1998.

11. "Defeating the Bad Guys," *The Economist*, October 3, 1998, p. 35.

PART II

Governance

3   The Difference between Charter Schools and Charterlike Schools

PEARL ROCK KANE

During the past decade a quiet revolution has taken place in New York City public schools. It has come in the form of small, theme-based schools developed by teachers and administrators in partnership with unions, colleges, neighborhood groups, museums, advocacy agencies, and even churches.[1] The idea for these schools was spearheaded by former schools chancellor Joseph E. Fernandez, who was encouraged by the successes of such schools created in District 4 in East Harlem. Fernandez considered small schools part of a strategy to reform secondary education by providing personalized environments for students, while simultaneously granting greater decision-making authority to administration and faculty so they could be responsive to students' needs. Despite unrelated controversies that led to Fernandez's ouster, these schools are seen as his major legacy. The idea of small schools is supported by many who feel they hold promise for meeting many of the needs of students who populate New York City's schools—especially the disproportionate number who are poor and from single-parent families, dependent on public assistance.

In 1991, with the support of the Annenberg Foundation and other contributors, Chancellor Fernandez approached four New York City organizations—New Visions for Public Schools, the New York Association of Community Organizations for Reform Now, the Center for Collaborative Education, and the Center for Educational Innovation—to help develop small, responsive, innovative schools for New York City. Collectively, the schools initiated by these four organizations now comprise a coalition of 140 small schools organized under the umbrella of the New York Networks for School Renewal.

At the same time that small schools were cropping up in New York City, charter schools—another reform aimed at establishing small, autonomous schools—began to sweep the nation. While these schools are created by laws that differ from state to state, charter schools can generally be defined as small public schools that are given greater latitude in decision making than district schools, and in return are held accountable for increased student performance. Following the introduction of such schools in Minnesota in 1992, many states began to adopt legislation permitting their establishment. As of September 1999, the charter school movement has given rise to over seventeen hundred schools in thirty-six states and the District of Columbia, and their numbers are projected to double within the next five years.[2]

In December 1998, New York State approved charter school legislation, paving the way for up to one hundred schools to open their doors in September 2000 and for an unlimited number of existing schools to convert to charter school status. Some may argue that the schools under the Networks for School Renewal already provide flexibility for innovation and personalization, eliminating the need for the more radical and perhaps risky reforms that charter school legislation will bring. In fact, the city's Networks schools are often referred to as "charterlike" schools, in that they are small and intended to foster decision making at the school level by means of a less bureaucratic governance structure.[3] A key issue to consider is whether the small schools in New York City have sufficient autonomy to fulfill their intended purpose, or whether charter schools hold greater promise for school reform. This chapter will attempt to address that question by analyzing one group of the Networks schools—the New Visions for Public Schools—in the context of progressive charter school legislation, particularly the New York State charter law.

Beginnings

When New Visions first called for proposals and announced $25,000 in planning grants with the promise of additional funds for schools that were chosen, the organization unleashed "an energy that no one quite expected" in the hundreds of people who were willing to take on the challenge.[4] The invitation was "to create an innovative and imaginative school," and the only requirements were that the schools be small, no more than five hundred to seven hundred students; that schools include grades 9–12, and as an option additional earlier consecutive grades; and that they have shared governance arrangements between Community School Districts and the High School Division.[5] Two hundred eighty-two proposals were submitted.[6] To assess the proposals, New Visions created an evaluation committee and subsequently chose thirty school designs to go forward. Twenty

New Visions schools opened their doors in 1993 with start-up grants from the Aaron Diamond Fund. In 1997–98, a second round of schools opened, supported by the Annenberg Foundation, bringing the total number of New Visions schools to twenty-nine. In addition, New Visions for Public Schools also sponsors ten small programs affiliated with conventional schools.[7] New Visions schools and programs serve over twelve thousand students in New York City and include approximately 40 percent of the population served by the New York Networks' small schools.[8]

New Visions schools and charter schools operate under different legal frameworks. Since New Visions schools are Board of Education schools— and abide by regulations imposed on all of the city's schools—no special legislation was required for their creation. This is not the case for charter schools, which are authorized by state legislation, and are usually autonomous of existing school districts. Charter laws vary from state to state since each law is a product of different interest groups such as unions, parents, and politicians, who shape the nature of the legislation. A state's charter school legislation, and the regulations established to implement the legislation, determine the number of charter schools allowed, how they are developed and approved, and the ways in which charter schools operate and relate to their sponsors.

For example, some states limit the number of charter schools that are allowed to operate, while other states allow an unlimited number. Some states permit only newly created schools, while others also allow preexisting public or private schools to convert to charter school status. According to a recent national study of charter schools, 70 percent of charter schools are new schools, 19 percent are public school conversions, and 11 percent are private school conversions (the latter only existing in the eight states plus the District of Columbia where private schools are eligible to become publicly funded charter schools).[9] Some states limit charter granting authority to one agency, while others allow multiple granting agencies. In states in which the authorizing body is restricted to the local school board, which may have a vested interest in discouraging the creation of new schools within its borders, the possibilities for charter schools are constrained. In states in which there are multiple charter granting agencies and in which charter developers can create new schools or convert preexisting public or private schools, the possibilities are extensive.

Although thirty-six states and the District of Columbia have charter laws on the books, only twenty-three of those states (including New York State) and the District of Columbia have provisions in their laws that encourage applications. These states are generally labeled as having "strong laws" or "expansive laws" in that they foster the development of numerous genuinely independent charter schools. At the other end of the spectrum are "restrictive laws" or "weak laws" with numerous constraints on autonomy and few incentives for charter school development.[10] The Center for Education Reform has developed criteria to use in determining whether a charter school law is expansive (strong) or restrictive (weak). Since there is no "typical" charter school, these criteria provide a framework for comparing the "charterlike" New Visions schools with charter schools.

We begin by considering similarities between New Visions schools and charter schools and then highlight the differences between the two types. To gather data on the New Visions schools, I worked with a team of researchers to conduct personal on-site interviews with a representative sample of principals, teachers, and students at eleven out of the twenty-nine New Visions schools and two of the ten programs affiliated with the New Visions organization.[11] Our team also conducted telephone and personal interviews with high school superintendents, and with staff members at the New Visions organization, the New York Networks for School Renewal, the central Board of Education, and the United Federation of Teachers. Approximately sixty-five interviews were conducted and many more hours were devoted to informally observing the schools in operation. Along with the data gathered through interviews and observations, newspaper articles and reports, press releases, and literature available from the schools were reviewed for relevant information. All of the research was conducted in the spring and summer of 1998.[12]

Similarities between New Visions Schools and Charter Schools

Although charter schools in New York State have not existed long enough to have a substantive record, data from several national charter school studies suggests what these schools are likely to look like. The studies, which also provide useful information for comparison, indicate that New Visions schools and charter schools share several defining characteristics: The schools serve similar student populations; founders often form partnerships with organizations outside of traditional education circles; and the schools are generally small in size, mission-driven, and staffed by teachers and administrators attracted by the schools' distinctive features.

Students

Demographic data on New Visions schools and charter schools indicate that the schools serve racially diverse populations that mirror the ethnic distribution of students in other public schools in the surrounding district. Insofar as charter schools are racially distinctive from their surrounding districts, they are much more likely to enroll students of color. A recent national study found that charter schools serve a slightly higher percentage (by less than 20 percent) of students of color than regular public schools.[13] The demographic situation is similar for the student population of New Visions and other small schools that are part of the Networks for School Renewal. Compared with students in other New York City public schools, these schools serve 13 percent more students who are black and 7 percent more students who are Hispanic.[14] Charter schools are estimated to serve about the same percentage of students with limited English proficiency (10 percent) as other public schools (10 percent)[15] but comparatively fewer students with disabilities (8 percent) than other public schools in the same state (11 percent).[16] The percentage of students in Networks schools who are designated as limited English proficient is slightly less (12.3 percent) than the percentage of limited English proficient students in other New York City public schools (16.7 percent),[17] and Networks schools serve slightly fewer students designated as requiring special education.[18] It is unclear whether New York Networks for School Renewal are actually serving fewer special education students or whether the schools are using different policies and practices for designating students as requiring special education.[19]

Partnerships

Another distinctive characteristic of both charter schools and New Visions schools is the diversity of affiliations of founders and the linkages the school have created with a number of organizations, many of which help to define the schools' missions. From the onset, the New Visions organization encouraged partnerships with parents, teachers, community-based agencies, civic groups, and representatives of the business sector. The schools' need for political allies and the economic necessity of providing space resulted in unprecedented linkages with organizations as varied as Cornell University, the American Museum of Natural History, the South Bronx Community Coalition, Outward Bound, and Prudential Securities. Similarly, newly started charter schools have a variety of founders and uncommon alliances between schools and institutions. For example, in New Jersey, twelve of the thirteen pioneering schools describe partnership arrangements with a university, a philanthropic organization, or other nonprofit organization in their charters.[20] Parents as school initiators appear to be more prevalent in charter schools, perhaps reflecting the difficulty of breaking long established traditions in district schools.[21]

Small Size

Small school size is another defining characteristic of New Visions schools and charter schools. On average, New Visions schools have less than one-third as many students enrolled (301) compared with the average New York City school (953). All of the New Visions schools fall within the bottom one-third of a ranking of New York public schools' sizes.[22] Nationally, 65 percent of newly created charter schools have fewer than two hundred students and only 10 percent have more than six hundred students enrolled, as compared with a median of 486 students in other public schools in the states in which the schools are located.[23]

New Visions schools and charter schools are designed to promote small class size. Both are likely to spread students across a larger span of grades than conventional schools, and they allocate budgets to favor hiring teachers and instructional aides over administrators and administrative support personnel such as secretaries and office assistants.[24] Class size in New Visions schools in the study ranged from eight to twenty-eight. In many schools, we observed classes with twenty or fewer students. Similarly, class size in charter schools tends to be small. In New Jersey, for example, classes ranged from eight to twenty students.[25] Studies of class size indicate that while all students show increased achievement in small classes, the benefits for children of color, largely the population being served by both types of schools, appear to be even greater, particularly in the primary grades.[26]

Teachers and principals in New Visions schools repeatedly extolled the advantages of small school and small class size as a way to get to know students and develop a sense of community. When we asked the students to describe the best aspect of being a student at their school, they talked about familial relationships with teachers and the school. As one student said, "It feels like a family here. Teachers really know me! I mean they really know me—my strengths." Another student offered, "When I start to slack they [the teachers] notice and make an effort to keep me on track."

Beyond the academic and social advantages of smallness, there may be economic benefits. A study of students enrolled in the Networks schools revealed that although small schools cost slightly more than the larger high schools, they have lower dropout rates and higher graduation rates. Comparatively, the schools have among the lowest cost per graduate. Smallness and personal relationships may yield the tangible benefits school systems are seeking.[27]

A Sense of Purpose

Charter schools and New Visions schools are founded with a mission in mind. In every New Visions school we visited, school principals were able to describe the school's mission and to give concrete examples of how the curriculum at the school serves the mission. This clarity of mission may be a result of the application process for both charter schools and New Visions schools, which require applicants to provide a well-thought-out vision statement and philosophy for their proposed school. A teacher commenting on why she chose to work in one of the New Visions schools pointed to the explicit expectations of the school's mission. "I wanted a school with a clear philosophy; a small school. In our other school we adopted everything that came along without really understanding it."

Community activism and meeting social and emotional needs are the dual purpose of most New Visions schools. The schools also embrace a variety of curricular themes such as focusing on the city's infrastructure, or vocational interests such as dance or law. Some schools give priority to unifying academic themes such as the humanities, sciences, or the arts. Some schools employ innovative techniques and theme-based curriculum to aid in the accomplishment of their mission. Many New Vision schools also target populations that are not well served by traditional schools, such as older students who had previously dropped out of school.

Choice of schooling is only useful if schools offer choices. Both charter schools and New Visions schools appear to have unifying themes and philosophies that are providing real choices for students and families. When schools attract like-minded students and families with common interests they are also likely to become cohesive communities.[28]

School Personnel

Many charter schools are born out of the dreams of educators who have not been able to achieve their vision in the norms, culture, and bureaucracy of conventional schools.[29] Similarly, several New Visions school principals we interviewed described their work as an "act of love" and expressed how lucky they felt at being able to "enact a dream" or "fulfill a lifelong goal." This sense of empowerment often translates into an intensive commitment; principals in both school types spend many hours working at their schools—many describing eleven- and twelve-hour workdays.[30] Their school day is often spent with students and teachers, and in fact many principals teach classes themselves and then stay extra hours to accomplish administrative tasks.

The leadership model that characterizes these schools also takes more time. New Visions principals were quick to say that leadership in their schools is a shared enterprise, with decisions being made "collaboratively" and with consensus in mind. There were few schools we visited in which teachers were not involved in curriculum development and making decisions about rules and regulations as well as teaching, advising, peer coaching, and leading various extracurricular activities.

Teachers in charter schools also like being involved in decision making, and they report being satisfied with their colleagues, the school's educational philosophy, the school's size, the students, the challenge to start a new school, and the administrators in the school.[31] Clearly, charter schools provide choice for teachers as well as for students and families, and they appear to attract faculty who welcome challenge and have a propensity for hard work.

The similar features shared by charter schools and "charterlike" New Visions schools—multiple partners, small size, unifying purposes, and committed personnel—have the potential to produce supportive and cohesive communities that may increase student learning and graduation rates. But schools exist in an organizational context that may either constrain or facilitate the attainment of their goals.[32] In the next section we consider the opportunities and barriers provided by the different organizational contexts in which charter schools and New Visions schools operate, using a framework provided by the Center for Educational Reform. The center has identified ten characteristics of state charter school legislation it considers expansive or "strong." Four of these criteria provide a setting for comparing the current reality of New Visions schools with the possibilities inherent in charter schools where there is a "strong" law. These characteristics include (1) multiple chartering authorities, (2) legal/operational autonomy, (3) automatic waivers from laws and regulations, and (4) exemption from collective bargaining agreements.

Differences between Charter and New Visions Schools

Legislation That Permits a Number of Entities, in Addition to or Instead of Local School Boards, to Authorize Charter Schools

The single most important factor in establishing a charter is the opportunity for those seeking charters to get approval from more than one institution, such as the local school board, the state department of education, or a university.[33] If the local school board is given exclusive authority to authorize charters, there may be a vested interest in approving only those schools that offer little competition for the district. Beyond providing a better learning experience for the small number of students who attend the school, a major purpose of charter schools is to break the local district's monopoly over education, and allow market forces to drive improvements in district schools. To accomplish this, states must have at least one other authorizing body and/or an appeal process that can overrule local district decisions that prevent the establishment of well-designed charter schools.

The New York State Charter School Act stipulates that three discrete chartering entities may approve applications for new charter schools: local school boards, the board of trustees of the State University of New York, and the state Board of Regents. Of these entities, the State University is tasked with approving fifty schools, and the remaining fifty are to be approved by either the state Board of Regents or local districts. The conversion of existing schools to charter school status calls for a different procedure, one that has direct implications for New Visions schools. While there may be an unlimited number of school conversions, the Charter Act contains two stipulations: schools must seek approval through their local district and, in districts with a population of one million or more, the chancellor is designated as the chartering entity.[34]

Former Chancellor Rudolph Crew was quick to express both praise for and discomfort with the passage of the Charter School Act. In a statement released in December 1998 he signaled that he intended to use his authority to charter schools "swiftly" and "in keeping with high standards for achievement." In the same statement, he declared that the Charter School Act was "fraught with peril," most notably because it threatens to drain funding from public education, it affords his office no ability to intervene in poorly performing charter schools, and it fails to "protect the rights and salaries of teachers, who are already woefully underpaid."[35] Crew's dissatisfaction stemmed from the act's stipulation that new schools with an enrollment of less than 250 students are not required to be affiliated with the local teachers' union and, while he has the power to limit the number of conversions from district to charter schools, those seeking to charter new schools may circumvent the chancellor and the New York City Board of Education altogether, and apply to the Board of Regents or the State University of New York.

New Visions Schools. The New York City Board of Education is organized into a central administration that oversees high schools and alternative schools, and thirty-two local community school districts to oversee elementary and middle schools, each with a district superintendent and local board. Whereas charter schools are (in most states) independent entities, the New Visions schools are an integral part of this bureaucratic structure. Until recently, applicants for small schools had only to obtain authorization from any of these divisions, which could grant approval without consultation with central headquarters.

This situation changed in 1998, when Chancellor Crew tightened controls on the creation of small schools by requiring all new schools to get approval from the central office.[36] This action made the central office the only authorizing agency for small schools and eliminated the previous option for new schools to seek approval through any of the community or borough districts. The new charter school law may have profound implications for the number, size, and type of schools that will be created in the future. However, the change in the approval process does not alter the way the small schools are organized within the system, since they will continue to be overseen by central authorities or local school districts.

Similar to charter schools, New Visions and the other small schools were intended as a departure from the huge scale and industrial atmosphere that characterizes many traditional schools in New York. They aim to accomplish this through a school design that replaces the factory model of education with a more personalized model focused on student learning and achievement. According to New Visions Vice President and CEO Beth Lief, the major advantage of remaining in the system is that the experience of principals in small schools will influence the behavior of principals of traditional schools. Lief claims that, "Administrators, mainstream and New Vision, sit at the table together in district meetings, so their effect is likely to be felt."[37] It is too early to gauge whether she is right, but it is clear that the small schools have paid a steep price to "sit at the table." The small schools have been subjected to the same bureaucratic demands imposed on large schools, even though they are not equipped to meet them. For example, a district office's demands on a school with a population of one hundred students are the same as those imposed on a large comprehensive high school with four thousand students. New Visions principals complained of being inundated with "paperwork," and pointed to stacks of papers on their desk, many a foot high. In these piles, there are daily, weekly, and monthly notices to read, forms to complete, and reports to write. Principals whose schools span both middle school and high school grades must comply with the demands of two different district superintendents. Principals also objected to being "pulled out" of their buildings too often to attend district meetings, both scheduled and emergency.

In large schools with a full staff of assistant principals, neither the paperwork nor the principal's absence to attend meetings is daunting. In small New Visions schools, where almost the entire faculty teaches, the school principal is often the only administrator, and there is no one else to whom the principal can delegate responsibility. Principals complained that meetings are lengthy and often do not relate to their unique pressing concerns. One principal of a school with an enrollment of one hundred students expressed the general sentiment: "I'm sitting in three-hour meetings with principals that have five thousand kids. They're talking about fights and weapons and we tell them we don't have any of those problems." A principal of a new school who said he was called to meetings several times a week exclaimed, "It's not enough to make [our school's] policy, we have to be there to implement it."

While most principals resented having to attend so many meetings, often irrelevant to their needs, some are equally troubled that they are not invited to principals' meetings or are simply ignored by district offices. Although a few principals talked about helpfulness and even support from superintendents and district staffs, many more principals expressed tension in these relationships. In some instances, there has been turnover in district superintendents and the small schools find themselves situated in districts that are now hostile to them. When asked about his school's mission, one faculty member was prompted to say, "Functionally, to stay in existence."

One reason for the tension is that the schools don't respond to the district office in a timely fashion. Many New Visions schools have been encouraged to be innovative, and many have changed long-established practices. One principal said that her school's goal was to "tear down the walls of traditional schools." This proves difficult when the school must fit into the system. For example, one school has chosen to issue six report cards a year instead of the usual three. "Our report cards are different," said a faculty member, "but we still have to use the Board format, which means we have to leave blanks in some of the boxes. This is confusing to parents. Schedules are different, but we have to open school on the day that the Board mandates it." Several principals used the word *challenge* in describing their relationship with the districts, but other principals were more graphic in expressing their frustrations: "We are a virus in the system," said one principal.

For their part, district superintendents are equally frustrated in having to deal with the small schools. Many district offices feel overburdened by their own responsibilities, and don't want to deal with small schools that one superintendent described as being "out of the box." Several superintendents fail to see the value of the small schools and consider them an annoyance. A high school superintendent lamented that the small schools "try to put all of their resources into teaching, then they can't get the paperwork done for us." Another noted similarly: "The schools place a priority on teachers and have very small administrations—typically just the principal who is the curriculum leader, building manager, decision maker, and filer of reports. Most other schools have assistant principals who help with these tasks, so often the paperwork does not take a higher priority. Each time the board of education wants a report done I need to make certain that all thirty-eight schools respond.—Thirty-four won't do."

Small schools with limited numbers of staff members, serving relatively few students, interfere with standard operating procedures and can be a nuisance for superintendents who are part of the larger chain of command. Furthermore, these schools were created with the support and enthusiasm of a previous chancellor, one whose ideas have given way to a more centralized view of management. The complex reporting relationships for schools that span more than one division, and the inflexibility of the system to bend to the needs and realities of small schools that are different by design, have sapped the energy of many New Visions schools' personnel.

Legislation That Allows Charter Schools to Become Legal Entities

Like New Visions schools, charter schools are public schools. However, they differ in that charter schools in states with strong laws are given legal status as corporate entities or nonprofit organizations. This status allows the schools to receive and disburse funds for legal purposes. The school is at liberty to purchase property and borrow money for capital investments. As a legal entity the school can contract for services such as building maintenance or after-school programs. The charter school has full control of budget allocations, personnel decisions, and the design of curriculum to meet state requirements. The school may also solicit and accept grants or gifts for educational purposes. To ensure that contractual agreements are met, the school may sue and be sued.

In New York State, charter schools are authorized to exist as corporate entities. Charter schools are granted a certificate of incorporation that legally designates them as "educational corporations." The Charter School Act goes on to define a charter school as an "independent and autonomous public school."[38] For purposes of local zoning, land use, building codes, and special education programs, the act stipulates that charter schools are to be treated as nonpublic schools. Like most charter schools in the nation, New York charter schools are nonprofit organizations.

As a nonprofit organization or corporate entity, a charter school is also assured autonomy through a governance structure that requires a voluntary board of trustees to oversee the school. The charter is granted to the board, which is vested with authority to ensure fiscal and managerial oversight. This includes responsibility for hiring and, if necessary, firing a principal, which helps to ensure that the school is well administered. Boards may also raise additional money for the school, and they provide a buffer against outside intervention. The majority of charter school boards act solely as a policy-making body, delegating full responsibility for the educational program and the day-to-day operation of the school to the principal and the staff.[39] This board support at the school level is important, since districts are often hostile toward charter schools in their locality. Most charter schools often achieve this support through a high representation of board members who are parents of current students. This assures a degree of parent involvement and a vested interest in the school's success.[40]

Unlike charter school boards that govern a single school, New Visions schools are overseen by local districts and the New York City Board of Education. The central Board of Education oversees all 1,129 public schools that are part of the New York City school system. To provide improved oversight, and to give those closest to the school a voice in shaping the goals and expectations of students, former Chancellor Crew released a plan to establish school leadership teams in each of New York City's schools by October 1999. The plan aimed to "decentralize school decision making" by involving parents, teachers, local administrators, and others in the community in creating a comprehensive educational plan for the school, as well as developing a school-based budget aligned with the school's goals and objectives.[41] However, unlike charter schools, these leadership teams have no authority to hire and fire the school's principal, or to formally evaluate the principal's effectiveness. Having responsibility without authority may ultimately undermine this plan's effectiveness.

New Visions and other small schools' freedom to regulate enrollment has become a source of contention within the New York City school system. The defining feature of the small school movement in New York City is scaled-down size. From the onset, New Visions for Public Schools called for small schools that would provide "personalized learning environments."[42] However, New Visions school principals often have to fight with district superintendents to maintain their small size, and there are indications that the battle will be more difficult to win in the future. In 1997, a staff report proposing minimum enrollment figures circulated by the chancellor's office set off a furor among those associated with the small schools, many of which did not meet the enrollment minimums. Chancellor Crew later retracted the memo and said that in approving future schools he would use "common sense and logic" to decide whether a proposed school was the right size.[43]

Small schools committed to low student enrollment may find solace in converting to charter school status. The Charter School Act stipulates that the number of students served at a single site shall be at least fifty; however, the school may serve fewer than fifty students if there is a "compelling justification." Since the chancellor of New York City is vested with the power to approve school conversions, it is unclear how or even whether school size will figure into the decision process.

Generally, New York City school principals have considerable power to use budgetary allocations creatively. However, the degree of budgetary autonomy a particular school enjoys often varies with the rapport the principal has with the district superintendent, and with the latitude the particular district accords. As one public school official said, "Often you can do what you want because no one is watching very closely." Several people described an informal merit system in which a school's level of autonomy is directly related to results. Schools with high retention rates, good attendance, good test scores, good college acceptance rates, and few "incidents" have a great deal of budgetary freedom.

The focus on results without careful consideration of the student population causes some schools to work hard at seeking high-ranking students. Most New Visions schools are in a category of "education option" schools for which student selection is determined by reading level. The schools are supposed to select 16 percent of students who score above reading level, 16 percent who score below reading level, and everyone else in between. To improve their outcomes, some New Visions schools are reputed to work with guidance counselors to attract higher achieving students. Charter schools may be less likely to engage in this type of manipulation, as they must be open to all who want to attend and schools that are oversubscribed must choose students by lottery.

Legislation That Provides Waivers from Regulations but Holds Schools Accountable for Results

CHARTER SCHOOLS. Some states give charter schools up-front waivers for all rules and regulations governing public schools in return for accountability. The essence of the charter idea is to give educators and parents an opportunity to create new schools or redesign existing schools that they believe will be effective in educating students if they accept responsibility for demonstrating student achievement. To accomplish this, charter schools are given "blanket" waivers or "superwaivers" exempting them from statutes and rules governing district schools (except those related to health, safety, and civil rights). Blanket waivers avoid the time-consuming and encumbered process of having to petition the state for exemptions one at a time.

In return for the freedom they are granted, the schools are subject to a review and a charter school renewal decision, usually every three to five years. If the school does not meet expectations, the charter may be revoked and the school will cease to exist. When the issue of accountability is well thought out, prior to granting a charter the applicants and the sponsoring organization agree on the school's measurable goals, the assessments that will be used to gauge achievement toward those goals, and acceptable levels of student performance.[44]

A national study on evaluation and performance of successful charter schools found that the schools used both standardized tests coupled with at least one other method of performance-based assessment such as teacher evaluations, student portfolios, and student presentations. Most schools in the study used three or four different approaches to assessment.[45] Many schools also issue annual reports, public documents that enumerate the school's goals and evidence that the goals have been achieved. Annual reports often cover student and faculty attendance and mobility rates, student behavior and attitudes, parental involvement and satisfaction, school climate, fiscal management, and program activities.[46]

The New York Charter School Act grants blanket waivers, stipulating that "a charter school shall meet the same health and safety, civil rights, and student assessment requirements applicable to other public schools except as otherwise provided in this [law]. A charter school shall be exempt from all other state and local laws, rules, regulations or policies governing public or private schools, boards of education and school districts, including those related to school personnel and students, except as specifically

provided in the school's charter or in this [law]." In return for this autonomy, charter schools are required to design educational programs that
meet or exceed the statewide standards of the Board of Regents.

Like all other public schools in the state, charter schools are required to
administer Regents exams to their students as an assessment of student
learning. If these assessments fall below a set level, and do not show improvement over the preceding three years, the state commissioner of education has the authority to terminate the charter and close the school.[47]

NEW VISIONS SCHOOLS. As part of the New York City school system,
New Visions schools are subject to the same regulations that apply to all
public schools. The schools' founding mandate—to be different, to enact
distinct philosophies, and to implement innovative learning approaches—
makes complying with these regulations difficult. For example, New Visions schools offer integrated activities and cross-grade courses that do not
fit the conventional school mold.

Although New York schools have the right to file petitions requesting
that the state waive code regulations, each regulation must be individually
negotiated. For example, waivers are required when a school wants to offer a humanities curriculum and needs one teacher for instruction in both
English and history. Most high school teachers are licensed in one subject
area. Teaching "out of field" is considered a violation of regulations,
even if the teacher has taken a concentration of courses in that discipline.
Waivers are also required to: change the sequence of subjects taught, such
as teaching global studies in the tenth grade instead of the ninth grade;
mainstream special education students into regular classrooms; or allocate
space in ways that fail to provide the per pupil footage specified by state
regulations. These regulations and statutes can be stifling for small schools
with limited staffing and which are often housed in buildings designed for
other purposes.

The thin administrative staff of most small schools does not afford
them the time required to work through the bureaucratic maze necessary
to obtain waivers, and many lack the political sophistication the process
requires. Even when waivers are granted, the state requires that schools
conduct an annual review comparing the objectives and outcomes of the
waivers, each year, for three years. In addition to state regulations, the
schools must also be responsive to local mandates and federal rules and
procedures connected with federal funding, such as Title I funding and
the Individuals with Disabilities Education Act, all of which come with
requisite paperwork. While charter schools are still subject to federal aid
program requests, blanket waivers from most local and state regulations
free the schools to make decisions, so long as they can demonstrate results.

New Visions schools continue to be stifled by regulations that limit school-level decision making and consume valuable time with paperwork intended to monitor compliance with regulations. However, the schools have no more fear of being closed than any other public school in the New York City system. New Visions schools do not operate with charters that assure a measure of longevity for positive outcomes, nor are the schools fearful they will be closed if student achievement is lacking.

Given the nebulous status of New Visions schools within the city system, imposing a rigid form of accountability may be in these schools' best interest. Indeed, this is the one area in which New Visions schools are asserting themselves by seeking waivers for alternative forms of assessment. New York State has recently imposed rigorous standards that require passing scores on six Regents examinations to earn an academic diploma. Cogent arguments have been made that a curriculum focused on such test scores may stifle intrinsic motivation and result in superficial learning.[48] New Visions schools are prepared to accept these new standards, but some schools feel that innovative curricula and efforts to meet students' social and emotional needs are incompatible with standardized testing. Additionally, many small schools are "last chance" schools for students who previously dropped out or were suspended. The schools are working hard to build student efficacy and to spark motivation to learn, goals they say would be undermined by the imposition of the state's tests. While all public schools in the state are struggling with these new requirements, the situation may be exacerbated in the small schools. To address these issues, some New Visions and other small schools have formed an alliance to seek waivers from the Regents exam and to substitute performance-based tests in their place.

Whether or not the state's new Regents requirements are realistic for most students, or even accurate measures of student performance, is a question practitioners in the state are grappling with. However, it may be impolitic or even unfair to argue that the tests should be waived for New Visions or other small schools' students. Many policy makers argue that standardized tests are the best mechanism we have for cutting through the culture of low expectations. While schools may rightly fight for public disclosure of "gain scores," which report progress over time rather than nationally normed scores, it is hard to justify abandoning standardized tests altogether. In a choice system, the New Visions schools must produce results that are easily understood by parents, policy makers, and taxpayers, so they can make informed choices and be assured that public money is wisely spent.

However, standardized tests should not be the sole form of assessment. New Visions schools are making an effort to develop "authentic assessments" of student learning that include portfolios, demonstrations, and exhibitions. These assessments, and the rubrics and observation protocols developed to review students' work, may be more relevant performance indicators for both students and teachers. While such alternative assessments may ultimately find their way into the school system as accepted practice, at the present time the schools may be too vulnerable to extinction if they abandon the state's Regents exams. Therefore, it may be in the best interest of New Visions and the various other small schools in the Networks for School Renewal to use school-developed measures in combination with standardized tests.

Legislation That Gives Charter Schools Control over Personnel Decisions

Some states allow charter schools to hire both state-certified and noncertified teachers who have sufficient experience and preparation in the field in which they teach, without providing disincentives to those already working in the system. Initial studies of charter school teachers show that the schools may be tapping into personnel who would not otherwise choose to teach in public schools. When charter school teachers were asked what they were likely to be doing if they weren't teaching in their particular school, only a third said they would choose to teach in another district public school. Almost half said they would be doing something other than teaching, or teaching in another charter school, or in a private school.[49] The likelihood that charter schools may be effective in attracting teachers from other sectors may be a practical advantage if predicted teacher shortages are accurate. It also turns out that even though charter schools are tapping into different sources for teachers, almost 90 percent are state certified teachers or working toward certification.[50]

In some states, certification protects teachers from losing seniority or accrued benefits such as local or state retirement plans. Teachers leaving another public school district to teach in a charter school are able to return to their former district school within a specified period of years without loss of status. Where such flexibility exists, teachers can choose to organize and bargain collectively, but separate from the district bargaining unit in which the school is located. Teachers can also choose to organize a cooperative or they can choose not to organize at all. Whether or not schools are unionized, small size and tight budgets dictate flexibility. Teachers who are sticklers for adhering to union guidelines would be uncomfortable with the multiple responsibilities that define the teacher's role in most charter schools.

Many states allow teachers who are not certified in administration to run charter schools. Charter advocate Ted Kolderie points out that such laws break with the long-held assumption that "if you want to be a teacher, you have to be an employee."[51] The desire to found and lead these schools usually evolves out of the desire for a better or different education than the public schools system can provide. Parents have started schools, as have both profit and nonprofit organizations and government agencies such as the U.S. Drug Enforcement Administration.[52]

The New York Charter School Act gives a school's board of trustees full discretion over contracting employment with teachers, administrators, and other school personnel. The act requires that the majority of charter school teachers hold state certification, but does give charter schools the flexibility to hire a limited number of experienced uncertified teachers, tenured college faculty, Teach for America alumni, and those "who possess exceptional business, professional, artistic, athletic, or military experience." The law does not set any certification criteria for charter school administrators.

New charter schools with an enrollment of fewer than 250 students are not deemed to be members of the district's existing collective bargaining unit, which allows these schools flexibility when negotiating contracts with teachers and administrators. Schools with an enrollment of 250 students or more and district schools that convert to charter status—the likely scenario for New Visions and other small charterlike schools—are covered in the district's preexisting collective bargaining agreements, and are considered part of the local collective bargaining unit. Ten of the fifty schools that can be converted or created by the State University can ask that these collective bargaining stipulations be waived.[53]

NEW VISIONS SCHOOLS. When the New Visions organization requested proposals, many teachers submitted applications and were given the opportunity to run a school. This changed in 1998, when Chancellor Crew mandated that only certified principals may head schools. If a school now wishes to hire someone other than a licensed and certified principal, a waiver must be requested from the State Education Department. Regular teaching assignments are also intended to be restricted to licensed personnel. However, a looming teacher shortage may make implementation of Crew's mandates unrealistic.[54] Consider, for example, that New York and other states throughout the nation already grant emergency licenses to more than fifty thousand people each year, and currently 27 percent of all teachers in the nation either have no teaching license or are working with a provisional or emergency license.[55]

Many New Visions schools have applied for a special "school based option" (SBO) arrangement negotiated with the teachers' union that allows a personnel committee at the school to select teachers. Administrators of schools that have SBO reveled in talking about hand picking their own faculty, and some use part of their funding from the New Visions organization for part-time nonlicensed consultants with special talents, such as musicians or choreographers. But not all schools have applied for School Based Options, perhaps as an outcome of preoccupation with the daily demands of school life. These principals are often obliged to hire teachers who are randomly sent to them by the district office.

"Charterlike" Schools and Educational Reform

Are the autonomy and accountability afforded New Visions "charterlike" schools sufficient for bringing about needed reform in New York City? Some educators and unionists have argued that there is no need for the more radical reforms that charter schools may bring. Clearly, the schools' small size, unifying sense of purpose, innovative instructional approaches, and committed teachers and administrators provide a more cohesive community than is generally found in conventional schools in New York City. The advantage of small schools is beginning to be documented by higher graduation rates, and the schools appear to be more humane places in which to study and work.

Nonetheless, this study points to the numerous constraints imposed on New Visions schools and the shortcomings of the current arrangement. Small schools are a misfit within the bureaucratized system of schooling in New York City. Rules and regulations imposed by districts and the accompanying paperwork to ensure their compliance sap the energy of school personnel whose efforts might be more productively directed toward student learning. These schools are constrained from decision making that would serve the best interests of students and parents, and at the same time, are annoyances to a district bureaucracy that must adhere to standard operating procedures.

Under present circumstances, the future for New Visions and other small schools in the Networks for School Renewal is uncertain. Even if existing schools remain, the reins have tightened on small schools, making it unlikely that small schools will be a force in New York City school reform. The lack of clear consequences and the schools' own movement away from state testing may increase their jeopardy. The schools have neither sufficient autonomy nor clear forms of accountability to ensure their continuance.

The implementation of "strong" charter legislation in other states has alleviated the kinds of limitations that are imposed on New York City's New Visions schools. Similarly, the New York Charter School Act of 1998 holds great promise for liberating teachers and administrators from the constraints of an encumbered system. Perhaps this explains why principals of Networks schools familiar with charter schools are consistently in favor of them. A large percentage of principals surveyed want more flexibility in the areas that charter schools provide: freedom to negotiate directly with teachers and support personnel, more control over budgets, and release from most federal, state, and local rules and regulations.[56] If

New Visions schools and the other schools in the Networks for School Renewal enjoy a degree of success, they do so despite the New York City public school system, not because of it. There is no simple answer to improving the quality of education for students in New York City, and charter schools are not a panacea. However, charter schools, in the hands of capable, caring, and committed teachers and administrators, do have the potential to instill new hope in the power of education.

NOTES

1. "Smaller, Better Schools," editorial, *New York Times,* June 2, 1995.
2. The Center for Educational Reform, "Charter School Highlights and Statistics-at-a-Glance," updated, December 20, 1999 [http://edreform.com/charters.htm].
3. "New York Networks for School Renewal: Helping Networks of Small Schools Revitalize Public Education" (New York: New York Networks for School Renewal, 1997), pp. 3, 5–6.
4. Peter Steinberg, program faculty, New Visions for Public Schools, personal interview, March 5, 1998.
5. Fund for New York City Public Education, "New Visions Schools: Request for Proposal" (New York: Fund for New York Public Education, 1992), pp. 1–2.
6. James Vlasto, communications director, New Visions for Public Schools, personal communication, December 14, 1998.
7. The "Memorandum" describes a school as "a self-contained, autonomous organization of students, using its own staff and budget to provide a full instructional program." A program is described as "affiliated with host schools and under the direction of the school principal." Programs are supported through resources that are part of the regular school budget. See Rudolph F. Crew, "Chancellor's Memorandum No. 2: Guidelines for the Creation of Learning Communities: Programs, Academies, and Schools," Board of Education of the City of New York, June 17, 1998, p. 3.
8. Enrollment figures supplied by telephone, Andrew Neuman, communications assistant, New Visions for Public Schools, September 3, 1998.
9. Paul Berman, Beryl Nelson, Rebecca Perry, Debra Silverman, and Nancy Kamprath, *A National Study of Charter Schools: Third-Year Report* (Washington, D.C.: Office of Educational Research and Improvement, U.S. Department of Education, 1998), pp. 5–6, 9.
10. Center for Educational Reform, "Charter School Legislation: State Rankings," October 1998 [http://www.edreform.com/laws/ranking.htm].
11. A random sample of twenty-five New Visions schools and programs was selected via a random-number generator from a list of all known New Visions schools and programs. Although response rates were low (52 percent), the enrollment of the New Visions schools that responded (mean of 218) correspond to the enrollment of all of the New Visions schools (mean of 301) according to enrollment data supplied by the New Visions for Public Schools, September 3, 1998. There still exists some danger of experimental bias in our study due to the small response rate. A further study should determine if there were significant differences between the schools that responded and those that did not.

12. Concurrently, I worked with another team of researchers to study the first year of New Jersey's charter schools. The findings, as reported in Pearl Rock Kane, "New Jersey Charter Schools: The First Year, 1997–1998" (Trenton: New Jersey Institute for School Innovation, 1998), provide comparative data.

13. Berman et al., *A National Study of Charter Schools: Third-Year Report*, p. 27.

14. Institute for Education and Social Policy, *Who We Are: Students and Schools in the NYNSR Project, 1995–96*, a report of the New York Networks for School Renewal (NYNSR) Research Collaborative (New York: Institute for Education and Social Policy, New York University, 1997), pp. 6–9.

15. Berman et al., *A National Study of Charter Schools: Third-Year Report*, p. 41.

16. Ibid., p. 38.

17. Institute for Education and Social Policy, *New York Networks for School Renewal and English Language Learners* (New York: Institute for Education and Social Policy, New York University, 1998), pp. 7–8.

18. Institute for Education and Social Policy, *Who We Are*, p. 10. At the elementary school level, 2.9 percent of the students in Networks schools are designated as requiring special education, compared to 4.9 percent of the students in other New York City public schools; at the high school level, 1.6 percent of the Networks' students are designated as requiring special education, compared with other New York City public schools. However, more Networks' middle school students are designated as requiring special education than other New York City public schools—8.1 compared with 6.9.

19. Ibid., p. iii.

20. Kane, "New Jersey Charter Schools," p. 15.

21. Brunno V. Manno, Chester E. Finn Jr., Louann A. Bierlein, and Gregg Vanourek, "Charter Schools in Action: How Charter Schools are Different: Lessons and Implications" (Washington, D.C.: Hudson Institute, 1997), p. 3.

22. Data on New Visions schools supplied by telephone, public information, New Visions for Public Schools, September 4, 1998; data on the New York City Public School System is derived from the 1998 State Report Cards. The raw data is available at http://www.nysed.gov/emsc/report 398/database.html.Disk 1 (March 11, 1998).

23. Berman et al., *A National Study of Charter Schools: Third-Year Report*, pp. 20–21.

24. Fund for New York City Public Education, "New Visions Schools: Request for Proposal," pp. 1–2; and Berman, Nelson, Ericson, Perry, and Silverman, *A National Study of Charter Schools: Second-Year Report*, p. 40.

25. Kane, "New Jersey Charter Schools," p. 14.

26. Jeremy D. Finn and Charles M. Achilles, "Answers and Questions about Class Size: A Statewide Experiment," *American Educational Research Journal* 27, no. 3 (1990).

27. Leanna Stiefel, Patrice Iatoarola, Norm Fruchter, and Robert Berne, *The Effect of Student Body on School Costs and Performance in New York City High Schools* (New York: Institute for Education and Social Policy, New York University, 1998). The study includes only high schools that enroll a majority of their students from junior high/intermediate schools at the ninth grade. Schools that enroll students transferring from other educational settings from which they may have dropped out or

have been suspended, often called "last chance schools," are not included in the study.

28. James S. Coleman and Thomas Hoffer, *Public and Private High Schools: The Impact of Communities* (New York: Basic Books, 1987), pp. 8–10.

29. Manno, Finn, Bierlein, and Vanourek, *Charter Schools in Action,* "How Charter Schools Are Different," part 6, p. 2.

30. New Jersey charter school directors, personal interviews, February through April 1998.

31. Manno, Finn, Bierlein, and Vanourek, *Charter Schools in Action,* "Charter Schools as Seen by Those Who Know Them Best: Students, Teachers and Parents," part 1, p. 6.

32. For a discussion on the institutional structure of schools see John E. Chubb and Terry Moe, *Politics, Markets, and America's Schools* (Washington, D.C.: Brookings Institution, 1990), pp. 141–84.

33. Ted Kolderie, "Model Charter School Bills" (Minneapolis: Center for Policy Studies, University of Minnesota, 1998), p. 2.

34. New York State Charter School Act of 1998, Article 56, sec. 2851.

35. Statement of Chancellor Rudolph F. Crew on the passage of charter school legislation in New York State, issued by the Board of Education of the City of New York, December 18, 1998.

36. Rudolph F. Crew, "Chancellor's Memorandum No. 2: Guidelines for the Creation of Learning Communities: Programs, Academies, and Schools," issued by the Board of Education of the City of New York, June 17, 1998, p. 4.

37. Beth J. Lief, president and CEO, New Visions for Public Schools, personal interview, March 13, 1998.

38. New York State Charter School Act of 1998, Article 56, sec. 2853.

39. Pearl Kane, Joe Conway, Chris Pryor, Morton Ballen, and Norman Atkins, "Charter School Governance: A National Survey," unpublished study, Teachers College, Columbia University, 1996.

40. Ibid.

41. New York City Board of Education, "Governance and Decentralization: School Leadership Teams, Core Principles Related to Schools," November 1998 (http:205.232.145.43/).

42. Fund for New York City Public Education, "New Visions Schools: Request for Proposal," 1992, p. 2.

43. Anemona Hartocollis, "No Enrollment Minimum Set for Small Schools," *New York Times,* October 18, 1997, sec. B, p. 3.

44. Stella Cheung, Mary Ellen S. Murphy, and Joe Nathan, *Making a Difference? Charter Schools, Evaluation, and Student Performance* (Minneapolis: Center for School Change, Hubert H. Humphrey Institute of Public Affairs, University of Minnesota, 1998), p. 20.

45. Ibid., p. 10.

46. Ibid., pp. 21–22.

47. New York State Charter School Act of 1998, Article 56, secs. 2854 and 2855.

48. Kennon M. Sheldon and Bruce J. Biddle, "Standards, Accountability, and School Reform: Perils and Pitfalls," *Teachers College Record* 100, no. 1 (1998).

49. Manno, Finn, Bierlein, and Vanourek, *Charter Schools in Action*, "Charter Schools as Seen by Those Who Know Them Best," Final Report, part 1, pp. 6–7.

50. Ibid., p. 7.

51. Kolderie, "Model Charter School Bills," p. 6.

52. Manno, Finn, Bierlein, and Vanourek, *Charter Schools in Action*, Final Report, part 6, p. 3.

53. New York State Charter School Act of 1998, Article 56, sec. 2854.

54. The National Commission on Teaching and America's Future, *What Matters Most: Teaching for America's Future* (New York: National Commission on Teaching and America's Future, 1996), p. 8.

55. Ibid., p. 8.

56. Mark Schneider and Paul Teske, *Does New York City Need Charter Schools? The View of Principals of Small Public Schools* (New York: Manhattan Institute with the Center for Educational Innovation, 1998).

4   Contractual Constraints on School Management: Principals' Perspectives on the Teacher Contract

DALE BALLOU

The contract between the Board of Education of New York City and the United Federation of Teachers is 204 pages long. It covers a wide range of subjects of concern to teachers who work in the city's schools: work loads, compensation, assignments, evaluation, promotion, pension and retirement programs, dismissals, and layoffs, to name only some. As such, it has a substantial impact on the way education is conducted in New York City. This is scarcely a novel or controversial observation. Supporters of teachers' unions as well as their critics agree that unions wield great influence over education.

> In less than a half century, teachers have risen from being under-paid, under-valued "semi-professionals" . . . to becoming the most powerful voice in education, key leaders within the larger labor movement, and prime movers in regional and national politics. To a large degree, this emergence from obscurity to prominence, from being exploited, sympathy-invoking martyrs to respected agents at the bargaining table and in the halls of government, is the result of the unionization of teachers . . . a phenomenon common in virtually every developed nation on earth.[1]

Consensus on the importance of teachers' unions gives way to disagreement, however, on the question of whether unionization and collective bargaining have helped or harmed public education. Not surprisingly, teachers' unions take the position that the influence has been beneficial. In the view of union leaders, the policies that teachers have sought through collective bargaining are merely those that an enlightened management would recognize for itself as in the best interest of public education. Union goals are, first, to achieve fundamental fairness for its members, and second, to improve public education by promoting reforms that the Board of Education would not otherwise have adopted on its own.[2] Contract provisions forestall autocratic administrators and misguided school boards from imposing working conditions that would prevent teachers from performing at their best, demoralize the work force, and make it difficult to attract capable individuals into teaching. More recently, with the advent of the "new unionism" espoused by the leaders of the National Education Association and the American Federation of Teachers, collective bargaining is seen as the primary mechanism ensuring teachers a collaborative role in the operation of the school system, collaboration that is ultimately in the best interests of students.

This portrayal of union activities is clearly self-serving. However, it should not be dismissed out of hand. In the first place, it is true that the contract in New York City (like teacher contracts elsewhere) contains many provisions that attempt to correct past abuses. Moreover, in several respects the current contract attempts to ameliorate some of the excesses of the old unionism. The contract does create more opportunities for collaboration. Some of it will likely be beneficial to students. On the other hand, several recent studies suggest that teacher unionization has not had an altogether benign influence on public education. Studies of the Boston and Milwaukee school systems and a review of teacher contracts in Michigan reveal significant ways in which collective bargaining has tied the hands of administrators, impeded reform, and made it more difficult to restore accountability for educational achievement.[3]

The discussion here continues this line of investigation by examining the impact of the UFT contract on the operation of the city's public schools. It does not attempt to consider all aspects of the contract. Rather, it focuses on the question: does the contract pose significant impediments to the efforts of school administrators to deliver educational services in their schools? Is it true that there is no fundamental conflict between the provisions of the contract and the policies that an enlightened administration would follow anyway? Or has the contract become an obstacle, a roadblock in the way of needed reforms?

How This Research Was Conducted

A close reading of the collective bargaining agreement between the Board of Education and the UFT turns up numerous provisions that constrain administrators. This is, of course, only to be expected, as it is the very purpose of a contract to restrict managerial prerogatives. But there is reason to be concerned about the nature of these restrictions. The UFT contract bears a strong resemblance to collective bargaining agreements in other urban systems that have been judged to have a negative impact on education performance. Among the features of these contracts that cause concern are excessively rigid work rules that deprive schools of the necessary autonomy and flexibility to carry out their educational missions, and numerous obstacles in the form of due process requirements that make it difficult to terminate incompetent teachers.

In addition to a study of the contract, this research draws on interviews with principals who work in the city's schools. Although the number of participating principals was small (eleven), they represented all levels of the system (elementary, intermediate, and high school) as well as both traditional and alternative schools. These interviews were useful for two reasons. First, they provided a check on conclusions based on the study of the contract. Second, these interviews provided specific examples of the way that administrators' efforts to improve the educational environment for students are frustrated by provisions in the agreement.

The sample of interviewees was small for several reasons. First was simply the cost of conducting interviews lasting forty-five minutes to an hour. Even with substantially greater resources than were available for this project, it would not have been possible to speak with more than a small fraction of the system's principals. Second was the need to assure principals of confidentiality. Many principals are reluctant to speak frankly on the subjects raised by this research. Securing cooperation required working through an intermediary whom principals trust, and even then some administrators who were approached were not willing to participate. Finally, there was substantial overlap in the concerns expressed by the participating principals. The interview process ended when it became apparent that further discussions would be unlikely to reveal new areas of concern, but would instead furnish only more examples of the problems already identified.

This does not mean the principals interviewed constituted a representative sample of New York City school principals. Indeed, the way that principals were selected for this study virtually ensures that they are not representative, since all of them have been involved in school reform, promoting changes within their buildings and throughout the district.[4] Thus they are more likely to be representative of an "activist" set of principals interested in improving the way education is conducted in the city than of the average or typical administrator.

While a wider sample of principals might have been more typical, in certain important respects it was useful to limit interviews to principals with a strong interest in education reform. Wholesale changes in the contract will not occur overnight, but rather in a piecemeal, incremental manner. In this process, reform-oriented principals will play a key role in demonstrating which changes are of greatest value. One change, for example, is that New York's new charter school law does not require charter schools serving fewer than 250 students to be unionized. Freedom from the constraints of the local collective bargaining agreement is of greatest value, of course, to principals who are interested in changing the status quo. Thus, the views expressed by the principals interviewed for this study indicate what may be at stake as faculty of charter schools confront the choice whether to unionize.

Principals' concerns tended to focus on matters close to their immediate responsibilities. As a result, these interviews dealt with such questions as who works in a school, what tasks they are assigned, how to deal with teachers who perform poorly, and how faculty and administration can work more cooperatively. Principals rarely commented on provisions of the contract that dealt with matters beyond their control, such as salaries. In keeping with their concerns, this chapter is also limited to aspects of the contract that constrain day-to-day decision making at the school level.

In the final stage of this research, the Board of Education was approached for statistical information to verify claims made by principals. In some instances these claims could not be corroborated, reflecting the fact that principals are not always well informed about the provisions of the contract or the impact that it has on the school system. Interviews with several officials at the board provided additional insight and perspective into the operation of the system and the role of the contract. The views reported here are not, therefore, the unedited opinions of the principals interviewed, but rather represent statements that were consistent with the language of the contract and with statistical evidence and other information provided by knowledgeable officials at the board.

As noted above, the agreement between the Board of Education and the UFT covers a wide range of personnel and educational practices. It is not, however, the only source of rules and regulations affecting the city's schools. The Board of Education has its own by-laws and directives. State education law also governs certain key personnel decisions. Principals themselves do not always know whether restrictions on managerial prerogatives are due to language in the contract, to regulations issued by the board, or to legislation.

This report concerns the contract, although at places it is also necessary to deal with the policies of the board and with education law, when the operation of the contract can only be understood within a broader context. In part this is because the contract is not the sole device by which the UFT presses its agenda. The political clout of the union ensures that its concerns will be taken into account both by the board and the state legislature. Full appreciation of contract language at times requires knowing how specific provisions of the bargaining agreement are complemented or qualified by directives and circulars issued by the board and by acts of the legislature.

There is a second reason why there is no hard-and-fast line between the collective bargaining agreement and the by-laws and regulations of the Board of Education. The contract subsumes many of the board's own policies in an article entitled "Matters Not Covered," quoted here in full.

> With respect to matters not covered by this Agreement which are proper subjects for collective bargaining, the Board agrees that it will make no changes without appropriate prior consultation and negotiation with the Union.
>
> The Board will continue its present policy with respect to sick leave, sabbatical leaves, vacations and holidays except insofar as change is commanded by law.
>
> All existing determinations, authorizations, by-laws, regulations, rules, rulings, resolutions, certifications, orders, directives, and other actions, made, issued or entered into by the Board of Education governing or affecting salary and working conditions of the employees in the bargaining unit shall continue in force during the term of this Agreement, except insofar as change is commanded by law.[5]

As a result, on a wide range of issues it is immaterial whether principals are constrained by provisions of the contract or by directives of the board. The latter are effectively as much a part of the contract as articles that were the specific subjects of negotiation.

Staffing

When discussing the problems that the contract poses, principals return to one issue again and again: under the terms of the contract, they are unable to control who teaches at their schools. This is not to say that principals lack any say in staffing decisions. By and large principals have a considerable amount of discretion in hiring teachers new to the school system. As a result, new teachers tend to share the principal's educational priorities and beliefs. This is not true, however, of veteran teachers in the system who can be forced on the school for one of three reasons: (1) they transfer into the school under the UFT's transfer system; (2) they are "excessed in" when jobs are eliminated in other schools in the system; (3) they are moved into the school when the system is downsizing and teachers are being laid off.

Under the UFT transfer system, principals post vacancies at their schools during spring "reorganization" when staffing and assignment decisions are made for the following school year. Teachers elsewhere in the system who hold the appropriate license(s) and have received satisfactory ratings for three consecutive years, including the year of transfer, may apply for the position.[6] The most senior applicant is awarded the job.

Excessing occurs when schools lose positions and thereby find themselves with a surplus of faculty. If not enough teachers volunteer for reas-
signment to other schools, teachers with licenses in the fields or grade levels that are in surplus are removed from the school in reverse order of
seniority, although this basic procedure is subject to an elaborate set of
rules that seek to minimize certain kinds of disruptions (e.g., in special education) and to protect teachers who are licensed in subjects other than the
ones they are currently teaching. Where possible, excessed teachers are
placed in vacancies within the same district. If there are no vacancies
within the district, they are placed elsewhere within the system. If there are
no vacancies within the system, the rules for excessing cease to apply and
layoffs take place instead following procedures established by state law.
These rules permit senior teachers to bump junior teachers with the same
licenses.

In a typical year some five to eight hundred teachers transfer under the
seniority-based system.[7] This averages to fewer than one per school, a figure that may not appear particularly high. Nonetheless, the principals interviewed for this study held the transfer and excessing rules responsible
for some of their biggest problems. One termed a principal's inability to
choose his staff the single worst feature of the contract. Principals who
have not had to accept incoming transfers are quick to acknowledge their
good fortune. Some have resorted to various stratagems to scare off teachers they don't want. One, for example, has asked prospective transfers
what they would do if a student brought a gun to class. Another has consciously cultivated a reputation of being a "bitch to work for." However,
not every principal is able to dissuade unwelcome teachers from transferring in. In fact, the contract does not even assure them of the opportunity
to try, since teachers who transfer into a school are not obliged to meet with
the principal before the first day of the school term. As one principal noted,
"I won't necessarily have the chance to discourage someone I don't want,
or even to find out if it's someone I will want or not."

In the past, principals have protected positions from the transfer system by withholding information on vacancies. For example, teachers who
were planning to retire were encouraged to wait until after the spring reorganization to submit formal notice. By this and similar devices, principals avoided posting their vacancies until the transfer period was over, at
which point they could fill these jobs with teachers of their own choosing.
These methods for circumventing the transfer system were unpopular
with the UFT, which subsequently negotiated language into the contract
to close this loophole, at least in part. Under the current contract, half the
vacancies in a school must be opened to the transfer system. (The principal can fill the other half with teachers of his or her choosing.) Moreover,
positions that were not listed as vacant the previous spring are treated the

following spring as if they were still vacant. Thus, unless such a position is among the 50 percent that the principal is able to protect from the transfer system, senior teachers from elsewhere in the system are permitted to bump the instructor who was hired in the meantime from the job.

The transfer system interferes with efforts to build an effective instructional team. Ironically, successful principals are most likely to be penalized. Many teachers are eager to transfer into schools that seem safer and better managed than those in which they have been working, even if they care nothing for innovations that the principal and other faculty are enthusiastic about. Their unwillingness to cooperate dampens morale and makes it harder to carry out improvements in the instructional program. Still worse are the ineffective teachers who are passed from school to school rather than terminated, a process characterized by one principal as a game of "pass the lemon." As principals have noted, it takes only one or two of these teachers to poison the atmosphere in an entire school.

Dissatisfaction with the UFT transfer plan and the obstacles it poses to educational reform at the school level were recognized by both the Board of Education and the UFT when the current contract was negotiated. The result was an alternative transfer plan operating under contract provisions governing School Based Options. Under the SBO transfer plan, schools may create a personnel committee to select staff for all vacant positions. These committees establish criteria for filling vacancies based on instructional needs, determine the process for recruiting teachers, conduct interviews, and make final hiring decisions. These committees are permitted to give precedence to non-senior applicants if their qualifications warrant it: "The personnel committee will select the most experienced qualified applicant of those candidates who apply for vacancies advertised under the transfer component of the SBO transfer and staffing plan. However, a less experienced applicant may be selected if the committee determines that the applicant possesses extraordinary qualifications."[8]

There were high hopes for this measure when it was introduced. The press and other local media took the Transfer and Staffing SBO, along with other school-based options, as signs of a new collaboration between the Board of Education and the UFT. The union pointed to this provision of the contract to answer critics who claimed that the union's rigid position on personnel matters was an impediment to reform. The contract itself contained an unusual statement boosting the reform: "It is our joint expectation that by the final year of the agreement all schools will have personnel committees and will receive the training necessary to undertake the process of staffing their schools."[9]

These words were written in 1995. The contract is now in its fourth year (1999–00), and the results have not justified this initial burst of optimism. Of the 1,136 schools in the system, 150 use personnel committees under the

Transfer and Staffing SBO. A year ago there were 138, and before that about 120. Although these numbers suggest slow but steady progress, the apparent trend is deceiving, as many of the schools now using the SBO are doing so for the first time. Fewer than half of the schools using the SBO in 1998–99 did so the year before. Clearly, many of the schools that tried it have subsequently reverted to the old system. Several factors appear to be responsible.[10] First, service on the personnel committee is voluntary; teachers are not compensated for a job that makes considerable demands on their time. Principals have also remarked on the cumbersome nature of the process. According to one, where it formerly took twenty hours to hire four or five persons, it now takes upward of one hundred. In some schools that initially embraced the Transfer and Staffing SBO, teachers and administrators appear to have burned out.

In some cases principals have been disappointed by the results. Fear of unsatisfactory outcomes has dissuaded other principals from pursuing the option in the first place. A majority of the members of the personnel committee must be teachers appointed by the UFT chapter leader. Principals have commented that they are unwilling to cede control of these decisions to such a committee, particularly when relations with the UFT chapter leader are not good. The committee must also contain parents selected by the school's parent association. As principals have noted, teachers and parents have not had the kind of training or experience that inclines them to look at the needs of the school as a whole when making personnel decisions.

In several ways, the SBO transfer and staffing plan actually diminishes the principal's authority over hiring. Whereas the contract allows principals to protect 50 percent of their vacancies from the traditional transfer system, a school that follows the SBO staffing plan must do so for all vacancies. Thus the personnel committee makes all hiring decisions, including the selection of new teachers, which was formerly under the sole control of the principal. Finally, although the SBO transfer and staffing plan allows the personnel committee to hire less experienced teachers whose qualifications are "extraordinary," these decisions can be appealed and taken to arbitration by senior teachers who are turned down. According to the Board of Education, about thirty schools were taken to arbitration last year. Although "only a handful" of decisions were overturned, these grievances add to the work involved and to principals' uncertainty about the outcome.

Finally, even where the SBO transfer and staffing plan is working well, it does not protect participating schools from excessing and layoffs, the effects of which can be worse than transfers. Such a case arose in one of the city's alternative high schools that had been among the first to implement a Transfer and Staffing SBO. The teacher who was excessed in had no interest in the school's innovative instructional program, which involved interdisciplinary team teaching, and she wished only to be permitted to teach her class in the traditional way. The personnel committee protested her assignment to the school. Teachers and parents wrote letters to the union and to the Board of Education. In the words of the principal: "It was a nightmare. It totally undermined the SBO process. Everyone was up in arms."

The final disposition of this case illustrates both the constraints confronting principals and the possibilities for circumventing the system in the right circumstances. A short-term solution was found when the principal obtained discretionary funds from the district superintendent to hire another teacher for the regular classroom. The excessed teacher was assigned to the school's resource room. The principal then began to document her failure to fulfill her duties, a task made easier in that the school was one of the system's alternative high schools, with additional faculty responsibilities stipulated in a "Memorandum of Understanding" between the staff and the Board of Education. (For example, teachers were expected to attend two weeks of summer meetings to plan curricula.) In the principal's words: "I started to put the heat on her." At the same time, he sought the union's assistance in arranging a transfer. Even so, the teacher turned down several offers of other jobs. She was finally persuaded to transfer only when the principal persuaded the Board of Education to finance a sabbatical for her on the understanding that when the sabbatical ended she was to transfer out via the seniority transfer system.

Teacher Evaluation and Termination

State education law grants teachers tenure after five years of continuous service. In New York City, this period is effectively shortened to three years by the contract, which assures teachers who have completed three years of service the same rights of appeal and review guaranteed tenured instructors.[11] In addition, as public employees, teachers are protected against arbitrary dismissal. As a result, tenured teachers enjoy an extraordinary degree of job protection.

Although it is a commonplace that teacher contracts have made it very difficult to fire ineffective instructors, the reasons are not as widely appreciated. The process of dismissing a tenured teacher begins with the documentation of professional misconduct.[12] Typically this means that the principal places letters and memoranda in the teacher's file, on the basis of which the teacher receives an unsatisfactory rating in the annual evaluation. Teachers must be shown all letters and other documents that are placed in their files and are entitled to file a grievance over any item. The first step in the grievance procedure is a meeting at the school between the teacher and the principal. At the teacher's request, the UFT chapter leader at the school may also be present at this meeting. If the grievance is not resolved to the teacher's satisfaction at this time, it can then be appealed to the district level. The superintendent or a designated representative meets with the teacher and union representative and renders a decision in writing. If this decision is not satisfactory, the union may appeal the matter to the chancellor's level, where the case is heard once again and another written decision issued.

If the union is still not satisfied with the outcome, the grievance can then be taken to arbitration, provided it involves the application or interpretation of the contract. As specified in Article 22C of the contract, this involves virtually any dispute in which there is disagreement over the facts of the case:

> Grievances involving the exercise of Board discretion under any term of this Agreement may be submitted to arbitration to determine whether the provision was disregarded or applied in a discriminatory or arbitrary or capricious manner so as to constitute an abuse of discretion, namely: whether the challenged judgment was based upon facts which justifiably could lead to the conclusion as opposed to merely capricious or whimsical preferences, or the absence of supporting factual reasons.[13]

After the teacher has exhausted all opportunities to remove material from his file through grievances, he may challenge the unsatisfactory rating itself by filing an appeal with the Office of Appeals and Reviews of the Board of Education. This involves another hearing at which the principal must present the evidence supporting this decision. Certain items are inadmissible. In particular, no evidence on the quality of the teacher's work can be presented from schools where the teacher may have worked previously, including schools within the New York City system.[14] The teacher may be represented by the union and has the right to submit evidence and call witnesses.

If the reviewing officer sustains the principal's rating, the superintendent of the district in which the teacher is employed may refer the case to the Office of Legal Affairs to seek termination of employment. If the board's lawyers decide there is sufficient evidence to bring the case to trial, it goes to a disciplinary hearing governed by Section 3020-a of the state education law. This is a legal proceeding in which the teacher is represented by attorneys from the UFT and the board by its own lawyers. The teacher has the right to subpoena and cross-examine witnesses. Teachers who are charged with incompetence have the right (invariably exercised) to have the hearing before a three-member panel of arbitrators; those facing other charges (e.g., chronic absenteeism) are heard by a single officer. The hearing officer (or panel) renders a decision on the facts of the case and on the penalties or other actions that the Board of Education shall take. Termination is the severest penalty, involving the loss of license. Alternatively, the officer may impose various types of remedial action, including a leave of absence, continuing education or study, counseling, or medical treatment. Finally, a teacher who is dismissed in a 3020-a proceeding has the right to appeal to the state supreme court under the relevant sections of the civil service law.

Principals contacted for this research agreed that terminating a teacher's employment is a difficult, time-consuming task. Principals speak of the need to establish an iron-clad case, to provide excessive documentation in anticipation that some of the evidence will be successfully challenged. In the words of one: "I need fifteen documented screw-ups, because some will be thrown out." Another principal, describing his efforts to remove an emotionally disturbed teacher from his school, displayed a three-ring binder filled with letters and other documentation he had prepared for a 3020-a hearing.

The number of tenured teachers who are dismissed through disciplinary hearings is quite small. Between February 1997 and March 1998, the Office of Legal Affairs won cases against seventeen teachers. Another seven cases were lost, and thirty-three more resulted in some other outcome, as stipulated by the hearing officer. These other outcomes often represent a kind of "plea bargaining" involving some lesser penalty. For example, teachers may be permitted to resign without loss of license. They may be fined, suspended without pay, or required to take a leave of absence. In some cases teachers must seek remediation (e.g., in the system's Peer Intervention Program).[15]

While these terminations may represent important victories, the number of cases is very small for a school system that employs 68,000 teachers. In part, this is the fault of principals. In a typical year only four to five hundred teachers in the entire system appeal unsatisfactory ratings.[16] The vast majority of teachers are rated satisfactory. Principals therefore bear much of the responsibility for the fact that many ineffective teachers are permitted to continue working within the district year after year. For this reason, claims that the contract is responsible must be regarded with caution. Such arguments can be self-serving, as principals seek to excuse their own failure as supervisors.

Yet the problem is not solely due to lax administration. As noted above, the principals interviewed for this study tended to be activist, reform-minded administrators. Several had sought, some successfully, to have poor teachers fired. Their testimony on this point is not an effort to scapegoat the contract for their own failings. On the contrary, these are principals who have tried to work within the structure established by the contract, Board of Education policy, and state law, to remove unqualified teachers from the classroom. Their comments are particularly useful in understanding why the present system discourages even conscientious administrators from attempting to dismiss poor instructors.

The greatest problem appears to be the time required to carry out frequent classroom observations and document teachers' failings. As one principal flatly stated: "You cannot go after more than one or two teachers at once. There simply isn't time." This burden is exacerbated by the challenges principals will face from union representatives and attorneys at these hearings. The union's standard position in these proceedings is that the problem is not the teacher but the principal, who has singled out an instructor for unfair, even malicious prosecution. Any inconsistency in the principal's actions will be exploited in an effort to substantiate this claim. As one principal related: "Suppose I have a teacher who is absent twelve days during the year. I put a letter in her file, which she grieves. At the hearing the union asks: 'Did you review everyone's cumulative absences register? Did you send this letter to every single person who was absent ten or more days?'" Other principals made the same point. A principal who wants to dismiss an ineffective teacher cannot scrutinize that teacher's performance to the exclusion of others in the school without giving credibility to charges of harassment. This can add considerably to the time required to document misconduct, particularly in schools in which the ratio of staff to supervisors is high. In one of the schools visited for this research, for example, the principal was the sole administrator with supervisory authority, overseeing a faculty of forty teachers. In these circumstances, it is very difficult to conduct even one formal observation on each teacher every year.[17] As this principal remarked: "I'm limited in what I can do with my time. I have to prioritize. The UFT knows this."

The burden on principals is increased by the expectation that the school system will attempt to remediate problems before seeking to terminate an employee. As one principal observed: "At the same time I am documenting misconduct, I have to make it appear that I'm helping this teacher, or I could be charged with harassment." Even when harassment is not a threat, failure to pursue remediation considerably weakens the board's case if charges are brought. State education law on 3020-a hearings states:

> In determining what, if any, penalty or other action shall be imposed, the hearing officer shall consider the extent to which the employing board made efforts towards correcting the behavior of the employee which resulted in charges being brought under this section through means including but not limited to: remediation, peer intervention or an employee assistance plan.

Often the Office of Legal Services will not charge a teacher until there is evidence that remediation has been tried and failed.

When hearings begin, principals can be called away from their schools for hours, even days. Substitutes must be found for staff who will be called as witnesses. There is also an emotional cost, as principals can look forward to having their motives and their professional judgment challenged throughout the proceedings. As one principal said: "The process sets you up for personal ridicule by the union." In the words of others: "The board of education doesn't show principals how to prepare the necessary documentation. You walk through a legal minefield with no help." "The deck is stacked against you." "You're outmatched."

Long delays in the process discourage principals from pursuing teachers who will continue to work under their supervision until the legal proceedings have finally ground to a halt. Grievances are one of the main sources of delay. Teachers are permitted to appeal every item in their files. In past years this played havoc with 3020-a proceedings. It was not unusual for lawyers for the Board of Education to learn in the middle of a case that evidence had disappeared from a teacher's file as a result of a grievance settlement. In recent years, policy has changed: charges will not be filed until all grievances have been concluded. But this in itself represents a delay.

The 3020-a proceedings are also protracted. State education law stipulates that within fifteen days of the selection of a hearing officer, a pre-hearing is to be held on each case. Within another sixty days a full hearing is to be scheduled, and within thirty days of that date, the hearing officer is to issue his final report. In reality these deadlines are routinely violated. Four to five months go by before hearings are scheduled. The delay is worst when the charges involve incompetence and a three-member panel must be convened, a circumstance that requires coordinating the schedules of three officers. According to the Office of Legal Services, the average 3020-a proceeding involving charges of incompetence takes 285 days to resolve from the date charges are filed. This, it should be noted, is a substantial improvement over past practice, when such cases often dragged on for several years. However, much of the improvement is due to the aggressive tactics of particular attorneys. If and when they leave their positions, multiyear cases may again become the norm. In the words of the departing deputy counsel of the Administrative Trial Unit: "The union's strategy is always to drag these cases out. It is an adage among lawyers: the longer a case goes, the harder it is to try."

Because the costs of terminating a teacher are so high, principals are cautious about initiating these proceedings. There is an understandable tendency to pursue cases that are relatively easy to document, such as those involving teachers who are mentally or emotionally disturbed (particularly if there have been incidents of corporal abuse) or instructors who are chronically absent or late. The hardest are those involving incompetence, a difficult charge to prove, as authorities on education law have noted:

> The ambiguity inherent in teacher evaluation and the job security
> of most teachers exert a powerful influence on administrators to

tolerate the incompetent teacher and to avoid the use of dismissal. Although incompetence is sufficient cause for dismissing a tenured teacher, it constitutes extremely problematic grounds for challenging the tenured teacher's employment contract with the district. Incompetence is a concept with no precise meaning; moreover, there are no clear-cut standards or cut-off points which enable an administrator to say with certitude that a teacher is incompetent. This ambiguity poses a serious problem for administrators because the burden of proof falls on them to demonstrate that a teacher is incompetent. Administrators can never be confident under these conditions that a Commission on Professional Competence or a court judge will uphold their judgment.[18]

As a result, many teachers of questionable effectiveness continue to teach in the system with no effort made to dismiss them. The worst are often assigned to positions as "cluster teachers" (e.g., in music, art, or resource rooms) where the damage they do is limited by the fact that students come into contact with them only once a week. Some receive unsatisfactory ratings and simply go on teaching in the same building. However, because teachers rated unsatisfactory are not allowed to transfer to other schools in the system, there exists an incentive for principals to conceal the full extent of the problem by rating a poor teacher satisfactory in the hope (or with the express understanding) that if they make life sufficiently unpleasant for the teacher in other regards, he or she will eventually move to another school.

Assignments

The contract restricts the way staff are assigned to various functions within in the school, significantly limiting administrators' flexibility. Principals lack the authority to assign the right person to the right job at the right time. Instead, they must function within the rules set by the collective bargaining agreement. As elsewhere in that agreement, teacher seniority regularly takes precedence over a principal's professional judgment. One example arises in the assignment of elementary school teachers to grade levels. Teachers' licenses at the elementary level typically qualify instructors to teach more than one grade. Decisions therefore must be made concerning which teachers are to teach which grades. Each spring teachers submit requests for grade assignments for the coming year. Of those "equally qualified" who seek the same assignment, the request of the more senior teacher is to be honored first.[19] Although the contract is not explicit about the meaning of the phrase "equally qualified," in a grievance hearing there will be a presumption that two teachers who have both been rated satisfactory and who hold the same license are equally qualified. Only if the principal has previously gone to the considerable effort to document his misgivings about the performance of one or the other will he have much hope of prevailing in a grievance hearing.

One of the principals interviewed for this study described his desire to reassign a first grade teacher to the second grade. In his judgment, this teacher had "gone stale" in the first grade classroom, while at the same school there were several strong second grade teachers who would, in his opinion, have helped to turn her performance around. The teacher, who had more seniority than any other first grade instructor, threatened to appeal the new assignment. "I would have lost," explained the principal. "The union would have bogged me down with detailed questions. 'How many times did you provide support for this teacher, if you thought she wasn't doing a good job? How many days did you go to her class? What actions did you take there? Did you consult with her afterwards? What was the result of that meeting?'" Despite the threatened grievance, this particular instance turned out well. The principal was able to work out a compromise by offering the teacher a desired room assignment in return for the move to the second grade. However, it is not always possible to strike such deals. Another elementary school principal, facing a similar problem, also sought to move a first grade teacher to an upper grade. He was unable to do it: the teacher's seniority posed too great an obstacle.

Restrictions on class and grade-level assignments are not the only ways that the contract can prevent principals from putting the right person in the right job. Many quasi-administrative tasks are carried out by teachers in the school system on what is known as a "comp time" basis. Teachers are not paid for assuming this extra work. Instead, their teaching load is reduced; that is, they are compensated with time. Such positions include deans, crisis intervention teachers, programmers, grade advisors, and attendance coordinators, though this list does not exhaust the possibilities. Each spring the principal meets with the UFT chapter committee to discuss the number and type of compensatory time positions and the basis for filling them. If an agreement is reached via this collaborative process, the principal fills the positions in accordance with the agreement. Individual teachers cannot appeal their assignments. The union can, though presumably it will not if the principal abides by the agreement.

When there is no agreement, positions are filled by the applicant with the most seniority in the school. If there are job-related qualifications for a position, it goes to the most senior applicant who possesses those qualifications. This provision is modified to the extent that an applicant who has not previously had a compensatory time position is to be given precedence over applicants who have.

None of these possibilities permits the principal to fill the position with the individual he deems most qualified. Principals who are on good terms with the UFT chapter leader may be able to reach an agreement that fills key positions with people of his choosing, but even when this process goes well principals will have to compromise and accept decisions that are determined by internal union politics rather than what they judge to be the best interests of the school. When there is no agreement with the UFT chapter committee, the principal will have trouble getting around the seniority provisions of the contract. This does not stop them from trying. Principals will sometimes write detailed job descriptions to screen out unwanted candidates. As one has said: "This leads to suspicion that there really is no job opening, that the job search is a sham. This breeds cynicism, all because I can't look openly for the right person for a job." These efforts also frequently fail. Assignments are appealed by senior teachers who have been passed over, and principals are told to rewrite the job descriptions in more generic terms.

When assignments are appealed, principals must try to prove that a less senior teacher was better qualified for the position. It is a difficult case to win. Arbitrators will not accept the mere perception that one teacher would be more effective in the position as sufficient ground to override seniority. They seek more tangible evidence in the form of licenses, ratings, past experience. If there are items in a teacher's file that call into question the teacher's ability to perform well in the position, the principal may be able to prevail at a grievance hearing. But as one principal remarked: "It takes lots of documentation to put a non-senior person in. Usually you won't have done it." Sometimes this is the supervisor's fault, as the union often points out. In the words of one principal: "The UFT's position is that there are sufficient safeguards in the system. The only impediments are administrators who drop the ball." However, those who suppose that principals should assiduously document every teacher's every failing in order to provide themselves with ammunition for possible future grievances are not taking due account of the complexity of managing a workplace. Principals must overlook many small failings in their staffs in order to avoid turning their schools into battlegrounds. As several noted, the problem with the contract is not that it forecloses all options, but that it often puts principals in the position of having to decide whether to go to war with their faculties or accept something less than what they deem best for their students. The steps principals would have to take in order to establish who is qualified for what are so disruptive to workplace harmony that the option is often not exercised, even by the most conscientious administrators. Beyond that, there is simply not enough time to document everything the principal learns about teachers' qualifications.

Ironically, sometimes principals find themselves in a position to play the game required by the contract, to the detriment of the teacher. One principal described the situation this way:

> I wrote a job description for a testing liaison person. The job qualifications were grieved as too specific and I had to rewrite the job description using more generic language. To keep out someone who wasn't right for the job, I had to find a letter in the file to explain why they [sic] didn't get it. Essentially, I had to make up a reason based on a past incident, rather than simply express my professional judgment. It's not really fair to the teacher, but the process doesn't allow me simply to say this isn't the best person for the job.

Perhaps the worst situations are those in which compensatory time positions are not created because the wrong people would get the jobs. This can forestall promising innovations. The following assessment of breaking up a large high school into academies—smaller programs or "schools within a school"—is an example: "I would like to create academies. For this I need teachers to lead them as deans. These would be comp time positions. Knowing who would get the jobs, I haven't pursued it: there would go my academies."

Compensatory time positions are not the only tasks teachers have taken on outside the classroom. Traditionally, teachers have also been responsible for the supervision of school yards, lunch rooms, hallways, and other sites where students congregate outside class hours. Teachers also have been assigned to inventory and distribute books and supplies, to collect money for school milk, lunches, and other purposes, and to engage in a variety of other nonteaching activities to keep schools running. These practices were changed by the current contract, which relieves teachers of such chores (except as described below). These noninstructional tasks are instead to be carried out by aides or administrative personnel, freeing teachers to use this time for more professional purposes. Well-intentioned as this reform is, it offers one more illustration of the way the contract hamstrings administrators while shielding weak faculty.

Teachers are expected to spend the time they would have devoted to these duties in some form of "professional activity." The approved list of such activities includes curriculum development, peer coaching and mentoring, peer computer training, small group and one-to-one tutoring, preparation of instructional materials, participation in school planning committees, community outreach, and enhancing extracurricular programs, to mention only a few. The actual menu of approved activities in any school is determined by the principal and the chapter committee each spring for the following academic year, with input from the school's parents' association. Disagreements that cannot be resolved at the school are referred to the district level and, failing a resolution there, to a joint chancellor-UFT committee.

Once the menu of approved activities has been established for the school, teachers are given the opportunity to state their preferences for positions. Principals are to honor teachers' preferences, favoring the more senior teacher(s) when there are multiple applicants for the same position. At the conclusion of the activity (typically the end of the following school year), teachers are required to submit an "activity evaluation report" describing what they accomplished and how it contributed to their professional development or student achievement.

Although the contract expressly prohibits teachers from spending their professional activity time on cafeteria duty or yard, bus, and hall patrol, there is one element of flexibility in the agreement. Like other provisions of the contract that govern assignments, this prohibition can be waived under the School Based Option provisions. Thus, teachers can assume cafeteria duty, for example, but only on the following conditions. First, 75 percent of voting nonsupervisory staff (teachers, paraprofessionals, support staff) must approve this waiver the preceding spring. Second, it must be approved by the union and administration at higher levels of the system (a formality). Third, unwilling teachers cannot be assigned to these duties; they must be carried out by volunteers.[20] The SBO can also be used to recreate compensatory time positions that would otherwise be eliminated by the contract's language on noninstructional activities.[21]

At the time principals were interviewed for this research, the school system was in its second year of coping with the new rules. In the first year there had been considerable turmoil as schools scrambled to find aides and administrators to assume tasks formerly carried out by teachers. By the second year, this chaos had subsided. Nonetheless, principals expressed several concerns about the new system. For various reasons, the school aides they had hired were not a fully satisfactory substitute for teachers. In some cases, aides lacked the training to supervise large groups of children. They tended to become distracted by problems involving one or two children, losing sight of the rest of the group. Some principals remarked that aides assigned to patrol halls and yards were hostile toward the students and that this hostility had exacerbated the problem of maintaining order. Others indicated that aides stood by and did relatively little to enforce rules of conduct. Several remarked that at the rates the Board of Education was paying, it was not possible to attract enough high-quality applicants for these positions. The public, and perhaps the Board of Education, did not sufficiently appreciate the complexity of some of these "routine" supervisory functions. As one elementary school principal remarked: "Supervising the lunch room is extremely important in an elementary school. You have to ensure that 125 kids, some as young as five, can eat safely in twenty minutes. This takes skilled people. Aides at $12 an hour don't do it."

Without criticizing their aides, other principals observed that relieving teachers of these noninstructional duties meant that teachers and students were no longer involved in many of the positive informal interactions that the previous system fostered, and that aides have proven to be no substitute for teachers in this respect. They are not viewed in the same way as teachers, and their exchanges with students lack the significance of interactions with teachers.

Principals also expressed some disappointment with the professional activities that teachers selected in lieu of these duties. As one remarked, he could not require faculty to participate in activities that might correct their weaknesses as instructors. Instead, he was required to honor their choices, however little the activity might do to improve their performance. Another noted that teachers frequently picked the least taxing items on the menu. Some put forth little effort even in these activities. Although this principal had contemplated monitoring what teachers were doing and "writing up" those who were essentially wasting time (i.e., putting letters in their files), given the absence of specific criteria for evaluating these professional activities she felt she would lose when the letters were appealed. As a result, provision of an official "professional activity" period had done little to improve her school. Teachers who were productively involved in these kinds of activities before the new contract was negotiated merely continued their involvement, while those who were not found make-work to occupy themselves. Some showed a total disregard for the purpose of the policy, as in the case of one teacher whose professional activity consisted of attending meetings of the school planning committee, at which he read the newspaper.

Principals also believed that the SBO alternative, while helpful, is a cumbersome process that frequently failed to function in the best interests of students. As several pointed out, the requirement that 75 percent of voting teachers approve any SBO permits a minority to block measures that most teachers approved. Sometimes the opposition appears to materialize for no other reason than a conviction that "the union had worked too long to achieve this for us to give it up." This argument is used to prevent teachers who were willing to patrol school yards, lunch rooms, and so forth from doing so.

The SBO also places inordinate demands on principals' time and energy. Each noninstructional position requires its own SBO waiver. Each has to be approved by a 75 percent vote every year. This requires that principals devote a lot of time and attention to lobbying their staffs for support. Principals speak of the need to placate teachers, to "play games" in order to make collaboration work. Even then they are concerned that a change of one or two votes could threaten school order and safety. Moreover, because SBO's must be approved the spring of the preceding year, schools lack the flexibility to respond to new and unforeseen needs.

Teamwork

Schools function best when teachers, administrators, and other staff work together as a team. Effective teamwork requires adjustments and concessions from all participants to promote the common goal of educating students. By specifying in rigid terms the hours and conditions of teachers' work, the collective bargaining agreement between the Board of Education and the UFT has made it more difficult for principals to elicit the necessary cooperation from their faculties. In some schools, principals and teachers work well together despite the contract. In others, where the principal and the UFT chapter leader are at odds and teachers insist on abiding by the letter of the contract, principals find the contract an impediment to changes that would benefit students.

The contract specifies a workday for teachers that is six hours and twenty minutes long. This is exactly the same time that students are to be at school. Teachers are therefore permitted to enter their classrooms at precisely the same time as their students and to leave when students do. Teachers need not make themselves available to students who want to talk to them before or after school hours. They need not be in the classroom to maintain order as students arrive in the morning before school or return from lunch. They can time their coming and going to avoid meeting administrators outside the six-hour-and-twenty-minute day. As one principal remarked: "I can't find teachers even ten minutes after school lets out to discuss something."

New York City teachers are expected to attend one faculty meeting per month of forty-five minutes duration.[22] Attendance at additional meetings is voluntary. Several principals observed that this was not enough time, and one complained about feeling "restricted in getting staff together for meetings. In business if I needed to conduct a team meeting, I would just call it. We are constrained in the number of meetings, confined to one official meeting per month. I have a good staff and have been able to work around it. But I was not so lucky in the past."

Requests that teachers voluntarily participate in additional meetings are often resisted by the union. One principal explained, "Teachers not only refuse, they also approach others, saying: 'Don't do it. This is a hard-won right. Don't go against the contract.' Often they are successful in influencing others, especially newer teachers, even though some of the newer teachers actually want to meet more often for guidance." Similarly, when another principal attempted to set up voluntary conferences with parents, the union chapter leader sought to discourage teachers from volunteering.

In the view of some principals, the limitation on faculty meetings does not allow enough opportunities for staff development. One proposed increasing instructional time by three to four minutes per day, thereby freeing up one Friday afternoon per month for professional development. The union would not even allow a vote on this proposal. Teachers who had initially expressed support for the idea backed off after they were approached by the union. Another principal mentioned that he had considered asking teachers to come after school hours voluntarily, but that most would not attend. Moreover, those in greatest need of staff development were the most resistant to coming in for anything beyond the contractual minimum. As a result: "We have less staff development than a worker in an auto plant."

The contract stipulates that teachers in junior and senior high schools are to spend no more than three consecutive class periods teaching. This can conflict with block scheduling, wherein students remain in the same group with the same teachers for an extended part of the day. One alternative high school that sought to establish a full-morning block, from 8:00 to 11:45, was able to do so only under the School Based Option (which required, as always, approval by 75 percent of the voting teachers each year). As the principal remarked, even this kind of restructuring would be a major effort for most schools.

Rigid limits on the workday make it difficult to deal with problems as they arise in the course of a school year. Because principals' authority to alter teachers' schedules is limited, to elicit the necessary cooperation principals often pay teachers a per session rate to take on extra work during the school day. This is a violation of Board of Education policy, which does not permit payment of per session fees (intended to compensate teachers for leading extracurricular activities) for other kinds of work done during school hours. Thus it is necessary to falsify teachers' time sheets in order to make these payments. In the words of the principal who described this practice: "I don't know a school in the system that hasn't done this. It allows you to buy your way out of a box. Of course, now the teachers have you, since you're violating the by-laws of the board of education by signing a false time sheet and they know it. But due to the lack of flexibility, the alternatives are to break the law or have the system come to a halt."

Like many contracts negotiated by teachers' unions throughout the country, the agreement between the Board of Education and the UFT puts limits on class sizes: thirty-two in elementary schools, thirty-three in junior high schools, thirty-four in senior high schools, with lower limits in schools serving Title I students and for certain types of classes (e.g., shop). Although it may seem that these limits are no more than what a wise policy would prescribe, writing them into the contract deprives administrators of the flexibility to exceed them when special circumstances arise. One high school principal described what happened when she attempted to exceed the class size limit in order to place additional students in an honors class. The teachers of the honors course were willing to take the extra students and wrote letters to that effect. Nonetheless, the union filed a grievance, taking its customary position that individual teachers cannot be permitted to renegotiate the contract. The upshot was that the class size restriction was respected; the students in question were returned to regular classes.

This was not an isolated incident. The principal of an intermediate school told a very similar story. The union insists that limits on class size be upheld even when all parties recognize that as a result of erratic attendance the actual number of students in class on a given day never exceeds thirty: "Once enrollment hits thirty-four on paper, the union targets the class for equalization."

The contract guarantees teachers a certain number of preparation periods during the week. (In regular junior high schools, for example, the number is five.) In the words of the contract: "'Preparation periods' are those periods during which the teacher is not assigned to a regularly programmed responsibility. Teachers are expected to utilize their professional preparation time in such manner as to enable them to further their professional work for the purpose of their greater classroom effectiveness."[23] In reality, teachers can use prep periods as they want. In the words of one principal, prep period has evolved into free period. Another mentioned that he could not compel a teacher to prepare during prep period: "They can sleep if they want."

Two of the principals interviewed for this study mentioned that they had concerns about teachers' dress. At one intermediate school, some teachers were coming to work in jeans and overalls. (Students at the same school are required to wear uniforms.) Yet the UFT resisted the principal's demands that teachers "present themselves professionally." In another case, a new elementary school teacher was coming to school in jeans, a t-shirt, and sneakers. The principal believed that her dress was losing her the respect of some students. But he was unsure whether to speak to her about it for fear his words would be misconstrued and that other teachers would think that he was attempting to impose a dress code: "There is a perception that it isn't the place of the principal to comment on things like dress, coming late, etc. All of this undermines the supervisor's role in subtle ways."

These kinds of issues can arise in any workplace, of course, and should not be attributed solely to the influence of the union and the contract. However, in the judgment of several principals, the union has been to blame for promoting an "us versus them" outlook that leads teachers to put their relations with their coworkers ahead of the interests and welfare of students. This is particularly troubling when teachers preserve an official silence about the misconduct of their colleagues. Because principals learn of these incidents only through information shared in confidence, they are unable to document them, let alone take the disciplinary measures called for. A principal explained that "hard-working, caring teachers will privately say, 'Such and such is happening, but you can't use my name.' I'm trying to change this culture. If peer pressure doesn't work, then I need to take more formal action, for which I need the cooperation of teachers who are now protecting their colleagues. The union is related to this attitude."

The Contract and the Future of Education Reform

The foregoing discussion may have created the impression that the principals interviewed for this study were uniformly hostile to the teachers' union and that they saw no merit in the contract. This was not the case. Some had worked in the district as teachers before the UFT negotiated its first contract and remembered abuses under the old system that led teachers to organize. One mentioned safeguards in the contract that she felt it was important to preserve. Several indicated that there was enough flexibility in the system to work around the contract: with sufficient administrative skill and luck (e.g., a cooperative UFT chapter leader), a talented principal in the New York City public schools can still manage to have a significant, positive impact on the direction of the school and the achievement of the students who attend it. Some principals (though none who were interviewed for this research) even go so far as to say that the contract is not an impediment at all, that there are always ways to finesse its provisions.

In some instances this may be true. But it is unwise to judge the systemwide impact of the contract by the achievements of a few exceptional administrators in fortunate circumstances. This was acknowledged in a particularly revealing manner during an interview conducted with the principal and UFT chapter leader of a Manhattan elementary school (the only one of the interviews at which the union representative was present). Both of these individuals stressed the importance of cooperation, and to all appearances, they had a remarkably good working relationship. When asked about problems the contract created for school management, they avoided a direct response and returned again to the importance of collaboration and shared decision making. Finally, to shift the focus from their own school, I mentioned the issue of charter schools and asked in what ways it might benefit charter schools not to be covered by the UFT contract. Immediately, almost in unison, both the principal and the chapter leader replied: "Freedom to hire and fire"—the very issues that most concerned the other principals interviewed for this study.

Defenders of the contract will sometimes admit that the contract occasionally prevents administrators from making decisions that would improve school performance, but argue that this is the necessary price to pay for protecting employees' rights and that on the whole public education is better off for these safeguards: abuses of authority are prevented that would discourage good teachers from working in the system and make it more difficult for teachers who remain to function effectively. Whatever validity this argument may once have had, it is much less clear that it remains relevant today. The picture of a school principal as an autocrat who must be restrained by a collective bargaining agreement is out of date. Principals are under pressure as never before to deliver results. Job protections such as tenure are in question. In New York City as elsewhere, policies are being shaped that will hold principals accountable when students fail to perform to acceptable levels on achievement tests. In this environment, an administrator who antagonizes his staff and diminishes their effectiveness through autocratic, arbitrary behavior does so at his own peril.

Several principals made this point when addressing the possibility that some charter schools may not be covered by the contract.[24] As one expressed it,

> A charter doesn't mean the principal will act autocratically. Instead, it gives you the freedom to use cooperative management more flexibly. Groups will form and dissolve to decide particular policies. This is a reasonable way to have collective input without autocracy. While you will do some things even without the contract that the contract now calls for, there are other areas where more managerial flexibility is needed: how to use prep periods, cover lunch hours, provide professional development. Everything can't be a teacher's choice, covered by contract language, if the school is to run.

As another principal said, "If a school is not at least partially teacher-run, it's going to be a dismal place." Even in the absence of a contract, good administrators will choose collaborative management practices because they are effective.

In some respects the contract actually inhibits collaboration. Principals frequently referred to a "tyranny of the minority" under the School Based Option, in which 25 percent of the voting staff can block reforms supported by the rest. Other innovations have been held up by excessive concern for the letter of the contract, as described above.

Precisely because cooperation is in the interests of good administrators and teachers, promoting collaboration is not the greatest challenge for public policy. Rather, the greater challenge is to ensure accountability so that administrators and teachers alike have incentives to adopt the best educational practices. Current efforts to hold administrators responsible for educational outcomes will fail to achieve the intended results if administrators are not given more authority over critical personnel decisions. Without authority there can be no genuine accountability. Or, as several principals put the matter, if the teachers' union is to share in school-based decision making, then it must also share in being held accountable for outcomes. By extending more power to UFT chapter committees and other committees dominated by the union, while at the same time preserving teachers' extensive job protections, the contract perpetuates a regime in which authority is divided, lines of responsibility are unclear, and reforms can be stalemated as various interest groups check one another.

Unfortunately, this seems to be the present trend of educational policy, as shown by other initiatives, such as the establishment of school leadership teams. These teams, composed of equal numbers of parents and school staff, are charged with developing long-term educational plans and school budgets. The former chancellor has extolled these councils as mechanisms for ensuring collaboration *and* accountability:

> Accountability is demanded equally of every member of each school leadership team and of every person who works within the school system. In this context, the Chancellor is as accountable as a classroom teacher, and a manager in the Division of Human Resources is as accountable as a principal. Every staff member, parent, union representative, or community member is responsible for making the best possible contribution, within the definition of his or her role, to improving the delivery of instruction to students.[25]

This statement is a triumph of good intentions over clear thinking. Nowhere in the document describing this policy is it explained how parents are to be held accountable. Indeed, they cannot, as parents are not employees of the Board of Education and cannot be disciplined for their actions. Nor is there any mechanism for holding teachers responsible. Principals are the only employees whose job evaluations will be affected by the activities of the leadership team. Although the chancellor's document recognized that "the principal is in an untenable position if he or she is held solely accountable for decisions of a team," there is no provision for assigning responsibility to anyone else. Yet by diminishing the principal's authority, the establishment of school leadership teams moves the system in the direction of less accountability, not more.

School leadership teams are part of a broader set of initiatives intended to make the school system "performance driven." To this end, former Chancellor Rudolph Crew and Mayor Rudolph Giuliani got legislation passed to eliminate tenure for principals, so that the chancellor and superintendents can demote or dismiss those who are ineffective. While this appears to be a step in the direction of enhanced accountability, it will prove to be more apparent than real if principals do not also receive the authority to make key personnel decisions and to manage their schools as they deem necessary. In the words of one principal: "I don't want tenure, not for me, not for anyone. We should be judged on doing the job." Unfortunately, the outlook for reforms that would establish this kind of accountability is not good.

NOTES

I wish to thank the New York City Board of Education for information about the school system and the United Federation of Teachers for its response to an earlier draft of this chapter. Most of all, I am indebted to the unnamed principals of the New York Public School System who consented to be interviewed for this research and to Bernard Zemsky of the Center for Educational Innovation for his assistance and guidance throughout this project.

1. Bruce S. Cooper, "Teacher Unions, Politics, and Organizational Adaptation," a paper prepared for "Teacher Unions: New Developments and Perspectives," a conference sponsored by the John F. Kennedy School of Public Affairs, Harvard University, September 23–25, 1998, p. 1. Source citations have been deleted.

2. This characterization of the contract was offered by Randi Weingarten, president of the UFT, at a meeting to discuss this report on January 5, 1999. Examples of such reforms include the Peer Intervention Program, initiated in 1987 to upgrade the performance of the system's weaker teachers, and an alternative to the traditional method of teacher evaluation, wherein the teacher formulates a personal plan of professional growth and is judged on the basis of progress toward these goals.

3. Steven F. Wilson, *Reinventing the Schools: A Radical Plan for Boston* (Boston: Pioneer Institute, 1992); Howard Fuller, George Mitchell, and Michael Hartmann, *The Milwaukee Public Schools' Teacher Contract—Its History, Content, and Impact on Education* (Milwaukee: Institute for the Transformation of Learning, Marquette University, 1997); La Rae G. Munk, *Collective Bargaining: Bringing Education to the Table* (Midland, Mich.: Mackinac Center for Public Policy, 1998).

4. All of these principals have been involved with the Center for Educational Innovation, a nonprofit organization that seeks to promote educational reform by shifting control from centralized bureaucracies to local schools. Funding for the center comes from various private foundations, including the Annenberg Foundation.

5. *Agreement between the Board of Education of the City School District of the City of New York and United Federation of Teachers Local 2, American Federation of Teachers, AFL-CIO Covering Teachers*, 1995, pp. 127–28.

6. In the past, teachers were not permitted to transfer unless they had served five years in their current schools. This requirement is being phased out under the current contract. Additional rules limit the number of teachers who can transfer from a given school or who teach the same subject in a single school.

7. Data furnished by Gary Barton of the Division of Human Resources of the Board of Education. These numbers are expected to rise as the current contract phases out the requirement that teachers spend at least five years in their current schools before they are eligible to transfer.

8. *Agreement*, p. 121.

9. *Agreement*, p. 120.

10. Details of the operation of the SBO staffing plan were provided by Gary Barton of the Division of Human Resources of the Board of Education.

11. "Teachers on probation who have completed at least three years of service on regular appointment in the school shall be entitled, with respect to the discontinuance of their probationary service, to the same review procedures as are established for tenured teachers under Section 3020-a of the Education Law" (*Agreement*, p. 129).

12. The rating and review process is described in New York City Board of Education, *Regulations and Procedures for Pedagogical Ratings*, 1997.

13. *Agreement*, p. 142.

14. In fact, the portion of the personnel file containing evaluations of performance does not travel with teachers who transfer within the system but remains at the old school, effectively under seal. Without defending this policy, the executive director of human resources for the Board of Education offered the following rationale. Because no teacher may transfer under the UFT transfer system who has not received satisfactory ratings each of the previous three years, the file at the former school ought not to contain material showing the teacher is currently unfit to teach. Items in the file that reflect unfavorably on the teacher's ability will date from an earlier period in the teacher's career and should not be considered relevant in evaluating current performance. However, this is not invariably true: more than 99 percent of teachers in the system are rated satisfactory, including many whose files contain letters that reflect negatively on their performance. Excluding this information denies the hearing officers any opportunity to decide whether it is relevant.

15. Data on 3020-a proceedings were supplied by the Office of Legal Services of the Board of Education.

16. Data from the Office of Appeals and Review of the Board of Education. These data reflect only the number of U ratings that are appealed; the total number of teachers rated unsatisfactory is unknown. However, a 1990 review of practices in the school system found that 99.7 percent of teachers were rated satisfactory, as reported in James Gill et al., "Findings and Recommendations of the Joint Commission on Integrity in the Public Schools," 1990, p. 178. Judging from the comments of the principals interviewed for this study, it is doubtful that this figure has changed very much.

17. Evaluating a teacher requires, in addition to each formal classroom observation, a pre-observation conference, a post-observation conference, and written comments on the teacher's performance.

18. Edwin M. Bridges, *The Incompetent Teacher: Managerial Responses* (Philadelphia: Falmer Press, 1992), p. 24.

19. *Agreement*, p. 31.

20. The one exception is home room. If the faculty approves an SBO establishing home rooms (in a junior or senior high school), faculty can be assigned to staff these positions involuntarily. However, they must rotate.

21. Some compensatory time positions can be re-created by an agreement of the principal and the UFT chapter committee. They are deans, crisis intervention teachers, programmers, grade advisors, and, for high schools, attendance coordinators.

Other compensatory time positions must be established through the SBO mechanism.

22. Language limiting faculty meetings to forty-five minutes per month does not actually appear in the contract. Instead, it is a Board of Education policy. However, by Article 20 of the contract, "Matters not covered," the board must negotiate any change in this policy with the union. Thus it is effectively fixed by the contract. Certainly it is perceived that way by principals. Even high-ranking officials of the Board of Education were surprised to learn that the policy on faculty meetings was not actually in the contract.

23. *Agreement*, pp. 26–27.

24. Under the recently passed charter school law, schools with fewer than 250 students are not required to abide by union contracts. The decision is left to a vote of the faculty of each school.

25. Board of Education of the City of New York, *The Chancellor's Draft Plan for School Leadership Teams*, September 1998, p. 43.

5 The Bronx Leadership Academy High School: The Challenges of Innovation

LEE STUART

This chapter traces the origin, formation, growing pains, successes, and challenges facing the Bronx Leadership Academy high school. The Bronx Leadership Academy (BLA) is a collaborative project between the New York City Board of Education and South Bronx Churches (SBC), which is a broad-based organization of religious institutions that has been instrumental in rebuilding the South Bronx, especially in the areas of housing development, education reform, and increased citizen participation in public life. The Bronx Leadership Academy began in 1991 as a dream of SBC parents and clergy who were deeply frustrated at the lack of quality public education in the South Bronx and angry at their inability over four years of effort with the local school districts and principals to gain even basic recognition as stakeholders in the education of their children.

SBC leaders worked for nearly two years to build the necessary relationships within the Board of Education to establish the new high school. The school opened in 1993 and immediately suffered from a crisis in leadership that threatened its very existence. Two and a half years in temporary quarters strained the ability of the faculty and staff to form a coherent educational community. Now, strong leadership from the current principal, a staff united behind high expectations and standards, and a new building complete with art studio, music room, and science laboratories have motivated the students to produce impressive results. Of students admitted in 1993 when the school opened, 93 percent graduated in four years. Of students admitted in 1994, all graduated on time. Forty-one of the forty-three students in this class applied to and were accepted into college, with a total of approximately two hundred thousand dollars in financial aid awards.

Despite this success, systemwide conditions continuously threaten the school. Among the threats are the lack of policies developed specifically for small schools, a pressure to increase enrollment to or beyond the maximum capacity of the building, centralized budgeting at very low levels, politically motivated "mainstreaming" of psychologically troubled children, and lack of concerted action on the part of the board to correct the "Dead Zones"—local school districts where fewer than 35 percent of the children in elementary and intermediate grades read at grade level. Ultimately a failure on the part of the chancellor to exercise his newly granted powers to remove principals for persistent educational failure and to hold principals accountable for the standards of education in their schools is responsible for the persistence of a two-tiered educational system in New York City, where, by an accident of birth, nearly 100,000 children in the South Bronx do not receive adequate education in the lower grades to prepare them for academic success in high school and beyond.

Origin and Vision

In order to understand the existence of the Bronx Leadership Academy, it is necessary to understand its development as an outgrowth of one of the primary issues of the public agenda of South Bronx Churches.[1] SBC was organized in 1987 as an affiliate of the Industrial Areas Foundation,[2] the nation's oldest and largest community organizing network. Clergy and lay leaders from over thirty congregations—Baptist, Catholic, Lutheran, Episcopalian, Presbyterian, Disciples of Christ, United Church of Christ, and United Methodist—came together to form the organization. They spent thousands of hours getting to know and trust one another, raising hundreds of thousands of dollars from their judicatories and bishops, pledging annual dues from each congregation to sustain the organization, analyzing the political and economic realities of the community, learning to build the power to participate fully in that political and economic reality, and developing an agenda for action on the most important issues facing their constituents. Not surprisingly, in the South Bronx, which at the time was a prime example of the nation's poverty, these issues included, in addition to improving public education, the development of new and renovated housing, providing better health care, increasing the availability of day care, and improving the economic life of families through increasing the minimum wage and a program of job development. Over one hundred thousand adults in the South Bronx signed petitions in support of SBC's agenda.

Unlike many community-based organizations before and since, SBC claimed the entire public domain as its own. With broad geographic representation throughout the South Bronx (and thus minimally limited by neighborhood turf boundaries), not at all limited on the range of issues on which they claimed the authority to act, and based in the only permanent institutions that had survived the decimation of the South Bronx, SBC was and is ethnically, religiously, and politically diverse. Inherent in the philosophy of SBC's leaders was a commitment to "stand for the whole" rather than for a narrow special interest, to practice the iron rule of never doing for others what they can do for themselves, and to hold both themselves and the public and private institutions of New York City to high standards of accountability. SBC leaders developed the power, both in terms of organized people and in terms of organized money, to engage those public and private institutions not as a supplicant, client, or victim but as a force to be reckoned with.

It was the attitude of self-determination that gave SBC leaders the courage and perseverance first to rid the local public hospital of a highly corrupt local political strongman, then to fight for control of abandoned land on which to build 750 new homes, and then to engage the local school boards and principals in order to have them do something to improve the dismal state of public education in the Bronx. Entrenched resistance to change, and in many districts, long-term corruption at the district level which starved resources from the classrooms, were formidable barriers.[3]

After being brushed off by principals and physically threatened by school board officials from one of the local districts, the leaders of SBC decided that it was impossible to work within the existing educational structures and personalities of the South Bronx. To get any change in education they would have to build their own school, as politically remote and impractical as this seemed. Then three young men were shot in a Brooklyn public high school, and their deaths forced the political moment that allowed the citywide new schools initiative under Chancellor Joseph Fernandez. When Chancellor Fernandez announced the formation of new, smaller high schools in collaboration with community groups as a way to reduce violence, improve education, and provide better links between the community and the schools, South Bronx Churches and its sister organization, East Brooklyn Congregations, decided to participate. Ultimately, East Brooklyn Congregations was successful in starting two high schools, one for Bushwick and one for Brownsville. South Bronx Churches started the Bronx Leadership Academy.

A group of about twenty-five parents and clergy constituted the Education Task Force of South Bronx Churches. They engaged the members of SBC in one-on-one and small-group meetings regarding the vision for a new school. The vision was shockingly simple, and therefore radical: SBC wanted an academically focused high school, which would admit students of varying abilities and train them for college and leadership in public life. The reason an academic, college preparatory emphasis is radical is that

fewer than one-third of high school freshmen in the South Bronx graduate in four years and only 2 percent to 4 percent of graduates typically receive Regents diplomas. In all but one of the six local school districts in the
Bronx (District 11), fewer than 35 percent of the students read at grade
level.[4]

SBC's internal organizing to create the new school was comparatively
simple compared to the need to organize the Board of Education itself for
the creation of the school. The process was new for both sides, and the advantage that SBC had internally over the board was that it had no preset
ideas, traditions, patterns, habits, bureaucracy, or procedures for dealing
with educational issues. SBC could start with (comparatively) a tabula rasa;
the board could not. The first step in the process was building the necessary relationships and respect between board personnel and SBC leaders.
The early exchanges, which went on for about six months, were almost an-
thropological in nature: two cultures, both good-willed but very different,
encountering each other. Attempts by SBC to engage professional educators as consultants in the process, however, were rarely successful or helpful. Eventually, a subcommittee comprised of the lead organizer of South
Bronx Churches and ten members of the Educational Task Force carried
out the bulk of the early negotiations.

This group researched new and effective models of school reform in
New York City and beyond. They met with educators from Fordham University and Columbia, visited innovative schools throughout the city, and
slowly developed their capacity to judge what made a good school and the
qualities they wanted theirs to have. Early in the process, the group met
with Joseph N. De Jesus, the Bronx superintendent of high schools, and
gained his wholehearted support of the effort. His support was key for the
establishment of the school and for meeting the challenges of the early
years.

During the early stages of the formation of the new schools throughout
New York City, a program called "New Visions" (see chapter 3) was established to provide financial and technical assistance to new school initiatives. SBC applied to New Visions, but upon learning that one of the requirements was collaboration with a local school district, did not pursue
the relationship. Thus the funding for SBC's efforts came from its core budget, supplied by congregational dues and grants from religious groups and
private foundations. The educational expertise also came internally from
teachers, principals, and other educators who were members of SBC congregations.

SBC, as do all the affiliates of the Industrial Areas Foundation, seeks to
build "relational" rather than "dominant" power, both internally and between itself and public and private institutions.[5] Whereas dominant power
is characterized by unilateral control, a position of one side over and

against another, and expansion of the strength of the dominant at the expense of the subordinate, relational power is characterized by mutuality, a position of "power with" rather than "power over," and the expansion and growth of both sides as they develop a mutually beneficial strategy for action. The nearly eighteen months of negotiations and relationship building prior to the formal establishment of the school in February of 1993 were required to build sufficient relational power between the Board of Education and South Bronx Churches. This relational power was necessary to overcome the extreme challenges encountered in getting the Bronx Leadership Academy from a proposal on paper to a smoothly functioning school.

The people most responsible at the level of the central board for the successful formation of the Bronx Leadership Academy were Cesar Previdi, Pat Haith, and John Farrandino. These three met over many months with delegates from SBC. They guided the writing of a sound proposal that would both meet SBC's objectives and board requirements for the establishment of a school. Both sides learned to compromise. At no time were the discussions hostile in any way, though there was mutual struggle to come to a meeting of the minds on some kind of reasonable time line. The guarded approach of the board representatives was appropriate in light of the absolute need to know and trust their collaborators from SBC. The last thing New York City needed was a narrow political or religious interest forming pseudo-public schools with an agenda other than quality education. The religious diversity of SBC allayed fears of violation of church and state separation: the Board of Education personnel realized that SBC would tear itself apart over the question of which doctrine to teach (if such had ever been the intent).

Learning by Doing: Early Obstacles and Successes

Neither the Board of Education nor South Bronx Churches had a track record of establishing new schools. It is only in retrospect that some of the processes and procedures of the early days can be seen as deeply flawed. The experience of playing out ideas that appeared worthy at the time, particularly ideas about staff selection and training, curriculum development, support for new principals and project directors, and the all-important issue of a building, has yielded significant changes in the approaches taken in more recent school start-ups.

The Bronx Leadership Academy developed along a path that now appears designed for a disaster. This is not to say that the planners were not intelligent, committed people but that they nevertheless made decisions which yielded great hardships down the line, and which proved to be nearly fatal to the endeavor. One example of this is the general sequence of events in the school's formation. Growing out of the immediate self-interest of SBC member congregations, the initial proposal for the school was developed in conjunction with the highest levels of the NYC Board of Education. Then, again with the help of people high in the board's bureaucracy, the political work of chartering the new school, namely, getting it past the vote of the Board of Education and officially recognized as a school, was accomplished.[6] The next step was to find the staff, and the final step was to find a building. The problem was that the initial staff had no part in the years of predevelopment work and relationship building that the board and SBC had undertaken together. It was as if a machine had been designed with no involvement of those who would be most responsible for making it run. The second problem was that a very important issue with respect to a school, its physical location, was left to the end of the process. Both staff issues and site issues nearly delivered a fatal blow to the Bronx Leadership Academy in its first two and a half years. These problems would not have had nearly the destructive potential had they been addressed earlier.

Although the initial project director was selected jointly by Board of Education and SBC leaders, and the director and the global studies teacher attended the national training of the Industrial Areas Foundation to become familiar with the work of broad-based organizations such as SBC, the relationship between the school staff and SBC quickly turned sour. At issue was what was meant by "collaboration"—whether that meant passive involvement on the part of SBC or whether the leaders of the Educational Task Force would be an integral part of the next stage in the school's formation such as curriculum development, particularly in the area of leadership for public life, internal practices and environment, and setting academic standards. The professional educators felt that SBC's involvement in these areas violated their professionalism; SBC leaders felt their exclusion to indicate lack of respect for the years of work already spent on the school. They felt that what had been "theirs" was now being "taken over" by people who had not participated in the struggle.

Also at issue was accountability. SBC leaders felt perfectly free to ask, and expected to get answers to questions such as: how will the mathematics curriculum be enhanced so that students weak in math can achieve Regents standards? How can we be assured that special education and ESL students make acceptable progress toward graduation? What support structures will be in place to build a sense of community and shared endeavor among students? Unfortunately, time and time again, such questions were interpreted as challenges to the authority of the project director and teachers. SBC leaders were concerned that even when given a blank slate to start a new school, the professional educators would reproduce the same structures and culture that had already failed the children of the Bronx.

The simple fact was that SBC leaders had spent far longer, years longer in fact, wrestling with the question of what makes a good school than had the initial staff. Complicating the situation was the fact that the project director had no experience at the high school level, was unfamiliar with the high school curriculum, and had a weak relationship with the Bronx superintendent of high schools. The stage was set for a series of highly damaging disagreements as SBC began working with a brand new staff under enormous pressure to bring together all elements of a new school. It had taken eighteen months for SBC and the high school division to develop a collaborative relationship in the school's formation. The timing of the opening of school allowed only one summer for the far more complicated task of turning the vision of one group (SBC) into action by another (school staff).

Space, Parents, and Race

As early as November of 1993, the tension between SBC and the staff was acute. Furthermore, efforts on the part of the superintendent's office to support the collaboration with SBC met stiffening resistance from school staff. Although a good effort had been made by both SBC and the Board of Education to find separate space for the new school, nothing had been found and the school opened in a wing of Samuel Gompers High School. The principal of Gompers made every effort to be welcoming, and most of the staff of the Bronx Leadership Academy made the same effort. Nevertheless, some Gompers students resented the presence of the BLA students. The BLA students felt both threatened by the far more numerous Gompers students and resentful that, having been promised their own school, they were now guests at another. The necessity of shared space became a wedge issue used by the staff of BLA to further discredit SBC's involvement; SBC was portrayed as having failed to live up to its obligation to find space for the school, a failure which now put the students at risk of physical harm.

Sadly, the parents became pawns in the struggle between SBC and the staff and board. SBC had always assumed that it would assist in organizing the parents association along the lines being undertaken by the Texas affiliates of the Industrial Areas Foundation.[7] This had been one of the core premises of the school. The Board of Education, however, has very set rules for establishing a parents association, most of which are completely impossible to fulfill in a start-up situation where no relationships exist. For example, the first order of business, according to the *Blue Book*,[8] the bible of parents associations, is to adopt by-laws and elect officers. SBC wanted to postpone this part until parents had a chance to meet one another, decide collectively on their goals and strategies, and take part in leadership training appropriate for building a relational model of a parents organization. The people from the central board responsible for parents associations held firmly to the traditional approach, and therefore the issue of the role of parents in the school was divisive. The picture was painted that SBC, in proposing a relational rather than a bureaucratic model for the parent association, was somehow denying parents their rights to organize!

The South Bronx is essentially a segregated society, in that whites make up less than 2 percent of the population.[9] The first student body of the high school was entirely African American, Caribbean American, or Hispanic. The staff included whites, but they were in the minority. Most of the leadership of SBC is likewise black or Hispanic, but the lead organizer was white, as were some, but not all, of the clergy. Some of the staff of the Bronx Leadership Academy repeatedly and publicly challenged SBC's participation in the school on the basis of the organizer's race and on the presence of white clergy in the organization's leadership.

In short, SBC was painted by some of the staff as, variously, threatening racial domination by whites, posing a sectarian takeover of public education, meddling in the work of educational professionals, and intentionally putting the safety of the children at risk by failing to provide a separate school building. That's a lot of freight for any organization to bear, and it was particularly hard on the SBC Education Task Force, who had worked so hard and long to establish the school.

As the polarization between the staff and SBC increased, SBC turned to the superintendent of high schools and requested support to reestablish a collaborative relationship. A series of meetings, retreats, workshops, discussion sessions, and so forth did nothing to ease tensions. Eventually it became obvious that collaboration was impossible with the existing leadership in the school, and in March of 1994, the project director was removed by the Board of Education.

Even six years doesn't give twenty-twenty hindsight on the first year of the Bronx Leadership Academy. What is clear is that the leaders selected for a new school should be among the most serious and seasoned professionals, with previous administrative experience at the level required for the job. It is entirely unclear whether, had the opening of the school been delayed from September 1993 to September 1994 to allow for the staff and SBC to work together on the next stage of the school's development, the extra time would have resulted in an atmosphere of collaboration.

The fact remains that the first year of the Bronx Leadership Academy was painful to all involved. The students were hurt educationally and emotionally by the turmoil and, perhaps worst of all, by the failure of the staff to provide a curriculum that met the requirements for New York City high schools freshmen.

The job of the new project director, Katherine Kelly, was to stabilize the situation for the remaining months of school, evaluate staff for transfers and training needs, win back the trust of parents and students, set up the appropriate structures and curriculum, and somehow, build a collaborative relationship between the school and SBC on the wreckage of the first seven months of the school's life. For its part, SBC was willing to take a back seat until things calmed down. The SBC leaders were nearly worn out because of the bitterness of the struggle, but they were confident in Mrs. Kelly's credentials and vision for education. All SBC had ever wanted was a good school, with high academic standards and a commitment to train students for full participation in public life. Endorsing Mrs. Kelly's plan for the academic curriculum and staff adjustments, SBC began working in earnest on the other vexing issue facing the BLA: a permanent home.

This took years. For most of the 1994 and 1995 school years, BLA was housed in a church education building. There were no labs, no cafeteria, the classrooms were too small, the gym was the banquet hall, and the elevator was shared with the church. Sometimes this proved awkward. Due to the topography of the site, it was easier for funeral directors to bring the caskets in through the school and down the elevator to the sanctuary than to climb the stairs from the street to the sanctuary. Mrs. Kelly made heroic efforts to boost morale and set the school on a good course. She brought in young, talented teachers, and provided the leadership required to produce a truly outstanding school. The parents voted to establish a dress code, over the protestations of their children. The teachers began considering school-based options in their contract which would help them meet the demands of a new school. SBC kept looking for a building.

Finally one was identified—a cinder-block shell, which could be remodeled from within to form a school. Lease and construction negotiations took months, and the school was ready for occupancy in February 1996. Finally the students had well-equipped labs, an art studio, a music room, and a gym. The design of the school was not perfect: Board of Education architects had allowed ventilating duct work to cross through the safe room where state-administered exams were to be stored. This nearly caused a denial of certification of the school because of the inability to protect the exams from theft. Eventually a type of jail cell was built which isolated the ducts from the safe room. In another mistake, the architects designed the gym with the outside dimensions of a basketball court, with no space between the boundary lines and the walls, much less for any spectators. Through months of design review, this error was not caught, even though, had it been, it could have easily been corrected because the site was large enough to accommodate a full gym.

During the construction of the school what became known as the school lease scandal hit the media.[10] In an effort to rapidly expand classroom space, the Board of Education and various landlords entered into highly unsatisfactory and exorbitant leases. The BLA lease was not part of the scandal, but nevertheless was highly scrutinized.

What Was Learned?

The Board of Education now requires staff educators to participate in the formation of new schools. While this might be seen as an attempt to co-opt the initiating role of the community group proposing the school, it avoids the situation encountered by SBC and BLA when the first staff were not adequately aligned with the vision of the school. It does place an additional burden, however, on community groups wishing to start schools, requiring them to organize carefully so that their views are not overwhelmed by people used to working within the system. Additional staff support and mentoring is now available for teachers and administrators in new schools, and the small schools have developed their own constituency.[11] It is now Board of Education policy that the leaders of new schools have the appropriate experience, and are not thrown into situations or administrative relationships entirely new to them. Many of the small schools started at the same time as BLA suffered from lack of permanent space. This has proven to be such an obstacle that current school start-ups require the designation of a site prior to the school's being established. While this can add years to the start-up process, it is probably wise because it provides for decent instructional space from the very first day of classes.

Establishing a Culture for Education and Learning

Most visitors to the Bronx Leadership Academy are instantly struck by two things: the cleanliness of the building and the focused order of students, both within the classrooms and when moving around the halls. Many New York City high schools have metal detectors; BLA has none. The school is rated above average in terms of safety. A standard design specification for New York City high schools is that the classroom doors be made of metal, because otherwise the students would destroy them. BLA has wooden doors. There is no trace of graffiti, either in the building or on its exterior. The students have their own committee to deal with anyone who defaces the building. Daily attendance is greater than 90 percent.[12] In many New York City public schools parents struggle to meet with teachers and principals. At BLA, there is an open door policy for parents. Without a playing field or standard gym, and with a small student body, BLA will probably never field a championship football, baseball, or basketball team. It does, however, field an excellent fencing team, coached by one of the judges in the most recent Olympics. Students win trophies in citywide debate.

Upon entering high school, many freshmen have studied literature only through excerpts. At BLA, there is an extensive summer reading list for all students, and novels, both classics and modern, are part of every year's curriculum. To make formal learning a year-round activity, all students in all grades have summer assignments in social studies, law, science, and mathematics in addition to the summer reading and writing requirements. Summer assignments are well integrated so that all teach vocabulary, writing, and reading as well as the content of the particular discipline. Students are responsible for summer work, and the work counts toward the first marking period grades.

BLA has a broad academic curriculum considering its size. French, Spanish, and Latin are taught. Advanced placement classes are offered in English, social studies, mathematics, and physics. General education and special education students are taught in the same classroom. The school has a band and a chorus and a spacious art studio. Extra ESL is offered after school for those who need it. Computers are accessible to students throughout the day, in the computer lab, in the library, and in some classrooms. With help from the Bronx borough president, BLA was one of the first high schools in the Bronx wired for the Internet.

The students contribute to the emphasis on academic achievement. In 1998, a student court was implemented as a means of self-discipline. Under the supervision of an adult, all students serve as jurors on a rotating basis. The students and staff collaborated to determine what would constitute a violation of the school community. Anyone in the school—staff or student—may give out violations for any breach of conduct, whether it is related to discipline, being late, being rude or disrespectful, being out of the dress code, defacing the building, or violating some other standard. Students with violations are given a "court date" and must appear before the jury to explain what happened. The students themselves decided that failing more than one subject should be considered a violation, particularly since tutoring is widely available and teachers are in the building at virtually all hours to help students with their courses.

Richard Baresch, a participant in the board's Principal of the Day program, came to BLA by the luck of the draw in 1995. He has continued his participation through the establishment of scholarships, additional financing for programs, and hiring graduates. Four attorneys are on the teaching staff; they have developed a curriculum theme of law as a way to promote leadership in public life and to integrate many academic skills. Each year the school sponsors trips to the traditional black colleges and to schools throughout the region so that students can gain a better understanding of what is available to them in terms of higher education. And then there's the dress code: white shirts, with blue, gray, or black trousers or skirts. Ties are required for the boys; Bloomingdale's has contributed ties so those who forget can borrow one for the day. In a noteworthy gesture of solidarity, the principal and many of the faculty adhere to the dress code. The school has gained the public's attention: four thousand students applied for the 125 available seats in the ninth grade in 1998.

The key to this remarkable enterprise is the school's principal, Katherine Kelly, and the able and dedicated staff she has gathered around her to provide the very best education to the students. The entire focus of the school is on learning and education. The grown-ups are clearly in charge. Antisocial behavior is simply not tolerated. Pride in one's self, one's school, and one's community is stressed. Hard work is the order of the day. Academic achievement is expected. Admission to BLA is by the board's "educational option" process. Students wishing to attend the school designate it in the standard articulation process used in middle schools throughout the city. Half of the entering students are selected randomly by computer from all applicants to provide a broad range of academic ability; the other half are selected by the school staff. It took weeks to comb through the four thousand applicants for the 1998 entering class (the process is not computerized at the school level), with staff placing a priority on attendance, reading scores, the presence of a sibling already in the school, and recommendations from the middle school.

What is important to realize is that nothing done inside BLA is in any way contrary to or an exception to the general high school policies of the New York City Board of Education. The quality of education and the educational environment at BLA are available within all existing regulations of the board. What is special about BLA is the absolute political will to make those regulations work to their limit for the sake of the students. The staff has the full support of South Bronx Churches and the Bronx superintendent of high schools to do whatever it takes to create a good school. For example, the United Federation of Teachers' contract allows for many school-based options if supported by 75 percent of the teachers in the school.[13] BLA faculty voted for a school-based hiring policy which does not allow automatic seniority transfers when staff openings occur. This allows for substantial transmission of the school's culture to any incoming faculty member. Vision and commitment to a particular quality and style of education must override tradition, the ease of following standard practice, and the inevitable bottom-seeking behavior of huge bureaucracies with histories of low accountability.

Measures of Success

The Bronx Leadership Academy was established to provide a rigorous academic program that would prepare all students to pass the Regents exams and attend college. Whereas the college admission rate is high, performance on Regents exams and the SAT is disappointing, and these scores are still below the city average. Most of the students entering BLA come from districts in which a third or more of the students do not read at grade level; thus current expectations are higher than they have been prepared for. The staff of BLA is not complacent or resigned, however, and various programs have been instituted to overcome educational deficiencies. As each year passes, student scores are expected to increase. The administration and staff are willing to be held accountable for their results.

Good progress is being made in certain areas. The state has recently set new standards that 90 percent of a school's eleventh grade students must meet in reading, writing, and mathematics. In the academic year 1995–96, BLA had nearly achieved the new state standards in reading (89.8 percent) and writing (87.8 percent), but was still low in math (77.6 percent). Therefore, all students began receiving double math instruction. Moreover, BLA is serious about students' learning to speak and write English, refusing to see LEP (limited English proficiency) as a permanent way of life. In 1995, 1996, and 1997, the percentage of LEP students achieving English proficiency was higher than the citywide average. In response to lower than average SAT scores, in 1998 BLA started Latin instruction for ninth graders, taught by a Ph.D. candidate in classics from Fordham University.

The results from the first marking period of 1998–99 are encouraging. The percentage of students achieving the honor roll (80–89 average) has more than tripled, from 8 percent at the end of the 1997–98 school year to 26 percent now. Similarly, the number of students achieving averages between 70 and 80 increased from 13 percent in 1997–98 to 27 percent in the first period of 1998–99. Fifty-five percent of the student body is passing all classes; 22 percent are failing one class, and 23 percent are failing more than one. Those who are failing are targeted for special support. Is BLA at its desired level academically? No, not yet, but the school personnel have implemented and will continue to implement programs to reach their goals.

Parents: Still an Unmobilized Resource

Parental involvement at BLA, while significantly higher than in many high schools in terms of school volunteers and accessibility, is still far below the potential envisioned by school staff and South Bronx Churches. The original by-laws of the parent association, adopted in the first year of the school, state a quorum of five for conducting business. While this is horrifying enough in a small school such as BLA, it is fairly standard for even much larger schools to have a parent association quorum of less than ten. The expectation in high school is low parental participation, and this expectation is usually fulfilled.

The problem is rooted in a basic lack of understanding. In particular, no one knows exactly what "parental involvement" means. Involvement is generally considered a good thing, but how it works and what it is meant to achieve are questions that usually remain unasked. Obviously parents are important in helping to create the environment in the home that fosters learning, and clearly parents are important in helping with a wide assortment of tasks within the school. Parents should care about their children's education, but how does this translate into action? Bake sale fundraising for school trips, chaperoning dances, signing report cards, getting the kids to school on time—all are important common tasks of parents. But, then what? If, as seems logically correct, parents are key stakeholders in education, what does that mean?

In New York City, as mentioned above, the sanctioned parent associations are bound by the *Blue Book,* a manual devised by the board to provide "legitimate" parental involvement in the school. In labor organizing, this would be anathema, the equivalent to a company in-house union. The distribution of power within New York City's educational system is dominated by the teachers' union (the United Federation of Teachers, or UFT), the principals' union (the Council of Supervisors and Administrators, or CSA), and—though to a lesser degree than previously—unions representing the custodians and other service workers. These are the groups that organize to shape most of what happens in the school. The groups wield tremendous power in the state legislature: in the first six months of 1996 the UFT reported $900,000 in lobbying expenses and political contributions. The UFT in New York City has an annual budget of $68 million, of which $8 million (12 percent) comes from the Board of Education.[14]

There is simply nothing comparable for parents, no union with any clout and no financing. The Board of Education allocation for the parent association at BLA is $100 annually. Because the rules for parent associations are written by "management," it is clear that accommodation of parents is the goal, rather than inclusion based upon an independent base of power. Even when a nod is given to the Presidents Council (the presidents of all parent associations within a district), the fact remains that the presidents of parent associations are presidents of groups that require a quorum of five to ten out of a membership of hundreds or thousands to operate. School-based parent associations are not designed for power; they are neither representative, democratic, nor accountable to a constituency, and the heads of these powerless associations are not, by extension, either. A constitution does not make an organization: organizing and relationships make an organization.

The issue of parental involvement at BLA, then, is not simply a local issue, but a systematic failing of the New York City Board of Education. SBC has proposed a different model of parental involvement that has grown out of years of work by the Texas affiliates of the Industrial Areas Foundation. The Texas program, the Alliance Schools Initiative, is a joint project of the Texas IAF affiliates and the Texas State Education Department. One hundred forty-six schools are now part of the Alliance Schools Initiative. Although test scores are only one method of evaluation, of the eighty-nine Alliance schools serving over sixty thousand students in 1996, nearly 90 percent increased the percentage of students who passed all sections of the state tests. The increase in 71.3 percent of the schools was higher than the state average increase.[15] In 1997, the Texas state legislature committed $8 million to support Alliance school campuses and to support the innovations developed through their interaction with the local IAF organizations. At the heart of the Alliance Schools Initiative, as defined by Dennis Shirley in his recent book *Community Organizing for Urban School Reform*, is the engagement of parents "as citizens in the fullest sense—[as] change agents who can transform inner city schools."[16]

After four years of watching the *Blue Book* approach to building a parents association falter and fail, SBA and the staff of BLA have just embarked on a new approach. With support from the Donors Educational Collaborative and the Public Education Association, SBC has hired a full-time organizer to build a model of parental "engagement," not parental "involvement." The organizer has begun a three-month campaign of individual meetings with staff, parents, and community leaders to find leaders, develop relationships, and exchange views and ideas related to issues in the school. As leaders surface, meetings of small groups of ten to fifteen will be held to find which issues are most important to the parents, and to develop an agenda for action on these issues. SBC expects that the organizer will know and be known by at least 150 of the parents through individual meetings, and even more through the small group meetings. A coherent issue agenda and a range of ideas, approaches, and viewpoints will have been developed, not through the ideas of the five or six who are the nominal heads of a typical parents association, but through hundreds of give-and-take conversations on what is important about BLA. A later step will involve Neighborhood Walks, whereby parents, teachers, and community members go door to door to solicit views on community issues that affect both the school and the broader community. Eventually, just as the parents, teachers, and staff develop an agenda for internal issues in the school, the school and community residents will develop an agenda for external issues. The effort is to link school and community again, and to engage both the school and the neighborhood in collective action that will improve education.

This is a work in progress. SBC, however, has also begun one-on-ones with principals of intermediate schools in the South Bronx, looking for principals who would welcome a new approach to parent organizing. When a principal is open to it, SBC will attempt to raise funds, along with the principal, to develop an Alliance School prototype for New York City. Despite the high expectations for school-based management committees, as long as the educational establishment in New York City sees parents as passive participants, with only a consultative role, parents will continue to be an undermobilized force in the reformation of New York City education.[17]

Pressures against Success

Although by most measures, BLA is a proven success, there are current and pending challenges that threaten the very nature of the place.

Enrollment

The school was intentionally designed for a maximum enrollment of 550. This small size allows for students to know one another and for each student to be known personally by faculty, and it also makes the school eligible for the addition of staff, including administrators, teachers, and guidance personnel to provide better student-staff ratios. Limiting size was also a factor in selecting the site. The square-footage allotment per student required a building of about fifty thousand square feet for a student body of 500 to 550. SBC knew that if the building they found was significantly larger, they would be under continuous pressure to increase enrollment.

Even with these precautions, however, there is pressure on BLA to increase its size. The 1998 registration was 613. Although this is somewhat over capacity, many schools in the Bronx are at 150 percent capacity, and so BLA is seen as an "undercrowded school," which can easily accommodate more students. This pressure to pack in more students raises an important question: what is the point of creating innovative, smaller schools if Board of Education policies work to undo the educational environment that makes them special and to turn them into replicas of the larger schools, which are better known for their problems than their success?

Arbitrary Assignment of Students Based on Political Criteria

SBC would be one of the first groups in the city to demand quality public education for all students, but recent decisions by the mayor and chancellor to eliminate special schools for emotionally troubled students are potentially damaging, both for the students themselves and for the schools to which they are "mainstreamed." For example, BLA is a target school for the transfer of so-called "SIE-7" students (for Special Instructional Environment). These students, while not having academic problems, are prone to emotional outbreaks. The original plan was for BLA to receive ten SIE-7 students, who would not be selected until well into the academic year—which would make any attempt at normal integration impossible. The students and their parents would have participated in none of the orientation sessions, the dress code would be a surprise, and the students themselves would be behind the BLA students, whose first weeks are spent on reviewing work that was part of the summer assignment. They would miss the all-important first days when the faculty and staff set the tone of the entire year.

Fortunately the principal of BLA was able to convince the board to make substantial revisions in their plan in order to make the inclusion of SIE-7 students as smooth as possible. Only four SIE-7 students were assigned to BLA, and they were enrolled at the start of school. What is instructive in this example is that the original decision to implement the SIE-7 transfers was made with incomplete analysis. Only one part of the picture was considered: how to close special schools and mainstream students. The impact on the receiving schools, or even on the students themselves, was not considered. Students are not things or pieces to be moved around at political whim. BLA has turned out to be a good place for its SIE-7 students, but if the original plan had been implemented, the situation could have been very different.

Budget

The non-personnel budget for BLA was $40,000—less than $80 per student—for the 1998–99 academic year.[18] This includes state allocations for textbooks ($12,096), as well as local allocations for science equipment ($2,549), software ($899), and general education ($8,153). Coincident with the budget is a board-ordered switch to world history from area studies, and with the switch, new texts are needed; a single copy costs $35. It is ludicrous to run a school on such a shoestring. It is only through the external fund-raising ability of the principal, various corporate leaders and corporations, and to a lesser extent SBC that the school has adequate resources to function. Obviously the question of budget is not unique to BLA but is a systemwide travesty.

Complicating the budget shortage is its restriction. Funds may only be used for designated purposes; there is no freedom on the part of the principal to move funds from one category to another. Although the principal of a high school, even a small school, is analogous to a CEO of a $5-$10 million corporation, the principal has no discretion with regard to the budget. While this might make sense to a system dedicated to central control, it does restrict local flexibility and innovation. School-based budgets would be a worthy improvement, even with budgets as tiny as $40,000 for five hundred students. The principal is the front line: he or she knows where resources should go.

Another budgetary practice of the board is a closed system of vendors. The reason for this is obvious, in that it limits the potential for corruption and has the potential of delivering the best prices for goods and services systemwide. However, the lack of competition does allow some prices (on books and computers, for example) to be available through board-sanctioned vendors at a cost significantly higher than the market price. Again, the principal's hands are tied. When every penny counts, the principals should be able to make the best deals they can for their schools.

The Heart of the Matter: Accountability
for Education Results

Although the statistics from BLA are encouraging relative to other Bronx high schools, and even throughout the city, many of the students are poorly prepared when they enter, and few graduate competitively at the highest level. At best, graduating classes from BLA will number 125–150. While educational "oases" are wonderful, they dramatize, rather than diminish, the need for systemic reform.

The changes in state education law in 1996[19] gave the New York City schools chancellor new powers to control local districts and to replace principals for persistent educational failure. Not until September 1998 was a definition of "persistent educational failure" forthcoming from the chancellor. Newly promulgated evaluation standards for principals state that the principals must have a plan to improve educational standards, but do not hold the principals to account for implementation of the plan or achieving the standards.[20] Newly set standards for "essential elements of exemplary schools" include monitoring of student achievement, collection of data, program development based on the data, distribution of diagnostic information to teachers, students, and parents from the data, and organizing student groupings based on the diagnostics. There is not one word about having students achieve some measurable level of ability in reading or mathematics.[21]

For the two years, the Public Education Association and the metropolitan area Industrial Areas Foundation affiliates urged the chancellor to use his powers, particularly to hold principals accountable for results in their schools. The PEA-IAF definition of persistent educational failure is robust: persistent educational failure exists in any school when, under the same principal, reading scores have failed to reach 35 percent for five or more years. The PEA identified fourteen school districts throughout the city in which persistent educational failure exists in the majority of the district's schools. PEA calls these districts "Dead Zones."

These districts, mostly in the Bronx, Harlem, Washington Heights, East New York, and Bedford-Stuyvesant, are attended primarily by black and Latino students. Many of the districts have been a dumping ground for what the chancellor himself calls the "Dance of the Lemons."[22] All of the districts commonly sending students to BLA are in Dead Zones. Although some have gained marginally in reading scores in recent years, the Dead Zones are still far below the city average. At the recent rate of increase, it will take seven years for Dead Zone schools to reach the present citywide average reading levels. Using as a model the widely acclaimed "COMPSTAT" approach credited with reducing crime in New York City through holding captains of police precincts accountable for crime in their precinct, the PEA and IAF have urged a similar approach in schools with persistent educational failure. Both the chancellor and the CSA have rejected this suggestion out of hand. Instead, the chancellor fought a losing battle in Albany to eliminate principal tenure, claiming that tenure, rather than performance, was the problem. At this moment the chancellor has the power to remove the principal from any school. Chancellor Crew chose, however, not to exercise this in the case of persistent educational failure. Admittedly, these are hard calls, but until a systemwide demand for accountability and such standards as are exemplified in schools such as the Bronx Leadership Academy, too many children will fail to receive the education they require for adult success. Creating a good school is not magic nor does it occur by chance: it takes firmness of purpose, a commitment to education, a willingness to make hard political decisions, and the good judgment to eliminate what does not work and to use what does. It takes leadership. While SBC and BLA can provide this kind of opportunity for five to six hundred students, a much larger effort is necessary.

This gets back to the question of "culture." The current Board of Education culture is still inherently bureaucratic and controlled by the interests of the teachers' and principals' unions rather than by the interests of the students. Occasional openings in this culture allow for the creation of schools like the Bronx Leadership Academy. What is required is a dramatic opening of the culture throughout the system.

What's Ahead?

Recognizing the need for the same kind of approach in lower grades as in the Bronx Leadership Academy, SBC leaders worked for two years with District 9 to create a middle school. Until recently, the lack of involvement by potential staff of the school and the lack of an available building have thwarted this effort. In October 1998, the district identified a potential site for a "school within a school" and several middle school administrators have joined the team working to create the new school.

On another front, the Bronx superintendent of high schools expressed interest in making BLA a grade 7–12 school. SBC and the current school staff have jumped at the opportunity. Available land exists immediately behind BLA, and the owner is interested in the site's being used for a school. SBC has relationships with alternative funding sources for school construction and with reputable private construction firms interested in doing the work in the most timely and cost-effective manner. SBC and BLA have formed a new Education Task Force, and meetings are beginning to make the middle school a reality.

Again, it is the opening of culture, not a Board of Education systemwide initiative that is at work. A few more children will be provided a decent shot at education. Most of their peers will continue to be trapped in Dead Zone schools. Glacial improvements will be celebrated. Throughout the city, in spite of tremendous odds, individual principals have shown what it takes to "turn a school around," and in some districts there has been significant improvement What is needed is more of that same level of commitment to "turn a system around." The local energy for the transformation exists. What is lacking is central leadership. In this, the most politically willful of cities, it is nonetheless the lack of political will that leaves the schools so far behind.

NOTES

1. Jim Rooney, *Organizing the South Bronx* (Albany: State University of New York, 1995).

2. Industrial Areas Foundation, *IAF: The First 50 Years—Organizing for Change* (San Francisco: Sapir Press, 1990).

3. Special Commissioner of Investigation for the New York City School District, "Preliminary Report: Corruption in Community School District 9," 1996.

4. Public Education Association, *Futures Denied: Concentrated Failure in New York City Public School System* (New York, 1997).

5. Bernard M. Loomer, "Two Forms of Power," *Criterion* 15, no. 1 (1976).

6. The Board of Education resolution officially chartering the Bronx Leadership Academy was passed on February 17, 1993.

7. Texas Industrial Areas Foundation, *Alliance Schools Concept Paper* (Austin: Interfaith Education Fund, 1997); Dennis Shirley, *Community Organizing and Urban School Reform* (Austin: University of Texas, 1997).

8. New York City Board of Education, *Parents Associations and the Schools: The Blue Book,* June 17, 1998.

9. U.S. Census, 1990; Citizens Housing and Planning Council, *Preliminary Assessment of Community Redevelopment in the South Bronx* (New York, 1998).

10. Special Commissioner of Investigation for the New York City School District, "Background Investigation into Board of Education Leased Properties," September 1996.

11. Leanna Stiefel et al., *The Effects of Size of Student Body, School Costs, and Performance in New York City High Schools* (New York: Institute for Social Policy, Robert F. Wagner Graduate School of Public Service, New York University, 1998).

12. New York State Education Department, *Summary of Findings, Bronx Leadership Academy High School,* March 16, 1998.

13. *Board of Education of the City School District of the City of New York and United Federation of Teachers, Local 2, American Federation of Teachers, AFL-CIO Covering Teachers,* October 16, 1995–November 15, 2000. Article 8, sec. B.

14. Sherry Giles, Public Education Association (unpublished report).

15. Texas Industrial Areas Foundation, *Alliance Schools Concept Paper.*

16. Shirley, *Community Organizing and Urban School Reform.*

17. Andrew Page, "Crew's Control," *Brooklyn Bridge* 4, no. 1 (1998).

18. New York City Board of Education, "FY 99 Preliminary OTPS Allocation to High Schools. Bronx Leadership Academy 72X525," 1998.

19. *An Act to Amend the Education Law,* December 17, 1996 (S. 1).

20. New York City Board of Education, "Principal Performance Review," 1998.

21. New York City Board of Education, "New York City Performance Assessment in Schools Systemwide (PASS)—Essential Elements of Exemplary Schools," 1997.

22. "Lemon Tree Not So Pretty," *New York Daily News,* October 31, 1997.

PART III

Defining Good Pedagogy

6 The Teacher Crisis and Educational Standards

STEPHAN F. BRUMBERG

The New York City school system is experiencing a severe teacher-quality and teacher-supply crisis. At the very moment when the city and the state of New York have launched ambitious initiatives to raise the standards of student achievement, there is a severe shortage of qualified applicants to teach in the city's public schools, especially in the essential areas of mathematics, science, English as a second language, bilingual education, and special education. And the gap between supply and demand is greatest in those areas of the city with the poorest records of student achievement and which, as a consequence, have the most acute problems in meeting new, enhanced learning standards. The future of public education in New York City depends on the resolution of this crisis.

Unless the Board of Education can find the desperately needed qualified and committed teachers, mandates for higher achievement standards cannot be realized. The dearth of qualified teacher applicants results in the hiring of unprepared and unqualified teachers and a growing gap between what many teachers are prepared to teach and what they are expected to teach. This, in turn, gives rise to a learning gap between those students who have competent teachers able to prepare them for standards-driven, high-stakes examinations and those who do not.[1] Since many of the schools in low-income, minority, and immigrant neighborhoods have the greatest difficulty in recruiting and retaining capable staff, the ambitious efforts to raise student academic performance may well result in harming the very students the city and state set out to help.

When the school system can no longer recruit and retain an adequate corps of competent, well-trained teachers, the system itself begins to break down. Students can neither acquire the knowledge and skills they need to function successfully in today's world nor earn the formal credentials needed to go on to further education or enter a good job.

Elements of the Crisis

In the past decade enrollments have grown by over 150,000, to nearly 1.1 million students.[2] In addition, the State of New York has mandated universal pre-kindergarten for four- year-olds, commencing in the fall of 1999. While this early education is not compulsory, the Board of Education must provide places for all four-year-olds who apply. It is estimated that 6,200 new teachers will need to be hired over the next four years to meet this mandate. Reduced class size in kindergarten through third grade has also been mandated in New York State, beginning in the fall of 1999. New York City needs 3,400 teachers to bring class size down to 20.[3] And higher standards for high school graduation make for particular urgency in hiring new mathematics and science teachers, specializations already extremely difficult to recruit.

On the supply side, the number of newly graduated and certified teachers in New York City has not kept pace with greatly increased demand, especially in hard-to-staff fields. Historically the constituent colleges of the City University of New York (CUNY) supplied the majority of new teachers to the city's schools. They now provide only about one-quarter.[4] Private colleges in the city are also a source of teachers, but the number of teachers they graduate is small, relative to demand. The State University of New York (SUNY) also provides teachers for the city, but the number of SUNY graduates attracted by the board is small.

Exacerbating the supply problem is the anticipated retirement of many senior teachers in the next few years. Over sixteen thousand veteran teachers already qualify for retirement. Many in this group are expected to retire in 2001 at the end of the current contract.[5] Taken as a whole, the number of qualified teachers prepared by the colleges and universities in New York City and their areas of teaching specialization is woefully inadequate to the city's needs. The board needs to find about eight thousand teachers a year for the next four to six years. It is unlikely that local colleges and universities will graduate more than two thousand, and not all of them are interested in New York City as a place to work, nor the Board of Education as their employer.

A difficult situation is made worse by the low retention rate of teachers in New York City's public schools. About half of all teachers hired leave the system by their sixth year. The figures are somewhat better for new teachers who are certified when first hired compared to those who are untrained and uncertified. Low retention means that the board confronts a revolving door: new, inexperienced teachers, who are hard to recruit, leave and are replaced by new, inexperienced teachers who were equally hard to recruit. Not enough stay around long enough to become trained and experienced teachers.

Recruitment is bedeviled by over-regulation. New requirements for entry into teaching recently promulgated by the New York State Board of Regents, examined below, will shrink the potential pool of recruits at the very time when the city's schools must recruit many new teachers. The Board of Education must simultaneously raise student learning standards while transforming its teaching force. Over the next six years close to half the teachers in the system will be replaced. The system's actual standards of expectation and performance ultimately reside inside the heads of classroom teachers. Hence efforts to raise learning standards are inextricably linked to the recruitment, training, and incorporation of these teachers into the schools.

The New York City Teaching Force

In the spring of 1998 New York City's Board of Education employed nearly 73,000 teachers (table 6.1), about 87 percent of whom were either regularly appointed or "Certified Provisional Teachers" (CPTs).[6] Most CPTs will qualify for and will receive regular appointments. More problematic are the 13 percent who are temporarily licensed teachers, known as "Preparatory Provisional Teachers" (PPTs).[7] These individuals have completed a bachelor's or higher degree, but lack the professional education to qualify for New York State provisional certification. By and large, they have had no prior classroom experience and are issued a temporary license to fill a vacancy until qualified staff can be hired, or until the PPT takes the requisite course work and passes the required state teacher's examinations.[8]

To a painful extent, staffing New York City's schools in the 1990s has depended upon hiring PPTs. Nearly 55 percent of all newly hired teachers from 1991–92 through 1997–98 were untrained, uncertified "temporary licensed" teachers. In 1991–92 PPTs represented 65 percent of new teachers, although their proportion declined to 44 percent by 1997–98. Nonetheless, the modal entry category into New York City classrooms is still the untrained teacher.[9] PPTs who wish to remain in the system must earn state certification within five years of initial hiring. About half do so, and most are then appointed to regular positions. The PPT attrition rate of 50 percent within five years, although higher than for newly hired regularly licensed teachers, is about the same as for CPTs. If trends in retention prevail, if PPTs continue to earn state certification at rates similar to the past, and the board is unable to substantially reduce its reliance on PPTs to fill new teacher vacancies, then teachers initially hired as PPTs—untrained and inexperienced novices—will represent about 40 percent of all New York City's pub-

TABLE 6.1 Employees on the Pedagogic Payroll of the New York City Board of Education, March 27, 1998

License Category	PPT[a]		CPT[b]		Regs.[c]		
	No.	%	No.	%	No.	%	Total
Teacher	7,367	12.4[d]	2,813	4.7	49,261	82.9	59,441
Teacher (special ed.)	2,038	15.1	566	4.2	10,909	80.7	13,513
Subtotals—Teacher	9,405	12.9	3,379	4.6	60,170	82.5	72,954
Other pedagogic personnel[e]	301	2.3[f]	528	4.0	12,244	93.7	13,073
Totals	9,706	11.3	3,907	4.5	72,414	84.2	86,027

Source: Based on information provided by the New York City Board of Education, H.R.S. Ad Hoc Report Unit, April 1998.

[a]Preparatory provisional teacher (lacks New York state provisional certification, or a state certificate of qualification).

[b]Certified provisional teacher (holds provisional or permanent New York State certification, but has not taken board interview exam; not regularly appointed).

[c]Regularly appointed teacher or other pedagogic personnel (tenured as well as those on probation, usually three years).

[d]Percents sum horizontally.

[e]Adult education (242), attendance teacher (231), community relations (4), guidance counselor (2,313), lab specialist or assistant (203), psychologist/psychiatrist in training (18), school psychologist (1,185), school secretary (3,297), school social worker (1,277), supervisor (4,257, all but 5 of whom are regularly appointed), and vocational assistant (46).

[f]Of whom 256 are school secretaries. This represents 7.8 percent of all school secretaries.

lic school teachers within the next ten years.[10] The salience of this situation needs to be fully acknowledged in any discussion of teachers and educational standards in New York City. We will revisit this issue below.

Any school district in the New York system can request waivers to hire PPTs if they cannot find state-certified applicants for teaching vacancies. But it is in New York City, with about one-third of all the state's teachers, that the vast majority of PPTs are to be found. In 1996–97 New York City teachers held over 88 percent of 10,252 temporary licenses issued statewide.[11] The city and the rest of New York State seem to exist in distinct labor markets, as we can see from table 6.2. The table presents all initial teaching certificates issued in 1996–97, separating temporary licenses (held by PPTs in NYC) from the total, and tabulated separately for the city and the balance of the state.[12] We can see a serious mismatch between categories of candidates and qualifications in New York City and a fairly favorable match in the rest of the state.

Critical shortages are reflected in those certification categories with large proportions of temporary licenses. In New York City the fields of special education (nearly 65 percent), the sciences (over 85 percent), mathematics (nearly 75 percent), languages other than English (83 percent), and teaching English as a second language (70 percent) must rely heavily on untrained teachers who are granted temporary licenses. And in bilingual education, nearly three-fourths of bilingual extensions were granted as temporary licenses.[13] If we look at the rest of the state, the only real area of shortage appears to be bilingual education. Relatively few temporary licenses were issued, even in mathematics, science, or special education. Perhaps most telling, in New York City 43 percent of credentials in elementary education were temporary licenses, whereas in the balance of the state virtually none were issued in elementary education. Looking at the aggregate of credentials issued, nearly 62 percent of licenses in the city were temporary, but only a little over 7 percent in the rest of the state.

Changes in teacher certification recently approved by the state Board of

TABLE 6.2 Selected Temporary Licenses Issued Compared to Total Certificates Issued, New York City and Balance of New York State, 1996–1997

Category	New York City[a]			Balance of New York State		
	Temporary Licenses	Temporary Licenses as % of All Certificates[b]	Total Certificates	Temporary Licenses	Temporary Licenses as % of All Certificates	Total Certificates
Biling. (exten)[c]	2,008	73.2	2,744	337	62.5	539
Elementary	1,870	43.0	4,344	14	0.2	5,824
Special ed.	1,448	64.8	2,235	354	11.5	3,067
Sciences	961	85.2	1,128	22	2.7	833
Math	564	74.5	757	5	0.9	536
Non-English[d]	517	83.0	623	65	16.9	384
Social studies	427	55.8	765	5	0.5	1,065
ESL[e]	358	70.2	510	13	6.4	204
English	269	42.7	630	6	0.6	957
Physical ed.	190	64.4	295	8	1.4	568
Vocational ed.	135	78.9	171	200	41.4	483
Business ed.	99	76.7	129	58	19.9	291
Totals	8,846	61.7%	14,331	1,087	7.4%	14,751

Source: Based on information provided in appendix A, New York State Regents Task Force on Teaching, "Teaching to Higher Standards: New York's Commitment" (approved July 16, 1998), Albany, N.Y., p. 40. The total refers to all initial as well as temporary certificates in each category.
[a]Determined by residency of teacher candidate.
[b]Temporary licenses as a proportion of all initial certificates in a certification category.
[c]Bilingual extension to an existing certificate or license.
[d]Languages other than English.
[e]Teaching English as a second language.

Regents, examined below, could easily lead to even greater recruiting difficulties for the public schools of New York City. While the Regents require the elimination of PPTs entirely by September of 2003, it is not clear what will happen in districts, such as New York City, under tremendous pressure to hire new teachers in a market that has had a hard time attracting sufficient numbers of qualified candidates. Can the city devise improved marketing and recruitment strategies to meet employment goals, and what will the board do if the numbers still fall short? Beyond recruitment, what needs to be realized is that the board must assume responsibility for the professional training of many new recruits who come with little or no prior professional education, in addition to the long-term professional development of all staff to help them meet rising educational standards.

Recruitment

Historically the New York City public schools recruited their teachers from the city's colleges. The constituent colleges of CUNY were the largest suppliers of teachers, along with the city's private institutions. The majority of new teachers were young women, often from first- and second-generation immigrant households. For many, this was the first step into the professions for female family members.

Until the recent past a candidate needed only a bachelor's degree with a major in education to become a common branches teacher in the elementary grades, and a disciplinary major along with a prescribed education sequence to become a high school teacher (and a music or art teacher for grades K–12). All prospective teachers sat for city licensing exams offered by the now defunct board of examiners. The training and recruitment system was generally adequate to yield sufficient candidates for all vacancies.

Much has changed in the past several decades. First, the sheer number of teachers employed by the system has increased dramatically. Enrollment in school year 1997–98 was nearly 12 percent higher than in 1958–59, but the teaching staff was 94 percent greater.[14] Hence the systemwide student-teacher ratio decline from 25.4 to 14.7. This reflects changes in the teachers' contract with the Board of Education (especially the additional teachers required to cover classes during every teacher's preparation periods), but also the rapid growth of special education from the late 1970s until the present.[15] Special needs classes have legally mandated small class size related to the nature of the services they are expected to deliver. But contract changes and special education cannot explain a near doubling of the teaching force. Mainstream classes are still large, with many children in the upper elementary grades and middle and high school in classes of well over thirty students. Clearly, there is a need to examine closely the actual deployment and utilization of teaching staff. At current staffing levels, however, today's board needs to recruit nearly twice as many new teachers each year to fill vacancies as it did forty years ago.

Other aspects of recruitment have changed as well. At one time graduates of CUNY colleges provided the majority of new teachers for the city's schools. In the past ten years, however, less than one-third of newly hired teachers were CUNY graduates. The remaining two-thirds came from institutions both in and outside of New York State. In the school year 1996–97, for example, CUNY produced just short of 1,400 provisionally certified teachers. The board hired almost 2,400 CUNY graduates, representing only 33.4 percent of the 7,153 teachers hired that year. Since CUNY "hires" exceeded graduates by about one thousand, some of these new recruits may have been teacher graduates from prior years, but most had to be uncertified "temporary teachers" (PPTs).[16]

The City University had been the natural institution to educate prospective teachers for the city's schools. That is not now the case, in part because the number of students who elect to take a professional sequence in education has declined relative to other majors, and in part because the absolute number of new teachers the board must hire each year has grown so enormously, forcing the board to greatly enlarge its recruitment pool.[17] Recruiters have attempted to reach potential teachers at SUNY campuses throughout the state, and have attempted to recruit nationally and internationally. A geographically broadened recruitment pool is a potential virtue, in that a diverse range of qualified teachers can be brought into the system. However, it greatly increases the cost and difficulty of recruiting, and it complicates the task of collaborating with the teacher training institutions who send teachers to the city's schools.

The composition of the recruitment pool has also undergone changes. Women, historically the mainstay of the teaching corps, now have substantially broader occupational horizons. They are not limited by gender discrimination to "women's" jobs. Schools must compete with all economic sectors for young women of talent. If potential job satisfaction, pay, career prospects, status, and working conditions are better elsewhere, schools must offer good reasons to choose teaching. Teaching candidates will tend to apply to schools and districts with the highest pay and the best work conditions. Table 6.3 compares 1997–98 starting and maximum salaries of teachers in New York City and selected cities and towns in the metropolitan region, including upper, middle, and lower income communities. All offered starting salaries that were from 5.9 percent to 29.8 percent higher than in New York; even Newark, New Jersey, a neighboring city with severe economic problems, offered new teachers nearly 10 percent more.

Prospective applicants also consider a district's maximum salary. Here New York City falls even further behind. The suburban districts around

TABLE 6.3 Initial and Maximum Teachers' Salaries in New York City Compared to Those in Selected Towns and Cities in the New York Metropolitan Region, School Year 1997–1998

Town/City	Entry Salary ($)	± NYC (%)	Max $ (MA+60)	± NYC (%)
New York City	29,611	—	61,801	—
Peekskill (W)	32,043	+8.2	81,266	+31.5
Ossining (W)	36,819	+24.3	77,754	+25.8
Greenburgh (W)	37,186	+25.6	82,658	+33.7
Newark (NJ)	32,501	+9.8	66,858	+8.2
Norwalk (CT)	32,750	+10.6	70,550	+14.2
Lindenhurst (S)	31,373	+5.9	85,466	+38.3
Copaigue (S)	35,783	+20.8	83,907	+35.8
Patchogue Medford (S)	33,737	+13.9	82,655	+33.7
Three Village (S)	32,531	+9.9	85,193	+37.8
Babylon (S)	33,858	+14.3	83,019	+34.3
Great Neck (N)	36,379	+22.9	84,720	+37.1
Manhasset (N)	38,450	+29.8	84,646	+37.0
Smithtown (S)	34,873	+17.8	83,542	+35.2

Key: CT = Connecticut, NJ = New Jersey, N = Nassau County (NY), S = Suffolk County (NY), W = Westchester County (NY).

New York held out the prospect of highly respectable salaries, in the $80,000 range,[18] about 26 percent to 38 percent higher than New York City. Even the older cities of Newark, New Jersey, and Norwalk, Connecticut, offered higher maximum salaries.

Competition is greatest for those who work hardest to prepare themselves for the teaching profession, those who are best qualified in terms of their own education, training, experience, area of specialization, and commitment. In light of the salaries offered by the Board of Education, New York City will find it hardest to compete for the best-prepared candidates and those in shortage areas such as mathematics and science.

The elaborate bureaucratic structure of New York City's schools and the very complexity of its application and appointment procedures are themselves disincentives to apply. The board has always been a highly elaborate bureaucratic system. Many of its procedures are needed to maintain teacher standards, guard students against teacher incompetence or criminal behavior, ensure equity in hiring and placement decisions, eliminate biases against candidates, and satisfy state or federal law. The advent of decentralization in 1969 not only complicated the schools' organizational structure but compounded problems of recruitment. The resulting Byzantine maze can confound all but the most undaunted candidate.

The board, to its credit, has labored to set up procedures and services to help prospective candidates successfully negotiate its own application system.[19] But the potential job seeker can never be sure, at the outset, if he or she should apply at the board's central office, at a community or high school district, or at a particular school. When can a candidate apply under the "alternative teacher selection method,[20] and who should initiate the action—the candidate, the school, or the community school district? Unless you have a relative in the system, how do you even know of such a procedure?

Recruitment has been further complicated over the years by the addition of specialized certificates (state) and licenses (city), most significantly special education and bilingual education. Although this may be desirable for enhancing classroom instruction, it segments the employment market. Thirty years ago a school district could search for common branch teachers to meet nearly all elementary instructional needs. Statewide there are still many more elementary certificates issued in a year than new elementary teachers hired.[21] At the same time there is a shortage of certified special education and bilingual teachers, with the gaps filled by teachers who are teaching out of their areas of expertise.

Traditionally the teacher market was divided into elementary and secondary levels (at present grades pre-K–6 and 7–12). However, the new Regents policy on teacher certification divides the world of childhood and youth into four categories: early childhood (birth to grade 2), childhood (grades 1–6), middle childhood (grades 5–9), and adolescence (grades 8–12).[22] The Board of Regents has not set forth a compelling rationale for such a classification scheme, nor does it cite research evidence which links narrowly age-specific training to enhanced student performance. Yet segmentation of the employment market will certainly exacerbate problems of recruitment, training, and placement of teachers.

A master's degree is effectively being made an entry requirement by the Board of Regents. While more formal education may be desirable, demanding higher levels of professional preparation results in costs to potential candidates in both time and money. Unless benefits are increased by more competitive salaries and better working conditions, increased certification requirements will increase the problems of teacher recruitment and quality in New York City.

We have heard much about the deteriorated physical condition of New York City's schools. Crumbling buildings have become a staple on the evening news. Substandard conditions have an especially negative impact on students but beyond damage to students, the sorry state of many school buildings is a powerful disincentive to apply for a teaching position in New York City.

The legitimate goal of ensuring that a diverse student population is re-flected in the teaching staff has also created problems for board recruiters. Just as women, once confined to gender-defined occupations, can now use their talents and ambitions to enter virtually any occupation, and can re-ceive the formal education to prepare themselves for such positions, so too can minority and immigrant youth. The law of the land, and increasingly the practice of the workplace, have opened a broad range of opportunities to youth of talent, ability, and drive. And while not all minority youngsters believe a bright social and economic future is open to them and feel them-selves constrained by poverty and prejudice, there are many who are in school and on tracks leading to desirable destinations. These are the very young people schools are seeking. However, teaching is but one of their options, and not necessarily the most attractive. One can serve the com-munity and oneself in better paying and higher status fields. What once was a ready teacher recruitment pool—the children of new arrivals and marginalized groups held down by convention and discrimination—has become among the most difficult to recruit.

The board has done a commendable job in the last few years in broad-ening its recruitment efforts and facilitating application procedures. It also has begun to move a greater share of the task of recruiting and hiring teach-ers to the schools themselves, and has successfully involved districts and schools in more aggressive recruitment efforts. At present, however, the board lacks the leverage to effect significant changes in the recruitment pool. Without substantial infusion of new funds, it can neither substan-tially raise salaries nor improve the working environment. These, in large part, are political decisions that the city and state have sidestepped.

The board, however, is not without influence. It can propose financial incentives linked to hard-to-staff specialties and districts. It can also pro-mote cash incentives to teachers that are tied to improvements in student performance, both at the class and school levels. The board can also im-prove its teacher retention record by improving the professional environ-ment within which teachers work. New teachers must know they will receive adequate assistance and guidance in their initial teaching assign-ments, and all teachers must be assured of participating in professional development linked to raising learning standards and new curriculum ini-tiatives. The board also can encourage staff initiatives by actively sup-porting teachers and administrators who propose reforming existing schools or establishing new alternatives.

The Board of Education has considerably improved its capacity to pro-ject its staff needs and has made real strides in framing recruitment plans.[23] But while planning occurs at the aggregate level, decisions to enter teach-ing occur at the personal level. One cannot compel people with talent to enter the field of education. Even if the projections were perfect and the recruiting message widely and effectively disseminated, would the board control sufficient incentives to attract talented individuals, especially in shortage areas?

At present the board provides scholarship and loan forgiveness programs to encourage college students and graduates to enter bilingual and special education.[24] The Board of Regents is proposing a scholarship and loan forgiveness program for the state as well, but this will require legislative action, never a certainty, before it can be implemented.[25] However, little has been done to encourage people to become mathematics and sciences teachers. And no financial incentives are available to attract such teachers to the city's schools or to encourage fully certified teachers in all fields to teach at hard-to-staff schools.[26]

Current trends in the labor market suggest that the board will be hard pressed, regardless of current initiatives, to sustain its recruitment pool, let alone expand it. And yet ideally one wants a pool in which there are more applicants than positions so that schools can interview and select the best available candidates. If entry into teaching is severely circumscribed by formal qualifications and the workplace itself is further subdivided into structurally distinct compartments for age group and type of learning (movement into each of which is controlled by further certification), there will be severe structural imbalances, even if the pool remains at the same size. We are confronted with the dilemma of specialization versus generalization and its impact on both the quality and quantity of the labor pool. Can we require that applicants possess knowledge in specialized content, developmental levels, and the particular conditions of learners, or do we seek the best-educated candidates who have demonstrated the ability to learn and achieve high standards, and who can be trained in the profession of teaching and particular specializations within the field? Put another way, to what extent can we demand fully formed professionals to fill the range of teaching positions the board must fill annually, and to what extent can and should schools and districts assume responsibility for the professional formation and specialization of "entry-level" teachers?

Restructuring the Teaching Corps

High qualifications are intended as an initial screen to eliminate unprepared candidates from the pool out of which new teachers are selected. In New York State outside of New York City, the supply of new qualified teachers is considerably larger than the number demanded. Hence districts have the real option to choose from among competing applicants. But within the city there is a dearth of qualified applicants. As a practical matter, anyone who has the formal credentials required by the state and applies to the New York City board will be hired, whether or not they are committed to children, can relate to and motivate students, support high standards of learning, or have the talent to teach. Nearly 55 percent of all new positions in the 1990s had to be filled by uncertified teachers: those who present themselves at hiring fairs or the board recruitment office, and agree to take professional courses leading to state certification.

The need to fill half of all teaching positions with untrained, uncertified teachers yields a mixed bag of recruits, ranging from potentially excellent teachers to decidedly marginal. A major part of the work of the Division of Human Resources must now be devoted to monitoring, counseling, and cajoling these uncertified teachers to take and complete college courses and to tutoring them for state certification examinations.

Regardless of prior education and training, however, certified and uncertified teachers, from their very first day on the job, have identical responsibilities for the education of all children placed in their charge. An inexperienced teacher with no professional preparation, no prior experience working with children, no knowledge of the curriculum or standards of student performance is expected to deliver the same curriculum and raise students to the same city and state mandated standards of performance as the most experienced and professionally prepared teacher.

In reality, the sad truth is that inexperienced, uncertified teachers are likely to teach in low-performing schools, especially "Schools under Registration Review" (SURR), and are themselves probable contributors to such low performance.[27] If actual learning standards are the outcome of teacher-student interactions in classrooms, then the current system of hiring, assigning, and supervising teachers works against raising standards. Where are the rules to support new teachers and protect their students? Where is the required internship for new teachers, and their gradual assumption of teaching responsibilities, rather than the present sink-or-swim approach, which, in the end, harms students more than teachers? A teacher can drop out and move on without incurring much damage, especially an untrained teacher who has not vested time and energy in professional training. But not so the student who is confronted by a succession of new, inexperienced, and often inept teachers. That student becomes a compulsory victim of poor teaching.

To ensure an adequate recruitment pool, the city and state need to acknowledge that for the foreseeable future there will be a mismatch between "qualified" candidates and vacancies. By all means reform teacher education, recruit better-trained candidates, and maintain high selection standards. But keep the uncertified channel open, screen for the best and brightest, and formally recognize that these aspiring teachers will need to be professionally "formed" on the job.

How can this be accomplished without harming the education of children as they are now? Rather than throwing professionally trained and untrained teachers into the classroom without differentiation, the board must construct a teaching ladder, each rung of which pairs the degree of responsibility for the instruction of children with demonstrated teaching competence. We want to encourage people of talent and commitment to enter teaching and to support them with relevant incentives such as scholarships for professional training. But the untrained person initially should work under the direct supervision of a fully qualified teacher (one who through study and demonstrated competence has earned professional standing). Responsibility grows as professional competence increases. Such a career ladder stretches from educational aide, to paraprofessional, to assistant teacher, teacher, and master teacher. A candidate's point of entry into this professional continuum is based on academic study, teaching experience, and demonstrated professional ability. A person progresses up the ladder on the basis of appropriate professional development and a demonstration of developed abilities. Hence, a newly hired teacher with some teaching experience and a provisional state certificate[28] would enter as a teacher. An uncertified candidate with a bachelor's degree but with no pedagogical training or prior teaching experience would start as an assistant teacher, working under the supervision of a qualified teacher. Under proposed Regents regulations, both would participate in a year of mentored teaching.[29] Each would also participate in a program of professional development designed to move those with talent and motivation up the professional teaching ladder.

A career ladder system can set out to recruit the best candidates at each step, provide relevant training and support, monitor performance, identify those who exhibit potential, and promote those who have demonstrated success, measured in terms of promoting student learning (as defined by student performance standards). This system simultaneously permits the board to maintain high hiring standards at each entry point and realistically acknowledges the nature of the potential recruitment pool. But it also places great responsibility for training on the system itself.

Teachers now enter the classroom at very different levels of developed competence, and those with the most limited professional skills often receive the least assistance. A career ladder (with salaries commensurate with degree of responsibility) would require that assistant teachers work under the direct responsibility of a certified teacher (as paraprofessionals do today) or master teacher. The assistant teacher might have his or her own class, but would be required to collaborate with a teacher or master teacher on such tasks as adapting and elaborating curriculum, lesson planning, selecting and developing materials, tailoring instruction for students with special needs, and assessing student learning.

The work schedule of assistant teachers would allow them sufficient time each day to work with their teachers or master teachers, to participate in training activities, and to observe teachers teaching. Each school would have at least one master teacher on its staff, and there would be a sufficient number of teachers and master teachers to mentor and oversee the work of assistant teachers. The performance ratings of teachers and master teachers would include how well they have mentored assistant teachers (determined by the measured achievement of the assistant teachers' students). The school's mentoring-training program would be directed by the principal or assistant principal or a department chair. In a system focused on instructional improvement, we can anticipate that the positions of principal, assistant principal, or chair increasingly will be filled from the ranks of master teachers or teachers who have successfully mentored novices.

New York State Regents' New Teacher Certification Requirements

The New York State Board of Regents is well into an ambitious process of raising the standards of instruction and student achievement in the state's elementary and secondary schools. They have now proposed reforms "in the way we recruit, prepare, certify, and continue to educate teachers" so that the quality of instruction will be consistent with new higher learning standards.[30] The Regents have identified four critical gaps in the current system:

1. New York does not attract and keep enough of the best teachers where they are needed most.
2. Not enough teachers leave college prepared to ensure that New York's students reach higher standards.
3. Not enough teachers maintain the knowledge and skills needed to teach to high standards throughout their careers.
4. Many school environments actively work against effective teaching and learning.[31]

The Regents propose to close the first gap by better monitoring of teacher supply and demand, teacher incentive programs, and efforts to stimulate student interest in the field of teaching. They intend to suspend, beginning on September 1, 2003, issuance of temporary teacher licenses, the category that accounts for over half of all newly hired teachers in New York City. Raising entry qualifications is laudable. However, even if their proposed incentive programs are enacted by the state legislature and approved by the governor, the Regents have not spelled out how these, in and of themselves, will bridge the gap between teacher supply and demand, especially in hard-to-staff specializations and geographic areas. Will instruction be suspended and entry into schools rationed if supply of qualified teachers falls short of demand?

The Regents propose to close the second gap, under-prepared new recruits, by raising entry requirements. They have voted to change teacher preparation standards (the substance of what prospective teachers must learn), and to reconfigure state certification categories. An "Initial Certificate" will require a master's degree and passing scores on all qualifying exams. A "Professional Certificate" will require a year of mentored teaching, three additional years of satisfactory teaching with more rigorous assessment of actual teaching performance, and a possible new advanced content specialty test. Acknowledging, however, that requiring a master's degree for initial entrance may have significant negative impact on both potential candidates and school systems, especially New York City's, they have proposed a "Transitional Certificate" which allows a candidate who has completed all requirements for an "Initial Certificate" except for the master's degree, up to two years to complete that degree.

There are several logical inconsistencies in the Regents' proposals. If a master's degree is needed to prepare oneself for classroom teaching, which will be assessed by state examinations,[32] how can the Regents require passing scores on all these tests by candidates for the "Transitional Certificate" before they have taken graduate course work? And if they, in fact, pass all tests before they earn a master's, why would they need to complete a master's degree? At present "Provisionally Certified" teachers have up to five years to complete a master's degree in an area related to their teaching. Will shortening this to two years raise qualifications or will it require candidates to focus more time on their own education and less on preparation to teach their students? If you allow a candidate to enter the classroom without a master's degree, but you maintain that it is prerequisite for teaching, what does this imply? And if someone enters the classroom without a master's and, over the course of the next two years, is mentored, gains classroom experience, and earns graduate credits, is it better to throw that person out of the classroom and replace him or her with a novice who also lacks a master's degree? If you determine that a master's degree is necessary for one to enter teaching, then it cannot be waived. But if it is not a prerequisite, then time to completion should not be so constrained as to overwhelm a new teacher. Conflating the time line also has an economic impact. At current salary levels, and in the absence of financial assistance for most master's degree students, especially part-timers, the new requirement places a heavy financial burden "up front," and is yet another disincentive for entering the teaching field.

An alternative to the Regents' plan has been suggested: a career ladder that enables candidates to apply for positions consistent with their level of professional preparation. As their preparation and demonstrated performance increases, so would their classroom responsibilities. Hence the candidate with less than a master's degree presents fewer concerns. He or she can serve as an assistant teacher, receive mentoring, and work under the supervision of a certified teacher or master teacher. Promotion to teacher only comes when academic requirements (and state exams) are satisfied and professional performance has been demonstrated. To the Board of Regents' credit, they propose that "an accomplished professional will ... mentor all new teachers."[33] It is, however, in the hands of the legislature to vote the funds required for such an invaluable program.

Gap 3 addresses the need for teachers to maintain the knowledge and skills required for effective teaching. The Regents' major recommendation is to require all newly certified teachers (after September 1, 2000) to complete a minimum of 175 hours of professional development every five years in order to maintain their certification. Such training must address student learning needs. In addition, "all districts will be required to develop a plan to provide all their teachers [newly certified as well as tenured teachers] with substantial professional development programs directly related to student learning needs as identified in the School Report Card, state initiatives and implementation of New York State standards and assessments."[34] It also calls for state financing of school district professional development.

Directly relating a school district's professional development to instruction can have real payoff. It is not clear, however, if a bean-counting approach to professional training measured in clock hours is as valid as an outcomes approach. Professional development, whether of individuals or entire staffs, might best be judged in terms of the measured improvements in student achievement which flow from such training rather than in terms of the number of teacher-seat-hours logged. The state might consider accepting a coherent, focused school district professional development plan which includes all the district's faculty in lieu of a fixed 175 recorded hours of training. However measured, it is heartening that the Regents recognize that all teachers can improve their practice by continued learning, and that teachers should be supported in that effort. As cited in the Regents' report, "New York City Community School District (CSD) #2 improved student performance in reading and mathematics in part by focusing staff development on students' needs. The success of professional development in improving student learning is persuasive."[35]

Professional development is not just an individual activity. Training also can be conceived as a group undertaking: school staff, administrators as well as teachers, can collectively and collaboratively learn strategies and skills designed to improve their students' achievement. Such training needs to be sustained over time. As CSD #2 demonstrates, instructional improvement requires "a long-term focus on a few important instructional priorities," and a successful strategy "depends on reaching teachers directly in their classrooms through a labor-intense consulting model and on using routine processes of management and oversight to educate principals and teachers to the centrality of their role in instructional improvement."[36] It is questionable if an accounting approach is consistent with

CSD #2's understanding of school management, which blurs the distinction between management and professional development.[37] "Management is about marshaling resources in support of instructional improvement and staff development is the vehicle by which that occurs."[38]

Gap 4 is concerned with enhancing the school environment, the world within which teachers perform their craft. The Regents recommend decreases in class size (in the early grades this went into effect in fall 1999), working to improve school safety, and increasing the use of technology in learning. They also call for repair or replacement of decaying schools. All these actions are certainly desirable, but they will require state and local funding. These issues go beyond the scope of this discussion, but it is clear that inhospitable work environments only make the job of recruiting and retaining able teachers that much more difficult.

The Education and Training of Teachers

We can distinguish three aspects of teacher preparation: general education, professional pedagogical knowledge, and craft development. At one time New York City's Board of Education was responsible for all three. Until 1933 most teachers who entered the city's public schools received their postsecondary education and training at one of three teacher training schools run by the board. The board not only prepared candidates in elementary and secondary school for entry into training schools but controlled recruitment into the profession (through selection into a training institution), general and professional education, hiring, placement, orientation, and tenuring. There was a nearly seamless web connecting the general education of prospective teachers, the school curriculum they were to teach, the teaching methods they were to use, and practical craft development. Teachers in training would observe model classes (taught by master teachers in model schools attached to the training schools) and then emulate these teaching strategies in their practice teaching conducted under the supervision of principals and teachers identified by the board, who would critique student teachers and model approved teaching practices. Successful graduates were hired by the system, being well trained in the curriculum to be offered and the teaching strategies to be used. Standards and expectations, introduced and modeled in training school, were reinforced at the school level by principals who had themselves been inculcated in, and were the products of, board philosophy and goals.

This system was weakest in providing a rigorous general education. The curriculum of the training schools was narrowly conceived as preparation for delivering the course of study of New York City's schools. It was strongest in linking professional preparation to actual classroom expectations and teaching practice. The art and craft of teaching, as it was understood by the board, was introduced and taught in the training school and continued to be developed in actual classrooms with the "principal teacher" overseeing (and rating) the adequacy and growth in performance of his or her new teachers.

One of the real weaknesses of the old system of teacher preparation was its inbred nature. Unless the board actively explored new ideas in curriculum and instruction and incorporated them into school practice, the old ways tended to become entrenched. And in a system as extensive as New York's, whose leaders learned their profession and came of age within the culture of the "system," there was an inherent tendency to refine existing ways of doing things and work to improve implementation rather than to launch new initiatives.

The system was also weak in enlarging the pool of prospective teaching candidates. Most teachers in training were themselves products of New York's schools. And all candidates had to make a vocational choice before leaving high school and commit themselves to entering a training school. But the training schools served the board well in their day, and yielded an adequate supply of common branch teachers so long as teacher salaries made the field attractive to high school graduates.[39] However, this system of teacher development was not intended for high school teachers, who needed to acquire a solid disciplinary base, which training schools could not provide. High school teachers, who early in the century enjoyed higher pay scales than elementary school teachers, were generally the products of colleges, especially the municipal colleges—City College for men and Hunter College for women.

In 1933 the training schools were closed as an economy measure in the depths of the Depression. No new teachers were being hired and none needed to be trained. Responsibility for teacher training was effectively transferred to the emerging system of municipal colleges as Brooklyn (1930) and Queens (1937) Colleges, both coeducational, joined City and Hunter. A significant proportion of all women who attended municipal colleges from the 1930s through the 1960s prepared to be teachers.

The link between professional studies and actual classroom practice of teachers was strained by the division of responsibilities. The activities of university teacher educators were shaped by the culture of higher education. Academic standards influenced decisions affecting these teacher trainers' own tenure and promotion and the universities' institutional culture encouraged research and academic study rather than practical development of teaching craft. The work of teacher educators was judged more by its academic nature than by its craft orientation. University faculty also lacked direct access to public school classrooms; even when they entered, they had no authority to intervene in classroom instruction. Different systems, with different institutional imperatives, led inevitably in different directions. As a consequence, the link between the academic preparation of teachers and their craft development was seriously strained.

Since enhanced classroom instruction is a prerequisite for raising student achievement, there is a critical need to repair the breach between the academic study of pedagogy and the actual practice of teaching in classrooms. As with any craft, the practitioner needs to combine cognitive knowledge with performance skills. He or she needs to acquire the professional knowledge and understanding out of which professional practice is built. Novice practitioners need to see examples of skilled craftsmen performing at the height of their abilities; they need to be able to imitate such models and have their performance critiqued by qualified and sympathetic craftsmen. Performance ability can grow if properly nurtured and supported, but achieving skilled performance takes time and much attention.

Colleges must take the lead in academic studies related to pedagogy: child development, learning theory, the history and philosophy of education, the social context of schooling. But colleges must work collaboratively with pre-K to 12 schools on studies related to the application of professional knowledge in the classroom: content pedagogy, instructional strategies, methods of instruction, curriculum development, and assessment of learning. Colleges will need to work in tandem with the schools in helping prospective teachers become comfortable working in school settings with children of various ages and backgrounds, and in their initial teaching efforts. Graduates of teacher education programs should possess skills sufficient for entry into their profession—as do newly graduated doctors, engineers, and accountants for theirs. However, the continuous development of craft is the joint responsibility of the new teacher and the employer, the Board of Education. Districts and schools are responsible for student achievement, the quality of which depends on the quality of instruction. It is the business of schools and their leaders, therefore, to enhance the practice of every one of their teachers, especially novices, to ensure the delivery of the curriculum to every student. As Richard Elmore has remarked with regard to CSD #2, "Professional development for teachers and administrators lies at the center of educational reform and instructional improvement."[40]

Exemplary professional development builds on academic and professional knowledge but brings it directly to the point of practice. It is linked to school and classroom: "It exposes teachers to actual practice rather than to descriptions of practice; it involves opportunities for observation, critique and reflection; it involves opportunities for group support and collaboration; and it involves deliberate evaluation and feedback by skilled practitioners with expertise about good teaching."[41]

Closing Comments

The shortage of qualified teachers in New York City is a structural problem and cannot be treated simply as a regulatory issue. Raising formal qualifications without providing tangible incentives to enter teaching will only aggravate the current situation. First and foremost, there is a need to make the field of teaching more attractive to talented individuals through better working conditions and better compensation for those who can demonstrate their proficiency as teachers as measured by their impact on student learning. It also calls for incentives to encourage people to prepare for shortage areas and to teach in hard-to-staff schools.

The teaching field needs to be restructured into a career ladder which will enable the school system to set high standards at each rung, match qualifications of entrants to teaching responsibilities (and in turn to salaries), guarantee appropriate mentoring and instructional supervision, and direct training to enhanced teaching performance. Promotion up the ranks of the profession will be based on demonstrated performance, that is, the ability to successfully teach children, and will enable talent and performance to be rewarded. Such "earned" promotion will be tied to commensurate salary increases.

A ladder also enables the system to recruit well-qualified liberal arts graduates into the New York City schools, a much larger pool of potentially talented teachers than the much smaller population of state-certified graduates of education programs. The board can guide new liberal arts recruits through professional studies linked to in-service professional development.

Moving more responsibility for recruitment to schools has merit and is critical if each school is to be held more directly accountable for its performance. But schools do not enter the game equal. There are desirable schools and districts that have far more applicants than vacancies and enjoy the luxury of choice. Schools in hard-to-staff districts, however, lack both the environmental conditions and financial incentives to compete with schools in more favored circumstances. They can offer the same salaries as in desirable schools, but often they have high proportions of uncertified teachers, old and poorly maintained buildings, and records of low student achievement. As a consequence they cannot attract enough qualified teachers and rely heavily on "temporary teachers," worsening an already bad situation. Less favored schools must be given additional resources to compete for good teachers.

Some districts are now providing scholarships to currently employed teachers to earn a second master's degree in a shortage area, often the area in which they are now teaching out-of-license but in which they have interest and talent. This is a promising way to meet shortages and to compensate for the inequitable position in which hard-to-staff schools find themselves, and should be supported by the city and state.

One important step schools can take to underline the importance of new teacher orientation and continuous professional development for all staff is to rescue the position of assistant principal and redirect its work to staff development. An assistant principal's day is now largely consumed with administrative duties: student transportation, food programs, routine disciplinary tasks, and bureaucratic paperwork. He or she needs to be relieved of many of these tasks in order to focus on the school's primary task—offering a high standard of instruction leading to enhanced achievement for all its students. School-based budgeting would give schools the power to direct their resources to meet identified objectives. Hence, a school could hire an administrative or clerical assistant to take over some of the current work of the assistant principal, freeing him or her to devote time to staff development.

Every school, regular or charter, public or private, must work to improve the performance of every member of its existing staff, and, through programs of professional development, to consistently focus on improving teaching and learning. When a school staff seriously commits itself to learning, it greatly increase the chances that the children will learn as well.

NOTES

I wish to thank the following individuals who graciously consented to meet with me to discuss the recruitment, orientation, and training of teachers in New York City: Mr. Anthony Alvarado, Superintendent of Community School District (CSD) #2, Mr. Samuel Amster, Personnel Director, CSD #21, Dr. Kathleen Cashin, Superintendent of CSD #23, Ms. Bea Johnstone, in charge of staff development for District #2, Mr. Ivor Lawson, Director of Operations, CSD #23, Mr. Howard Tames, Executive Director, Division of Human Resources, New York City Board of Education, and Mr. Robert Reich, also of the Division of Human Resources. I benefited greatly from their considerable knowledge and insight. Our conversations, and the information provided, helped to enlarge my understanding of issues related to teaching in New York City. However, I am solely responsible for the interpretation of issues, and for opinions expressed and positions taken in this chapter.

1. See the work of Andrew Porter on opportunity-to-learn as defined by students' rights to receive competent instruction in the content of the curriculum: "Opportunity to Learn," Center on Organization and Restructuring of Schools, University of Wisconsin-Madison, no. 7 (1993) and "A Curriculum out of Balance: The Case of Elementary School Mathematics," *Educational Researcher* 18, no. 5 (1989).

2. Calculated from data provided by the New York City Board of Education, Office of Student Information Services.

3. Reducing class size will also require several thousand additional classrooms, no small task for a system already severely overcrowded and with a poor record of building new schools and classrooms.

4. New York City public schools, Division of Human Resources, Ad Hoc Report Unit, March 4, 1999.

5. Large-scale retirements are expected on the part of teachers with many years of experience in the system who will benefit from the relatively high salary at the final step of the current pay scale in the union contract, which serves as the basis for calculating retirement income.

6. Regularly licensed teachers meet state certification requirements, and CPTs have met New York State certification requirements but have not yet sat for the Board of Education's interview examination. If successful in the interview exam, nearly all will be regularly appointed to a teaching vacancy.

7. The number and proportion of PPTs in teaching lines have declined since the early 1990s. In 1990–91 there were about 13,000 PPTs and by spring 1998 PPTs had declined to about 9,400, or from over 15 percent of all teachers to a projection of about 10 percent of teachers in the fall of 1998. And whereas uncertified staff were found equally in shortage and non-shortage areas earlier in the decade, they are now largely confined to the shortage areas of mathematics, the sciences, special education, and bilingual education. The numbers fluctuate over the course of the school year, with the proportion of PPTs tending to rise, especially when certified teachers leave or retire during the school year and cannot be replaced with certified teachers. Data provided by the Division of Human Resources, New York City Board of Education.

8. All candidates must take the liberal arts and sciences test (LAST), the test of pedagogical knowledge (Assessment of Teaching Skills-Written) and, for secondary school candidates and specialty areas, a content-area specialty test (Content Specialty Test).

9. Of the 16,586 teachers hired as PPTs, over 53 percent went on the obtain New York State Teacher Certification (provisional and permanent). However, 30 percent of the PPTs hired in this period are no longer working for the Board of Education, with attrition highest among those hired in the early 1990s. There attrition rates are only slightly higher than the rates for CPTs (27 percent for the period). New hires who were regularly licensed teachers had the lowest attrition rates, 15 percent.

10. New hires in the seven years starting in 1991–92 and ending in 1997–98, and still working in 1997–98 accounted for 30.3 percent of all New York City teachers in March of 1998. PPT new hires in this period still employed in 1997–98 represented 15.8 percent of all teachers. If PPTs continue to represent 40–45 percent of new hires over the next decade, and if their attrition rates remain as they have been in the 1990s, the proportion of teachers who enter the system as PPTs could easily grow to over 40 percent.

11. Regents Task Force on Teaching, "Teaching to Higher Standards: New York's Commitment," approved July 16, 1998 (Albany: University of the State of New York, 1998), p. 10.

12. Ibid., p. 40. Unfortunately the Regents' report gives data only by candidates' place of residence. It does not indicate which candidates were hired or if they were hired by the New York City public schools or another jurisdiction. We do not know who was hired among those newly certified or temporarily licensed, or where, but we can reasonably assume that candidates who apply for temporary licenses do so only if they have secured a teaching position, and since New York City has been

granted the vast majority of waivers issued by the state, we can assume that candidates with temporary licenses who live in the city were hired by the New York City public schools.

13. Teachers receiving bilingual extensions are usually certified in another field.

14. There were 37,593 teachers in New York City's schools and 5,607 vacant positions in 1958–59; there were 72,974 in 1997–98. *Annual Report of the Superintendent of Schools,* Board of Education, City of New York, 1960, p. 309, and Board of Education, Division of Human Resources, Ad Hoc Report Unit, April 1998. It is not known if vacancies in 1958 were filled by substitutes. If so, growth of the teaching force in this forty-year period would have been 69 percent.

15. The exact number of special-needs children enrolled in New York City's schools is hard to determine, since the categories and the conditions of children who qualify have changed over time. However, in 1959 there were 20,021 children assigned to special-needs categories, 45,153 in 1979, and 84,996 in 1998 (exclusive of children assigned to resource rooms). Sources: *Annual Report of the Superintendent of Schools,* Board of Education, City of New York, 1959; "1981–82 Annual Report of the Chancellor," Board of Education of New York City, 1982; and Board of Education, Office of Student Information Services, ad hoc report, March 1998.

16. Data on the undergraduate college of newly hired teachers was provided by the New York City Board of Education Ad Hoc Report Unit, based on information provided by the City University of New York. The number of CUNY graduates who became provisionally certified, 1,396 in 1996–97, was provided by the New York State Education Department. Certainly not all of those who graduated from CUNY and became certified would have taken a position with the New York City Board of Education. Hence the number of PPTs would be greater than one thousand in 1996–97. Unfortunately no data exists to determine the colleges of the two-thirds of non-CUNY graduates hired. Of the one thousand plus PPTs who graduated from CUNY, some proportion would represent those who had completed an education sequence and had yet to pass the state teachers examinations. But the vast majority would have been B.A. graduates with no prior training in education.

17. Due to changes in state teacher certification requirements in the late 1980s, virtually all candidates for a teaching certificate must major (or have a concentration) in a liberal arts discipline. Professional education can be taken as a co-major or minor sequence. The additional liberal arts requirements may have had the unintended consequence of discouraging some potential teachers from taking an education co-major or minor sequence, in part explaining the decline in the number of students, especially at CUNY, who graduate with the pedagogical prerequisites for state provisional certification.

18. Actual salaries are based on number of years of service and the degrees and credits earned. Districts also vary in the number of salary steps from the bottom to the top of their scale.

19. NYC Board of Education, Division of Human Resources, "Recruitment and Staffing Initiatives," April 1, 1998.

20. Section 2590-j-5 of New York State Education Law. According to this section community school district schools that are ranked at the 45th percentile or lower on the statewide reading exam may refer nominations for regular appointment to ORPAL, Division of Human Resources, if the candidate meets state certification

and has passed the LAST and the ATS-W. Nominations must be submitted before May 1.

21. In 1996 the Regents reported that 21,500 teaching certificates were issued, the majority in elementary education, and 5,900 newly certified teachers hired in all fields of specialization. Regents Task Force on Teaching, "Teaching to Higher Standards: New York's Commitment," July 16, 1998, p. 10.

22. "To ensure teachers have sufficient knowledge and skills, certification requirements should reflect students' developmental levels. This will require adjustments for teacher education programs, school districts, and teachers themselves. However, the potential academic gain for students justified the change." Ibid., p. 18.

23. New York City Board of Education, Division of Human Resources, "Recruitment and Staffing Initiatives," April 1, 1998. The Division of Human Resources is now actively working with community school districts and high school divisions to improve both their ability to make projections of teacher needs and to actively recruit such personnel.

24. The Loan Forgiveness Program is directed toward bilingual special education and currently enrolls twenty-five participants. The Bilingual Special Education Teacher Training Program, for first-year uncertified bilingual teachers, has sixty-nine participants and forty graduates employed in this shortage area. The Scholarship Program supports students at thirty-six participating colleges to prepare for state certificates and city licenses in the bilingual specializations of special education, speech improvement, deaf and hard-of-hearing, visually impaired, school psychologist, guidance counselor, and school social worker. Through spring of 1998, 1,017 participants have graduated from the program, and most are still serving in the system. New York City Board of Education, Division of Human Resources, "Recruitment and Staffing Initiatives," April 1, 1998 (unpaginated).

25. Regents Task Force on Teaching, "Teaching to Higher Standards: New York's Commitment," Teacher Incentive Program, p. 8.

26. The proposed Regents' Teacher Incentive Program includes a $10,000 bonus paid to permanently certified teachers who agree to teach for at least three years in a high-need school. Ibid., p. 8.

27. While 11 percent of New York City teachers were not certified, this proportion rises to 16.4 percent in SURR schools. Outside of the state's five largest cities, only 4.5 percent of teachers were not certified. Regents Task Force on Teaching, "Teaching to Higher Standards: New York's Commitment," p. 10.

28. The Regents intend to recast this as an "initial certificate."

29. Regents Task Force on Teaching, "Teaching to Higher Standards: New York's Commitment," Teacher Incentive Program, p. 14.

30. Ibid., p. 3.

31. Ibid., pp. 4–5. The New York Board of Regents approved new teacher certification requirements on September 17, 1999. While a few requirements varied from earlier drafts, and some implementation timetables changed, the underlying structure and philosophical orientation of the regulations were basically unchanged from the draft released July 16, 1998. *New York Times*, September 18, 1999.

32. The Liberal Arts and Sciences Test, the Assessment of Teaching Skills, and the Content Specialty Test.

33. Regents Task Force on Teaching, "Teaching to Higher Standards: New York's Commitment," p. 17.

34. Ibid., p. 28.

35. Ibid., p. 30.

36. Richard F. Elmore, with Deanna Burney, "Investing in Teacher Learning: Staff Development and Instructional Improvement in Community School District #2, New York City" (New York: National Commission on Teaching and America's Future, and the Consortium for Policy Research in Education, 1997), pp. 27–28.

37. "Each district will maintain a professional Development transcript for each teacher affected by the 175-hour requirement. . . . Wherever possible the transcript should be accessible to the State Education Department through electronic transfer and will be used to assess a teacher's completion of the requirements for continuing certification." Regents Task Force on Teaching, "Teaching to Higher Standards: New York's Commitment," p. 29.

38. Elmore and Burney, "Investing in Teacher Learning," p. 25.

39. After the First World War the legislatively fixed teachers salaries fell well behind prevailing wage rates due to raging inflation experienced in the postwar period and high demand for educated workers in a boom economy. As a result, there were severe teacher shortages in New York City in the early 1920s.

40. Elmore and Burney, "Investing in Teacher Learning," p. 2.

41. Ibid., p. 2.

7   Teaching Reading: Phonics and the Whole-Language Method

JOANNA P. WILLIAMS

Who would have thought that the perennial debates—some would say wars—over how to teach reading would ever lead to actual laws mandating specific teaching methods? Presumably classroom teachers are best qualified to make decisions about instruction because of their training and their intimate knowledge about the particular needs of the children in their classes. But some policy makers have decided not to leave all the decisions to teachers—or to school boards or to the writers of the basal readers, the textbooks that over the years have determined the way reading is taught in many of our schools. Several states, including Texas, have rewritten their standards of instruction to require the use of particular instructional methods, and, according to Monaghan,[1] in at least three states (Alabama, California, and Ohio), laws have been passed about how reading must be taught.

There is no such law at this point in New York, but, as in the rest of the country, educational issues are currently at the forefront of public concern. Improving the nation's schools, via hiring more teachers and cutting class size, repairing physical plants and increasing security in the schools, is high on everyone's agenda. All of this is happening in the context of a major shift back to a traditional model of schooling in which basic skills, discipline, and accountability are emphasized. The press for national standards is strong, and there is a loud call for reform of teacher education. It is no surprise to find that much of current discussion about educational policy has to do with reading. Reading has been and will always be the most important ingredient in the elementary school curriculum. If children do not learn to read with accuracy and ease in their early years in school, they will have difficulty in all of their other school subjects and will fall further and further behind.

For New York City, as for all large urban centers, the task of providing all students with the education they deserve, including quality reading instruction, represents a real challenge. The latest news on the reading front is disappointing. A test administered by New York State in 1998 indicated that New York City third graders and sixth graders scored substantially lower than they had in 1997. Over one-third of the city's third graders were reading below remedial level—a year or more behind where they ought to be.[2] (In a new test that was administered to fourth graders in 1999 by the state, 67 percent of the city school children failed to meet the state standards in English.[3])

But whatever the test, citywide statistics mask the large variation in scores among the city's thirty-three community school districts, many of which are larger than the entire school system of a small city. Ninety-seven of the city's 1,100 public schools are on the state's list of failing schools; all but four of the schools on the state's list are in the city.[4] Not surprisingly, the student population in the low-achieving districts and in the failing schools is in large measure an economically disadvantaged one. Clearly there is much room for improvement.

New York City has no consistent policy about how to teach reading. The semiautonomous nature of the city school districts presents a challenge to the establishment of any citywide policy about curriculum. But there is a large body of research on reading, and we do indeed know a great deal about the best methods of teaching it. Given the research evidence, plus the fact that this evidence supports the current swing toward teaching the basics, the districts should recognize that the time is ripe for change.

What does the research say? The first thing it says is that we should teach phonics. Phonics is the method of instruction that capitalizes on the fact that written English represents spoken English by mapping speech sounds to print. Phonics teaches students how letters and letter combinations correspond to speech sounds. Many of the recent mandates around the nation specify phonics as the approved instructional method. To many of us involved in research on reading, this is merely a return to sanity. Not giving phonics its rightful place in the curriculum, which is to say a central place, means seriously depriving children of quality reading instruction. It is certainly true that some children are able to pick up on their own the relationship between sound and letter and attain an effective understanding of the structure of the language after only a small amount of instruction. But most children will benefit from some systematic instruction, and some children will need very intense and extensive instruction.[5]

Teachers need to be able to meet the needs of all children, whether they are slow learners who need a full complement of phonics instruction or children who may merely require limited help at advanced stages. Teachers must be able to provide a complete program of instruction. They also must be able to correct errors and to answer specific questions that a child might ask. Doing the latter adequately, that is, taking an opportunistic stance in which the child's immediate need provides the "teachable moment" for an impromptu phonics lesson that is precisely targeted to that need, presumes substantial knowledge on the part of the teacher and arguably even more teaching skill than does moving competently through a structured program of instruction.

Understanding the alphabetic principle, that is, decoding printed words into their spoken equivalents, and doing this quickly and easily, is the first and foremost task of the beginning reader. It is not the only one: The ultimate goal of reading is comprehension. But decoding must be mastered so that the child's attention can be given over to understanding what is read.

The second thing that research says is that we should teach comprehension. Children do not necessarily understand a text just because they can decode it. There are important differences between written and spoken language, and students need instruction and guidance in getting meaning from texts. Such instruction continues throughout the school years, for the challenges of understanding texts continue as what the student is asked to read becomes more complex. Indeed, we expect that students will not only understand what is written but that they will draw inferences from it, learn from it, and critique it. In short, comprehension is text-driven thinking, and that is what we are teaching when we give instruction in reading comprehension. Such comprehension instruction is not something to start after children have learned to decode; focus must be on meaning right from the start, both as an integral part of decoding instruction and in other ways as described below.

The Alphabetic Principle: Why Phonics Is Important

Written English is an alphabetic system: letters are associated with speech sounds. This makes English orthography very productive, in that only a relatively few written symbols are necessary; they are combined in many ways, and the combinations suffice to represent the entire spoken language. Consider the difference between this type of orthography and the Chinese writing system, in which the written characters incorporate elements that correspond not to sound but directly to meaning.[6] As such, these elements are similar to the "pictures" or "ideographs" that comprised the earliest writing systems. Because of the large amount of rote learning required, it takes years of hard work to achieve a substantial written vocabulary in Chinese. The memory load of our alphabetic system is much lighter.

It is thought that the alphabet was invented only once in the history of mankind—by the Phoenicians—and that it took the Phoenicians and the Greeks several centuries to complete the development of a representation of, first, consonant sounds and, later, vowel sounds. This discovery that spoken language is made up of very small sound units, called phonemes, that appear in many combinations and permutations, could not have been easy, because of the abstract nature of the phoneme. It is not likely that children will discover on their own a principle that is considered to be a major intellectual advance for the world; the principle needs to be taught.

Discovering the alphabetic principle would be especially difficult for speakers of English. A particular feature of English orthography, unlike, for example, many other alphabetic orthographies such as Italian or Finnish, is that the correspondence between letters and phonemes is not simple and regular. That is, there is not a one-to-one correspondence between letter and phoneme. Rather, the letters of the alphabet, singly and in combination, map onto the language's forty-odd phonemes in complex ways. Some letters and letter combinations represent more than one phoneme (*church, chasm, Cheryl*), and some phonemes correspond to more than one letter or letter cluster (*gem, jam, edge*). Moreover, the size of the relevant written unit varies (*so* vs. *crow* vs. *though*).

Such a difficult and abstract principle cannot be taught simply by explaining it to a beginning reader, although explanation helps. As examples are provided—simple ones at first, like "*M* stands for m-m-m," and as children acquire more and more phonics knowledge—what letters and what sounds go together, they are also acquiring an understanding of the principle.

Whole Language: Another Point of View

There has always been controversy over how to teach reading, and the field has become accustomed to debating, sometimes vociferously, about methods. No one disagrees with the idea that the goal of reading instruction is for students to understand what they read; this is only common sense. The debate revolves around how best to get students to that goal. What is in contention is usually the question of phonics: should we, in acknowledgment of the fact that English is an alphabetic language, focus instruction on the alphabetic principle and the acquisition of letter-sound relationships? I have argued yes. The other side of the debate is typically framed in terms of the need to orient instruction around meaningfulness and motivational concerns, which (the debaters argue) are ill-served by phonics instruction.

The phonics approach has recently been challenged by the whole-language movement, which has enjoyed great popularity all over the English-speaking world for the last couple of decades. This is a major challenge because whole language is presented as much more than an alternative method of teaching reading; it is almost a philosophy of education. According to proponents of this approach, such as Goodman[7] and Weaver,[8] the tasks of learning to read and write are not fundamentally different from the tasks of learning to listen and speak. Just as oral language is learned naturally in the absence of formal instruction, as long as a child is in a language-rich environment, reading and writing will be learned naturally by children in a rich literacy environment. Highly structured instruction in which natural (wholistic) language is fragmented into meaningless bits and pieces like letters and sounds will not help. Rather, the curriculum should feature authentic text—high-quality fiction and nonfiction—and authentic reading and writing tasks.

A great deal of writing (composing) is usually done in whole-language classrooms. But the low-level aspect of writing, spelling, is not given much specific attention because it is felt that spelling will improve gradually and naturally over time. Since basal readers are believed to embody all the faults of the "old" reading instruction, including unengaging text, fragmented language, and meaningless tasks, they have been banished from many whole-language classrooms.

Other attributes of whole-language instruction are less tied to the task of beginning reading but are still integral to the approach, such as a focus on the varied needs of individual children and respect for diverse cultural and linguistic backgrounds. Most important, teachers are empowered to handle their classrooms in accordance with their own professional judgment instead of having others—the school district or the basal reader—make instructional decisions. Indeed, this list of attributes, along with the fact that there is wide variation in what goes on in language-based classrooms, underscores the characterization of whole language as a philosophy.

The important question of the role that phonics should play in reading instruction is still central. While some whole-language teachers do incorporate some phonics training in their instruction, many more do not—after all, phonics certainly violates the tenet that whole language should keep language whole. Those whole-language teachers who do teach some phonics are most likely to do it only on an as-needed basis, in context. That is, if a child makes an error while reading, the teacher will at that point step in and provide a minilesson—which may be totally disconnected from the rest of the lesson and therefore not highly effective even when well taught.

But there is no evidence that points to the superiority of whole-language approaches. Recent reviews conducted by Stahl and his associates contrasted whole-language instruction with basal reader approaches, which are considerably more structured and contain more phonics instruction. Stahl and Miller found that whole language may be more effective in kindergarten, where teaching is focused on developing a basic understanding of the purpose of reading and writing, but less effective in first grade, where children must learn to decode in order to become independent readers.[9] They also found that whole language did not fare as well when the students were disadvantaged and of low socioeconomic status, the very children who need the most help. Most telling, these findings held even when the "naturalistic" criteria favored by whole-language theorists were used, as well as when more traditional measures were administered.

In 1994, Stahl et al. did a second review.[10] Surprisingly, there seemed to have been a shift in the goals of the research. Fewer than half of the studies they included in their analysis used any measure of reading achievement at all. Many of the studies used affective measures such as attitude and orientation toward reading and self-esteem—outcomes that have been promoted heavily over the years by the whole-language movement. As important as motivation is, it seems rather foolish to decide that instruction intended to increase motivation to read is more important than instruction intended to improve comprehension, as the design of these studies would suggest. That is, it is perfectly plausible that if children become interested in reading, greater reading proficiency will follow. But that does not mean that any intervention that increases children's interest can be counted on also to improve comprehension; a demonstration of the latter outcome would have to be provided as well. In any event, the analysis of these studies showed no advantage for whole language, whether reading achievement (word recognition or comprehension) or attitude toward reading was compared.

Notwithstanding the lack of empirical evidence in its favor, for many years whole language enjoyed enormous support, especially from teachers.[11] The widespread enthusiasm for this approach surely had to be taken seriously, and it was. People began to realize that what was going on was a revolt against instruction that had often become rigid and stale. Writing had been given short shrift in many classrooms. There was certainly room for improvement in the selection of stories and articles. And in truth, sometimes instruction did focus too heavily on phonics and give too little attention to comprehension.

The 1995 results of the National Assessment of Educational Progress, however, indicated that the whole-language movement had gone too far. The NAEP test scores showed that California, which had moved strongly to whole-language instruction, was ranked with Louisiana, thirty-ninth out of thirty-nine participating states. California guidelines were immediately reexamined, and curriculum modifications made. Other states followed soon thereafter, and today much of the country is turning back to teaching phonics.

Teaching Beginning Reading and Phonics

Following is a general outline of the major components of a phonics program. Then the many other essential features of a good beginning reading program are listed.

Letter Differentiation

Before children can make associations between letters and sounds, they first must have some knowledge of the letters as entities and the sounds as entities. For one thing, the letters must be visually differentiated. Some specific training in identifying letters and, usually, producing them (writing instruction) is necessary. However, in recent years the field has judged that this aspect of the task is not too much of a challenge; that is, most children will master it without inordinate difficulty.[12]

Phonemic Awareness

But the ability to differentiate the phonemes in words—which is necessary in order to be able to map the spoken units onto the orthographic units—is quite difficult for many children. This is a step in phonics instruction whose importance was neglected until a Russian psychologist, Elkonin, pointed it out.[13] Elkonin recommended that explicit phonemic analysis training—that is, practice in taking apart the phonemes in a word and putting them together (blending)—should precede reading instruction.

We call this ability phonemic awareness, to underscore the notion that what is important is the understanding that words are composed of separable sounds and that these sounds (phonemes) are combined into words. This is a necessary forerunner to the understanding of the alphabetic principle and to the actual acquisition of the correspondences between phonemes and letters and letter combinations. Phonemic awareness is one of the best predictors of how successful students will be in learning to read in school, and continued low phonemic awareness through the elementary grades is associated with poor spelling and, in severe cases, dyslexia.[14] Some types of phonological structures, including words themselves, syllables, even onsets and rimes (c-at), can be segmented fairly early in life, and they do not prove to be a challenge in the way that phonemic structure does. Even illiterate adults, after a lifetime of speaking a language, are typically unable to segment phonemes.

Intervention studies have demonstrated that phonemic awareness training in preschool leads to superior decoding in beginning readers[15] and in older disabled readers.[16] An extraordinary amount of research has been conducted on this topic, and the field has been persuaded of its importance. The emphasis on phonemic awareness represents a genuinely new and very important refinement of phonics instruction. Recently several commercial instructional programs have become available for use in schools and also for parents of preschool children.

Decoding

Understanding of the alphabetic principle will deepen as a child learns and practices the code. Initial lessons keep the code simple and consistent; only a few letter-sound correspondences are introduced at a time and with a single value for each. For vowels, this usually includes the short vowel sounds only. Phonics instruction is most effective when done explicitly and systematically, allowing for sufficient practice at each step of the way.

Because the orthographic code in English is complex, the child must learn how letters are pronounced in particular contexts. For example, *c* is pronounced like *k* if it precedes *a, o,* and *u* (*cap, cop, cup*) and like *s* if it precedes *e* or *i* (*cent, city*). Critics argue that, because English is so irregular, there are too many such "rules," and, moreover, too many exceptions, for phonics to be a successful teaching method. But this criticism is unwarranted. In good phonics instruction, children do not learn rules. It is the developers of phonics programs, and teachers, who organize words according to rules, that is, according to spelling patterns. These words are presented, appropriately grouped and sequenced, and are contrasted with words having other spelling patterns. Children pick up these patterns, helped by their ability to use analogy, a natural, automatic cognitive process. That is, if they know how to read *rain, pain,* and *main,* they will more easily read *gain.*

Sight Words

It is important that children be introduced early to connected text, for meaning does not reside simply in words alone. Many common words are not made up of highly regular letter-phoneme correspondences, but they are important because without them the simplest sentences are impossible: *a, the, is, if, they.* These are taught as sight words. That is, they are simply presented as unanalyzed wholes and associated with their spoken equivalents. Because these words are relatively few, and because they appear frequently in text and therefore have much exposure, they are easily learned.

But consider the difficulties for someone who has no systematic way of decoding words and who must independently memorize every word in the language—what a daunting task that would be! This is theoretically what happens in a nonphonics approach to instruction. In fact, no one ever learns to read with proficiency without at some point achieving some knowledge of letter-sound relationships. But it is a great burden for beginners to have to discover on their own that there are such relationships, and to parse letter strings and (especially) spoken words, and to learn the correspondences without a teacher's guidance or opportunity for systematic practice. Many children never succeed under such tutelage.

Automaticity

Proficient readers, of course, do not actually sound out each word as they read. As children practice reading, the connections between the visual pattern (the letter string) and the spoken word are strengthened every time a word is encountered and sounded out. After much practice the letter sequence becomes represented in memory as a unit. At the same time, the word as a visual unit becomes more strongly connected to its meaning; eventually the reader sees the word and automatically thinks of the meaning of the word.[17] This happens more and more quickly, and the child gains automaticity, or fluency.

Instead of putting all one's attention on laboriously sounding out the words, some attention can then be given over to comprehending the text. In fact, unless decoding is sufficiently rapid, comprehension is extremely difficult, because of the memory load required to keep all the words in mind until enough information is gathered (a sentence or a phrase) so that the meaning can be figured out. (This is not purely a reading phenomenon: if someone speaks slowly enough, it can prove impossible to get the meaning of what has been said.)

Syntactic and Semantic Cues

If text were merely a string of unconnected words, each to be read as if it appeared in isolation or on a list, then the teaching of word recognition as described above would suffice. Text, of course, is not like that: text contains many cues to word identification that have little to do with decoding. Language is redundant, and often one can identify a word even when it is completely missing, as in "For her fruit bowl, Sally bought apples, pears, grapes" or "Kevin put on his shoes and tied the   ." In fact, this is the basis for one method, the *cloze* method, of assessing how well people understand what they read. Every fifth (or so) word is omitted, and the task is to fill in the blanks. Here useful cues are both syntactic and semantic. In the sentence about Kevin, we know that the missing word is a noun, and we also know that shoes have laces (and that usually they are tied).

Use of syntactic and semantic cues is an integral part of proficient reading, of course. But overdependence on them in the beginning stages of reading is detrimental, because relying on context instead of phonic and orthographic structure cues impedes the development of fluent decoding. It is the poor reader who relies on context cues in an effort to compensate for poor decoding skills.[18] And it is the poor teacher who overemphasizes guessing at words on the basis of context cues (or on the basis of the illustrations).

Advanced Decoding Instruction

A good decoding program will teach advanced elements of word structure well beyond initial phonics instruction.[19] Attention to syllabic patterns aids the automatization process described above. Meaning comes into decoding through morphemes, smaller-than-a-word units that represent meaning. (For example, *cover* has one morpheme, because there is no meaning in any smaller segment of the word, and *uncover* has two.) A focus on morphemes helps comprehension in two ways, by enhancing automatization and by contributing to vocabulary development. Henry has shown that the study of word structure, including spelling patterns related to word origins (differences among Greek, Latin, and Anglo-Saxon roots), can continue profitably even through middle school.[20]

Spelling and Writing

Spelling is a phonics task that involves encoding oral language into written language, rather than decoding writing into speech. Even before they learn to read, many children express rudimentary phonics knowledge in their attempts to print or write (spell) words, attempts that may not succeed according to orthodox spelling rules but that reflect some emerging ability (*ppl* for *people; grl* for *girl; blun* for *balloon*).[21]

The original studies of invented spelling were used to argue that as they grow older, children conform more and more to acceptable English spellings without formal instruction in phonics. But lately the same evidence has been used to promote the use of spelling in phonics instruction. Spelling offers valuable practice on phonemic analysis. From another point of view, however, there is a danger in invented spellings. When they do not conform to orthodox spelling, they provide a poor visual/orthographic image of the word. Children who see the result of an inaccurate attempt at writing a word may remember it, and this will only interfere with learning to spell and read. (So teachers might be wary of displaying children's invented spellings on the bulletin board.)

Comprehension: The Ultimate Goal

The focus here on word recognition via phonics and more advanced study of word structure does not mean that a good elementary reading program that features phonics ignores comprehension. From the very beginning of instruction, children should be given a wide variety of experiences with books (and other print, such as magazines). They should hear many stories, selected from quality literature, and participate in discussions about them. Teachers should ask questions that focus attention on important aspects of a story and they should encourage their students to tell and retell stories and to play-act.

Other types of text, in addition to stories, should be introduced, from expository pieces to poetry. Vocabulary training should be provided, to increase not only the children's store of words but also of concepts. Children should be learning about the world, through discussion, field trips, classroom visits from parents and others who talk about their jobs or hobbies, and so forth—to gain knowledge, of course, but also because one's general knowledge store helps mightily in reading comprehension. All of these activities promote oral language development as well as reading and writing. The earliest instruction, necessarily involving listening comprehension, will enhance reading comprehension later.

In the phonics portion of the beginning reading curriculum, too, attention should be directed to meaning: The meaning of words as they are decoded should be called to children's attention, and simple sentences discussed. There should be games that focus on meaning as well as on structure. Teachers should show their students how they themselves get value and pleasure out of reading. And last but not least, children should read and then read some more; practice will improve decoding and hasten automaticity, and it will also foster reading comprehension.

Teaching Comprehension beyond Beginning Reading

A simple view of reading might posit that once a reader has attained automaticity and can decode a text into spoken language, the text will be understood without further ado. However, even among children who have successfully acquired decoding skills, there are many who cannot grasp the meaning of what they read. Many children do not have problems until they are expected to use reading as a tool. Then they start to have difficulty understanding school texts in social studies and other content areas.

Until about twenty-five years ago, little attention was paid to reading comprehension as an ability that had to be addressed in its own right. At that time, comprehension instruction was perfunctory. The basal readers really needed improvement. They included texts that were fragmentary and often not engaging. The questions designed for teachers' use in classroom discussion were low-level, requiring mainly surface-level memory of text details. There was little attempt to explain the comprehension process.

But if reading is really text-driven thinking, then thinking is what must be taught. And thinking is a complex and covert mental activity that is notoriously difficult to teach. In the 1960s, the new information-processing theory of cognition provided theoretical impetus for change. Reading was conceptualized as a process of integrating various sources of information. The reader does not merely extract the information that is in the text, for since no text is complete in and of itself, it cannot constitute a complete message. Rather, text information is integrated with additional information, that is, what the reader already knew prior to reading the text (background knowledge). Thus it can be said that the reader is "constructing" meaning.[22]

This new conceptualization of reading led researchers to focus on the question of what proficient readers actually do when they construct meaning. Researchers began to ask people to "think aloud" as they read and to stop after every few sentences to report their thoughts and images. Whatever these activities were might prove to be the things that young readers should be taught. This work provided the underpinning for the new comprehension instruction, which focuses on strategies, that is, procedures that a reader can perform, actively and consciously, to gain comprehension. There are two main strands to this instruction.

Strategies Involving Text Structure

First, children are taught how text is structured and organized, because structure helps guide comprehension. This knowledge will help them to identify the most important information, to make inferences, and to remember main points and details. Each of the two basic text types, narrative and expository, has conventional structures or frameworks that assist comprehension. Most children come to school with a reasonable sense of narrative structure, from hearing stories and watching TV and movies, but expository text is more unfamiliar and more difficult. There are several types of expository structure: description, collection, causation, problem/solution, and compare/contrast. Explicit instruction in these text structures helps students to comprehend texts.[23]

Strategies Involving Active Thinking

The second major strand of strategy training involves teaching young readers to think actively as they read. Certain strategies are commonly used. For example, a good reader often scans a text before reading it, reviewing headings and picture captions, in order to get a general idea of what the text is about. During reading, a good reader might find a particular sentence ambiguous and, at that point, decide to go back over the text for clarification. After reading, a good reader sometimes reflects, drawing inferences that relate to other texts or information gleaned elsewhere. All of these strategies presume an active awareness of one's comprehension.

When comprehension strategy training was first introduced, most intervention studies focused on teaching a single strategy, for example, how to create mnemonic images while reading. But such training was found to be rather artificial and awkward. People do not, typically, single out one cognitive strategy and apply it as they read. So investigators began to combine several strategies into a training "package." One of the best-known multiple-strategy packages is Reciprocal Teaching.[24] In it, children are taught to raise questions about the text, summarize, predict what might come next, and clarify any unclear content. Instruction is conducted in a small group setting, where discussion allows the students to hear each other's attempts at strategic comprehension and to practice it themselves. However, teaching even this combination of four specific strategies has come to be seen as rather artificial. Recently, there has been movement toward a more flexible and fluid approach in the classroom, in which the emphasis is still on reading as an active thinking process but in which a focus on specific strategies that are practiced individually is deemphasized.

Arguably, the most fully developed and most demonstrably effective training package is Transactional Strategy Instruction, introduced by Pressley and his associates, which represents the newer flexible approach.[25] Several strategies are taught in concert, and student discussion is paramount. Pressley has found it takes a substantial amount of time for students to show positive effects of such strategy training, time measured in months, not weeks. Moreover, this type of instruction takes enormous skill and experience on the part of the teacher. This means that educating teachers to be successful at strategy instruction takes considerable time and effort.

Vocabulary

There are other aspects of good comprehension that are not emphasized in today's strategy-based approach. Strategy-focused instruction is generic, that is, strategies apply across the board, regardless of content. But text comprehension depends strongly on the knowledge that the reader brings to the reading task, and texts must contain content of some kind. Traditionally, one important way to bring content into comprehension instruction was to teach vocabulary. The better one's vocabulary—knowledge of words as well as the concepts the words represent—the better one's comprehension. But there is relatively little emphasis on vocabulary instruction these days, at least in part because recent research suggests that it is quite difficult to enhance vocabulary by any kind of direct instruction. Most vocabulary growth seems to be achieved via extensive reading, during which new words are encountered in meaningful contexts. However, it is likely that as we continue to move toward more traditional, structured approaches to reading instruction, some sort of systematic vocabulary training will make a comeback; it certainly should.

Further Issues

Teachers of social studies and science, not only in elementary and middle school, but even in high school, are now being urged to help their students improve their reading as well as their knowledge of subject matter. But there is a paradox here. In recent years, much attention has been given to modifying texts to make them more comprehensible. Secondary school textbooks have, in fact, become more readable—and presumably more effective in communicating content. But adaptations of text (or supplements to texts, like outlines or visual-graphic organizers) are designed to circumvent students' difficulties rather than to improve their ability to comprehend text in general.[26] In some sense, these efforts work against the enhancement of reading comprehension.

In fact, results indicate that such adapted texts do help students learn and understand the specific content presented. However, no improvement is seen when students move on to read a new text. Content-area instruction currently also includes a great deal of nonprint material—films, videos, and so forth. Having poor readers listen to and watch their lessons may be a great boon for social studies instruction, but the lessened reading practice that results certainly works to the detriment of reading comprehension goals.

As described above, strategy instruction has moved from teaching individual strategies to a more flexible and fluid approach. But it retains its structured, analytic underpinnings. However, much current comprehension instruction is quite unstructured, and it is not surprising to find that it is more effective with above-average students than with students for whom reading is a challenge. Students at risk for failure are usually not prepared to take advantage of such instruction. On the contrary, they respond well to explicit and well-structured instruction, which is quite antithetical to this new constructivist teaching paradigm.[27]

An important point to consider is that constructivist goals and constructivist teaching techniques do not necessarily go hand in hand. In the case of beginning reading, one can fully subscribe to the whole-language philosophy, namely, that the ultimate goal of young readers is to get meaning from written language. But one can still believe that the best way of getting readers to that goal is to make sure that they receive well-structured, explicit phonics instruction.

The situation is similar in comprehension instruction. One can emphasize the holistic nature of the comprehension process and the importance of instruction that highlights the relation of text to readers' own concepts and experiences, and yet still endorse a more direct and structured type of instruction. Perhaps such a direct approach will be most useful for children at risk—but of course teachers must be fully prepared to respond effectively to the needs of all children. In any event, we are just beginning to try to incorporate the tenets of the new comprehension instruction and the traditional principles of instruction that are appropriate for students who are having difficulties.[28]

Teacher Education

Much of the call for reform across the country has focused on the quality of teachers. Because women and minorities now have more options in terms of career choice, and because the salaries and working conditions of teachers have deteriorated, it has become increasingly difficult for schools to attract and maintain a well-qualified teaching staff. New York, like other states, has had to start to recruit outsiders, going as far as Austria this past year for mathematics and science teachers.

There has been a move to raise standards. Recently, the New York State Board of Regents put an end to lifetime licensing for teachers. From now on teachers will have to take continuing education courses in order to renew five-year licenses. As described in the previous chapter, the Regents have also voted to close teacher preparation programs that do not prepare their students well enough to pass state teacher certification examinations. This new policy will motivate schools to raise their admissions standards, but it raises other issues.

The curricula of the teacher-education programs should also come in for a general overhaul. While it is likely, in response to the Regents' actions, that performance criteria in courses will become more stringent, more needs to be done. The actual content of certain courses should be evaluated. What should a teacher preparation program in reading education include? Ehri and Williams suggest that prospective teachers should get a thorough grounding in the nature of the reading process itself, including a study of reading disabilities.[29] The fact that there are substantial individual differences in achievement in any classroom, whether due to the impoverished environments of some students, to cultural differences, including a native language that is not English, or to other factors, makes it mandatory that instruction in how to organize the classroom also be offered, including various types of grouping.

Future teachers should know the characteristics of sound general instruction, the tried-and-true classic principles such as providing sufficient practice, offering timely corrective feedback, incorporating demonstration and explanation, introducing prerequisite tasks in appropriate sequence, and so forth. They should learn how a child's age matters in the selection of teaching techniques and evaluating performance. They should learn about the strengths and limitations of standardized tests and the uses of informal assessment. They should get some training in critical inquiry so that they will not be seduced by claims about innovative untried methods.

Overall, a good program starts out with heavily supported and prescriptive course work and then turns to the practical, offering prospective teachers the chance to practice their developing skills under the guidance of an experienced mentor. As teachers' own experience in the classroom increases, they will gain a repertoire of useful instructional materials and activities, a reasoned knowledge base for making the myriad decisions required during every class session, and a flexibility in responding to the immediate needs of their students whenever they arise.

The most frequently mentioned gap in today's teacher education is instruction in phonics. This is to be expected, given that phonics has been far from universally valued in the recent past. Such instruction is very much needed. Moats surveyed experienced teachers and found that they had very little knowledge about the structure of language.[30] Only 25 percent could count the number of phonemes in *ox* and in *precious*, for example, and only 10 percent could consistently identify consonant blends. These teachers may have achieved a level of linguistic awareness sufficient to have learned to read themselves, but a greater depth of knowledge is needed when it comes to teaching others.

Teachers who themselves know about language structure will appreciate the importance of teaching it to their beginning readers. They will also be more appreciative of teaching materials that provide explicit lessons with extensive, well-sequenced practice opportunities and of decodable texts designed to highlight a particular phonics element or word pattern.

A number of teacher preparation programs in the New York City area do not currently require their students to take courses in the structure of language and the teaching of phonics; in some that do, the courses do not necessarily require them to acquire a depth of knowledge and expertise sufficient for them to go out and teach phonics successfully. Prospective teachers have often been exhorted to be "eclectic" in their own instructional approach—reasonable advice unless, as sometimes occurs, it is presented in conjunction with the notion that no approach has to be learned thoroughly because a variety of approaches will be used.

But it would be unfortunate if adding a course in language is all that is done in the quest for quality teacher education. The challenge for teacher education is even greater when it comes to preparing teachers to teach reading comprehension. When all children are given high-quality literature to read (as whole-language proponents insist on), this situation will be improved. But the use of good literature is far from sufficient. As Pressley has noted, long and intensive training is needed in order to prepare teachers to implement a strategic approach skillfully. Indeed, the essence of such an approach is skill and flexibility.[31] There is no specific content, such as phonics, that exists to be taught. Therefore, courses of study would be helpful; but even more helpful would be extensive immersion in the classroom as an apprentice to an experienced teacher and extensive study of one's actual teaching performance, via discussion with a mentor, videotapes, and so forth.

Schools of education are under the gun, because alternative ways of acquiring teacher certification are coming to the fore. Some New York City schools are beginning to establish their own mentoring and apprenticeship programs for their teachers. Teachers' unions, notably the American Federation of Teachers, which includes New York City's United Federation of Teachers, have also developed extensive teacher-education programs.

Results of a recent survey by Public Agenda, a nonpartisan research group, indicated that professors of education hold a different view from that held by both the public and classroom teachers.[32] The latter two groups are concerned with the teaching of basic skills, test scores, and discipline, whereas professors have a more idealized vision of the process of education; they do not consider assessment and discipline to be issues of high priority but rather hold as a major goal instilling children with a love of learning. In recent years such values have not typically been accompanied by the teaching of intensive phonics or of any other type of highly structured instruction. These results suggest that one important audience to reach with discussion of the research evidence is the faculty in schools of education.

Summary

In the New York City public schools, as in many other locales, there is no consistent policy on how reading should be taught. However, there is a sound body of research that informs good pedagogical practice. Indeed, not all of the teacher-preparation programs in the New York City area are training their students to use methods that have been shown in empirical studies to be most effective. We should take the steps required to get the research evidence out to teachers, principals, and district superintendents, as well as to professors of teacher education. Reading is, after all, the most important component of elementary school instruction. It is the foundation for all of school learning as well as for much of life learning.

NOTES

1. E. Jennifer Monaghan, "Phonics and Whole Word/Whole Language Controversies, 1948–1998: An Introductory History," in *Finding Our Literacy Roots*, Eighteenth Yearbook of the American Reading Forum, ed. Robert Tefler (Whitewater, Wisc.: American Reading Forum, 1998).

2. Anemona Hartocollis, "City Reading Scores Fall in a State Test," New York *Times*, November 26, 1998.

3. Anemona Hartocollis, "Most Fourth Graders Fail Albany's New English Test," New York *Times*, May 26, 1999.

4. Anemona Hartocollis, "Nine Percent of the City's Public Schools Are Failing, State Says," New York *Times*, November 14, 1998.

5. Jeanne S. Chall, *Stages of Reading Development* (New York: McGraw-Hill, 1983).

6. Charles Perfetti, *Reading Ability* (New York: Oxford University Press, 1985).

7. Kenneth Goodman, *On Reading* (Portsmouth, N.H.: Heinemann, 1996).

8. Constance Weaver, *Understanding Whole Language: From Principles to Practice,* 2nd ed. (Portsmouth, N.H.: Heinemann, 1994).

9. Steven A. Stahl and Patricia S. Miller, "Whole Language and Language Experience Approaches for Beginning Reading: A Quantitative Research Synthesis," *Review of Educational Research* 59 (1989).

10. Steven A. Stahl, Michael C. McKenna, and Joan R. Pagnucco, "The Effects of Whole Language Instruction: An Update and Reappraisal," *Educational Psychologist* 29 (1994).

11. Michael C. McKenna, Richard D. Robinson, and John W. Miller, "Whole Language: A Research Agenda for the Nineties," *Educational Researcher* 19 (1990).

12. Frank R. Vellutino, *Dyslexia: Theory and Research* (Cambridge, Mass.: M.I.T. Press, 1979).

13. D. B. Elkonin, "The Psychology of Mastering the Elements of Reading," in *Educational Psychology in the USSR,* ed. Bruce Simon and June Simon (London: Routledge and Kegan Paul, 1963).

14. Hollis S. Scarborough, "Prediction of Reading Disability from Familial and Individual Differences," *Journal of Educational Psychology* 81 (1989).

15. Ellen W. Ball and Benita A. Blachman, "Does Phoneme Awareness Training in Kindergarten Make a Difference in Early Word Recognition and Developmental Spelling?" *Reading Research Quarterly* 26 (1991).

16. Joanna P. Williams, "Teaching Decoding with an Emphasis on Phoneme Analysis and Phoneme Blending," *Journal of Educational Psychology* 72 (1980).

17. S. Jay Samuels, Nancy Schermer, and Scott Reinking, "Reading Fluency: Techniques for Making Decoding Automatic," in *What Research Has to Say about Reading Instruction,* ed. S. Jay Samuels and Alan E. Farstrup (Newark, Del.: International Reading Association, 1992).

18. Tom Nicholson, "Do Children Read Words Better in Context or in Lists? A Classic Study Revisited," *Journal of Educational Psychology* 83 (1991).

19. Miriam Balmuth, *The Roots of Phonics: A Historical Introduction,* 2nd ed. (Timonium, Md: York Press, 1992).

20. Marcia Henry, "The Decoding/Spelling Continuum: Integrated Decoding and Spelling Instruction from Pre-school to Early Secondary School," *Dyslexia* 3 (1997).

21. Marilyn J. Adams, *Beginning to Read: Thinking and Learning about Print* (Cambridge, Mass.: M.I.T. Press, 1990).

22. Janice A. Dole, Joanna P. Williams, Jean Osborn, Jacqueline J. Bourassa, Kathy Bartisias, Sue Greene, and Doreen Terry, *Reading Comprehension Instruction* (Washington, D.C.: American Federation of Teachers, 1998).

23. Russell Gersten, Joanna P. Williams, Lynn Fuchs, and Scott Baker, *Improving Reading Comprehension for Children with Disabilities: A Review of Research* (Report to Office of Special Education Programs, U.S. Department of Education, 1998).

24. Annemarie S. Palinscar and Ann L. Brown, "Reciprocal Teaching of Comprehension-fostering and Monitoring Activities," *Cognition and Instruction* 1 (1984).

25. Rachel Brown, Michael Pressley, Peggy Van Meter, and Ted Schuder, "A

Quasi-Experimental Validation of Transactional Strategies Instruction with Low-Achieving Second Grade Readers," *Journal of Educational Psychology* 88 (1996).

26. Isabel L. Beck and Margaret G. McKeown, "Social Studies Texts Are Hard to Understand: Mediating Some of the Difficulties," *Language Arts* 68 (1991).

27. Karen K. Wixson and Marcia Y. Lipson, "Perspectives on Reading Disability Research," in *Handbook of Reading Research*, vol. 2, ed. Rebecca Barr, Michael L. Kamil, Peter Mosenthal, and P. David Pearson (White Plains, N.Y.: Longman, 1991).

28. Joanna P. Williams, "Improving the Comprehension of Disabled Readers," *Annals of Dyslexia* 48 (1998).

29. Linnea C. Ehri and Joanna P. Williams, "Learning to Read and Learning to Teach Reading," in *The Teacher Educator's Handbook*, ed. Frank B. Murray (San Francisco: Jossey-Bass, 1996).

30. Louisa C. Moats, "The Missing Foundation in Teacher Education," *American Educator* 19 (1995).

31. Michael Pressley, *Reading Instruction That Works* (New York: Guilford Press, 1998).

32. Somini Sengupta, "Are Teachers of Teachers Out of Touch?" *New York Times*, October 22, 1997.

8   Teaching Language Minorities: Theory and Reality

CHRISTINE H. ROSSELL

New York City has been providing special programs for language minorities since the 1960s. The most controversial of these is bilingual education. Critics complain that it produces low-scoring students with poor English language skills. Supporters counter that short-term achievement in English is not the goal and that ultimately language minority children who learn to read and write in their native tongue will be more cognitively developed than language minority children who learn to read and write in English. In my opinion, almost everyone is confused to one degree or another, in part because bilingual education is ill defined and inconsistently implemented, and in part because people are generally confused about what test scores mean.

This chapter will attempt to clear up some of the confusion. First, bilingual education needs to be defined because it has, unfortunately, come to mean many things to many people, a problem that has contributed to the disagreement over it. In fact, people who appear to be in disagreement about the effectiveness of bilingual education may just be talking about different policies.

There are currently three *very* different instructional programs for limited English proficiency (LEP) students: (1) native-tongue instruction with transition to English, (2) structured immersion—all English instruction in a self-contained classroom, and (3) regular classroom instruction with English as a second language (ESL) instruction in a pullout setting. All three are being implemented in the New York City public schools and all are being called bilingual education by state and local administrators, legislators, reporters, and educators. Thus there is no treatment called "bilingual education" in the sense that it is implemented in the same way and understood to be the same thing by everyone, and this is true not just in the New York City public schools but throughout the United States.

According to state law (sec. 3204 [3] of the education law), state regulations (Part 154, Title 8), and city regulations, bilingual education in New York City must consist of five parts:

1. Instruction in native language arts
2. Social studies instruction in the native language
3. Science instruction in the native language
4. Math instruction in the native language
5. Instruction in English as a second language (ESL)

In a transitional bilingual education program (TBE), students learn to read and write first in their native tongue and they learn subject matter in their native tongue, but they are gradually transitioned to English until they are taught completely in English. In a dual immersion or maintenance program, students not only learn to read and write in their native tongue and learn subject matter in their native tongue, but this is continued throughout the program, along with language instruction in English, since its goal is to develop full proficiency in both the native language and English. I am referring to both types of programs when I use the terms *bilingual education* and *bilingual education taught according to the theory*.

There are also two all-English techniques for educating LEP children—structured immersion, and regular classroom instruction with ESL pullout. ESL pullout is a program in which the LEP student is in a regular classroom with fluent English speakers but is pulled out for an hour a day, or several hours a week, for small-group instruction in English. Structured immersion is all-English instruction in a self-contained classroom containing only LEP students. The teacher teaches in English, but at a level the student can understand. At the secondary level, these programs are sometimes called sheltered classes. Both of these techniques are practiced in the New York City schools, although structured immersion is called "bilingual" education, and ESL pullout is occasionally called "bilingual" education, despite the fact that both are taught entirely or almost entirely in English.

Structured immersion is called bilingual education by school systems because the teacher is usually bilingual, the students are in a self-contained classroom separate from fluent English speakers, and the classes are typically formed with the declared intent of providing native tongue instruction. In some of these classrooms there may be a bit of native tongue instruction as an enrichment, but it is not a means of instruction nor of acquiring literacy. Occasionally ESL pullout programs are called bilingual education if the students receiving the ESL instruction are of the same language minority group and the teacher is bilingual. The fact that these so-called bilingual classrooms are actually taught in English is ignored by the administrators, the policy makers, the parents, and the advocates of bilingual education—indeed, the advocates passionately *deny* it.

In general, teaching LEP children of the same language group and grade only in English in a self-contained classroom could be a violation of state and board policy because, according to section 3204 (3) of the education law and Part 154 (Title 8, Chapter 2, Subchapter 1) of the New York Codes, Rules, and Regulations, if there are twenty students in a grade of a single language group—enough to fill a classroom—bilingual education must be offered. School districts that want to be eligible for state funds for LEP programs are supposed to teach LEP students completely in English only if they have fewer than twenty students in a grade of a single language group.

New York City board policy goes even further than state policy. According to board policy, bilingual education must be offered if there are only fifteen students in *two* contiguous grades in elementary through junior high schools, meaning 7.5 students per grade, rather than the twenty required by the state. For high school students, city policy is the same as the state's—bilingual education must be offered when there are twenty or more LEP students with the same language background enrolled in the same grade within a school.

Parents do have the option of withdrawing their children from bilingual education, but doing so is difficult and discouraged by administrators and teachers. Chinese parents appear to exercise this right more than other language minority parents because Chinese is defined as one language, although immigrants from China speak dozens of dialects such as Cantonese, Mandarin, Toisanese, Fujianese, and so forth. In fact, although there is a Chinese written language, there is no Chinese spoken language, only the various dialects.

A school in New York City with fifteen Chinese LEP students in two contiguous grades is required to offer a Chinese bilingual program with instruction in "Chinese" even if each Chinese LEP student speaks a different dialect. This is obviously senseless, and so most schools just teach the children in English, and *all* of the schools teach the Chinese LEP children to read and write initially in English, either in a regular classroom with ESL pullout or in a self-contained classroom that is labeled "bilingual" education. Many parents also refuse to allow their children to enroll in a "Chinese" bilingual program in the first place, since a child's dialect may not be spoken by the "Chinese" bilingual program teacher.

The Facilitation Theory

The theory underlying bilingual education is the facilitation theory, developed by Jim Cummins.[1] This theory has two parts: (1) the "threshold" hypothesis, which states that there is a threshold level of linguistic competence in the first language that a bilingual child must attain in order to avoid cognitive disadvantages, and (2) the "developmental interdependence" hypothesis, which states that the development of skills in a second language is facilitated by skills already developed in the first language.

It is a limited theory, however, because it ignores the issue of the great variation in written language. In particular, it is silent on how you would teach Asian children to read and write in their native tongue and why you would want to do that. The majority of Asian languages use an ideographic system of writing, rather than an alphabetic or phonetic system, and have no similarity to English in appearance,[2] thus reducing the number of transferable skills, such as sight recognition of words, sounding out of words, and so forth. These languages also take much longer to master than English. In other words, learning to read in the native language, if it is ideographic (i.e., Chinese or Japanese), may actually be harder than learning to read and write in the second language, if the latter is English or another phonetic, alphabetic language. Indeed, some Chinese bilingual teachers in New York City are not literate in their native tongue because they were educated in the United States and becoming literate in Chinese is so difficult that even fluent speakers of a Chinese dialect cannot do it on their own. As a result of these problems, I have not found any nonalphabetic bilingual education programs that actually teach initial literacy in the native language, although many of them are taught in self-contained classrooms, are called bilingual education, and receive bilingual education funding.

I also have not found any non–roman alphabet bilingual education programs, even if the alphabet is phonetic (e.g., Hebrew, Arabic, the Indian dialects, Russian, and Khmer), that teach initial literacy in the native language. I suspect this is because educators perceive it to be too difficult or distracting to teach initial literacy, particularly to young children, in a language with a completely different alphabet from English. One Russian "bilingual" program teacher in New York City explained to me that she was not teaching her Russian LEP students to read and write in Russian because she thought it would be too confusing until they had a solid foundation of English language literacy.[3]

Interestingly, neither the federal and state laws nor bilingual education theory recognizes these limitations to the facilitation theory. According to bilingual education theory and New York State law (and that of many other states), all LEP students are to be taught initially to read and write in their native tongue regardless of the language. Indeed, I have not read any official document that addresses any particulars other than the numbers of students of the same language group and the number of certified teachers in that language group.

Moreover, this silence has been going on for two decades. In 1977, the

Board of Education negotiated a Lau agreement with the U.S. Office for Civil Rights and issued Special Circular No. 69, which defined the criteria for identifying non-Spanish-speaking LEP students and the program they would receive. This six-page memo solemnly describes the program that non-Hispanic LEP children, most of whom are Chinese, would receive in exactly the same terms used for Spanish speakers. Not one word of explanation was offered about how one teaches native language arts or substantive subject areas to children who have a non–roman alphabet language and for whom there are no textbooks. Indeed, there is not a single non-Hispanic language minority group with textbooks in their language written for the U.S. curriculum. But this and subsequent board memos are silent on this problem. So are the state laws and regulations.

Figure 8.1 is a flow chart that predicts instruction in a self-contained classroom and native tongue instruction across different language groups, not according to the numbers of speakers of that language, but according

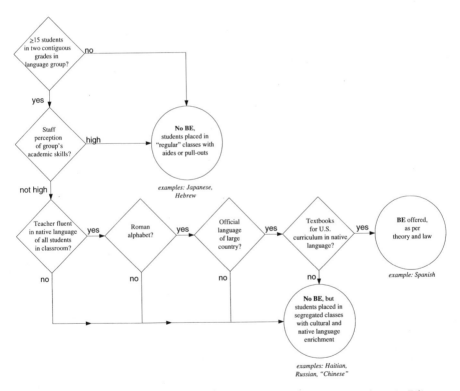

Figure 8.1. Predicted Criteria for Placement of LEP Elementary Students in Bilingual Education in New York City

to important practical criteria, all of them ignored in the theory and in policy statements. This chart is based on logic and on my classroom observations in schools in New York City, as well as in Minnesota, California, and Massachusetts. Assuming a language minority group meets the minimum New York City criterion of fifteen students in two contiguous grades (7.5 students per grade) of a single dialect or language, my flow chart predicts that if the elementary LEP student is of northern European or more affluent Eastern origin (e.g., Japan or Israel), that student will be in a regular classroom where he or she will receive instruction in English with pullout support or in-class ESL tutoring, although there may be a bilingual teacher or teacher's aide for support. Elementary LEP students from poor Asian countries such as China, Cambodia, Laos, the Philippines, or Vietnam; poor southern European countries like Greece or Portugal; or a Latin American country are likely to be in self-contained classrooms because they are thought to need the protection of a specialized classroom for LEP students.

However, students in self-contained TBE classrooms may or may not receive native tongue instruction. As shown in figure 8.1, even if the students are in a self-contained classroom consisting only of the same country of origin LEP students, they will be taught to read and write in their native tongue only if (a) their native tongue is a phonetic language with a roman alphabet, (b) their teacher is fluent in their dialect/language, (c) all the students in the classroom speak the same dialect, (d) there are published textbook materials in the native tongue written for the U.S. curriculum, and (e) the dialect or language is the official language of one or more large country.

The bottom line is that it is pretty much only the Spanish speakers who receive bilingual education according to the theory, because they are usually the only ones who fulfill all the conditions for receiving it: that is, there are enough of them to fill a classroom by combining two grades *and* they have a native tongue that is a phonetic language with a roman alphabet, *and* they are likely to have a teacher who is fluent in their language, *and* all the students in the classroom speak the same dialect since Spanish has no dialects, *and* there are published textbook materials in the native tongue written for the U.S. curriculum, *and* the dialect or language is the official language of one or more large country.[4]

The causal path for secondary students is different and is not shown here. Secondary schools (defined by the grade at which departmentalization of subjects occurs) differ from elementary schools in the rationale for bilingual education, since the typical secondary LEP student already knows how to read and write in the native tongue and has many years of cognitive development. The purpose of bilingual education for secondary students is to protect the LEP students from the competition and, it is believed, an assault on their self-esteem found in the regular classroom and to enhance their self-esteem by showing respect for their native tongue and culture. Some of the secondary programs also have another purpose—to keep at-risk LEP high school students from dropping out and to enable them to attain a high school degree by offering as many required courses as possible in the native tongue or in a "sheltered" environment on the assumption that they would have trouble passing the same course in a regular English-language classroom and / or would feel alienated to the point of dropping out.

But the reality at the secondary level is that it is rare for a school to have enough resources to offer all courses in the native tongue, even if it is Spanish, since teachers have to be certified in both the subject matter and a foreign language. Therefore, bilingual education at the secondary level is a hit or miss proposition. If it is offered, it is usually in one or two subjects, although this does not stop many junior and senior high schools in New York City from declaring that they have a bilingual program.

At all grade levels, claims are made in reports to the state about offering bilingual education when the numbers indicate there couldn't possibly be a bilingual program taught according to the theory and state law. For example, one intermediate school claims to have a Chinese bilingual program for two students in seventh grade and six students in eighth grade, although there is no "Chinese" bilingual teacher at that school. At the same school, there are apparently four Haitian students in seventh grade and eight in eighth grade receiving "bilingual" education from three Haitian bilingual teachers, a pupil-teacher ratio of four to one. Another school claims to have a Haitian bilingual program for eight Haitian students across three grades: third, fourth, and fifth—a pupil-teacher ratio of eight to one even if all three grades were combined. This same school claims to have a French bilingual program for six students in grades four and five—a pupil-teacher ratio of six to one.

In a city bulletin titled "Facts and Figures: Answers to Frequently Asked Questions about Limited English Proficient (LEP) Students and Bilingual / ESL Programs, 1996–97," the Office of Bilingual Education in the New York City schools lists the "Languages in Which There Are Bilingual Programs" and the number of LEP students of that language. The city claims to be offering a bilingual program for 648 Korean LEP students, 310 Bengali LEP students, 269 Polish LEP students, 144 French LEP students, 142 Arabic LEP students, 48 Urdu LEP students, and 47 Vietnamese LEP students in hundreds of schools across the city—which works out to only a few LEP students in each school supposedly receiving bilingual education from a bilingual teacher.

It is hard to believe that the New York City public schools can actually do this, since it is certain they cannot afford it. What is more likely is that these students are in a regular classroom and the bilingual teacher is in fact an ESL pullout teacher who is bilingual. For example, I visited a Bengali "bilingual" program at an elementary school in New York City which was not only taught completely in English but the sign on the teacher's small room clearly said "ESL Content Instruction." Why was it called a bilingual program by the city, the principal, and the teacher? Probably because the teacher was bilingual in English and Bengali and all the students who came to see him were Bengali speakers. Nevertheless, because English was the means of instruction—reading and writing was taught in English and all subject matter was taught in English—*and* because these students spent most of their day in a regular English language classroom, this is not a bilingual education program. It is exactly what the sign on the door says—an ESL program. If the students had been in the ESL teacher's classroom all day, it would have been a structured immersion program.

Figure 8.2 shows the outcome of these policies and practices for the five largest language minority groups in New York City in 1994–95 and 1997–98. The 1994–95 data come from a 1994 Board of Education report called "Educational Progress of Students in Bilingual and ESL Programs: A Longitudinal Study, 1990–94." The 1997–98 data come from individual school reports that are sent to the Office of Bilingual Education at the state department of education. Reports were not filed for the high schools in that year (and perhaps not in other years) and so the 1997–98 data are for elementary and middle school students only. As shown, 76 percent of Hispanic LEP students in 1994–95 and 65 percent in 1997–98 were enrolled in nominal bilingual education classes. The decline from 1994–95 to 1997–98

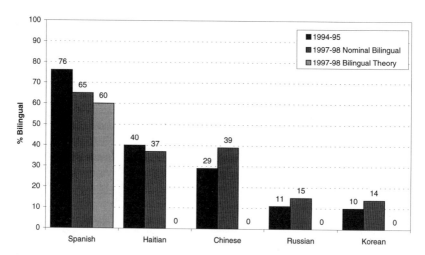

Figure 8.2. Percentage of Bilingual Education by Language Group, New York City, 1994–1995 and 1997–1998

is due to a 1996 change in policy. The board had previously administered the L.A.B. ("language assessment battery") to all Hispanic students, but in 1996 began to administer the exams only to Hispanic students who came from language minority families. The eleven-point decline suggests that at least 11 percent of Hispanic students classified as LEP in 1994–95 were from families for which English was the home language. They were eliminated from the LEP category when the home language survey became a screening device.

Although the Spanish bilingual classes are the most likely to be taught according to the theory, some unknown percentage of them are not, either because of a shortage of Spanish-speaking teachers or because not all the students in them can speak Spanish or because the teacher or principal has a philosophy of emphasizing English. I have reduced the percentage of Spanish LEP students in bilingual education in figure 8.2 by five percentage points—my estimate of the percent not enrolled in bilingual education taught according to the bilingual education theory. This is just a guess derived from my classroom observations—the actual percentage is truly unknown since this is a topic that no one discusses and on which there is not an ounce of information.

Figure 8.2 also shows that in 1994–95, 40 percent of Haitian LEP students, 29 percent of Chinese LEP students, 11 percent of Russian LEP students, and 10 percent of Korean LEP students were in nominal bilingual education. In 1997–98, 37 percent of Haitian LEP students, 39 percent of Chinese LEP students, 15 percent of Russian LEP students, and 14 percent of Korean LEP students were in nominal bilingual education. However, since there are no textbooks in any of these languages for the U.S. curriculum and three of the languages do not have a roman alphabet, these students will, contrary to bilingual education theory, learn to read and write initially in English and learn science, math, and social studies from English-language textbooks, although explanations may be given in the native tongue in some classrooms. Therefore, the percentage of Haitian Creole, Chinese, Russian, and Korean students predicted to be in a bilingual education program taught according to the theory is zero.

These Chinese, Russian, Korean, Haitian, and other languages represent only 10 percent of the enrollment in "bilingual" education programs, however. This is an important fact that has the following implications. First, it means that bilingual education is really a program for Hispanics *even* if you believe that the other bilingual programs are truly bilingual education. Second, it means that the program evaluations that do not distinguish between nominal and actual bilingual education programs do not have a lot of error in them, since 90 percent of the bilingual education enrollment is Spanish-bilingual and these are the programs that are likely to be taught according to the theory.

Across all language groups, only about half of all LEP students are in bilingual education. In 1994–95, 55 percent of LEP students were in nominally bilingual education programs. A total of 47 percent of LEP students were in Spanish bilingual programs—the only programs likely to be taught according to the theory—and some unknown smaller percentage—perhaps 42 percent—were in bilingual education taught according to the theory. In 1997–98, 52 percent of LEP students were in nominally bilingual programs, again with 47 percent in Spanish bilingual programs and some unknown smaller percentage—perhaps 42 percent—in bilingual education according to the theory. Thus there has been a small reduction from 1994–95 to 1997–98 in the percentage of LEP students in bilingual programs, largely because of the elimination of the automatic L.A.B. testing of all Hispanic students.

Since most LEP students in New York City are receiving instruction only in English, including many of those enrolled in programs called "bilingual," critics of bilingual education are wrong when they blame the low achievement of LEP students solely on bilingual education. Even the relatively lower Hispanic achievement cannot be blamed solely on bilingual education since, although 65 percent of Hispanic LEP students in New York City are in bilingual education, only one-third of Hispanic students are limited-English-proficient. Hence only 21 percent of all Hispanic students are in bilingual education. This is an important fact since it means that doing away with bilingual education is unlikely to dramatically improve the relative achievement of Hispanic students in the New York City schools and in the nation.

The History of Bilingual Education in New York City

Indeed, we know that eliminating bilingual education will not dramatically improve the achievement of Hispanic students because the impetus for bilingual education was the relatively low achievement of Hispanic students taught completely in English. Long before bilingual education was on the scene, the New York City Board of Education and the Fund for the Advancement of Education undertook a major research project on the education of Puerto Rican students in the city, published in 1958 as the Puerto Rican Study.[5] This study found that Puerto Rican students had the lowest graduation rate of any identifiable ethnic or racial group. That report recommended English language orientation classes for new immigrants and the classification of students according to their English language ability.[6]

It was not until the 1960s civil rights movement that Hispanic activists put bilingual education on the political agenda nationally and in New York City specifically by depicting Hispanic students as victims of an educational system that had deprived them of their native tongue and culture. The first bilingual programs in New York City were established in 1968, one in the Ocean Hill–Brownsville School District in Brooklyn at P.S. 155 and another at P.S. 25 in District 7.[7] More followed in quick succession.

With bilingual education, Hispanics in New York City continued to have lower achievement rates than Anglos, just as they had with all-English instruction. So in 1972, the *Aspira* lawsuit was filed, named after the organization (Aspira of America) that had first begun building the legal case on behalf of "Spanish-speaking or Spanish surnamed" children "whose English language deficiencies prevent them from effectively participating in the learning process and who can more effectively participate in Spanish." A consent decree was signed between Aspira and the Board of Education which required that such children be so identified and classified at least once a year and be provided an appropriate program of Spanish and English literacy and content area instruction in Spanish.

However, determining the eligible class of children to receive this program turned out to be difficult and contentious, and the litigants found themselves back in court. The Board of Education had created the group of tests called the "language assessment battery" [L.A.B.] in both English and Spanish. Those who scored higher on the Spanish version than on the English version would be enrolled in bilingual education programs, but only if they scored above the tenth percentile on the Spanish L.A.B., indicating that they did function in Spanish to some degree.

The plaintiffs demanded that there be no cutoff at all—that every Spanish-surnamed student receive the Spanish L.A.B. and be assigned to the bilingual program if he or she scored better on it than on the English version, regardless of how high the student's test scores were. After listening to the conflicting testimony, the court concluded: "The most vivid point to emerge from all the argumentation is that we confront an enormous amount of speculation and uncertainty."[8] But "without approaching confidence or certainty," the court defined the plaintiff class as Hispanic students who scored at or below the twentieth percentile on the English L.A.B., but higher on the Spanish L.A.B. The court then went on to say: "The crudity of this formulation is acknowledged on all sides. It is not possible to say with precise and certain meaning that an English-version score at a given percentile is similar to the same percentile score on the Spanish version. . . . But we are merely a court, consigned to the drawing of lines, and we do the best we can."[9]

Identifying a Child as Limited English Proficient

The judge in the *Aspira* case accurately portrayed the state of knowledge. Unfortunately, this situation has not improved with time. Moreover, his decision reflects the continuing willingness of people to select criteria despite their understanding that these are arbitrary and meaningless.

The identification process in New York City, typical of that in other school districts in New York and in other states, involves the following steps:

—STEP 1: Administer home language questionnaire to all students.
—STEP 2: Administer the oral portion of the L.A.B. (English proficiency test).
—STEP 3: Administer the written portion of the L.A.B. to end-of-year kindergarten and older students.
  (If the student scores at or below the fortieth percentile on the L.A.B., but is not Spanish speaking or Spanish surnamed, he or she is classified as LEP and placed in an appropriate program; if the student scores at or below the fortieth percentile on the L.A.B. but is Spanish speaking or Spanish surnamed, he or she is classified as LEP and goes to STEP 4.)
—STEP 4: Administer the Spanish portion of the L.A.B. to Spanish-surnamed or Spanish-speaking students and assign to bilingual education even if the student scores the same or lower on the Spanish L.A.B. (called "comparably limited").

Step 1 in the identification process has changed since *Aspira*. As shown in table 8.1, from 1975 through 1996, all Spanish-surnamed or Spanish-speaking students were eligible to take the L.A.B. regardless of whether a language other than English was spoken in their homes. The practical effect of this is that from 1975 to 1996 some unknown number of Hispanic students from English-speaking families were assigned to bilingual education.

In 1977, a home language survey began to be administered and used as a screening device for non-Hispanic entrants into the public schools as part of the Lau agreement with the Office for Civil Rights. Thus, from 1977 until 1996, non-Hispanic students were more accurately identified as LEP than Hispanic students because the only non-Hispanic students classified as LEP were those from families in which a language other than English was spoken.

It was not until 1996 that the city decided to stop automatically testing all Spanish-speaking or Spanish-surnamed students regardless of their home language and to start using the Home Language Identification Survey (HLIS) as a screening device for all students. This policy has continued to the present day. Students must come from a non-English-speaking environment, as determined by the HLIS, to be eligible to take the L.A.B. In short, some twenty-one years after *Aspira*, Hispanic students were finally treated equally with non-Hispanic students. Ironically, it was their advocates who had demanded their unequal treatment.

TABLE 8.1 New York City and State Standard for Classifying Student
as LEP, 1975–1998

Year	Board Standard		State Standard
	Spanish Surname or Speakers	Non-Hispanic Students	
1975–89	*Aspira:* at or below 20th percentile on English L.A.B. and higher score on Spanish L.A.B. for *all* Spanish-surname or Spanish-speaking students		
1978–89		*OCR:* 20th percentile on English L.A.B. for non-Hispanic students identified as having a home language other than English	
1980–89			At or below 23rd percentile on an English-language assessment test
1989–96[a]	At or below 40th percentile on English L.A.B. for all Spanish surname or speaking students regardless of Spanish L.A.B. score	At or below 40th percentile on English L.A.B. for students identified as having a home language other than English	At or below publisher's cut-off on oral English proficiency test; if pass oral test, at or below 40th percentile on standardized achievement test in English reading
1996–	At or below 40th percentile on English L.A.B. for students identified as having a home language other than English	At or below 40th percentile on English L.A.B. for students identified as having a home language other than English	Same as above

[a]Note: that 40th percentile was optional in 1989–90 for state aid; required by 1990–91.

Step 4 also represents a departure from the *Aspira* decision. As shown in table 8.1, *Aspira* required Hispanics to be assigned to bilingual education only if they scored at or below the twentieth percentile on the English L.A.B., and their Spanish score was higher than their English score. But in 1989, the policy changed to one of administering the Spanish L.A.B. to low-scoring Hispanics, but disregarding the score. If a student scored at the thirty-ninth percentile on the English L.A.B., but zero on the Spanish L.A.B., he or she was nevertheless classified LEP, and assigned to a program (and called "comparably limited").

These assessment tools may give the appearance of being scientific, but it is an illusion. Every single step in this process is capable of classifying a student who is fluent in English as a limited-English-speaker, and this was even more of a possibility from 1975 to 1996, when Hispanic students didn't even have to be from a Spanish-speaking family to be classified as LEP and assigned to a bilingual education program.

THE HOME LANGUAGE IDENTIFICATION SURVEY. The home language survey in New York City, the first step in the identification process, consists of the following questions:

1. What language(s) does the child *understand?*
   ( )English   ( )Other_____
2. What language(s) does the child *speak?*
   ( )English   ( )Other_____
3. What language(s) does the child *read?*
   ( )English   ( )Other_____   ( )None
4. What language(s) does the child *write?*
   ( )English   ( )Other_____   ( )None
5. What language is spoken in the child's home or residence most of the time?
   ( )English   ( )Other_____
6. In what language does the child speak with parents / guardians *most of the time?*
   ( )English   ( )Other_____
7. In what language does the child speak with brothers, sisters, or friends *most of the time?*
   ( )English   ( )Other_____
8. In what language does the child speak with other relatives or caregivers (e.g. babysitters) *most of the time?*
   ( )English   ( )Other_____

A student is potentially LEP and eligible to take the L.A.B. if any one response to questions 1–4 *and* any two responses to questions 5–8 include a language other than English. So if the parent answered "English and Cantonese" to question 1 and 2, only "English" to questions 3 and 4, "Cantonese" to questions 6 and 8, but only "English" to questions 5 and 7, the child is considered potentially LEP despite the fact that he or she speaks English and can only read and write in English. In short, the problem with the home language survey is that it does not try to determine if the child in question is fluent in English. The wording of the questions are intentionally broad in order to identify children who come from language minority backgrounds, not children who are limited in English.

NORM-REFERENCED TESTS. The overinclusiveness of the home language survey would not be a problem if the subsequent steps accurately identified who was not fluent in English. Unfortunately, they do not. On the other hand, as I explain below, it is only the home language survey that keeps 40 percent of all New York City students from being classified as limited English proficient.

The oral part of the Language Assessment Battery (L.A.B.) was normed in 1981–82 on a citywide population that consists mostly of native English speakers. The written part of the L.A.B. was normed in 1985 on the same citywide population. In other words, questions were selected so that their answers produced a normal distribution of scores among a sample of all students in the city's public schools.

The criterion for determining whether a child is limited English proficient is currently the fortieth percentile. It is a mathematical principle that 40 percent of the population scores at the fortieth percentile. If the L.A.B. were administered citywide, 40 percent of the children in the city, almost all of whom are English native speakers, would be classified as limited English proficient.

An important question is why people set norms for limited English proficient students that cannot be met by 40 percent of the citywide student population. One reason is ignorance. Educators seem to have been misled by the constant criticism they receive from intellectuals, policy makers, and reporters who castigate them for such sins as having "only half their students at grade level." In my discussions with school personnel, I have found most of them ignorant of the fact that nationally it is only possible to have half the population at grade level.[10]

Another reason why people adopt a standard for LEP students that cannot be met by 40 percent of the students in the city is confusion. Educators apparently believe that children who score below average—any score below the fiftieth percentile—are children who are in academic difficulty. Since the home language survey identifies those who are from a home in which a language other than English is spoken, many educators believe that setting a standard such as the fortieth percentile identifies children who are academically in trouble because they come from a home speaking a language other than English.

Indeed, the judge in *Aspira* reiterated this common misperception when he stated that "a Hispanic student scoring better than a fifth of his English-speaking peers on the English-version L.A.B. has a level of proficiency enabling him to participate effectively in English-language instruction." The implication of his statement is that a student scoring worse than a fifth of his English-speaking peers on the English version L.A.B. has a level of proficiency that *prevents* him from participating effectively in English-language instruction.

This is, however, wrong. The twentieth percentile is that point at which 20 percent of the population scores—no more and no less. All of the students, including those scoring below the twentieth percentile, could be extremely smart and highly knowledgeable (let us say by comparison to previous generations). Conversely, all the students, including those scoring above the ninety-ninth percentile, could be stupid and ignorant (let us say by comparison to previous generations). We just can't tell from percentiles, or from any score computed in order to differentiate children. They are rank orders, not absolute standards.

Unfortunately, we human beings do not know any other way to evaluate than comparatively, either explicitly with norm-referenced tests which are designed to produce a bell-shaped curve or implicitly with criterion-referenced tests that have larger categories—what the average student knows at a certain age, what the below average student knows at a certain age, and sometimes what the advanced student knows at a certain age. Moreover, people do not agree on these categories, and the tests are constantly being "renormed." In short, we are more or less stuck with the problem that we do not know how to impose realistic and accurate absolute standards and must therefore fall back on rank orderings that can be misleading and misused.

ORAL PROFICIENCY TESTS. All New York City students identified by the home language survey as potentially LEP have to take an oral proficiency test—the listening and speaking portion of the L.A.B.—as well as the written portion. Beginning kindergarten students take only the oral portion. On the face of it, oral proficiency tests would seem to be better than written norm-referenced achievement tests at determining whether a child knows enough English to function in a regular classroom, because the child doesn't have to know how to read to take an oral proficiency test. Unfortunately, oral proficiency tests are no better than standardized achievement tests and for many of the same reasons.

Oral proficiency tests are known to be unreliable—that is, you cannot get the same outcome in subsequent tests of the same child[11]—and invalid—that is, they do not accurately determine who is LEP.[12] Like standardized achievement tests, language proficiency tests cannot tell the difference between a student who does not know English and a student who does not know the answer—that is, they confuse intelligence with knowledge. In addition, they have the same arbitrary cut-off points that standardized achievement tests have. There have been several experiments in which oral proficiency tests have been administered to English monolingual students. Between 40 and 50 percent of these children who know no language other than English received a score that classified them as limited English proficient.[13] Other studies have found that the tests classify students as limited in their native language as well as in English.[14] In addition, the tests do not agree with each other. A student can be classified as limited English proficient by one test but not by another.[15]

An experiment in Chicago suggests that even above-average students are not immune from being classified as LEP by an oral proficiency test. The Chicago Board of Education administered the Language Assessment Scales (LAS) to students who spoke *only English* and were *above* the city-wide ITBS norms in reading. Almost half of these monolingual, above-average, English-speaking children were misclassified as non- or limited English speaking. Moreover, there is a developmental trend. Seventy-eight percent of the English monolingual five-year-olds, but only 25 percent of the fourteen-year-olds were classified as LEP.[16] Similar results would be found with the L.A.B. Since the cut-off point is the fortieth percentile established by a citywide population, 40 percent of the citywide population would be classified as LEP by the L.A.B. even though they are overwhelmingly fluent English speakers. Teachers are better than tests in determining whether a child is proficient in English, but even they make mistakes and for the same reasons. Like the tests, they can become confused as to whether a child does not understand English or does not know the answer, particularly if they do not know the child very well.

In short, the procedures and criteria used by New York City (and every other school district in the United States) to determine if a child is LEP identify more children as LEP than actually are because they cannot tell the difference between a child who does not know English and a child who does not know the answer. Second, the criterion used—the fortieth percentile as determined by a mostly native English-speaking population—guarantees that at a minimum 40 percent of the students who are administered the L.A.B. will be classified as LEP no matter how fluent they are in English.

Not only does this occur, but these students get assigned to bilingual education. I visited a first grade Spanish transitional bilingual education class in New York City composed only of Hispanic students. Nevertheless, during the Spanish reading period the teacher translated most of what she said in Spanish into English because there were Hispanic students in her class who understood little or no Spanish. They had been assigned to the bilingual program because they had scored below the fortieth percentile on the L.A.B.

The original *Aspira* decision required dual language testing. A student was classified LEP only if he or she scored higher in Spanish than in English among those who scored below the twentieth percentile in English. This reduces error, but it does not eliminate it because the two tests are not equivalent. The fortieth percentile on the Spanish L.A.B. does not indicate the same ability level as the fortieth percentile on the English L.A.B. For one thing the tests are normed on different populations—Spanish speakers in the case of the Spanish L.A.B. and all students in the case of the English L.A.B.—and for another we do not yet know how to make questions equally difficult in two languages. Even if we were able to, few educators would be able to resist concluding that a language minority student who scores at the tenth percentile in Spanish and the eleventh percentile in English is limited English proficient. Educators are as confused as the general public as to what tests mean, and most of them appear to believe that a low score has some absolute meaning.

Moreover, there appears to be no concern about the fact that more students are identified as limited English speaking than actually are because (a) city officials believe in the value of bilingual education or, at the very least, extra help for children from language-minority homes and classifying them as LEP gets them extra help, and (b) it means more state and federal money for their students, something few school districts in the country would turn down. In a June 28, 1989, memo,[17] the chancellor ordered the community districts to implement the new state standard of the fortieth percentile as of fall 1989, because students scoring between the twenty-first and the fortieth would now "generate State LEP Aid." This is apparently all the explanation he felt he needed to offer.

Even if a language-minority student is accurately identified as LEP upon entering the school system, the classification criterion guarantees that at a minimum 40 percent of the students will never get *re*classified as fluent English proficient (FEP) no matter how good the program is and no matter how proficient they are in English. Moreover, the principals and bilingual education directors appear to know this. A large number of the program narratives in the reports to the state refer to LEP students who have been in ESL and bilingual programs for years only because they cannot reach the fortieth percentile.

Not surprisingly, the number of LEP students in New York City has increased dramatically, at a much faster rate than the number of students and the number of immigrant students. As shown in table 8.2, the number of LEP students in the New York City public schools increased by about thirty-five thousand students from 1987–88 to 1990–91 as a result of the 1989 change in the LEP standard from the twentieth to the fortieth percentile. However, enrollment growth slowed with the 1996 decision to no longer automatically administer the L.A.B. to Hispanic students regardless of whether they come from a language-minority background.

As shown in table 8.2, there are currently 154,311 children in regular education classified as LEP. If we add to this LEP children in special education, the percentage of LEP in the school system is 16 percent, down from a high of 18 percent before the 1996 policy change regarding Hispanic stu-

TABLE 8.2 New York City Limited English Proficient (LEP) Student Enrollment 1987–1998

Year	Total Enrollment[a]	LEP Enrollment			Immigrant Enrollment[a]	Annual Change in Enrollment (%)			% LEP	% Immigrants	Ratio of LEP to Immigrants
		General Education	SPED	Total		Total	LEP	Immigrant			
1987–88	939,933	93,637	12,641[b]	106,278					11		
1988–89	936,153	90,915	12,274[b]	103,189		-0.4	-3		11		
40th %ile*											
1989–90	940,000	110,246	14,883[b]	125,129		0.4	21		13		
1990–91	957,000	121,777	16,440[b]	138,217	94,003	1.8	10		14	10	1.5
1991–92	973,000	125,984	17,008[b]	142,992	119,780	1.7	3	27	15	12	1.2
1992–93	995,000	134,124	18,107[b]	152,231	137,796	2.3	6	15	15	14	1.1
1993–94	1,016,000	154,526	20,861[b]	175,387	124,827	2.1	15	-9	17	12	1.4
1994–95	1,034,000	163,558	22,080[b]	185,638	127,195	1.8	6	2	18	12	1.5
1995–96	1,075,605	167,602	24,000	191,602	133,565	4.0	3	5	18	12	1.4
LM Only**											
1996–97	1,075,635	162,154	20,439	182,593	134,875	0.0	-5	1	17	13	1.4
1997–98	1,083,943	154,311	20,832[b]	175,143	139,777	0.8	-4	4	16	13	1.3
Change											
1987–97	144,010	60,674	8,191	68,865	45,774	15	65	49	5	3	-0.2

[a]Includes special education.
[b]Estimated from 1995–96 and 1996–97 data.
*Change from the 20th to the 40th percentile on L.A.B. as criterion for classifying LEP.
**L.A.B. only administered to language minority (LM) students; elimination of automatic L.A.B. testing of Hispanic students.

dents. From 1987–88 to 1997–98, total enrollment grew by 15 percent, immigrant enrollment by 49 percent, but LEP enrollment by 65 percent, as shown in the bottom line of table 8.2. LEP enrollment is about one and a half times that of immigrant enrollment. If the L.A.B. were truly detecting limited English ability because the children come from families speaking a language other than English, you would expect LEP enrollment to be lower or at least the same as immigrant enrollment.

What all of this research indicates is that national, state, and local estimates of the number of LEP students cannot be relied on. It is an absolute certainty that the true number of LEP students is much smaller than the published estimates, and the only uncertainty is exactly how much smaller.

Program Effectiveness—Reclassification Rates

State law requires that students be in bilingual education for no more than three years. However, this may be extended for another three years with the approval of the commissioner. But even this does not end bilingual education for a LEP student in New York City, since according to a letter written by a special assistant to the chancellor[18] to the attorney for the Bushwick Parents Organization, the school district serves LEP students until they reach the fortieth percentile no matter how many years it takes. They simply do not use state funds to pay for the special program after six years. Thus the state laws and regulations that govern bilingual education are merely funding requirements as interpreted by the city. If schools want state money, they must abide by these rules. If they are willing to do without state money, they can ignore state rules. And they do.

There is very little information on how long students are classified LEP and how long they stay in special programs. The New York City public schools, like almost all school districts in the country, do not do real (i.e., scientific) program evaluations. In general, the reports they produce to evaluate their programs are simple descriptions of what the program's goals are, what the program did, which schools had the programs, and how many students were served. On occasion, there will be aggregate statistics on achievement for the students served. But even aggregate statistics are rare.

A scientific (or real) program evaluation has the following four characteristics.[19] First, there should be a treatment group—for example, LEP students in a bilingual program—and one or more comparison groups—for example, similar LEP students in one or more types of all-English programs. Second, the achievement (or any other outcome) of these students should be compared after some time period in their respective programs. Third, any differences between the students initially should be controlled for statistically in order to give each group a level playing field. (This is not necessary if there is random assignment.) Fourth, the same students must be followed over time, since there is no way to statistically control or match on initial differences, nor would it make any sense to do so, if different students are in the study at different points in time.

The only data on the effectiveness of bilingual education programs in New York City that is even close to being scientific is the 1994 report published by the Board of Education.[20] Typically such educational reports list the authors on the title page, but this one is anonymous. Apparently, the report's conclusions were thought to be so controversial that nobody in research and evaluation wanted to take credit for it.

According to this study, the percentage of LEP students still classified LEP after three years (from 1990–93 or 1991–94) is 41 percent for those entering in kindergarten, 52 percent for those entering in first grade, 62 percent for those entering in second grade, 67 percent for those entering in third grade, 85 percent for those entering in sixth grade, and 89 percent for those entering in ninth grade. One way to interpret these results is to compare them to a citywide student population consisting mostly of native English speakers. When the L.A.B. was normed in 1981 (oral) and 1985 (written), 40 percent of the citywide population received a score that would designate them as LEP. Since for most of them this is their true score (i.e., it is not caused by the fact that they do not understand English), 40 percent of these English monolingual students would still be classified as LEP no matter how many years they were in bilingual education.

Using this standard, the results for the kindergarten cohort are excellent. They are achieving what children citywide would achieve, because 41 percent are still LEP after only three years in the public schools. Even the results for the first grade cohort are very good—52 percent are still LEP after only three years in the public schools compared to 40 percent of the citywide population. The results after that do not look good, culminating in 89 percent of the ninth grade LEP cohort still classified LEP after three years. We do not know, however, whether the problem is the test or the students or the programs. The report itself offers no explanation for this pattern across the grades. Part of the answer may be the L.A.B. itself. It was normed almost fifteen years ago. It may no longer reflect the curriculum in the later grades, and if so, the increasing percentage across grades still classified LEP is simply an artifact of the test.

Part of the answer may also be that the earlier a child enters a school system, the more his educational experience is a product of that system and the sooner he is on an equal footing with his peers. Older children will have had a varied early educational experience ranging from good schools to bad schools to none at all. Indeed, there are older children who enter the New York City public schools illiterate in their native tongue. These students not only don't know English, they don't know how to read and write at an age when everyone else does. The kindergarten child, by contrast, is only disadvantaged by not knowing English, since very few students at that age know how to read and write.

Figure 8.3 shows the percentage of LEP students still classified LEP after three years by program enrollment in ESL or bilingual education. Unfortunately, the nominal bilingual education program category includes all the Chinese, Korean, Russian, and Haitian "bilingual" classes in which native tongue use in instruction is minimal or nonexistent. But since the Spanish bilingual education students represent 85 percent of all bilingual education students in this sample, the inclusion of these structured immersion programs does not bias the results much.

Figure 8.3 indicates that at every grade students in ESL classes get reclassified as fluent English proficient at a much faster rate than students in nominal bilingual education programs. For students who entered in kindergarten, only 21 percent of the ESL students were still classified as LEP after four years compared to almost half of the bilingual education students. From kindergarten through third grade, the differential between the ESL programs and the bilingual education programs in the percentage of students who are LEP favors the ESL program by about forty percentage points. The ESL advantage narrows to fourteen points by ninth grade. A difference this large across grades is unlikely to be due only to the characteristics of the children enrolled in the two programs. Unfortunately, we do not know how much, since in this sample 85 percent of the students in the bilingual programs were Spanish speakers and 70 percent

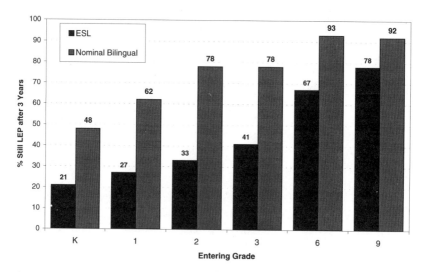

Figure 8.3. Percentage of LEP Students Still Classified LEP after Three Years by Program Enrollment, New York City, Fall 1990–1993 or 1991–1994

of the students in the ESL programs were non-Hispanic students, most of them Asian.

Even controlling for social class does not adequately eliminate the differences in student characteristics between the two programs because it does not eliminate the cultural difference between Asian students and all other American students. Asian students study more and watch less television than other American students and as a result learn more and get better grades than would be predicted from their social class.[21] Thus the difference between the two programs cannot be accurately determined unless this cultural difference is controlled for. This can be done by comparing the reclassification rates of Spanish speakers in bilingual education to Spanish speakers in ESL programs, controlling for student characteristics such as L.A.B. score upon entry into the school system, free/reduced lunch status, parents' occupation, and so forth. Since 35 percent of Spanish-speaking LEP students are in ESL programs, it is in fact possible to do this analysis.

Unfortunately, the school district did not do it. They did control for the student's L.A.B. score upon entering the school system. The results of this analysis for students who entered in kindergarten are shown in figure 8.4. At every level of initial English language proficiency, the bilingual program has a much higher rate of students still classified LEP. For students scoring at the first percentile when they entered the school system in kindergarten, the percentage of students still classified LEP after four years is 20 percent for the ESL program and 50 percent for the bilingual program—a thirty point disparity. The disparity is less for students who know some English and/or are of higher ability. For those entering in kindergarten with scores between the second and fortieth percentile, the advantage of being in an ESL program is only fifteen percentage points.

The analysis shown in figure 8.4 controls for the student's English language ability upon entering the school system, but it is still confounded by the large ethnic difference between the bilingual and ESL programs. Figure 8.5 addresses this issue by breaking the data down by ethnic group and program enrollment for students entering in kindergarten. The percentage of LEP students still classified LEP after four years is compared to the percentage of that ethnic group enrolled in nominal bilingual education and the percentage enrolled in bilingual education taught according to the theory.

The only comparison in this chart that I feel is meaningful as a measure of the relative effectiveness of the two programs is that between the Haitian and the Spanish LEP students classification rate. Only 23 percent of Haitian LEP students are in nominal bilingual education compared to 75 percent of Spanish LEP students. Although Haitian students have lower test scores and lower social class than Hispanic students, they have eight points fewer students still classified LEP after four years. If we were able

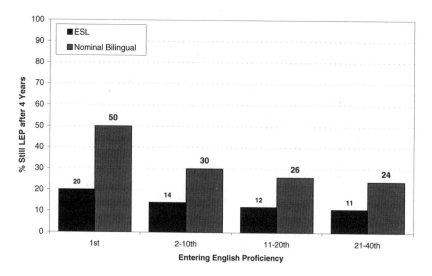

Figure 8.4. Percentage of LEP Students Entering in Kindergarten Still Classified LEP after Four Years by Program and Initial English Proficiency (L.A.B.), New York City, Fall 1990–1994

to control for the lower test scores and social class of the Haitian students, the gap would be even larger favoring ESL. Thus I feel confident in concluding that LEP students in ESL classes get reclassified as FEP at faster rates than do similar students in bilingual programs and that this has something to do with the characteristics of the program. Indeed, the authors of the Board of Education report themselves conclude: "That students in ESL classes exit their programs faster than students in bilingual classes is not surprising, considering that proficiency in English is the criterion for exiting LEP entitlement. As would be expected, the greater the time on task, the greater the level of proficiency on that task."[22]

Although the greater reclassification rate for students in ESL is probably a true program effect, we do not know why. Is it a function of the greater exposure to the English language or the organizational structure or both? It may be that students are tested more and pushed to be reclassified more in the ESL alternative because they are already in a regular classroom and the ESL pullout is a disruption of their education. Getting them reclassified means ending the disruption. The reclassified students in an ESL program continue in the same classroom and program they have been in.

Just the opposite dynamic is operating in any program with a self-contained classroom, even one taught completely in English. When the student is in a self-contained classroom with second-language learners, getting them reclassified disrupts their education. They are pulled out of their classroom and put into a new classroom taught by a new teacher. Many "LEP Program" teachers believe these regular teachers will not provide the LEP students with proper support and a nurturing environment.[23]

In addition, there is a cultural enrichment that goes on in the bilingual programs, even the ones taught completely or almost completely in English, that some parents and teachers may be reluctant to give up by having their children reclassified. In short, the reclassification rate might be lower for students in a self-contained classroom than in ESL pullout for reasons not related to the language or quality of instruction. What is most likely, however, is that some of the differential favoring ESL pullout is due to the organizational issues discussed above and some to the greater exposure to English. The proper analysis to determine how much is due to each would be to compare the Chinese students in "bilingual" education classes to those in ESL pullout. If the Chinese students in "bilingual" classes have lower reclassification rates than Chinese students in ESL pullout, we would know that the organizational structure is a factor causing it since the language of instruction is English in both situations.

These data are from 1994. By 1996, the reclassification rate for bilingual education had not only not improved, it had generated a lawsuit against the state by the Bushwick Parents Organization.[24] The lawsuit was filed against the state because of its policy of mass approvals of the three-year time limit for enrollment in bilingual education.[25]

There is no information on whether things have improved since 1996.

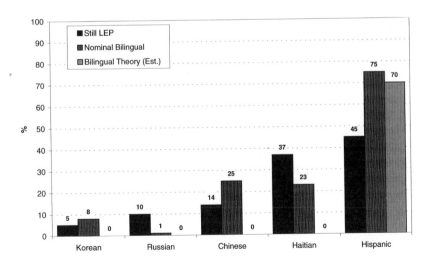

Figure 8.5. Percentage of LEP Students Entering in Kindergarten Still Classified LEP after Four Years, by Ethnic Group and Percent in Bilingual Programs, New York City, 1990–1994

Each year, the Board of Education produces annual report cards with basic statistics and achievement data for each of the 1,100 New York City public schools.[26] These report cards show that approximately 25 percent of elementary school LEP students and 14 percent of middle school LEP students were reclassified as FEP in 1996–97.[27] The previous year's percentage is 23 percent of elementary students and 11 percent of middle school students. This may look like a miserable statistic, but in fact it is too good to be true. If these were the same students over time (unfortunately, they are not), almost all elementary school students and half of middle school students would be reclassified fluent English proficient within four years. It is hard to imagine that things have improved this much since the 1994 longitudinal Board of Education study. It is also hard to imagine that all elementary LEP students are above the fortieth percentile when only 60 percent of the city student population was above it. But there is no breakdown by program or ethnicity, nor do we know what a true longitudinal study (the same students over time) would show.

Program Effectiveness—Student Achievement

The 1994 Board of Education study looked at the achievement of students who had been reclassified from each program. They found that once students had been reclassified, the students who had been in ESL programs continued to outscore the students who had been in the bilingual education programs on the Degrees of Reading Power and the CAT/5 tests of reading and mathematics. The problem with this analysis is that it did not control for ethnicity, social class, years in the program, or initial proficiency in English.

The only recent student achievement data comes from the 1996–97 Annual School Report for New York City. These report cards show that approximately 13 percent of LEP elementary students and 8 percent of LEP middle school students were reading above grade level as of 1996–97. These are good results since we would expect no students to be above grade level, because LEP students are defined by their below average achievement on the L.A.B. and since the definition of grade level is the average for a grade. Indeed, the only reason there are any LEP students above grade level is that the L.A.B. is administered in the fall and the CAT/5 in the spring and because the tests are not perfectly synchronized. To put it another way, if the tests were administered at the same time and were equivalent, it would be an "error" to have any LEP students reading at or above grade level, since LEP students are defined as below-grade-level students.

To conclude, we cannot tell from aggregate achievement statistics what kind of a job the New York City public schools are doing for LEP children. Nor can we tell from a LEP child's test scores what kind of job the schools are doing educating that child. We can assess the effectiveness of alternative programs and we can determine whether a child is achieving more or less than would be predicted from the given IQ and home environment, but that requires a massive amount of data and a sophisticated statistical analysis that is simply not available at this point. For now, we know only that ESL programs are more effective than bilingual education programs in teaching children enough English to get themselves reclassified FEP. Unfortunately, only about half of the LEP students are in the more effective program.

Although the school district continues to favor bilingual education, LEP children are no longer excused from the promotional standards for New York City students. Those promotional standards, however, make no more sense than the L.A.B. criterion for classifying a child as LEP. In order to be promoted in New York City, a child in grades three through eight must achieve a score at or above the fifteenth national percentile on the CAT reading test—for grades three, six, and eight, the state Degrees of Reading Power (DRP) may also be used—and on the CAT math test in English or in translation. LEP students who are exempt from taking the CAT and DRP must meet the promotional standard for reading in English on the L.A.B.

The only problem with a promotional standard such as the fifteenth percentile is that it means that at a minimum, 15 percent of the students will not be promoted no matter how learned they are. Indeed, since New York City students are poorer and more likely to be from non–English-speaking families than the national student body on which these tests are normed, we can expect more than 15 percent will not be promoted. Why does the city set standards for itself that cannot be achieved by at least fifteen percent of a more affluent, native English-speaking population? My guess is politics. The public wants standards and the school district is willing to give them what they want, even though the standards are arbitrary and meaningless, and individual students will suffer from them.

At the same time that the city is imposing standards that can never be met by all LEP students, the state of New York is revising its policies in two contradictory directions. On the one hand, LEP students can now take the Regents exam in their native tongues. This means they can graduate without learning English. On the other hand, the state department of education is proposing to modify Part 154 of the regulations so as to triple the amount of ESL instruction for high school LEP students at beginning levels of English language proficiency and double it for those at intermediate levels of fluency. This proposal will also double the amount of time for ESL instruction for elementary and middle school students at beginning and intermediate levels of English language proficiency. Finally, the proposal will double the amount of time for English language arts for elementary and high school LEP students at advanced and transitional levels of English language proficiency.

Although I have no confidence that anyone can accurately determine "beginning," "intermediate," "advanced," and "transitional" levels of English proficiency, the increase in the amount of English is a step in the right direction. If this is approved by the Board of Regents, it is not clear how New York City will respond nor whether they will be exempt because of the *Aspira* consent decree and the Lau agreement with the Office for Civil Rights.

Conclusions

Bilingual education began as an Hispanic program and it continues to be an Hispanic program, although Hispanic intellectuals and bilingual education advocates deny this. With rare exceptions, only Hispanic LEP students are taught according to bilingual education theory—that is, learning subject matter in the native tongue, learning to read and write in their native tongue, and transitioning to English when they have attained native tongue literacy. The most successful language-minority students—Asians—are taught completely in English. The implications of this are that there is something wrong with the theory that children will be cognitively disadvantaged unless they are taught to read and write in their native tongue. This is undoubtedly why bilingual education advocates vehemently deny the fact that only Hispanic students are receiving native-tongue instruction according to the theory. To acknowledge the ethnic apartheid that exists is to raise troubling questions about the efficacy of the program and the civil rights of Hispanic LEP students.

We cannot tell how effective bilingual education is simply from the aggregate reclassification rates of LEP students. The procedures used to identify a child as LEP and to reclassify him or her as FEP guarantee that at a minimum 40 percent of students from language-minority homes will never be reclassified no matter how good the program is and no matter how fluent the student is in English. Indeed, the test used to reclassify a student as FEP is one that classifies 40 percent of the city's students as limited English proficient. Nor is there any real solution for this involving testing on a mass scale. Teachers do a better job than tests in identifying whether a students is LEP, but they are fallible also.

One reform that would improve the classification process is to revise the home language survey so that it determines whether the child in question is fluent in English. This process could be a three-step one:

1. Administer a short home-language survey to all entrants into the school system to find children who speak a language other than English.

2. Administer a longer home-language survey to entrants who speak a language other than English to determine how limited the child is in English and how proficient the child is in the non-English language.
3. Identify children who are of a language-minority background.

Children would never be reclassified because their identification would not be as limited English proficient, but as language minority, a classification that is not dependent on misleading test scores. This is an identification they would have all their school careers and it would avoid the impossible task of deciding when a child is, or is not, LEP. The instructional staff would give these students the academic support they need, as it does for any other child in the school system.

I have two recommendations regarding program characteristics for language-minority children. First, language-minority children should be taught in English if the goal is to reach the highest level of English language ability. Scientific research indicates that language-minority children generally have higher achievement if they are taught in English rather than in their native tongue.[28] Second, even when taught in English, LEP children should not be in a self-contained classroom (as in the Chinese, Russian, and Haitian "bilingual" programs) for more than a year. Such time limits are necessary because, just as we do not know how to tell if a child is initially LEP, we do not know how to determine when a child is no longer LEP.

If a fluent English-speaking child is misclassified as LEP and placed in a self-contained classroom of second-language learners, he or she will be slowed down by the children who truly do not know English. If formerly limited students become proficient in English while in a self-contained classroom, their teachers will nevertheless tend to keep them in what they perceive as a nurturing and supportive environment, and they too will be slowed down. Therefore, a time limit on enrollment in a self-contained classroom must be imposed to protect LEP children from being trapped by good intentions. Bilingual education, like many educational programs, is an example of good intentions that were not well thought out.

NOTES

1. Jim Cummins,"The Construct of Language Proficiency in Bilingual Education," in *Current Issues in Bilingual Education,* ed. J. E. Alatis (Washington, D.C.: Georgetown University Press, 1980); Jim Cummins, "The Entry and Exit Fallacy in Bilingual Education," *NABE Journal* 4 (1980).

2. The exceptions are Hmong and Vietnamese, whose written languages were created by Westerners with roman alphabet languages.

3. There is, however, a Russian bilingual program called Globe, for gifted students from Russian-speaking homes, in which literacy is taught simultaneously in

Russian and English. But even in this program, the emphasis is on English, and Russian is taught only because it is believed these gifted students can handle it.

4. Occasionally, other roman alphabet language groups will have the numbers to fill a classroom—in Massachusetts this is sometimes true of Portuguese speakers—but even in these cases, it is rare for a true bilingual program to be offered.

5. Isauro Santiago, "A Community's Struggle for Equal Educational Opportunity" (Princeton, N.J.: Educational Testing Service, 1978); C. J. Morrison, "The Puerto Rican Study 1953–1957: A Report on the Education and Adjustment of Puerto Rican Pupils in the Public Schools of the City of New York" (Board of Education of the City of New York, 1958).

6. Board of Education, cited in Santiago, "A Community's Struggle for Equal Educational Opportunity."

7. Delia Wilfredo Romero, "The Puerto Rican New Yorker in the New York City Schools: Did Bilingual Education Make a Difference?" (Ph.D. diss., University of Massachusetts, Amherst, 1987).

8. *Aspira of New York, Inc., et al. v. Board of Education of the City of New York, et al.*, 394 F. Supp. 1161, 1975.

9. Ibid., at 1168.

10. The concept of grade level and reading below grade level is almost universally misunderstood, not only by laymen but by educators. Grade level is simply the average achievement for a particular grade; it has no "absolute" meaning. It is not possible, for example, for all students in the norming population to be above grade level because it is not possible for all students to be above average; only half can be.

11. J. David Ramirez, Sandra D. Yuen, and Dena Ramey, "Second Year Report: Study of Immersion Programs for Language Minority Children" (Alexandria, Va.: SRA Technologies, 1986).

12. See Keith Baker and Christine Rossell, "An Implementation Problem: Specifying the Target Group for Bilingual Education," *Educational Policy* 1, no. 2 (1987), and Christine Rossell and Keith Baker, "Selecting and Exiting Students in Bilingual Education Programs," *Journal of Law and Education* 17, no. 4 (1988).

13. Robert Berdan, Alvin So, and Angel Sanchez, "Language among the Cherokee: Patterns of Language Use in Northeastern Oklahoma, Part 1, The Preliminary Report" (Los Alamitos, Calif.: National Center for Bilingual Research, 1982); U.S. Bureau of the Census, Data for the Office of Planning, Budget, and Evaluation, Decision Resources, "1984 Analysis" (Washington, D.C.: Department of Education, 1984).

14. Sharon E. Duncan and Edward A. De Avila, "Relative Language Proficiency and Field Dependence / Independence," paper presented at the annual meeting of TESOL, Boston, 1979.

15. D. Ulibarri, M. Spencer, and G. Rivas, "Comparability of Three Oral Language Proficiency Instruments and Their Relationship to Achievement Variables" (Report submitted to the California State Department of Education, 1980). G. Gillmore and A. Dickerson, "The Relationship between Instruments Used for Identifying Children of Limited English Speaking Ability in Texas" (Houston, Tex.: Education Service Center [Region IV], 1979); Robert A. Cervantes, *Entry into and Exit from*

Bilingual Education Programs (Washington, D.C.: E. H. White, 1982); Sol Pelavin and Keith Baker, "Improved Methods of Identifying Who Needs Bilingual Education" (paper presented at the annual meeting of the American Research Association, Washington, D.C., 1987).

16. C. Perlman and W. Rice Jr., "A Normative Study of a Test of English Language Proficiency" (paper presented at the annual meeting of the American Educational Research Association, San Francisco, Calif., 1979).

17. Special Circular 42, 1988–89, Board of Education, New York City.

18. Ariel Zwang, "Correspondence with Mr. Gary Stein," March 31 (attached as Exhibit B to *Bushwick Parents Organization v. Richard P. Mills, Commissioner of Education of the State of New York*, Verified Article 78 Petition, 1995).

19. See Christine H. Rossell and Keith Baker, "The Educational Effectiveness of Bilingual Education," *Research in the Teaching of English* 30, no. 1 (1996); Christine H. Rossell and Keith Baker, *Bilingual Education in Massachusetts: The Emperor Has No Clothes* (Boston, Mass.: Pioneer Institute, 1996); Christine H. Rossell, "Mystery on the Bilingual Express: A Critique of the Thomas and Collier Study," *Read Perspectives* 5, no. 2 (1998).

20. New York City Board of Education, "Educational Progress of Students in Bilingual and ESL Programs: A Longitudinal Study, 1990–94" (New York City Board of Education, 1994).

21. See Ruben G. Rumbaut, "Transformations: The Post-Immigrant Generation in an Age of Diversity" (paper presented at the annual meeting of the Eastern Sociological Society, Philadelphia, Penn., March 21, 1998).

22. New York City Board of Education, "Educational Progress of Students in Bilingual and ESL Programs: A Longitudinal Study, 1990–94," p. 29.

23. According to the Ramirez study (J. David Ramirez, David J. Pasta, Sandra D. Yuen, David K. Billings, and Dena R. Ramey, "Final Report: Longitudinal Study of Structured Immersion Strategy, Early-Exit and Late-Exit Transitional Bilingual Education Programs for Language-Minority Children" [San Mateo, Calif.: Aguirre International, report to the U.S. Department of Education, Washington, D.C., 1991]), by the fourth year in immersion, having been taught completely in English since kindergarten, only 58 percent of the immersion students were mainstreamed. This is only somewhat higher than the percentage mainstreamed from the early-exit bilingual program—42 percent. What these results tell us is that teachers will keep their students in these sheltered programs far beyond the time period when they can benefit from them regardless of the language of instruction.

24. *The Bushwick Parents Organization against Richard P. Mills, Commissioner of the State of New York* (Index No. 5181–95)

25. While the parents lost their case because the court concluded that the state had the right to approve the extensions to the three-year limits, there is a possibility that the lawsuit was the impetus for the Board of Education's 1996 decision to require the home language survey as a screening device.

26. Most of this data is also available from the New York City Board of Education web page. For some odd reason, the web pages for each school do not include LEP achievement data.

27. I am indebted to Public Education Associates in New York City and Ray Domanico, in particular, for computing this figure from the Annual School Reports.

However, their table labels this as the percentage attaining proficiency in English. In fact, it is the percentage reclassified as fluent English proficient, since a student can be proficient in English—indeed, they can be English monolingual—and still not be reclassified.

   28. See Rossell and Baker, *Bilingual Education in Massachusetts.*

9　The Education of Handicapped Children

FRANK J. MACCHIAROLA

It is virtually impossible to make a generalized statement about the education of handicapped children that does not disturb the sensibilities of someone with any awareness of what children seeking an education are entitled to receive from our society. This is true across the nation, and particularly true about New York City. This is not to say that on an individual basis, in some places and circumstances, no students benefit from their classroom experience in special education. There are too many effective programs, and too many caring and capable people who work in the New York City schools for the system of special education not to benefit some of its students. But the issue is not whether particular individuals fare well. The issue is whether the system—in its rationale, its design, and its implementation—provides a quality education for the overwhelming number of students in its charge. On that basis, special education has to be judged an utter failure and it cries out for radical change.

This chapter deals with the students in special education classes who are not severely handicapped, though many of them are in need of special services of some kind. The students considered here make up a staggering 13.5 percent of the total population of the New York City school system— a figure which has not given enough educators reason to pause, even though it significantly exceeds the national average for urban school systems (10.4 percent).[1]

There is ample evidence of the system's failure as an academic enterprise. Only 37.4 percent of the students in self-contained special education classes graduate.[2] As of 1997, there were 8,200 youngsters in high school over the age of twenty-one. This does not include students in citywide classes for the severely challenged, whose graduation rate is only 8 percent. Students in special education classes in the city do not even fare (nearly) as well as their peers in the rest of the state, as indicated by the percentage of those who perform at the minimum reference point in the state standardized tests (see table 9.1).

Why the System Fails

The reasons for the failure of special education are many and interrelated. To begin, the basic federal statute governing special education—The Individuals with Disabilities Education Act—did not lay an adequate or appropriate foundation for an effective system of education.[3] Its design and interpretation over time have required school systems like New York City's to devote enormous resources and energy to following confusing and exacting procedures and rules that have little relation to the quality of student education. Worse, while spelling out in painful detail the procedures for referral and the rights of the children served, the statute and interpretations thereof are silent on what constitutes an effective special education program. It's all system and little service.

With the special education system now in place, individual student interests too often give way to the special interests of various constituencies that have powerful roles to play within the program. Since measures of program effectiveness for students are nonexistent, service providers are inordinately powerful and tend to control the way the system is managed. Sadly, the system customarily is judged effective on the basis of factors having little or nothing to do with whether or not children within the program are well served.

Once the failure to adhere to certain standards occurs, agencies charged with oversight, most notably the state education department, establish additional rules and enforcement mechanisms to ensure compliance. As a result, there are more monitors, more deadlines, and more personnel to sat-

TABLE 9.1   Percentage of Students Performing above State Reference Point in 1997

	New York City	New York State
Reading		
Grade 3	32.2	70.0
Grade 6	26.2	66.9
Math		
Grade 3	77.6	96.2
Grade 6	67.4	88.4

Source: Data derived from State of City Schools '98, Public Education Association.

isfy a huge bureaucracy. But this compliance does not make the system work properly—even if this could be attained. Instead, these rules increase the overall costs of special education, intensify the antagonisms within the system, and act to exacerbate the difficulties faced by special educators.

The rules intensify the problem because the system is without direction. Its major purpose seems to be to warehouse children, since there are no measurable goals apart from the numbers served. The system serves more and more students, but doesn't bother to ask if it serves them well or how to do a better job. The special education system appears to operate under the maxim "If you don't know where you are going, any road will take you." And often, the fact that something is "being done" will allow for some relief from bureaucratic supervision. Special educators always seem to be buying time, hoping (often without reason) that a solution will somehow emerge. Without a system of measurement, and without meaningful objectives and standards related to pupil performance, it is impossible to have a system of true accountability. In essence, since we do not have a definition of what success is—and hence cannot reward it—we are at a loss to identify failure. Marginal performance with poor quality is the working standard of the special education system. Superior programs are often determined by anecdotal evidence alone.

Beyond all of the above, the most important reason for the failure of special education is that its youngsters are considered "not as good as" the youngsters in regular education programs. Even the label "special," which is considered to be a positive one, conveys a negative meaning, and gives society and the school system a basis for further marginalizing students in the program. By focusing on what is deficient in the children, what is different about these youngsters, we single them out and hold them apart from others. There have been many efforts by many dedicated professionals to break through the labeling and segregation of students in special education. These people are, however, fighting against a prevailing culture that would prefer that these youngsters just go away.

The lowly status of special education programs is indicated by the unusual patterns of representation of limited English proficiency (LEP) and minority youngsters in them and the incredible differences in referral rates among the city's school districts for LEP students. In District 5 (Central Harlem), for instance, only 2.64 percent of the LEP students were referred to special education programs in 1996–97, while in District 31 (Staten Island), 21.85 percent were referred.[4] In fact, in November 1998 the Office for Civil Rights of the United States Department of Education once again challenged the city's placement of minority students in special education, a matter that was addressed as recently as 1997 when the federal government and the Board of Education entered into an agreement to modify practices that have still not been corrected. It is also mind-boggling to realize that in two of the city's districts (21 in Brooklyn, 1 in Manhattan) more than 20 percent of the black students are in special education programs.

In order to operate successfully, special education needs to have effective alternative programs, with high expectations for the reduced numbers served and a strong belief in the capacity of youngsters to overcome the difficulties they face. The special education program must be premised on the idea that students are more alike than different, and that all children should, as much as possible, be afforded the same education. Getting to that point from where we are today is a tough trek, and we are without the will, the methodology, or the design to get there on a systemwide basis. Again, this is not to say that there aren't model schools that see the handicapped youngster as part of the whole school community. But all too often, the programs that have these qualities are at odds with monitors who want to manage the system at a central level and who lack the capacity to have it succeed.

The Legislation

The root of the problem in special education lies in PL 94-142, now called the Individuals with Disabilities Education Act. Signed into law in 1975 by President Gerald Ford, the law provided a free and appropriate education to all disabled children, until the age of twenty-one. The law was well-intentioned. Before its passage students with disabilities were regularly excluded from schools and deemed "uneducable" by state and local authorities who did not know how to treat them or simply did not want to incur the expense. As recently as 1973 there were more than one million children in the United States who were denied enrollment in public schools solely because of their disabilities.[5] The statute seemed to open schools to these children, but it has proven to be a major failure for two reasons.

First, the federal government has failed to deliver anything near the amount of funding that it promised. Funding has been grossly short of the amount needed to serve children with handicapping conditions. Typically, the federal government supplies only about 10 percent of the cost of special education, although Congress had made a promise to assume 40 percent of the cost when it originally passed the act. Moreover, according to the statute, the federal government will not provide funding for more than 12 percent of the general school-age population, even though state and local authorities are legally required to provide services to all students who are identified as having disabilities. While the funding limit was designed to discourage inappropriate placements—ostensibly a reasonable objective—it also served to increase the financial obligations of the states and localities.[6] It has become a classic example of federal mandates without federal financial support and, as a result, has created antagonism within the school community and among local governments and state government officials.[7]

Moreover, an educational program based on the statute has not been developed. Rather, enactment has been driven by advocates whose clients had been frustrated by the unavailability of schooling for youngsters who were classified as "uneducable" by several states, and who had been excluded from public schools. PL 94-142 established the right of the handicapped to an education, and set up guidelines for how children would be introduced into the schools. The statute was civil rights legislation rather than an education act. It did not define who was eligible for these services in terms of the handicapping conditions, or what eligibility meant in terms of the type of schooling and the content of the curriculum to be offered. In other words, Congress provided only the setting for adjudication of the rights of disabled students, guaranteeing that an advocacy process would be available to those youngsters affected. It did not define what those rights would entail.

The rush to the courts was occasioned by a process that encouraged advocates to sue, even though the law did not specify what could be sued for. It was particularly encouraging to advocates in New York City because the lawyers bringing suit were paid for by the city's school system. Hence they had incentive to sue, and never to settle. The legislation turned out to be the goose that laid the golden egg, for lawyers at least.

Almost simultaneously with the enactment of the federal law came the New York City financial crisis, which resulted in severe cutbacks in city services in the public schools. In 1979, the Bureau of the Budget refused to yield to advocate pleas for city-funded special services—a plea that I, as chancellor, made in vain to the city in 1979. Advocates then went to court and sought federally guaranteed rights denied by the city. Instead of spending less than $430 million, which the special education advocates were asking for, the resultant *José P. v. Ambach* consent decree was entered into, at the insistence of the City Corporation Counsel. Its cost is currently $2.6 billion per year. And with it all has come increasingly greater chaos within the system.

The early and rapid assertion of federal rights, and the significant demand for personnel to evaluate the claims for special education services, had an extraordinarily disabling effect upon the system as it was bracing for the transition of tens of thousands of students from general education to special education. While it is clear that some significant benefit occurred for students who had previously been excluded from public school—a circumstance not the case in New York City, which had well-recognized and relatively effective programs for physically handicapped youngsters—the federal law's mandates landed on the school system without a staff or programs ready for them. It was this program, which was designed by tremendous advocacy input, that could never be implemented according to the standards of the federal courts. The advocacy nature of 94–142 and the demand for services, even if not warranted, led to a massive shift in the number of students served. In essence, if someone demanded special education service, whether merited or not, the system had no effective way of examining the real need of the claimant. At the beginning, special education referrals actually meant special education placements at levels in excess of 90 percent. Resources denied to these youngsters by city budget cuts were replaced by high-cost alternatives mandated by the federal court. The mindless push for expansion of special education services was the bane of the school system from the late seventies to the present. In 1996–97, the average acceptance rate for youngsters to special education across the city's districts starts at 85 percent, with seven districts at 90 percent or more.

In June 1998, the Mayor's Task Force on Special Education, chaired by former first deputy mayor Peter J. Powers and consisting of City Corpora-

TABLE 9.2 Special Education Enrollment and Budget

Year	Enrollment	% Increase	Billions of Dollars	% Increase
1980	71,850	—	0.4344	—
1981	87,261	21.45	0.5157	18.72
1982	96,194	10.24	0.5961	15.59
1983	102,768	6.83	0.7122	19.48
1984	112,715	9.68	0.8516	19.57
1985	117,330	4.09	0.9578	12.47
1986	116,592	−0.63	0.9949	3.87
1987	114,786	−1.55	1.111	11.67
1988	114,823	0.03	1.3219	18.98
1989	117,150	2.03	1.3629	3.10
1990	119,589	2.08	1.52	11.53
1991	125,091	4.60	1.6336	7.47
1992	128,674	2.86	1.7213	5.37
1993	134,124	4.24	1.9112	11.03
1994	136,559	1.82	1.9878	4.01
1995	145,124	6.27	2.1951	10.43
1996	151,419	4.34	2.1603	−1.59
1997	161,006	6.33	2.1936	1.54
1998	166,950	3.69	2.3824	8.61
Total increase	95,100	132.36	1.948	548.43

Source: Reforming Special Education in New York City: An Action Plan, Mayor's Special Task Force on Special Education, June 9, 1998.

tion Counsel Michael D. Hess and then Chancellor Rudolph F. Crew, found that "decades of misclassification and over-placement of students have distorted the original purpose of Special Education."[8] Their study cited a report by a previous panel commission chaired by former Board of Education member Richard Beattie, which said: "More than 116,300 students are enrolled in Special Education programs in the City of New York's public schools. A significant number of these children may not necessarily be handicapped and should not be there. They are placed, and remain in, Special Education because they need educational counseling, or therapy services unavailable in regular education, and because the Special Education assessment process fails to differentiate between children who have handicapping conditions and those who do not."[9] As the Powers Task Force reports, "These words still ring true today, with a single exception: the Special Education enrollment is no longer 116,300, but rather 161,006 students."[10] What is alarmingly true is that this law for the disadvantaged has now come to embrace 161,006 students (as compared with 34,803 in 1975), or 13.5 percent of the total student population. The growth rate over the last decade has been 45.4 percent (as compared with a 14.4 percent overall growth). The costs have also grown at incredible levels from a budget of $434.4 million in 1980 to $2.38 billion in 1998. On a per student basis, the average cost for each special education student is $20,767 as compared with $6,183 for a student in general education. Students receiving resource room services and other services that are not for the severely handicapped cost $12,284 per year in 1998.

After the Beattie Commission report, special education numbers saw signs of stability, going from 117,330 in 1985 to 119,589 in 1990. Since 1990,

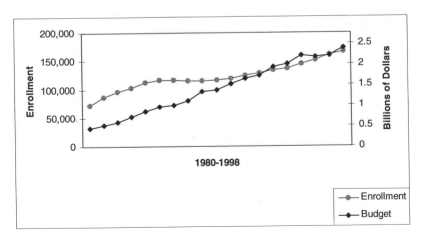

Figure 9.1. New York City Special Education Enrollment and Budget, 1980–1998

however, a veritable explosion in these numbers has occurred. The major reason rests with the underlying law and the way it has been interpreted and applied. The decisions are in the hands of those whose rights are encouraged by an advocacy-friendly statute.

Mislabeling

Approximately 55.3 percent of all students in special education in New York City are labeled "learning disabled," which is somewhat higher than the national average of 50 percent.[11] Despite its widespread use in the profession, the classification "learning disabled" (LD) does not describe a single disorder. It is a general category that refers to seven different kinds of disabilities: receptive language (listening), expressive language (speaking), basic reading skills, reading comprehension, written expression, mathematics calculation, and mathematical reasoning.

A study completed by Lerner in 1989 showed that the primary difficulty of 80 percent of the children classified as LD is learning to read.[12] G. Reid Lyon, director of the National Institutes of Child Health and Human Development, pinpoints the problem more specifically as the deficit of phonological awareness in reading. This is a reasonable conclusion, given that educators who supposedly teach reading generally place a low priority on phonics instruction. Moreover, the LD label is more a social construct rather than a clinical diagnosis. As Lyons explains, "'LD' is not a distinct disability, but an invented category for social purposes. Some argue that the majority of students identified as having learning disabilities are not intrinsically disabled but have learning problems because of poor teaching, lack of educational opportunity, or limited educational resources. In addition, because the label of LD is not a stigmatizing one, parents and teachers may be more comfortable with the diagnosis."[13]

While the problem of mislabeling may be more widespread among disadvantaged communities, it is an occupational hazard that cuts across class and racial lines. An interesting illustration of this phenomenon took place in the mid-1980s at New York's prestigious Dalton School, a private institution located on the Upper East Side of town.[14] It began when a wealthy alumna donated $2 million to the school to set up a remedial program for students with "learning disabilities." Within a few years, a special education industry grew up at Dalton that nobody, including the donor, could have anticipated. It included fourteen full- and part-time professionals, a secretary, a board of directors, and an executive director—all serving this one part of a primary school with twenty master teachers and four hundred students. Though kindergartners are not known to be reliable test takers for purposes of evaluation, 36 percent were nonetheless identified with learning problems. As one evaluator commented, "the attitude was that it didn't hurt to give them help even if they didn't need it."

By 1992, half of Dalton's students entering the fourth grade had received remedial help for such disabilities as "potential visual motor problems" and "sequencing ability defects." That year, a new principal abruptly dismantled the program, declaring that too many children were being burdened with harmful and unreliable labels. Despite hundreds of thousands of dollars spent on consultants from Teachers College and New York University, no outside evaluators were able to produce objective evidence that the program helped students. Fortunately, in this case, the costly and ineffectual system was put out of existence. But bureaucracies that are allowed to crop up in the public school system are not easy to do away with, especially when they are backed by a powerful network of advocates who claim to be representing the best interests of students. As a result, special education gets substituted for sound pedagogical practice, like the proper teaching of reading.

The Advocacy System

In a more sensible system of placing youngsters in classes, a teacher's decisions made under the supervision of the school principal would be the rule. While the choice would rest with the professional, there would be room for other input, including consultation with parents. Nothing like this system exists in special education, where the process for referral, evaluation, and placement are strictly regulated by federal and state law.

It would seem reasonable that at or before the time a youngster is referred to special education, there would be more serious consultation at the home school. An evaluator would ask whether the child is actually disruptive or whether the placement in a particular class or school might explain the student's behavior. Any reasonable attempt by the school system to address this problem has been frustrated by advocates seeing this as an effort to thwart the provision of warranted service. The desire on the part of the system to relate referrals to school climate was seen by advocacy groups as an effort to deprive students of their rights. The state education department continually has frustrated any effort to stop unwarranted referrals, basing its reasoning on the "rights" argument that prevented the search for what might be a real cause of the student's difficulty. Once a student has been referred, the commissioner's regulations also make it almost impossible to introduce intervention and prevention strategies. Such a position by the state bureaucracy makes it difficult for professionals to assist the child or to do more than just "process" the student into special education.

There have been some attempts to shift the focus from referring students to providing resources where they are needed. The city budget for FY 1999 contains school funding for initiatives such as prevention programs and supplemental services in an effort to stem the growth of special education, but the quality of these services and how they will be delivered remains quite problematic. There is deep mistrust of the city's commitment to education. Some people doubt whether in the long term these services will continue to be provided or the needs of the youngsters will be addressed absent legal entitlement provided by PL 94–142. Thus, as helpful as the effort to replace special educational services with greater general education funding is, we are still left with an adversarial climate that gets in the way of sound pedagogical judgment.

Suspicions about the lack of commitment to youngsters in need of special help means that too many professionals have come to see special education as the only answer for the student in need. While not a perfect system, they say, it at least gives an important service to the handicapped youngster, even if that handicap is mild. Thus, at the present time, about 85 percent of the students referred for evaluation are classified as handicapped, notwithstanding the fact that most experts concede that this number is excessive. A New York University study, for example, found that only 15 percent of sampled children who were classified as learning disabled in New York City's public schools actually met the state's mandated criteria for learning disabled.[15]

Requirements in federal, state, and city regulations demand an individual evaluation for every student who is referred for special education. The evaluation, though not necessarily made by a teacher, requires a team to determine whether the student is handicapped, and then, whether the disability will affect the student's ability to learn in the regular school setting. The School Board Support Teams (SBST) conducting these evaluations are multidisciplinary, and include a school psychologist, a school social worker, and an educational evaluator. Until the summer of 1998 the SBST had an incentive to provide special education services, since the extra services would be provided by additional staff represented by the same union. In addition, they were accountable to the central board and not to the principals or superintendents in the schools and districts affected. While the reforms of summer 1998 created independence for the SBSTs, the vested interest in continuing to maintain the flow of students referred to special education remains.

The groups conducting these evaluations include almost three thousand staff members, and they have an extremely limited function—they evaluate referred students. They are isolated from school settings and do not provide prevention services or any services to students already in the special education program. The productivity of these workers is low, and there has been little or no attempt to require them to provide any services to children. Recent changes promise some improvement, yet special education has a huge feeding operation and momentum driving its growth.

Added to the difficulties with the SBSTs are the significant procedural safeguards for parental consent. The alert parent negotiates with the SBST for a "better" placement, which usually means whatever program the parent associates with the highest costs. Those less informed and with a more limited capacity to advocate, the SBST pressures into a less desirable placement. The best protected get the most desirable offers, and often this means private schooling at public expense. The rest get the public school system. The educational basis for the placement is trumped by an expedient need to move the system along.

The results of this system of referral and placement can best be explained by the advocacy character of the process. As mentioned previously, the placement data across the system do not show a consistent application of educational judgment. Rather, they indicate a number of things about politics, not the least of which is the desire to get the child out of the queue. When parents are more savvy of their rights, they are able to block the queue by demanding a favorable placement for their children. When the parent is unaware, the child is more rapidly placed. The data show a tremendous variability among community school districts, ranging from only 76 percent of referrals accepted into special education (D. 31, Staten Island) to 96 percent (D. 5, Central Harlem) accepted. Perhaps they are explained by factors other than the characteristics of the youngsters themselves, factors associated with the socioeconomic status of the parents, the quality of the general education program in the districts, the quality of the SBST evaluators, or a combination of these. In a poorly performing school, all too often there is a tendency to refer more children to special education, and hence to blame the children for the system's failure.

The advocacy model expects that a correct result will emerge from the process and it lacks the means to self-correct. And when the process is judged solely by the way the hearing has been conducted, incompetence is undetected, prudential judgment surrenders to formality, and the result is a system in failure. The data show that minority students are significantly discriminated against in the number of referrals to programs for the emotionally handicapped. In terms of its impact on racial minorities, further, the federal government's study of special education placements found that in nine districts black and Hispanic students were more than twice as likely to be referred to special education. It also determined that black students were three times more likely than whites to be referred to the most restrictive of special education classrooms.[16]

One highly regarded researcher found that more than 80 percent of the overall student population could be classified as learning disabled by one or another of the definitions presently in use.[17] Such variation in the standards for labeling is further proof that the system itself cannot adequately deal with mislabeling, and that the labeling of children as handicapped is taking place for reasons unrelated to the condition of the child. It shows that in the name of helping children we are harming them. The educational program that results costs the taxpayers more than three times as much for a youngster wrongly placed in special education as it would for alternative services in a general education program. The $20,767 average cost per pupil burdens the New York City taxpayer, only a bit less than the charge for the tuition at an Ivy League college. The report of the Powers Task Force suggested major reforms in work rules, productivity, and the role of outside evaluators. The report is on the right path, but its policy suggestions will encounter major difficulties because of the enormity of the task, the inadequacy of current staff, and a lack of commitment by those charged with the responsibility for educating our children.

Unfortunately, the cure for failure has been increasing regulation. Sadly but typically, bureaucracies deal with failure by imposing standards that lead to further failure. No bureaucracy I know of has greater nuisance value in this respect than the New York State Education Department. Its strategy for its own survival has been to pick on those incapable of defending themselves. In special education, the key issue has been compliance with rules that limit class size, strengthen the advocacy position of interest groups, and ensure that educational judgment does not substitute for rigid rules in the placement of students. Continued pressure by local school boards on the legislative and executive branches have resulted in a softening of the rule making functions of the department, but significant damage has already been done. Moreover, the dynamic that caused it, a mistrust of local school personnel, continues.

The problem of a system that does not respect those who work in it is made even more tragic because the system of special education does not know what it is supposed to do. Experts present the students and system with an "Individual Educational Profile" that is supposed to plot an academic program, but it is very often a "no education" substitute for schooling. Students are continued in special education programs without any real chance of escaping the system. In 1996–97, only 3,854 students (2.4 percent of the 161,000 enrolled) were decertified out of special education.[18] Remarkably, this tiny number represents a substantial gain over the practice of the last decade.

At bottom, while many children are served, the system fails because it has no educational mission, save the constant increase and containment of children in its programs and the protection of jobs. Special education, moreover, is a system wherein individual evaluations are made without reference to objective standards. Neither test scores, graduation rates, or college acceptance rates are used as measures of success. There is no achievement; there is no success. It is an elementary proposition that what youngsters need does not occur in a system that largely marginalizes and segregates. Any advocate who wants to treat the special education youngster like a student in regular education is often seen as a "traitor to the cause" by other advocates.

Too many special interests see the success of special education in increased spending, increasingly smaller class sizes, and costly additions to the basic school program. They see increasing costs per pupil as a positive thing in and of itself, and modifications to artificially enriched programs are seen as an unwarranted reduction of real service. In a world in which there are no educational values, educational expenditures demonstrate the commitment. It is a misplaced commitment, for it diverts attention from the failed system itself and from our own obligations as educators to help these children. In 1999 the New York State legislature passed a bill, signed by Governor George Pataki, that is designed to provide financial incentives for school districts to retain students in regular education programs rather than channel them into special education. The new law is well meaning, but it runs against the tide of a system that has habitually placed students in special education who did not belong there. It remains to be seen whether the law will succeed in making this hidebound system responsive to the true needs of students.

Conclusion and Recommendations

The men and women teaching in special education programs are engaged in important and often difficult work. In many instances they try to educate children with less support and guidance from the school system than they need and deserve. The recommendations that follow are intended to make their work more efficient, more productive, and more rewarding for them and their students.

1. Special education students are often first placed in remedial programs in general education. All too often these programs are poorly funded or not effective. Strengthening general education—most especially with prevention and early remedial programs—is an important step to reducing the number of students who will be referred to and placed in special education. The relationship between quality in special and general education programs must be better appreciated.

2. Special education referrals and placements should not be made under the time constraints that are currently found in the commissioner's regulations and the law. These time periods should be extended and time should be allotted to permit a thorough exploration of educational alternatives within the mainstream setting. The labeling of students as handicapped should be treated as a last step rather than an easy solution. The school system should be forced to

explain why a student is not succeeding. The student should not be presumed to be inadequate.

3. The recommendations of the Powers Task Force are thoughtful, intelligent, and mindful of the interest of the school children. They call for, among other things, an evaluation process that is more efficient, more consistent, and less likely to result in placement. The recommendations should be adopted as school system goals, and monitoring the progress of their implementation should be the major activity of a collaborative effort between the mayor's office and the Board of Education.

4. The referral rates of individual schools should be made an explicit element in the evaluation of the school's effectiveness. These rates should be monitored on a districtwide and systemwide basis. These rates should also be considered as factors in declaring schools in need of state monitoring and intervention. The referral rates have to be dealt with aggressively and there must be systemwide goals that reflect the reduction of referral rates overall.

5. There must be an effort to rewrite federal and state laws to discourage the tendency of people to perceive special education primarily as a legal process, and only secondarily as an educational process. To this end a task force composed of state and city experts must work toward moving special education benefits away from the legalistic, adversarial, and constituency-driven model that currently exists. This will require an extensive effort, for it flies in the face of entitlement models that have long dominated the provision of social and educational services.

6. Special education must be truly special. The numerous mild and moderate categories that exist within special education must be eliminated. At the same time, interim programs must be made available to students who need them. These interim programs must be structured toward returning youngsters to general education programs more frequently than assigning them to programs in special education.

7. Special education must be seen as something that, except for providing additional services to youngsters in need, is not desirable. Thus labeling of children should be avoided; categories of special education must be truly meaningful descriptions of handicapping conditions; and everything must be done to ensure that the students are able to leave the system as quickly as possible. Their placement in special education should be regarded as temporary, and the school system should promote policies that facilitate the result.

8. The recent trend toward first localizing decisions about special education in the classroom should be strongly reinforced. Professionals

need to be encouraged to make decisions that affect the children in their charge. In delegating decision-making responsibility to the level closest to the children, teachers and supervisors will gain greater confidence in their own ability to advance the interests of students.

9. All of these improvements will come to naught if teacher preparation does not adjust to the changes that have to be made in special education. Teachers must be encouraged to understand that the differences that exist among students must not be used to diminish their faith in the same children. They must see children in terms of their capabilities rather than in terms of their liabilities. It is an appreciation of the tremendous possibilities for these youngsters that is at the heart of the transformation of special education.

NOTES

1. This chapter does not address the schooling of severely handicapped youngsters who are served in the New York City public schools by what is called District 75—a designation originally so designed to accommodate the need for a separate budget classification. The students in District 75 number 16,000 of the 164,000 in the special education population.

2. *State of the City Schools, '98* (New York: Public Education Association, 1998), p. 12.

3. IDEA legislation, 94–142.

4. Mayor's Task Force on Special Education, "Reforming Special Education in New York City: An Action Plan," June 1998.

5. "Executive Summary, Special Education for Students with Disabilities," *The Future of Children* 6 (1996).

6. See "Restructuring Special Education Funding in New York to Promote the Objective of High Learning Standards for All Students," prepared for the New York State Board of Regents Education Finance Symposium on School Finance for High Learning Standards, November 17, 1997.

7. For an excellent analysis of the gap between funds provided and funds delivered by the federal government, see Joseph P. Viteritti, *Across the River: Politics and Education in the City* (New York: Holmes and Meier, 1983), p. 187.

8. Mayor's Task Force on Special Education, "Reforming Special Education in New York City: An Action Plan," 1998.

9. Commission on Special Education, *Special Education: A Call for Quality: Final Report to Mayor Edward I. Koch*, 1985, p. 20.

10. Mayor's Task Force, "Reforming Special Education in New York City," p. 2.

11. The New York City data is based on "The IDEA report" submitted to the state education department by the Board of Education of the City of New York, December 1, 1998.

12. J. W. Lerner, "Educational Interventions in Learning Disabilities," *Journal of the American Academy of Child and Adolescent Psychiatry* 28 (1989). See also K. A.

Kavale, "Potential Advantages of the Meta-Analysis Technique of Special Education," *Journal of Special Education* 18 (1984).

13. G. Reid Lyon, "Learning Disabilities," *The Future of Children* 6 (1996): 63. See also chapter 7.

14. Michael Winerip, "A Disabilities Program That Got Out of Hand," *New York Times*, April 8, 1994.

15. Jay Gottlieb et al., *Focus on Learning: A Report on Reorganizing General and Special Education in New York City*, New York University Institute for Education and Social Policy, October 1995, p. 17.

16. "U.S. Questions the Placement of City Pupils, Its Study Suggests Bias in Special Education," *New York Times*, November 21, 1998.

17. James E. Ysseldyke, "Classification of Handicapped Students," in *Handbook of Special Education: Research and Practice*, vol. 1, ed. Margaret C. Wang, Meynard C. McReynolds, and Herbert J. Wahlberg (New York: Pergamon Press, 1987).

18. Mayor's Task Force, "Reforming Special Education in New York City."

PART IV

Nonpublic Schools

10   Catholic Schools

PAUL T. HILL AND MARY BETH CELIO

In 1995 Catholic schools in New York City served 151,352 students in 356 schools. If ranked among the nation's public school systems, the New York and Brooklyn Catholic schools would serve the eleventh largest number of students, more than Dallas or San Diego, and run the fourth largest number of schools, more than Philadelphia or Detroit.[1] In 1995 the Catholic schools in New York City educated over eighty-six thousand minority children (African American, Latino, or Asian), almost ten thousand more minority children than were enrolled in the District of Columbia public schools that year. They served more non-Catholic children (over thirty-four thousand) than the total number of children served by such city school systems as Jersey City, New Jersey, Providence, Rhode Island, Tacoma, Washington, and Richmond, Virginia.[2]

A schooling enterprise of this size clearly makes a major contribution to the education of New York City's children. One simple measure of that contribution is financial: if all the children served by the city's Catholic schools were returned to the public schools, a conservative estimate of the annual cost of their education would be over $1.1 billion.[3]

By reputation, however, the contributions of the Catholic schools are more than financial. Many parents—both Catholic and non-Catholic—regard Catholic schools as rare places where their children can be kept safe, learn the mainstream academic skills expected of middle-class students, be taught to function as responsible members of society, and leave with a good chance to attend college or get a decent job. Many business leaders and college admissions officers also treat a Catholic education as a marker for a student who can read, write, and figure, who will do a job faithfully and with some imagination, and who will maintain a civil attitude.

How did Catholic schools gain this reputation? Are the Catholic schools the same as they were when they served an almost entirely Catholic population? Is their only real advantage based on their ability to reject "bad apple" students and to impose iron discipline on those who remain in the schools? Or have the schools adapted to the needs of a non-Catholic population that looks to the schools for strong educational experiences but cannot be treated as captive members of a potentially fractious Catholic community? Do they represent an alternative kind of education that offers real advantages to New York City's increasingly low-income and minority public school population?

This chapter relies on data provided by the New York City Catholic schools offices and the state of New York. It draws on new research in selected Catholic schools, a substantial literature on how Catholic schools in general work for low-income and minority students,[4] and the authors' own earlier research.[5] The first section provides a historical and statistical profile of the city's Catholic schools. The second section examines how the Catholic schools educate: their goals, approaches to teaching and student motivation, ways of hiring and improving teachers, and relationships with parents. The third section considers the future of the New York Catholic schools as an asset in the broader community-wide effort to educate its children.

How the Catholic Schools Came to Be

The Catholic Church started schools in New York City in an effort to ensure that immigrants from Catholic countries did not lose contact with their religious roots, as well as to protect children against anti-Catholic bias in the city's public schools and larger society. They were created to serve children of Catholic parents and to ensure that bonds weakened by immigration and loss of village ties were rebuilt in the New World. Because few immigrants had extensive religious education, and many had never established regular habits of church attendance and support in their countries of origin, the schools were meant to serve essentially missionary purposes within the Catholic-born population. The city's Catholic schools were, in effect, intended to be an instrument in the creation of an American church.

Now, at the beginning of the twenty-first century, the New York City population and the Catholic schools have both changed significantly from those early beginnings. The nineteenth-century Irish, Italian, Polish, and German immigrants have largely retained their Catholic identities while becoming economically and culturally assimilated and, often, moving from the city of their birth. The city is still a settling-place for immigrants, but now from the American South, the Caribbean, Central America, Asia, and the former Soviet Union. The schools remain Catholic but their mission is no longer simply to preserve the church: they are to be part of the church's contribution to the broader society, especially to the poor. Mainstream education, and equipping disadvantaged children to participate fully in American economic and political life, have become predominant concerns of Catholic schools. The schools still proclaim their religious foundation and aggressively teach Christian values and morality, but preservation of the church itself is no longer their primary purpose.

New York City's Catholic schools are split between the Archdiocese of New York and the Diocese of Brooklyn. Like the boroughs prior to their consolidation into New York City in 1898, the two dioceses run independently. Data in this chapter concern only the parishes and schools within the boundaries of New York City.

Schools for the Church

The hundreds of Catholic schools now found in New York City trace their roots to the former St. Peter's on Barclay Street in Manhattan. St. Peter's opened in 1800 and was headed in 1805 by the first U.S.-born saint, Elizabeth Ann Seton. As the population and the demand for education grew, more Catholic schools opened. A Catholic newspaper, the *Freeman's Journal*, noted in 1842 that classes were often held in the basement of the church, where children were "so closely pushed together that they hardly had room to move."[6]

The sorry state of the Catholic schools and even sorrier state of thousands of newly arrived Irish immigrants led the new bishop of New York, John Hughes, to engage the Public School Society in political maneuvering, public oratory, and street fights around the issue of financial support for Catholic schools. Bishop Hughes objected to Catholics' paying taxes "for the purpose of destroying our religion in the minds of our children."[7] He recognized that the newly arrived immigrants from Ireland and Italy and Germany were as untutored in their faith as they were in their letters and sums.[8] Education in both secular and religious subjects was necessary.

What came to be known as the Great New York School War between Bishop Hughes and the Public School Society ended with a clear decision that public funds would not be available to pay for sectarian schools. But this decision did not end either the Catholic schools or Archbishop Hughes's crusade for them.[9] The results of the bitter conflict set the stage for national policies in both the secular and the religious arenas because, denied access to public money to support schools serving thousands of Catholic children, Hughes led the fight for an entirely separate school system for Catholics. Hughes's battle cry to the bishops, "to build the school-house first, and the church afterwards," became embedded in church policy. It was at this time that a committee of theologians working for the bishops defined parochial schools as "institutions, in which none but Catholic children are admitted, and which are conducted by teachers who have the approbation of the pastor, exercising their office under his direction and superintendence, and making the catechism the frequent subject of their instructions to those under their charge."[10]

The initial purpose of the Catholic schools was to provide education untainted with the prevailing Protestant mind-set and to protect the fragile cultural and religious heritage brought to America by immigrants from a number of heavily Catholic countries in Europe. Religious instruction was paramount, but church leaders also insisted on good instruction in secular subjects. Teachers in the Catholic schools had to prove their competency by passing examinations administered by boards of examiners.[11] By the time Michael Corrigan was archbishop of New York in 1898, only about one-half of the parishes in the diocese had schools, but the cost of these schools, simple as they were, was overwhelming. Corrigan faced a $7 million debt at the end of the nineteenth century.[12]

In New York the number of Catholic schools increased rapidly but not according to any definite plan. Some were built to serve the needs of specific immigrant communities—Germans, Poles, Italians; others served the more general Catholic community. By 1967, the year of peak enrollment in city Catholic schools, 488 schools were serving a total of 360,200 students.

From the very beginning and out of necessity, the Catholic schools in New York City adopted a number of practices that helped them maintain quality despite low budgets and limited resources for central supervision. First, the parish schools at all times during their history have been site-based, neighborhood schools responsive to the population in the specific area served by the school.[13] Second, each of the Catholic schools in New York has been able to turn to two kinds of sources of support, religious order networks and the diocese.

Most of the religious sisters and brothers in the schools originally came to America to teach in schools catering to their own countrymen. However, just as the Italians, Polish, Irish, Germans, and others became part of the fabric of American culture, so did religious orders. Dozens of religious orders were either newly founded in America or established outposts in the United States designed especially to create and teach in Catholic schools. In 1967, there were 5,335 sisters from fifty-seven different religious orders serving in the schools of the New York or Brooklyn dioceses, along with 1,035 men from ten congregations of brothers and priests.[14]

The religious orders provided all the benefits of a school system with few of the negative bureaucratic side effects. The sisters, brothers, and priests who taught in the schools did not function as independent and low-paid contractors or freelance educators; they were trained and served by their religious orders, each of which had its own *charism* (guiding philosophy and mission) and way of operating. Whether the order provided organization and staffing for a number of parish-based schools or operated schools independently of parishes (and many did both), the end result was a number of different mini-systems.[15] These provided the intellectual and personnel resources for the site-based parish schools while maintaining strong connections to citywide, regional, national, and even international networks. The orders selected curriculum, trained teachers, assigned, monitored, and evaluated staff, conducted long-range planning, and often designed and owned the school buildings.

The second support system for Catholic schools, the diocesan structure, is probably better known to most Americans than the religious order networks. Like most bishops in the United States, both of the bishops serving New York City delegate the day-to-day responsibility for overseeing the Catholic schools to professional staff who function somewhat in the manner of the public school system central office, but on a much smaller scale. Thus, in 1967 the diocesan staff overseeing 202 Catholic schools in New York and 286 Catholic schools in Brooklyn totaled no more than twenty staff members. Their functions were limited to oversight and technical assistance, with little time for or interest in standardizing curriculum or monitoring achievement.[16] According to the time-honored principle of subsidiarity in the church, decisions are to be made at the lowest appropriate level. Day-to-day operation of the schools was to be done at the parish and school level, or by the religious orders.

Schools for the City

Until 1967, the academic quality of the Catholic schools was assumed, or at least not questioned. The emphasis in the years up to and immediately after 1967 was on responding to the staggering demand for classroom space in Catholic schools rather than on evaluation of the effectiveness of the school. Much was made of the size of classes in both private and public schools and this has often been linked to judgments about academic quality. In 1967, the average number of students per classroom in the Catholic elementary schools in the New York archdiocese was 38.4 and the students per classroom in the high schools was 19.9; the equivalent classroom sizes in Brooklyn were 44.7 and 21.4. Some elementary schools served over one thousand students, and Cardinal Hayes High School was split into several campuses because of the overwhelming number of students requesting admission there.

In 1967, Catholic schools in New York City were operated for, paid for, and staffed almost entirely by Catholics. Almost 80 percent of the parishes in the city operated a parish elementary school and twenty-seven also operated a parish high school. In addition, there were twenty-five diocesan high school sites, three "commercial" high schools, and forty-eight private high schools, most of them single sex. Over 360,200 children attended these schools.

Catholic schools were financed in a manner roughly parallel to taxation for public schools: all church members, whether or not they had children in the schools, paid part of the schools' costs. As much as 80 percent of the parish income went directly to the school. Small contributions built and maintained huge schools that, the bishops hoped, would be free. The very low salaries of the teachers provided an additional subsidy that could keep costs low. In the words of one observer, "Education in the American Catholic Church . . . is more accurately described as the philanthropy of the poor."[17]

In the late 1960s, a number of major demographic and cultural shifts took place that severely challenged the health and the prospects of Catholic schools throughout the country. The changes were particularly traumatic in New York City because the number of students was so great and the Catholic schools were so numerous. The changes included the upward mobility of the Catholic population, which led to massive movement to the suburbs and away from existing parishes and schools; a drop in the birth rate following the postwar baby boom; an increase in the educational expectations and standards of many Catholics; the loss of thousands of women and men from the teaching orders after the Second Vatican Council called by Pope John XXIII (1962–65);[18] and the relative decrease in financial support forthcoming from Catholics.[19] All of these events combined led to crises of identity and viability for the Catholic schools in New York City, as in the country as a whole. The period has been characterized by one observer as "the institution hemorrhaging."[20]

By 1977, Catholic school enrollment in New York City had dropped by over 37 percent, to 226, 571 students. The number of sisters, brothers, and priests teaching in the schools had dropped over 51 percent, from 6,270 to 3,059. The empty places at the front of the classrooms were filled by lay people, who were paid significantly more than the sisters and brothers, though still less than what public school teachers could make. Lay teachers became the majority, their number rising from 4,092 to 5,767. The consequent increase in costs forced schools to raise their tuitions above the very low levels required in prior years, and this led to further decreases in enrollment.

Decisions had to be made, but they could not be made in a vacuum divorced from what was happening in the Catholic Church as a whole. Vatican Council II produced a change in direction for Catholic schools, exhorting pastors and the faithful "to spare no sacrifice in helping Catholic schools to become increasingly effective, especially in caring for the poor, for those who are without the help and affection of family, and those who do not have the Faith."[21] This statement of ideals was heard in the United States at a time when many urban Catholic educators had come to their own conclusion that the mission and clientele of the schools should change. One prominent educator noted that the availability of a nonpublic school "in a disadvantaged or semi-segregated residential area tends to hold certain people in the area who would otherwise move out, and thus tends to encourage residential integration."[22]

But many Catholic educators questioned whether continued support of the Catholic schools should be the church's highest priority. Many wondered whether the schools were equipped to respond to the needs of new kinds of Catholic immigrants, and whether they could effectively perform a larger public-service function. As a priest participating in a 1968 Washington symposium on Catholic education noted, "It is not enough to demonstrate . . . that the products of the Catholic schools are in no way inferior to those of the public school systems. Rather, to rationalize the expenditure of additional dollars on Catholic schools, it must be shown that the returns, however defined and measured, must be greater than those from the same expenditure on some other church activity. If it cannot be shown that the products of the Catholic schools are actually superior to their public school counterparts, it may be difficult to justify additional expenditures in terms of maximizing returns from Church resources."[23] In other words, the existence of a Catholic school system should be decided on the basis of its "returns." In the late 1960s, for the first time in many years, there was real doubt in many minds about the purpose, and thus the future viability, of Catholic schools.

By the mid-1970s, these doubts and questions had risen to such a peak that the United States Catholic Conference (USCC) commissioned a report summarizing research on inner-city Catholic schools. The report concentrated on Catholic school systems in New York, Brooklyn, Chicago, and Philadelphia. It concluded that by the late seventies inner-city schools often belonged to the "shells" of parishes, where there were buildings and staff and territory, but very few Catholics. The author of the report wrote that "pastors who decide to close inner-city schools often note that these schools no longer provide Catholic instruction, follow Catholic traditions, or have any Catholic students. They conclude that the school is not necessary to families in the parish."[24] In essence, the central problem was not whether the church could support the schools, but why it should support them. He concluded, "If the church has reasons to support the schools, it has the ability."[25]

In 1977, when the USCC report was issued, there was little research on the effectiveness of the inner-city Catholic schools or, for that matter, public schools. From the evidence available, however, the author concluded that inner-city Catholic schools "provide improved educational opportunities for minorities; strengthen families, stabilize and organize neighborhoods; foster urban integration; force the improvement of inner-city public schools; provide religious and moral education for Catholics and non-Catholics alike; and help build parishes and extend a bridge between the church and non-Catholic minorities."[26] Some of these results match the purposes for Catholic schools proclaimed by Archbishop John Hughes in the mid-1800s, but others implied a commitment to take on tasks generally considered to be the province of the local, state, or federal government.

By 1977, fifty-five elementary schools and thirty-one high schools had closed in the dioceses of New York and Brooklyn. Although enrollment had dropped by over a third, the number of schools had dropped by less than 18 percent overall. Thus schools were much smaller but most of them still survived. Smaller schools and moderate-sized classes made Catholic education more attractive to middle-class Catholics and others who wanted more intimate, personalized instruction. And the news from the research community was exceptionally good: Catholic schools, especially those serving low-income and high-risk students, were found by Coleman and others to be particularly effective in bringing up test scores and preventing early school exit.[27] Whether because of the increasingly favorable reports from the media about inner-city Catholic schools or because parents in the neighborhoods saw and approved of the alternatives offered by the Catholic schools, non-Catholic children began filling seats in the Catholic schools.

A doctoral dissertation focusing on parents' response to the new, religiously integrated Catholic schools found that both Catholic and non-Catholic parents ranked academic program and the teaching of moral and spiritual values as the top two reasons to send their children to a Catholic school. Religious atmosphere ranked third for Catholic parents and fourth for non-Catholic parents. Two factors that came to serve as a shorthand for the parents' assessment of their children's education were "solicitude" (the care taken for the growth and welfare of the children within the entire school community) and academic quality, with both Catholic and non-Catholic parents rating both factors very favorably. Catholic and non-Catholic parents alike responded that they did not wish to see future changes in religion programs, prayer services, or sacramental programs. On the other hand, there was no desire or intention on the part of any of the respondents to use the schools as a means of gaining Catholic converts.[28]

Catholic schools remain, as they have been since the early 1800s, a high-priority concern for Catholic Church leaders in New York City, particularly the bishops. As Reese reports, the decision to close a school can very often lead to picketing of the archbishop by its parents, students, alumni, and neighbors. And if the school is in the inner city, the uproar is markedly more vigorous, with the closure decrees viewed as an example of the church's neglect of the poor and people of color.[29]

Reese reports that "when [today's incumbent] Archbishop O'Connor arrived in New York, he found a number of schools that were waiting for approval to close. He refused because he did not want to become known as the archbishop who closed schools his first year in office."[30] O'Connor has been vociferous in his support for Catholic schools, especially those in the poorest and often least-Catholic neighborhoods. Brooklyn's Bishop Daily is also credited for helping to rebuild the strength of the schools in his diocese.

O'Connor has strengthened the small central Catholic schools office. The staff are responsible for screening all school principals, who must all be active practicing Catholics, and for providing continuing education with special emphasis on what is known as "Values Infusion." Many of the few remaining men and women of religious orders in the system serve as principals, but their teachers are predominantly lay people. In the entire Catholic school system within the city in 1997 there were only 103 priests, 144 brothers, and 895 sisters serving along with 6,640 lay teachers and administrators.

Cardinal O'Connor has launched an endowment fund drive for inner-city schools, which has already reached 50 percent of its $50 million goal. The diocese also helps individual schools in crisis, whether finding money to replace a roof or providing yet another scholarship for a needy child.

From the time of Archbishop John Hughes to the present, the Catholic schools in New York City have been haunted by financial uncertainties. Tuitions for city Catholic elementary schools in 1998–99 ranged from $1,300 to $2,000, with a median of $1,900. However, the average cost to educate each student at a parish elementary school is over $2,900. The difference between tuition and cost is provided by parish subsidies, gifts from the diocese, and contributions from small shopkeepers, private donors, and major foundations. Financing now depends on the philanthropy of the rich as well as of the poor. But every year is a struggle.

The two New York City dioceses' efforts to maintain the Catholic schools have a good chance to succeed. But much has been lost: 136 schools with close to 210,000 (very closely spaced) desks since 1967. The two bishops with overall responsibility for the Catholic schools in New York City speak clearly of their commitment to the community beyond the church membership, and research continues to bolster the spirits of those who lead, teach in, and send their children to the schools.

The Results Catholic Schools Get and How They Work

Over the past twenty years a small industry of statisticians has struggled to judge the effectiveness of Catholic schools and other schools that admit students by choice, not at random. Statisticians like to infer the effectiveness of an instructional program by comparing two groups that are identical in all ways except that one has had the program in question and the other has not. However, such comparisons are difficult to make because choice presumably confers advantages that go beyond any difference in schools' instructional programs. Families that choose schools are presumably more interested in education than those that do not. Further, the fact of having chosen affects the parents' and students' trust for a school and the likelihood that they will take its demands seriously. In statisticians' terms, students in Catholic schools differ from students in public schools in three ways: they experience a different instructional program, they come from families that presumably care more about education, and they have the added benefit of having made a commitment to a particular school.

In the face of such complexities, the best comparisons are the most straightforward ones. Studies of Catholic school effectiveness over the past twenty years have consistently shown that outcomes for Catholic school students are markedly better than results for demographically comparable groups of public school students.[31] The advantages of Catholic schools are especially significant for low-income and ethnic minority students. This is true for both elementary schools and for high schools, as reflected in short-range measures like test scores, persistence in school, rates of credit accumulation, and passage of "solid" courses like algebra, laboratory science, and English literature. It is also true for long-range outcome measures like post–high school employability, entry into college, and college completion.[32]

Results of the RAND Study of New York City High Schools

From 1989 through 1991, Paul T. Hill led a Rand study of low-income minority students attending New York City Catholic schools. Students' tuition was paid by the Student Sponsor Partnership program, which selected troubled public school students who had not previously attended private schools. The study results confirmed the Partnership program's initial impression that its students were doing unusually well in school. In 1990, the last year of the Rand study, graduation rates for private voucher students were more than half again higher than New York City public high school students, and nearly as high as the tuition-paying students in the Catholic schools they attended.

The study was able to compare the 1990 Scholastic Aptitude Test (SAT) scores of Partnership students and students in the public schools. The vast majority of private voucher students graduating from the Catholic schools take the SAT, which is required for admission to most selective colleges and universities, while less than one-third of their peers in public high schools do so. Despite the fact that public school students taking the SAT were a select group, Partnership students' scores were much higher. Though all the scores in table 10.1 are below the national average for all students, the scores for Partnership students are well above average for the most similar national norm group, all African American students. Mean scores for all New York City students fall far below the national average for African American students. Private voucher students scored nearly as well as their tuition-paying Catholic school classmates.

Partnership private voucher students' advantages extend to college admission and completion. Since the first Partnership graduating class in 1990, an average of 90 percent of participating students has attended college; of those attending college 90 percent have enrolled in four-year B.A.-granting institutions directly out of high school. The first Partnership class, which graduated high school in 1990, sent thirty-three of its thirty-nine graduates (85 percent) directly to college, and twenty graduated with bachelor's degrees only four years later—a four-year graduation rate higher than that of the vast majority of public four-year colleges and universities.

Results from the New York State Education Department

Valuable data on New York City schools are available from a New York State study published in 1993,[33] the annual reports[34] to the governor and legislature on the educational status of the schools, and district-level Comprehensive Assessment Reports[35] (CAR) on Catholic schools in New York City.

The 1993 study was conducted by the Office for Planning, Research, and Support Services of the state education department to assist the members of the education commissioner's Blue Ribbon Panel on Catholic Schools during their deliberations about the declining enrollment in Catholic schools and its implications for the State of New York. The study provided

TABLE 10.1 Comparative Performance of Graduating Seniors in Public and Partnership Schools, 1990

Schools	Percentage Taking SAT	Average Combined SAT Score	Percentage above Mean for Blacks
Public	33	642	<30
Catholic Partnership students	85	803	>60
All students	85	815	>60

Source: This table first appeared in Paul T. Hill, Gail Foster, and Tamar Gendler, *High Schools with Character* (Santa Monica, Calif.: RAND, 1990). The sources for the data include the Student-Sponsor Partnership Program and the New York City Board of Education.

extensive comparative data on New York State and City public and Catholic schools.

The following brief paragraphs highlight the Blue Ribbon Panel's main findings, updated by our own analyses of more recent data.

—In 1991, one out of five Catholic schools in New York City served a student body with over 30 percent of the pupils from families receiving public assistance. There are no comparable data for 1997–98, but the racial distribution of the schools this past year along with the stated policies of the schools would suggest that there have been no significant changes in the makeup of the Catholic schools in subsequent years.

—Catholic schools in New York City had a minority enrollment of 57 percent in 1991 and this percentage had grown to 60 percent by 1997. Hispanics represent the largest minority group in the Catholic schools, followed by blacks. In 1991 over 40 percent of the Catholic schools served student bodies that were 80 to 100 percent minority. Again, there is no reason to believe that this has changed since that year.

—In 1991 the public and Catholic schools in New York City had essentially the same proportion of students with multiple risk factors (i.e., family income below $15,000, single parent household, parents not completing high school, and student with a sibling who dropped out of school). The 1988 National Education Longitudinal Study showed that in New York City 26 percent of public school students and 24 percent of Catholic school students had multiple risk factors. There is no reason to believe that this situation has changed in recent years.

—For New York State, Catholic school students are only slightly more likely than public school students to score at the Statewide Reference Point (SRP) on all examinations. In New York City, however, Catholic schools had a significantly higher percentage of students passing the exams than the public schools in both 1991 and 1997. Major percentage differences were found in grade 3 reading, grade 3 mathematics, grade 5 writing, grade 6 reading, and grade 6 mathematics. The greatest differences in Catholic and public school achievement in 1991 were found when schools with the highest levels of minority composition were compared. (For additional data see the Appendix).

—A comparison of New York City public and Catholic schools with the highest minority composition showed that the Catholic school students were far more likely than comparable public school students to pass Regents Competency Tests (RCT). In 1991 these differences were evident in reading (+29 percent), writing (+23 percent), mathematics (+24 percent), science (+26 percent), history and government (+21 percent), and global studies (+23 percent). Information on RCT pass-rates for 1996 could not be broken down by minority composition, but an overall comparison of the rates for all New York City public and Catholic schools in 1991 and 1997 show similar results: in all subject areas, participants from Catholic high schools passed at significantly higher rates than participants from public high schools. (For additional data see the appendix).

—The 1993 Blue Ribbon Report did not include information on the percentage of participants in New York City schools passing the Regents examinations in the various subject areas (although statewide information was available for the two types of schools). However, information is available for the June 1997 testing and it shows, again, a significantly larger percentage of students enrolled in Catholic schools than in public schools passing the Regents examinations.

—The 1990–91 dropout rate for New York City Catholic schools was 0.1 percent versus 7.1 percent for public schools. For the same year, the college-going rate of graduates from the New York City Catholic schools (75.6 percent) surpassed the rate for graduates from New York City public schools (57.4 percent). Graduates from New York City Catholic schools with a minority composition of 81–100 percent entered college at a rate far higher than students from demographically comparable public schools (66.9 percent to 52.6 percent).

Summarizing the results of the study completed for its use, the Blue Ribbon Panel concluded, "There is no doubt that Catholic schools are effective learning environments. Their educational effectiveness is evident through analysis of standardized examination results, minimal dropout rate, and high college attendance rate. The success of Catholic schools is most dramatic in the education of students with at-risk characteristics." Although it is not possible to replicate the Blue Ribbon study and thereby test this conclusion using 1997 data, the new performance data cited above make it highly unlikely that there would be any significant change, given the continuity in the leadership and mission of the Catholic schools.

Why are the city's Catholic schools effective? The answers are complex. Carnoy et al. claim that there are few immediately visible differences between private and public schools,[36] and they have a point. Catholic schools look and smell very much like public schools. They group students by grade, and into separate classrooms. Their teachers are trained in many of the same education schools that train public school teachers, and many Catholic school teachers have taught in public schools (though more are likely to have their degrees from private colleges and universities). Some of their principals have been principals in public schools, though many Catholic school principals have extensive experience in other Catholic schools, including schools run by a particular religious order. Catholic schools also draw from the same pool of textbooks and other instructional materials as do public schools.

However, few people who have worked in or closely studied public schools think that these similarities mean that Catholic and public schools are the same. A series of independent studies of Catholic schools, conducted by investigators from different disciplines, at different times, and in different places, has identified a number of distinguishing traits.[37] Catholic schools are driven by a vision of the desired graduate as a competent, responsible person. They believe that learning is good in itself and also good because it brings the power to protect one's family and help others. They believe that innate ability is a fact of human life but that achievement comes from effort. They believe in parenting, adult leadership by example, and protecting students from noise, physical dangers, and emotionally upsetting disruptions of the school day.

Catholic schools are based on the belief that life has value and meaning and that knowledge is a route to personal salvation. These beliefs are based on religion—on faith in God, on absolute good and evil, and an afterlife. But in the context of Catholic schools these beliefs are also practical. As parts of parishes, Catholic schools are close to the essential events of life, to births, passage to adulthood, marriage, family dissolution, success and failure, illnesses, care of the sick, death, and mourning. They do not shield children from these realities but try instead to make them meaningful within the context of community and religious life.

These are highly conventional beliefs that are acceptable to most Americans. They also set extremely challenging standards. Because Catholic schools profess these beliefs, they are also vulnerable to charges of inconsistency when they do not take proper care with a student or when teachers' personal lives are less than exemplary.[38] Catholic schools are human and imperfect institutions, and no one associated with them—least of all the leaders of the New York and Brooklyn diocesan schools—thinks they are as good as they should be.

There are many paradoxes about Catholic schools. Despite being part of one of the most hierarchical organizations in the world, they are highly independent. Despite having a religiously focused mission, they spend more time on basic academics than do most secular schools. Despite depending on financial support from the middle and upper classes, Catholic schools are often focused on the needs of poor, minority, and immigrant children.

Perhaps the most significant paradox about Catholic schools is that despite being embedded in the church, they are more linked to the outside world than public schools. They are not bound up in educational fads. New practices reach them, but slowly. They have to contend much more directly than public schools with the misgivings of pastors, parents, old graduates, and donors. The schools also use external validators—colleges, universities, and desirable employers, high-status alumni, and students and faculty from similar schools—to assure students and parents that the school's offerings and demands make sense. They are also less able to devote time to learning new techniques and developing instructional innovations that are not evidently linked to what students need to know. These are attributes that could be both strengths and weaknesses, and they are both.

Five characteristics of New York's Catholic schools provide a more concrete picture of how they operate and how they differ from public schools: simplicity; universalism; intellectualism; assimilationism; and authority.

Simplicity. Catholic schools have simple curricula and offer far fewer options than most public schools. Among Catholic educators, a good school is one that accomplishes the fundamentals well—producing students who are literate, able to write and reason, possess an understanding of fundamental mathematics and science, and have a conscience, a sense of history, and a belief in citizenship. A school with a long list of classes and many separate courses of study for many separate groups is not necessarily a good school.

Catholic schools probably have too little money and invest too little in technology or professional development. Catholics who want their children to get highly innovative or technology-based instruction, or favor advanced arts experiences, often send their children to public schools or specialized non-Catholic independent schools.

But Catholic schools make the most of what they have. Catholic schools have what we have called elsewhere centripetal curricula that draw all students toward learning certain core skills and perspectives.[39] The school's dedication to preparing students for a certain kind of adult life means the school must work to ensure that all students master core subject matter; students cannot be left behind because the teacher does not have time to explain a key point, and no student may be relegated permanently to basic skills workbooks. Students who enter with basic skills deficits are given special instruction and required to study nights, summers, and weekends in order to catch up. But they are all ultimately exposed to the curriculum that the school defines as essential for all its graduates.

Like public schools, Catholic schools in New York City are serving an increasingly disadvantaged and poorly prepared student population. Many work continuously to find ways to bring young children up to grade level in reading and mathematics and to teach authentic high school mathematics, history, and literature to students who enter with a weak grasp of basic skills. Many are continually experimenting with teaching methods and materials, especially in the early grades. Catholic schools do group students by achievement levels, but they do not let low achievement exclude a student from rigorous materials.

A recent report on ability grouping in U.S. schools singles out the Catholic schools' approach:

> Intellectually stimulating low track classrooms do exist, however, and researchers have found the most productive of them in Catholic schools. Margaret Camarena and Adam Gamoran have described low-track classrooms, lively discussions, and ample learning take place. In 1990, Linda Valli published her study of a heavily-tracked Catholic high school in an urban community. The school's course designations publicly proclaimed each student's track level. Textbooks and instruction were adapted for each track. Yet Valli discovered that a "curriculum of effort" permeated the entire school, even at the lowest tracks. The school centered around academic progress . . . students of all abilities were aggressively pushed to learn as much as they could. Every year, low-track students were boosted up a level. By the senior year, the lowest track no longer existed.[40]

Bryk et al., Coleman et al., and Hill et al. (all cited above) provide highly detailed accounts of Catholic schools' methods for introducing struggling students to challenging adult materials. As all these analyses show, the Catholic schools are not infallible and some students do not succeed. However, disadvantaged minority students' high rates of school completion, college entry, and college completion show that the Catholic schools' basic approach to the instruction of all students works remarkably well.[41]

UNIVERSALISM. Catholic schools regard every student as a child of God and therefore equal: equally able to learn, in need of knowledge, and in need of guidance. They are not blind to individual differences but resist concluding that these differences justify different performance standards. They resist labeling on the basis of ethnicity or "handicapping condition," which gives them an advantage with the vast majority of children. Children who have been labeled with mild learning or behavioral disabilities are educated in regular classes: by some accounts Catholic schools in New York City educate the same proportion of children labeled "handicapped" as do the public schools.[42] However, Catholic schools are generally unable to serve severely, neurologically handicapped children.

A remarkable recent book, *Growing Up African American in Catholic Schools,* provides detailed analysis of the experience of children from groups that are most often considered educationally disadvantaged.[43] Though the book does not explicitly discuss the New York City Catholic schools, the authors' conclusions are strikingly similar to those expressed by New York City minority high school students interviewed for *High Schools with Character.* Written by professionally successful African American women who discovered that a striking number of other successful non-Catholic African

Americans had, like themselves, attended Catholic schools, *Growing Up African American in Catholic Schools* provides formal analysis and personal memoirs of the Catholic schooling experience. The authors emphasize the importance of Catholic schools' rigorous academic standards, simple curricula that ensure that all students are exposed to "mainstream" academic courses, emphasis on hard work and individual responsibility, and caring atmosphere.

Lisa Delpit, in a chapter entitled "Act Your Age, Not Your Color," writes, "There was no assumption that being Black meant you couldn't learn. . . . In fact the assumption was that we had to be smarter than white kids if we were going to be able to do anything. The other message was not that we could learn but that we *would* learn. . . . The careful attention to language structure focused our attention on the difference between our spoken language and written edited English. . . . But even with the very teacher-centered instruction and adult-administered discipline, there was a great deal of responsibility given over to children. . . . As I think back on the attitudes of those teachers I realize that they never equated ignorance with a lack of intelligence . . . they assumed their students had the academic sense to learn anything they were taught—if they were taught correctly."

Like many of the other authors in the same book, Delpit notes a certain lack of cultural sensitivity in Catholic schools, as do many older minority students in New York City Catholic schools. The schools consider a student an individual first, and do not assume that ethnicity, skin color, or cultural background justifies different expectations or exposure to material. Irvine notes in her chapter, "What the Catholic nuns and priests shared with my parents and the African American community were strong and dogmatic beliefs in the power of education over oppression and discrimination, and values such as discipline, resilience, achievement, and hard work."[44] Irvine notes a lack of "cultural synchronicity" between Catholic schools and the African American community, but concludes that shared values about work and learning were sufficient for an effective partnership.

As others in the same book recall, Catholic schools treat African American children as children of God like all other children, who can and must learn certain core facts, skills, and habits. Accidents of birth and family background should not interfere with the basic learning process. In many ways, the schools described are culturally insensitive, by design. They appeal to the universal and downplay the racially or culturally specific. In so doing, the schools sometimes offend and even wound students who feel that their ethnic or cultural identity is more important than the characteristics and needs they share with all other students. In the one strongly negative article about the Catholic school experience, Kimberly C. Ellis argues that the school's effects on achievement come at too great a cost of neglect of students' racial identities.[45]

Catholic schools in New York and other cities continue to struggle with the question of how much to accommodate the cultural sensitivities of African American and other minority students. Though most want to project respect and openness toward minority families, their commitment to a rigorous core curriculum, principles of hard work, self-denial, and personal responsibility make some Catholic schools seem insensitive. Most rely on families to provide culturally specific teaching and exemplars, assuming that it is up to the minority community to maintain what Foster (quoting W. E. B. Du Bois) calls the "double consciousness" of membership both in a universal community of learning and in a more specific community of family and neighborhood ties.[46] Few Catholic schools would claim to be the proper educational environments for children whose parents think the route to learning is through linkage with race- or ethnicity-specific experiences. High school principals and teachers frequently tell of their struggles to show respect for students' growing consciousness of ethnic identity, without surrendering the school's commitment to universalism.

INTELLECTUALISM. Catholic schools are committed to literacy in its fullest sense—using language in all its subtlety, as a tool for inquiry, dispute, and deductive reasoning as well as for self-expression. City high schools, even those dedicated to the education of immigrants and the poor, value classic texts. They use reading and discussion to help students learn how fully formed adults—lawyers, government leaders, philosophers, and fiction writers—use language. Principals and teachers interviewed in New York City Catholic schools say that an educated person is one who expects to use her mind productively, both by critiquing others' ideas and forming her own. This involves seeing the connections between disparate ideas, reasoning productively, using analogies imaginatively, and holding all ideas, including their own, to high standards of logic and evidence.

The goal of producing a graduate who fits a particular image obliges a Catholic school to make commitments about what is good for the student and for the society and what is not. However, it does not require a commitment to elitism or exclusion of minorities. Despite their trappings of elite education, the vast majority of New York City Catholic schools are not selective or designed only for the wealthy or highly motivated. Catholic schools occasionally come under criticism for imposing elite perspectives on students from diverse backgrounds. While admitting that the forms of education they offer should be chosen, not imposed, school leaders argue that the abilities they teach are and will remain pathways to understanding society, succeeding within it, and influencing it. As one principal argued, children from low-income and minority groups are precisely the ones who most need to develop such abilities in school.

Catholic schools' prominent ethical and moral agenda make it easy for them to be driven by clear visions of their desired graduates. Unlike public schools, which try to be all things to all people, Catholic schools make definite judgments about the goodness of knowledge and the importance of preparing people to use their minds for the betterment of society. Catholic schools in New York and elsewhere are conservative in that they aspire to readying students to live in today's society, not for some society that is utterly unlike or at war with what we have. They intend to help students understand the ideas that have created our economy and society, analyze social situations well enough to take constructive action, know their interests while appreciating the perspectives of others, and argue issues clearly and fairly.

ASSIMILATIONISM. New York's Catholic schools were founded to preserve the links between European immigrants and the church, but they have never held their graduates apart from the mainstream of American society. To the contrary, Catholic schools were meant to help immigrants remain Catholic yet be fully American and succeed in the context of New York City and America. This orientation has helped Catholic schools serve non-Catholic immigrant and minority children effectively.

It seems ironic that schools sponsored by a church that is itself founded on belief in divine revelation and a life lived for the hereafter would be so closely tied to the here and now. The American church might criticize individual practices of businesses and the materialism that leads individuals to ignore religion in their quest for money and success. But the church is not opposed to the two quintessentially American routes toward social and economic mobility, capitalism and politics. To the contrary, the American church thinks that lay Catholics and non-Catholic graduates of the schools should be active in democratic politics at all levels, and encourages students to learn skills that lead to success in business. The numbers of New York city and state political leaders who have come from the Catholic schools—including minority persons like former public schools Chancellor Rudy Crew—attests to their success.

Of course, the institutional church benefits directly from having Catholic school graduates in high elected office and in senior positions in business, the professions, academic institutions, law firms, and the judiciary. All church-related institutions also benefit from Catholic school graduates' having high enough incomes to permit generous donations to the archdiocese, universities, hospitals, and other institutions. But the church values professional and material success beyond their effects on church income. The church values success because it expects Catholic school graduates to be full members of American society, to influence and lead the city and its major institutions.

These concerns distinguish Catholic schools from many public schools. Though, as Crain and others have documented, some public schools in

New York City expressly devote themselves to linking students with careers in mainstream institutions,[47] many public schools disdain such connections. They reflect the attitudes of college of education professors, as recently revealed by surveys conducted by Public Agenda. Education school professors overwhelmingly distrust competition, the emphasis on productivity in economic life, and economic rewards incentives for productivity.[48] As education school professor Alex Molnar says in his speeches attacking business's role in education, "All business wants to do is to sell things you don't need and can hurt you." Though many public school teachers resist these views, the teachers who accept them often mistrust business and express ambivalence about preparing students for careers in a capitalist system.

AUTHORITY. New York's Catholic schools were not built on the assumption that families strongly support education and can be counted on to fill any gaps in instruction or motivation that the school cannot fill. To the contrary, the city's Catholic schools were constructed as missionary institutions, intended to strengthen a relatively weak bond between nominally Catholic European immigrants and the church. The schools expected to deal with families that had left their home countries because they could not succeed there and did not greatly value home country institutions, including the church. The schools also expected to deal with families fractured by the forces that beset so many economic refugees—poverty, out-of-wedlock birth, family separation, alcoholism, and violence.

Catholic schools did not condone these attributes of highly stressed families, but they were organized to educate children despite them. The schools tried to provide warm and supportive environments for children. As *New York Times* reporters frequently observe, Catholic schools are striking for their studiousness and serenity. Maintaining such an environment in the midst of a chaotic city is no small accomplishment. But principals and teachers say that it is necessary to ensure that pursuit of the schools' religious and social service goals do not drive out academic learning.

Teachers and administrators in Catholic schools believe they have a moral warrant for taking the above positions; that the school has important things to teach and that students benefit from learning them; that character and conscience development are inextricably linked with the rest of a child's education; and that the school has the right to protect itself against political, parental, or individual student demands that would weaken the above characteristics.

Catholic schools in New York City struggle with the student peer culture, but they are equipped to deal with it. Their advantages are composed of clear expectations to which students and parents subscribe when they choose the school: strong academic demands and evident links between what is taught in school and consequences for students' future lives.

Schools use these advantages. Many, especially those in low-income and high-crime areas, consciously intervene in the student peer culture, tapping exemplary students for prominent roles in the school, working directly with parents to discourage negative exemplars, and, rarely, expelling students who will not be reconciled to the school's demands.

In general, all schools, particularly high schools, must deal with the same paradoxes of youth development: that students need both structure to protect them and help them learn efficiently, and freedom to test alternative behaviors. They must also deal with a paradox of parental behavior, that parents want safe and academically serious schools for their children but will also object strenuously if their own children are subject to discipline. Catholic schools, especially those that are now trying to serve non-Catholic African Americans, are struggling to show respect for parents' expectations without surrendering the bases of the school's influence and effectiveness. In general, Catholic schools do not adopt the attitude prevalent in some public schools that educators serving racial or ethnic majority students must also adopt the manners, forms of address, and language prevalent in students' homes and neighborhoods. To the contrary, most Catholic school principals and teachers assume that making traditional demands for student effort and behavior is the best way to gain parental support and have influence on students.

Catholic schools do not think that introducing mainstream expectations into the lives of poor and minority children is cultural imperialism. Most assume that parents have high hopes for their children's effort, behavior, and ethical development, but many are worn down by pressures from popular and "street" culture.[49] The schools, principals and teachers claim, must show the institutional strength to help parents realize their deep aspirations for children.

Catholic schools are also strengthened by choice: parent choice of school and mutual choice between school and teachers. The need to keep promises made to parents makes the school's overall reputation of great importance to staff. This focuses their attention on instructional effectiveness first and all other issues second. Most staff members in New York City Catholic schools are eligible to work in regular public schools for equal or greater pay. They stay in the Catholic schools out of commitment to the mission or because they prefer the working conditions. They therefore value their jobs, which they know would end if the school were forced to close. From our interviews, it is clear that Catholic school teachers know that the continuation of their jobs depends on their own performance and that of their co-workers. They are also very reluctant to give up on a student, knowing that too many failure stories can wreck a school's reputation. Staff members treat students as if they are educable, not frozen in either their academic abilities or their attitudes.

Choice also conveys the parent's authority to the school, creating a legitimacy for the school's demands on the student that an assigned school does not enjoy. This grant of parental authority greatly increases the school's leverage over its students. School staff are able to use the parent's grant of authority to make demands on students. As a young woman interviewed for our report *High Schools with Character* said, "Your mother didn't send you here to hang out in the rest room. She sent you here to learn." As another New York City principal explained, a child who skips school, does not study, or displays a sullen attitude is risking a confrontation with her parent. The fact that parents have chosen a school, and that the school has an incentive to be as helpful as possible, creates a relationship of trust. Families that deal with the same school over a long time, especially those who have sent several children there, develop especially strong bonds of sentiment and loyalty toward the school.

Students gain from being in a situation in which they themselves must make commitments and take them seriously. If a student has any preference for the school she now attends over other schools she might have to attend after failing in the current one, she is susceptible to influence. Though they may prefer not to do all the school requires, students know that failure to do so could result in their being forced to leave the chosen school and go to another that is less attractive to them. Once they have accepted the schools' demands, they have given the schools leverage: teachers and administrators can assign homework, take attendance, grade performance, and administer consequences just as they said they would.

As a scientific proposition, the superiority of Catholic schools is not proven beyond a shadow of doubt. As a practical proposition, the likelihood that an individual child—especially one from a disadvantaged background—will benefit from a Catholic education is very high. The results noted above justify the widespread belief among African American and other minority parents that Catholic schools give their children a chance for success that public schools frequently do not.

Catholic Schools and the Education of New York's Children

Based on their numbers alone, Catholic schools are a major asset to the city. They are a promising route to integration into the larger society for tens of thousands of children. They provide rare opportunities for struggling parents to do something positive to protect their children from forces that imperil their futures. They are social glue for some otherwise chaotic neighborhoods. Their scale and importance to the poor and minority families that rely on them make the Catholic schools a major civic asset—one that, as Bryk and others have observed, serves a fundamental public purpose.

Catholic schools are also struggling institutions, charging low tuitions and relying on private charity to meet expenses. Though fewer have closed in recent years than in the 1970s and early 1980s, many run deficits. The Archdiocese of New York spends an average $7 million each year in emergency funds to keep schools about to close from doing so.

What can be done to preserve this asset and maximize its potential service to the city's children? Perhaps more importantly, what can be done to make schools like the Catholic schools available to all city families that want them?

Making the Most of the Catholic Schools

In most other Western countries the city's hundreds of Catholic schools would receive public financial support, and be recognized as public institutions. In Britain, for example, they would be regarded as privately operated public schools, coexisting with public schools operated by other religious groups and by local government bodies, the local education authorities. The United States is one of the few Western countries that define public schools only as schools operated by local government agencies and staffed by public employees.

The American tradition of making sharp distinctions between publicly and privately operated schools is based partly on a strict construction of the Constitution's separation of church and state.[50] It is also reinforced by the political activism of public school administrators and employees who do not want government funds to leak out of the institutions under their control. But the strict construction of the Constitution is now under fire in the courts, and many states and localities are experimenting with new ways to support students in Catholic schools. Parent pressure, especially among urban minority families, is also beginning to countervail the political power of public education provider groups.

New York State's Blue Ribbon Panel on Catholic Schools concluded that it is "educationally and fiscally prudent for New York State to develop and adopt programs of assistance which will contribute to reversing the trends of declining enrollments and school closings so Catholic schools will continue to be an asset to education in New York State."[51] This support, according to the panel, should include education tax credits for tuition and for donations to schools, programs, and scholarship funds. The panel also recommended "equitable participation of nonpublic school students in State-funded learning technology initiatives, such as distance learning, . . . interactive media, . . . [and] computer-based instruction."

It is possible that New York and other cities will soon be able to support Catholic schools more aggressively. The most obvious form of such support would be paying tuition to fill the two thousand seats in Catholic schools that the New York City archdiocese estimates are still available.

A direct per-student subsidy, to assist with the education of all the children whose parents pay taxes but do not receive any benefits from the New York City public school system, would assure the Catholic schools' survival.

Making Coherent, Effective Schools Available to All

No matter how much public support they received, the existing Catholic schools could not possibly expand to serve all of New York City's children. The only way to make such schools available to all children is to create new public schools modeled after Catholic schools, adapt existing public schools that demonstrate the capacity to change, and make a permanent change in methods of public funding, staffing, and control.

The key to such changes in public education can be seen in a comparison of how differently the city's Catholic and public school systems have responded to demographic change and more challenging students. In many ways the urban Catholic schools have faced the same problems that the big-city public schools have had to cope with. The students they serve are much poorer, more affected by crime and family disintegration, more often foreign born, and from less well educated families than was the case in the 1950s and 1960s. Since that time, like the public schools, Catholic schools' economic base has also eroded and (due to loss of the nuns) their costs have risen, and their school buildings are much older and more in need of repair. However, unlike the public schools, the Catholic schools have not collapsed, nor do Catholic school leaders claim that the schools' problems are due to the deficits of the families they serve.

Catholic schools' better adaptation to the same circumstances that beset public schools can be laid to two factors: lack of detailed central control of the schools and reciprocal choice among schools, families, and teachers.

DECENTRALIZATION. Catholic schools are independent organizations, run almost entirely by pastors and school heads. They share the basic goals of the bishops under whose authority they operate, but they are not subject to the creation of new mandates that constantly change the way they do business, or to compliance-based inspections.

The Catholic schools operate under an ancient principle of subsidiarity, that every action must be taken at the level of organization most likely to understand its consequences. Subsidiarity was a necessity for a worldwide church represented by provincial bishops, pastors, and missionaries who might not communicate with Rome for decades at a time. It emphasized universal agreement on goals and fundamental principles of operation, and forswore any effort to control day-to-day decisions. The results were not always perfect, as occasional scandals and even regional heresies arose. But it was the best feasible adaptation to the circumstances of a very large organization with little central capacity and great dependence on the quality of actions taken in the field. Other large and far-flung organizations, including diplomatic services and navies, also work on the principle of subsidiarity. It requires explicit and highly stable basic doctrines, a central organization dedicated to supporting, not thwarting, local initiative, and a capacity to intervene in exceptional cases of local failure.

CHOICE. Catholic schools are places of voluntary association. Parents are not compelled to send their children to any Catholic school. Teachers choose to work at a particular school, rather than being assigned by a centrally administered civil service system. Similarly, school leaders decide what mix of skills they need on their faculties and, within the constraints set by the labor market, whom to employ.

Choice reinforces the organizational strength of individual schools. The schools are able to lead parents by setting and enforcing standards for student effort and behavior, and they are able to enforce these standards by credibly threatening to expel students who disrupt the education of others. Though expulsions are rare—far more rare than dropouts and administrative suspensions in public schools serving similar populations—their possibility is a great asset for Catholic schools. Catholic schools are also able to choose and keep their own principals, set clear expectations for teachers, offer extra pay and benefits (including spousal employment) to excellent teachers, create strong incentives for weak teachers to upgrade their skills, and reject teachers who cannot or will not perform up to standard.

Faced with similar challenges, urban public school systems have employed dramatically different strategies. They have strengthened central control of spending, staff hiring, hours, and working conditions. They have subjected individual schools to waves of new mandates created through citywide and even statewide political bargaining, and through litigation. They have compelled families to send their children to certain schools, including some that no one wants to attend, have controlled staff assignment to schools via districtwide seniority rules, and have moved principals out of schools that wish to keep them and into schools that may not want them.

Why would this system be more likely to serve the public interest than one based on subsidiarity and choice? Why should the existing public school system be the way society tries to educate its most disadvantaged children? What do mandates, politics, regulations, and constraints on choice contribute to the education of the poor? Why is this system more public than the Catholic school system which serves the same population and operates with no more money, with more respect for individual dignity, and with better results for students?

The answers to these questions have nothing to do with the needs of disadvantaged urban children and everything to do with accidents of political and legal history. There is no reason why public education needs to be centralized or why individual schools need to be disabled by the rules, mandates, and lack of leverage over staff. There is no reason why public education cannot respect parents' choices.

This is not the place for all the ideas about how public schools can gain the advantages that have made Catholic schools so effective. But there are serious proposals for applying the lessons of Catholic education throughout the public school system.[52] They show that communities like New York City can have a public school system that values school independence, consistency, and accountability for performance responsibility. As we have argued elsewhere, government need not (and should not) operate schools directly. Rather, it should support independently operated schools via contracts. School boards should guarantee equitable student access to schools and take responsibility for closing and replacing schools that are failing their students, but they should not exercise day-to-day control of school curriculum, teaching methods, or staffing.[53]

Such proposals do not turn over the education of all children to the Catholic Church or any combination of sectarian organizations. But they do show how we can have schools that serve the public interest in the ways that the Catholic schools do.

NOTES

1. New York City Catholic school and enrollment figures are taken from entries for the Diocese of Brooklyn and the Archdiocese of New York in *The Official Catholic Directory*, published annually by P. J. Kennedy and Sons, Providence, N.J., since 1817.

2. All public school enrollment figures are taken from the U.S. Department of Education, *Digest of Education Statistics 1997* (Washington, D.C.: Office for Educational Research and Improvement, 1997), tables 92 and 93.

3. The section on "cost effectiveness and fiscal challenges" in *Roman Catholic Schools in New York State: A Comprehensive Report* (University of the State of New York, State Department of Education, Office of Planning, Research, and Support Services, 1993), p. 28, reports that in 1991–92 the total expenditures per enrolled students in New York State were $8,374, which includes funds that go to Catholic school students for transportation and special services, amounting to $529 per Catholic school student. Deducting the total of these funds from the public school expenditures would mean that slightly over $8,100 is spent per pupil in the New York State public schools. If 150,000 plus Catholic school students were in public schools, it is estimated that they would cost city and state taxpayers approximately $1.1 billion per year, although the elasticity of the public school system might permit the absorption of some of these students at less expense if they entered the system gradually.

4. See, for example, Jacqueline Jordan Irvine and Michele Foster, eds., *Growing Up African American in Catholic Schools* (New York: Teachers College Press, 1997); Anthony S. Bryk, Valerie Lee, and Patrick Holland, *Catholic Schools and the Common Good*

(Cambridge, Mass.: Harvard University Press, 1993); James S. Coleman and Thomas Hoffer, *Public and Private High Schools* (New York: Basic Books, 1987); James Coleman, Thomas Hoffer, and Sally Kilgore, *High School Achievement: Public, Catholic, and Private Schools Compared* (New York: Basic Books, 1982); James G. Cibulka, T. J. O'Brien, and D. Zewe, *Inner-City Private Elementary Schools* (Milwaukee, Wis.: Marquette University Press, 1982); Robert Crain et al., *The Effectiveness of New York City's Career Magnets* (Berkeley, Calif.: National Center for Research on Vocational Education, 1992); University of the State of New York, *Roman Catholic Schools in New York State: A Comprehensive Report*, May 1993; Blue Ribbon Panel on Catholic Schools (Hugh L. Carey, Chair), *Report to New York State Commissioner of Education, Thomas Sobol*, June 1993.

    5. Paul T. Hill, Gail Foster, and Tamar Gendler, *High Schools with Character* (Santa Monica, Calif.: RAND, 1990); Paul T. Hill, "Private Vouchers in New York City: The Student-Sponsor Partnership Program," in *Private Vouchers*, ed. Terry M. Moe (Stanford, Calif.: Hoover Institution Press, 1995); Mary Beth Celio, *Building and Maintaining Systems of Schools: Lessons from Religious Order School Networks*, Working Papers of the University of Washington Graduate School of Public Affairs, 1995.

    6. Quoted in Jay P. Dolan, *The American Catholic Experience* (Garden City, N.Y.: Image Books, 1985), p. 263.

    7. Harold A. Buetow, *The Catholic School: Its Roots, Identity, and Future* (New York: Crossroad, 1988), p. 24.

    8. Roger Finke and Rodney Stark, *The Churching of America, 1776–1990: Winners and Losers in our Religious Economy* (New Brunswick, N.J.: Rutgers University Press, 1992), p. 140.

    9. Diane Ravitch, *The Great School Wars—New York City, 1805–1973: A History of the Public Schools as Battlefield of Social Change* (New York: Basic Books, 1974).

    10. Dolan, *The American Catholic Experience*, p. 268.

    11. Ibid., p. 272.

    12. Ibid., p. 275.

    13. Bryk, Lee, and Holland, in *Catholic Schools and the Common Good*, contend that "no current effort to promote decentralization in the public sector approaches this level of school-site autonomy" (p. 299).

    14. Some of the religious order networks staffed only a handful of schools in the city, while others had dozens: the Sisters of St. Joseph staffed seventy-three schools in Brooklyn in 1967 at the same time the Dominican Sisters of the Third Order of St. Dominic-Brooklyn staffed forty-eight schools in the same diocese. In the same year, the Sisters of Charity of St. Vincent de Paul staffed thirty-seven schools in the New York archdiocese and another nine in Brooklyn. Particularly active men's orders in 1967 included the Brothers of the Christian Schools (twenty-three schools in the city), the Marist Brothers of the Schools (nine schools), and the Congregation of Christian Brothers (nine schools).

    15. For a more extensive discussion of the different networks of religious order schools and their characteristics, see Mary Beth Celio, "Building and Maintaining Multischool Networks: Lessons to be Learned from the Catholic Schools," Working Paper 94-12 in Public Policy Analysis and Management, University of Washington, Graduate School of Public Affairs, May 1994.

    16. Francis M. Ouellette, "Interdependent Administrative Linkages between the Diocesan Education Office and Diocesan High Schools" (Ph.D. diss., Boston

College, 1989); Stephen J. O'Brien, ed., *A Primer on Educational Governance in the Catholic Church* (Washington, D.C.: National Catholic Education Association, 1987).

17. Ernest Bartell, "Efficiency, Equity, and Economics in Catholic Schools," in *Catholic Education Today and Tomorrow*, ed. Michael P. Sheridan and Russell Shaw (Washington, D.C.: National Catholic Educational Association, 1968), p. 32.

18. The Second Vatican Council was a meeting of all bishops of the Roman Catholic Church, called by Pope John XXIII to consider ways in which the church could respond to the modern world in more effective ways. It is best known for its liberalization of the church and "ecumenism," an effort to seek common ground with people from other religious traditions. The three-year council resulted in a number of major policy documents and in significant shifts in the focus of many church organizations. Many religious orders of men and women rethought their purposes and, in the process, thousands decided to leave their religious orders. The reasons for this massive exodus have never been fully explained, but the impact is still being felt throughout the church.

19. There has been considerable discussion about the level of, and changes in, charitable giving by Catholics since Vatican II. Research in this area was reviewed and summarized for the National Conference of Catholic Bishops in Mary Beth Celio, "Catholic Contributions to the Church: An Examination of Recent Research," October 1995.

20. Bryk, Lee, and Holland, *Catholic Schools and the Common Good*, p. 339.

21. "Gravissimum Educationis," October 28, 1965, in *Vatican Council II: The Conciliar and Post Conciliar Documents*, ed. Austin Flannery, OP (Northport, N.Y.: Costello Publishing, 1981), p. 735.

22. Robert J. Havighurst, "Social Functions of Catholic Education," in *Catholic Education Today and Tomorrow: Proceedings of the Washington Symposium on Catholic Education*, ed. Michael P. Sheridan, S.J., and Russell Shaw (Washington, D.C.: National Catholic Educational Association, 1968), pp. 1, 17.

23. Bartell, "Efficiency, Equity, and the Economics of Catholic Schools," p. 38.

24. Thomas Vitullo-Martin, *Inner City Catholic Schools: The Future* (Washington, D.C.: United States Catholic Conference, 1979), pp. 37–38.

25. Ibid., p. 50.

26. Ibid., p. 74. See also Caroline Minter Hoxby, "The Effects of Private School Vouchers on Schools and Students," in *Holding Schools Accountable: Performance-Based Reform in Education*, ed. Helen F. Ladd (Washington D.C.: Brookings Institution, 1996), pp. 199, 201. Hoxby assessed the "natural" voucher system provided by the subsidies to Catholic school children from their parish and diocesan supporters. Looking at school achievement levels in both private and public schools in metropolitan areas, she found that "a $1,000 voucher would improve student performance across the board: both public and private school students would increase their educational attainment (about 2 years), test scores (about 10 percent) and wages (about 14 percent). The improvement would be greater for Catholic students, African American students, and all student with college-educated parents. The improvements are almost entirely among public school students." In other words, "private school tuition subsidies force public schools into higher productivity."

27. Coleman, Hoffer, and Kilgore, *High School Achievement*; Bryk, Lee, and Holland, *Catholic Schools and the Common Good*.

28. Catherine Tighe Hickey, "The Impact of Non-Catholic Students in Catholic Schools of a Large Eastern Diocese" (Ph.D. diss., Fordham University, 1983), pp. 91–93, 99.

29. Thomas J. Reese, S.J., *Archbishop: Inside the Power Structure of the American Catholic Church* (San Francisco: Harper and Row, 1989), p. 278.

30. Ibid.

31. See, for example, Bryk, Lee, and Holland, *Catholic Schools and the Common Good;* Coleman and Hoffer, *Public and Private High Schools;* Coleman, Hoffer, and Kilgore, *High School Achievement;* Hoxby, "The Effects of Private School Vouchers on Schools and Students"; Hill, Foster, and Gendler, *High Schools with Character;* Darlene E. York, "The Academic Achievement of African Americans in Catholic Schools: A Review of the Literature," in Irvine and Foster, eds., *Growing Up African American in Catholic Schools;* Valerie Lee, "Catholic School Minority Students Have a Reading Proficiency Advantage," *Momentum* 17, no. 3 (1986); George F. Madaus and Roger Linnan, "The Outcome of Catholic Education," *School Review* 81, no. 2 (1973); Adam Gamoran, "Student Achievement in Public Magnet, Public Comprehensive, and Private City High Schools," *Educational Evaluation and Policy Analysis* 18, no. 1 (1996); Derek Neal, "The Effects of Catholic Secondary Schooling on Educational Achievement," *Journal of Labor Economics* 15, no. 1 (1997); William Sander, "Catholic Grade Schools and Academic Achievement," *Journal of Human Resources* 31, no. 3 (1996); William N. Evans and Robert M. Schwab, "Finishing High School and Starting College: Do Catholic Schools Make a Difference?" *Quarterly Journal of Economics* 110, no. 4 (1995); William Sander and Anthony C. Krautmann, "Catholic Schools, Dropout Rates, and Educational Attainment," *Economic Inquiry* 33, no. 2 (1995).

32. See, for example, Hill, "Private Vouchers in New York City."

33. *Roman Catholic Schools in New York State: A Comprehensive Report* (University of the State of New York, State Department of Education, Office of Planning, Research, and Support Services, 1993); Blue Ribbon Panel on Catholic Schools, Hugh L. Carey, chair, *Report to the New York State Commissioner of Education, Thomas Sobol,* June 1993.

34. *Statewide Profile of the Educational System: A Report to the Governor and the Legislature on the Educational Status of the State's Schools* (University of the State of New York, State Department of Education, 1996, 1997, 1998).

35. Comprehensive Assessment Reports on high schools in the Archdiocese of New York and the Diocese of Brooklyn for 1995, 1996, 1997.

36. Martin Carnoy, Luis Biveniste, and Richard Rothstein, "How Different Is Private from Public Education?" PACE Newsletter 1, no. 2 (Berkeley, Calif.: Policy Analysis for California Education, 1998).

37. See, for example, Irvine and Foster, eds., *Growing Up African American in Catholic Schools;* Bryk, Lee, and Holland, *Catholic Schools and the Common Good;* Coleman and Hoffer, *Public and Private High Schools;* Coleman, Hoffer, and Kilgore, *High School Achievement;* Cibulka, O'Brien, and Zewe, *Inner-City Private Elementary Schools;* Hill, Foster, and Gendler, *High Schools with Character;* and Adam Gamoran, "Achievement in Public Magnet, Public Comprehensive, and Private City High Schools," *Education Evaluation and Policy Analysis* 18 (1996).

38. As the present authors' own ongoing research on effective schools has

shown, such charges are extremely common in high schools, and are most often made by students, always alert for adult inconsistency.

39. Hill, Foster, and Gendler, *High Schools with Character.*

40. Thomas Loveless, *The Tracking and Ability Grouping Debate* (Washington D.C.: Thomas B. Fordham Foundation, 1998). The research cited is in Linda Valli, "A Curriculum of Effort: Tracking Students in a Catholic High School," in *Curriculum Differentiation: Interpretive Studies in U.S. Elementary Schools,* ed. Linda Valli and Reba Page (Albany: SUNY Press, 1990).

41. See, for example, Coleman, Hoffer, and Kilgore, *High School Achievement.* See also Paul T. Hill, "Private Vouchers in New York City: The Student-Sponsor Partnership Program," in *Private Vouchers,* ed. Terry M. Moe (Stanford, Calif.: Hoover Institution Press, 1995).

42. Public charter schools, perhaps in imitation of Catholic schools, also "de-label" a child with moderate learning and behavioral disabilities. See, for example, Chester E. Finn, Bruno V. Manno, and Louann Bierlien, "Charter Schools in Action: What Have We Learned?" (Washington, D.C.: Hudson Institute, 1996).

43. Irvine and Foster, eds., *Growing Up African American in Catholic Schools.*

44. Ibid., p. 92.

45. Kimberly C. Ellis, "Topsy Goes to Catholic School: Lessons in Academic Excellence, Refinement, and Religion," ibid.

46. "Mea Culpa, Mea Culpa, Mea Maxima Culpa: The French Catholic School Experience," ibid.

47. Robert L. Crain et al., *The Effectiveness of New York City's Career Magnet Schools: An Evaluation of Ninth Grade Performance Using an Experimental Design* (Berkeley, Calif.: National Center for Research in Vocational Education, 1992).

48. Steve Farkas, Jean Johnson, and Ann Duffett, *Different Drummers: How Teachers of Teachers View Public Education* (New York: Public Agenda Foundation, 1997).

49. We could not validate these claims directly by interviewing parents, but the principals' assertions were wholly consistent with Public Agenda's findings on minority parents' aspirations for their children, as summarized below. As one outstanding former inner-city principal commented, it is the job of a school to introduce children of all backgrounds to universal standards of studiousness, work, performance, and self-control. Ethnic and social background differences between student and teacher are no excuse: "If white teachers can't figure out how to educate Black children we are all in big trouble. The numbers of African American graduates from schools of education are shrinking, while the numbers of African American schoolchildren are growing. Most Black children are going to be educated by white teachers, and white teachers have to take responsibility for learning how to do it."

50. For a review of likely consequences of litigation on the church-state issue in education, see Jesse Choper, "School Choice: Federal Constitutional Issues under the Religion and Speech Clauses of the First Amendment," in *School Choice: Politics, Policy, and Law,* ed. Stephen Sugarman and Frank Kemerer (Washington, D.C.: Brookings Institution Press, 1999).

51. Blue Ribbon Panel on Catholic Schools, *Report to New York State Commissioner of Education,* pp. 3–4.

52. See, for example, John E. Brandl, *Money and Good Intentions Are Not Enough;*

Or, Why a Liberal Democrat Thinks States Need Both Competition and Community (Washington, D.C.: Brookings Institution Press 1998); Paul T. Hill, Lawrence C. Pierce, and James W. Guthrie, *Reinventing Public Education: How Contracting Can Transform America's Schools* (Chicago: University of Chicago Press, 1997); Adam Urbanski, "Make Public Schools More Like Private Schools," *Education Week*, January 3, 1996; Paul T. Hill and Mary Beth Celio, *Fixing Urban Schools* (Washington, D.C.: Brookings Institution Press, 1998).

53. For a succinct summary of this proposal, see Paul T. Hill, "Contracting in Public Education," in *New Schools for a New Century*, ed. Diane Ravitch and Joseph P. Viteritti (New Haven, Conn.: Yale University Press, 1997).

APPENDIX: DATA FOR YEARS AFTER PUBLICATION OF THE NEW YORK STATE BLUE RIBBON PANEL REPORT

Since publication of the Blue Ribbon Panel report, the state education department has collected additional data on Catholic and public school performance, but it is not broken out in the same way or to the same degree of detail as that for the Blue Ribbon Panel. The tables on this and the following page present demographic and assessment data on New York City public and Catholic schools for the years indicated and in the detail permitted by the various state education department data sources.

TABLE 10.2 Percentage of Pupils in Public and Catholic Schools Scoring above State Reference Points on Pupil Evaluation Program (PEP) Exams

	1991		1997	
	NYC Public	*NYC Catholic*	*NYC Public*	*NYC Catholic*
Grade 3				
Reading	60	77	69	86
Math	81	90	92	98
Grade 5				
Writing	84	91	86	92
Grade 6				
Reading	69	80	69	84
Math	80	90	88	96

TABLE 10.3 Percentage of Pupils in Public and Catholic Schools Passing Regents Competency Tests

	June 1992		June 1996	
	NYC Public	NYC Catholic	NYC Public	New York Archdiocese
Mathematics	57	78	55	76
Science	63	89	52	87
U.S. government	60	78	73	86
Global studies	51	76	43	68
Writing	62	81	80	89
Reading	62	91	69	94

TABLE 10.4 Percentage of All Students Enrolled Passing Different Regents Examinations

	June 1997	
	NYC Public	NYC Catholic
Comprehensive English	39.2	72.9
Sequential mathematics I	39.2	49.8
Sequential mathematics II	28.1	42.9
Sequential mathematics III	22.3	37.0
Biology	17.9	63.6
Chemistry	17.1	40.7
Earth science	12.2	22.8
Physics	12.2	19.4
Global studies	29.3	61.7
U.S. history & government	31.8	57.5

11 Jewish Day Schools

MARVIN SCHICK

According to a recently completed census, in the 1998–99 school year there were 76,414 students from the four-year-old preschool level through the twelfth grade enrolled in more than two hundred elementary and secondary Jewish all-day schools located in New York City.[1] Because enrollment certainly grew in the 1999–2000 school year and some schools may not have been included in the survey, the current enrollment is probably close to eighty thousand students. While these numbers represent a small proportion of New York's school-age population, enrollment in these schools has grown steadily for more than a generation, and this trend is certain to continue, despite the substantial overall decline in New York's Jewish population in the post–World War II period.

About three-fourths of the students attend elementary schools, which in many instances encompass a substantial preschool program. Nearly an equal proportion of the schools and an even higher percentage of students are located in Brooklyn, primarily in Borough Park, Williamsburg, and Flatbush, the neighborhoods with the largest concentration of Orthodox Jews.

The city's Jewish schools include students who live outside of the five boroughs, primarily in suburban New York counties and nearby New Jersey areas. There are also some New York children of school age who attend Jewish schools outside of the city. If one considers Jewish school enrollment in the New York metropolitan area as a whole, there are more than 250 schools with an enrollment of 110,000 students, constituting sixty percent of all Jewish elementary and secondary school enrollment in the United States.

These figures highlight the centrality of New York in the profile of American Jewry and yet they also give a somewhat distorted picture. New

York is the center of American Jewish life, but in demography and much else, its pattern is quite different from what is found elsewhere in the country. The contrast is most pronounced in religiosity, a factor that has a substantial bearing on the schools attended by Jewish children. Because of the far higher concentration of Orthodox Jews in New York than elsewhere, Jewish school enrollment on a per capita basis is substantially greater in the city.

Jewish schools are usually referred to as day schools, although the more intensively religious institutions are also called yeshivas. While the two terms are at times used interchangeably—including in this chapter—there are important educational differences that reflect the specific religious orientation of the various schools. The differences encompass nearly all of the academic program, school ambience, curriculum, school hours, dress code, admission policy, mission, and even approaches to tuition and scholarships, as well as the attitudes and expectations of administrators, faculty, parents, and students.

Typically, American Jews identify with several different subdenominational groups, most familiarly, Reform, Conservative, or Orthodox. Because religious education is central in their belief system, Orthodox Jews have led the way in establishing day schools. Among the non-Orthodox, these schools were long regarded as the place for other people's children, as full confidence was conferred on public schools as the instruments for incorporating Jewish youth into American life.[2]

During the past decade especially, there has been a reassessment of attitudes toward day schools, so that there is now a growing number of schools sponsored by the Conservative and Reform groups, as well as transdenominational institutions that seek or claim to accommodate students from across the religious spectrum. Still, the Orthodox continue to predominate in the day school world; and in New York City they account for about 95 percent of the schools and all but 2 percent of the enrollment. A half-dozen years ago, there was not a single non-Orthodox high school in the city. There is now a small Conservative high school in Manhattan and there is a larger one in Nassau County that is accessible to city students. Several additional non-Orthodox high schools are in the planning stage.

Although they constitute but 10 percent of American Jews and about one out of six Jewish New Yorkers, the Orthodox are a far from homogeneous lot. They encompass modern and centrist elements, a collection of Chassidic subgroups, and Jews of a traditional yeshiva-world orientation. These differences, some of practice and belief and others of nuance, profoundly affect the character of Jewish schools. In order to appreciate the nature and educational role of yeshivas and day schools in New York, it is necessary to appreciate the variations in Orthodox life.

Jewish Schools as Religious Institutions

Like all schools, Jewish elementary and secondary schools are educational institutions that aim to convey knowledge about different subjects and to develop patterns of study that will provide students with the intellectual and informational tools and skills that permit them to function successfully as they reach maturity. They are also the means chosen by a growing number of Jewish parents to comply with state compulsory educational laws.

It would seem remarkable if Jews, who are often referred to as "the people of the book," did not give the highest priority to formal education, to classroom experiences that center on text and knowledge. In Chassidic families, there is a custom that appears to express the importance of learning. When a boy of three or four is given his first religious text—a Hebrew prayer book or Bible—a bit of honey is dabbed on the page and the boy kisses the book and tastes the honey. The hope and prayer is that Torah study, including the Bible, Talmud, and many other classic religious texts, will remain sweet for him for all of his days.

Another message is conveyed by this experience: the hope and prayer that a religious lifestyle will remain sweet for this young child. While there were times and places when Jewish schools were essentially educational institutions, that was in periods when there was scant prospect that the hostile outside world would wean children away from Judaism. With the acceptance of universal education and the nearly contemporaneous clash between modernity and religious life, the mission of religious Jewish schools has been altered to incorporate the more fundamental role of religious socialization and reinforcement.

For all yeshivas—and depending on where they are located on the religious spectrum, for day schools as well—formal education is foremost a process of religious socialization, of students being taught the observances and beliefs that are the core of the Jewish religious tradition. They are constantly given reinforcement to practice what is being preached to them, the goal being that when formal schooling has ended they will retain not merely the knowledge but the attitudes and practices that they have been taught.[3] In line with this mission, students are rarely expelled, especially in the elementary school grades, because of academic deficiencies. There is a far greater likelihood, including in some more modern day schools, that students may be asked to leave if they do not adhere to the expected normative or religious standards.

Viewed from this perspective, the reputation of a Jewish school is primarily predicated on its success in creating an environment of religious purposefulness that affects the lives of the students and, at times, their families. It would be misleading to suggest that there is no concern for ordinary educational outcomes, for how well students do in class or on tests. Educators and parents are endlessly preoccupied with educational performance, but this outlook assumes that the religious norms are being acquired and adhered to.

Jewish schools are, of course, parochial schools, which is to say that they are religiously sponsored, a status that they share with thousands of Catholic and other religious day schools. Actually, most parochial schools are minimalistic in their religious programs; their curriculums are not all that different from what is offered in public schools. In Jewish schools, however, and especially in the New York area, the religious element is pervasive, and not only in the institutional mission and ambience. Religious education more often than not stretches across more than half of the school day. Unlike Catholic schools, which are increasingly catholic in their recruitment efforts, Jewish schools admit only students of the Jewish faith.[4]

In a majority of Orthodox schools in New York, few if any of the students come from non-Orthodox homes, with the exception of those schools that have a special outreach mission or focus on immigrant families. There is, in fact, an element of self-selection, as parents seek schools that accord most closely with their own religious orientation. A deeply felt religious commitment invariably begets insularity and a measure of estrangement from the larger society. It is evident, particularly in New York, that yeshivas and more than a few day schools have become more stringent in their religious code. This reflects, to an extent, what is occurring in a variety of seemingly disparate faith communities, as they confront the attitudinal and behavioral challenges arising from modernity. In Orthodox circles, the secular environment and its manifestation through forms of popular culture is usually viewed as antithetical to Torah living.

Put otherwise, most Jewish schools regard the outside world as a threat to the fulfillment of their mission. As society becomes more permissive and promiscuous, the response of Jewish schools has been to raise the religious standard, whether this be indicated through dress codes or the strong discouragement of movie attendance, television and video watching, and surfing the Internet. These are regarded as attributes of a culture that is hostile to what the Torah requires of observant Jews.

Of course what the schools want is what most Orthodox parents now believe in, as they have come to regard a sincere religious lifestyle as incompatible with accepting much of what modernity has to offer. As a consequence, there is greater homogeneity in behavior and outlook in the school population than was evident a generation ago. However, it would be a mistake to conclude that deviation from the standard does not occur outside of the schools or that yeshiva students and some day school students are collections of junior Stepford wives. Compulsion yields diminishing returns, and persuasion is always the more effective means of ensuring compliance. What has happened in Orthodox life and therefore in Orthodox schools is substantially the product of choice among people who fiercely want to maintain their religious way of life. They have come to believe that the only way to accomplish this is to reject much of what the outside world offers.

This is the prevalent pattern in the New York area, where there are few non-Orthodox schools and even the Modern Orthodox institutions share some of the concerns of those that are more stringently religious. Elsewhere, the pattern is more varied, as a growing number of non-Orthodox schools compete with the more established Orthodox institutions and offer programs and approaches that are more welcoming of outside culture and influences and far less committed to the standard of religious purposefulness.

Types of Schools

While religion permeates the program of nearly all Jewish schools, it does not account for everything. There are inevitable variations arising from grade level, as well as from other factors that tend to distinguish schools everywhere. The most fundamental classification is whether schools operate on the elementary or secondary level. The larger schools—they are generally regarded as those with an enrollment above seven hundred—operate at both the elementary and secondary levels, at times in a single facility, but always as separate divisions. These larger schools probably account for more than half of all Jewish school enrollment in New York.

Yeshivas, as distinct from day schools, that operate at the elementary school level tend to have full-blown preschool programs that may begin with three-year-old nursery school children. Whereas such programs may elsewhere be regarded as day care and not formal education, here they are integrated into the institution's educational program because of their religious content. Four-year-old students attend kindergarten and those who are a year older are in what is usually called pre-1A; thus by the time these Orthodox children reach the first grade, they may have as much as three years of schooling under their belts. Yeshiva children are expected to read Hebrew before they reach the first grade.[5]

High school encompasses grades 9–12, although yeshiva high schools for boys that operate at the postsecondary or seminary level—as many of them do—increasingly tend to integrate all or part of the twelfth grade into the seminary component—in what may be regarded as a form of early admissions. There is also a tendency for high school graduates, both boys and girls, to devote at least an additional year to religious study, in Israel or here, often as a prelude to college study.

Jewish schools in New York, especially below high school, are neighborhood based, with students traveling short distances to the site. In the key Brooklyn Orthodox neighborhoods, where most students live in relative proximity to their schools, busing is ordinarily provided by the institution, a service that many regard as vital in view of the length of the school day. A relative handful of yeshivas have dormitories to accommodate students, usually high schoolers or older, who come from out of town or who prefer to live at the school. Most yeshivas, but a decreasing number of day schools, provide school lunch. The boys' yeshivas that are open from early in the morning into the night may offer three meals a day at the school.

Jewish schools tend to be small, certainly when they are compared with the nearby public schools, although the enrollment average in New York is considerably higher than it is elsewhere. As noted, there are some fairly large institutions, but even in New York most Jewish schools enroll fewer than five hundred students. Some schools—notably at the high school level—are astonishingly small, with perhaps two dozen or so students. Obviously, school size is a factor in determining the scope of the academic program.

The pattern of Jewish day school enrollment in the United States is pyramidal, with significantly more students enrolled in the first grade than in the eighth grade and certainly in the high school classes. This mirrors, to an extent, the demographic trend, as an escalating Orthodox birth rate results in more children in the lower grades. It is also the consequence of parental choice, especially among those of marginal religiosity who believe that after a limited number of years in a Jewish school there are compelling social and/or educational reasons to transfer students to a public school or non-Jewish private school. As an example, Rodeph Sholom, located in Manhattan and the only Reform day school in the city, as well as the oldest Reform day school in the country, terminates after the sixth grade. Overall, because of the large concentration of Orthodox Jews for whom an intensive religious education is an imperative and not an option, this phenomenon is less of a factor in New York.

Coeducation is one of the issues that divide Jewish schools. Because it is not acceptable to the vast majority of New York's Orthodox, there are separate schools for boys and girls or, in some of the larger schools, separate divisions with entirely separate facilities. The non-Orthodox and Modern Orthodox insist on coeducation, as they believe that it is progressive and desirable. However, a number of day schools that attempt to accommodate modernity with a more Orthodox inclination have separate Jewish studies classes, if not from the outset then in the middle or upper grades.

Curriculum

A school is defined by its curriculum, by the classroom and other educational experiences that give shape and substance to its mission. For Jewish schools, the curriculum also encompasses much of what ordinarily might be regarded as informal education, as well as issues relating to the school day.

In Orthodox institutions, daily prayer is expected of all students. Depending on grade level, gender, and the precise character of the school, this may take place prior to the start of classes in a room that is used specifically for this purpose or in classrooms—or, for some boys, in synagogues near where they live, or at home. In non-Orthodox schools, there is no preferred pattern, and while school officials usually emphasize the importance of prayer, there is recognition, at times also resignation, that this goal is more of a hope than an expectation, in view of the orientation of many of the students and their parents.

In yeshivas and the parallel schools for girls, the morning hours—and in many boys' schools, part of the afternoon, as well—are reserved exclusively for the Jewish component of the curriculum. This is a clear manifestation of the priority that is assigned to it. The arrangement varies in Orthodox day schools, with the more intensively religious adhering in a general way to the yeshiva pattern, albeit with fewer hours for the religious subjects. In other Orthodox day schools, the tendency is to intersperse religious and secular subjects throughout the day, an arrangement that arises to some extent from the necessity to make maximum use of the faculty. In non-Orthodox schools, Jewish subjects constitute a relatively small proportion of the curriculum, as priority is given to the academic subjects, much the same way that the Catholic schools emphasize secular subjects.

The length of the school day varies according to grade level, gender, and the school's orientation. Classes begin at 8:30 or 9:00 A.M., at times preceded by prayer services and breakfast, and rarely end before 4 p.m. Obviously, even in the Jewish schools in which the religious program is curtailed, the school day is usually a good deal longer than it is in nearly all non-Jewish schools.

In boys' yeshivas, the day can be remarkably long, especially for the upper elementary school grades and above, where classes can extend past 6 p.m.[6] Beginning with the fifth grade, yeshiva students are expected to be in school at least one evening a week, usually Thursday, for a program of self-study in religious subjects. As the yeshiva world has veered toward ever more rigorous standards of religiosity and more intensive Jewish education, the school day has been lengthened. Apart from its immediate educational implications, this development has resulted in a narrowing of the prospect that students will have an opportunity to be confronted by outside secular influences.

Sunday classes are another distinguishing feature in the world of Jewish schools. All yeshivas are open on Sunday, usually with a somewhat curtailed school day since secular subjects are not scheduled. In the parallel girls' schools, Sunday classes depend on the grade level, so that the younger students generally are not in school on that day. Few day schools operate on Sunday, although in the religious tug that many of them experience, there are parents who push for more religious intensity, including Sunday classes, while the majority contend that Sundays should remain a family day.

There is, as might be expected, substantial variation in the implementation of the Jewish curriculum, although there is a fair degree of homogeneity in the lower grades. For the youngest students, the emphasis is on basic skills, such as learning to read and write Hebrew, the essentials of prayer, Bible study, and knowledge of the holidays and relevant observances. In the more intensive girls' schools, this is the general pattern throughout, with history, Jewish thought, and the intensive study of religious texts figuring more and more prominently as the grade level rises.

By the fourth or fifth grade in the yeshivas, the study of the Talmud emerges as the main subject, and by high school it is nearly all that is taught. Accordingly, at a certain point in Jewish education, academic status for boys is determined almost exclusively by progress in a single subject, one that is commonly regarded as arcane. More than a few students fail to master the logic and the language of the Talmud.

The Talmudic orientation of yeshivas is rooted in the religious education system that prevailed in Europe, where formal education was far more selective than it now is. Educators and parents alike agree that this is an aspect of contemporary Jewish education that is most problematic, since the failure to succeed in Talmudic study often severely undermines a student's self-confidence, and such discouragement may offset much of what the schools hope to accomplish through their efforts at religious socialization.

Talmudic study is not an option in the intensively religious girls' schools, for reasons that arise out of a very long tradition. In day schools, especially in the New York area, the picture is diverse, and while many of these institutions now offer some form of Talmud study for girls, it is usually quite curtailed. However, the issue of Talmudic study for women generally has become a rallying point for Orthodox Jewish feminists, and a growing number of schools, particularly girls' high schools, now emphasize it in their curriculum.

The religious education provided in Orthodox schools is, as a rule, classroom centered, consisting of lessons and lectures and much discussion. It is also exceptionally text driven, as students are taught to understand the range of ever more difficult or intricate commentaries on the principal texts. In yeshiva high schools, for instance, students are expected to prepare for their Talmud lectures by studying the text in advance.

The intellectual rigor demanded of yeshiva students is quite high, certainly above what is required of students of comparable age in other schools. It may well be that the strongest Jewish high schools are at the intellectual level of fairly intensive higher education. It also may be that the strain of looking at religious texts for many hours accounts for the prevalence of eyeglasses among religious Jewish students. Of course, genetic factors may also play a role.[7]

There are interesting variations in the language employed for Judaic instruction. Hebrew is always a factor, if only because prayer books and other essential texts are in that language. However, except in some day schools, it is not used as the primary language for lectures and class discussions. The schools that stress spoken Hebrew tend to prefer the Sephardic dialect that is accepted in Israel and not the Ashkenazic or Western dialect, a choice that narrows the pool of available faculty.

There was a time when yeshivas used to employ Yiddish quite a bit, and Chassidic institutions still do. But once the Talmud is introduced, the strong inclination is to revert to English, as educators recognize that the subject matter is sufficiently difficult without the additional encumbrance of a language that is not readily spoken by most students.[8] In girls' schools, the usual pattern is for English to be interspersed with Hebrew, again with the exception of Chassidic institutions, where Yiddish is usually predominant.

Secular education in yeshivas and most day schools is powerfully affected by two constraints. The first is the concentration on Jewish subjects, a factor which severely limits the hours available for any other instruction or programming. The second restraint is financial, which at the least limits the variety of the secular academic program. Essentially, Jewish schools strive to meet the basic requirements established under state law and regulation.

There are exceptions, primarily in the large day schools, such as Ramaz in Manhattan and the Yeshiva of Flatbush in Brooklyn, both Modern Orthodox institutions that cater to a relatively affluent clientele. In the main, even at the high school level, there are few electives and extracurricular activities are primitive. Auxiliary educational facilities, such as gyms and libraries, pale when compared with what is available elsewhere. In short, secular education in Jewish schools is a straightforward classroom experience of lectures and discussion, some homework and exams.

Just the same, in nearly all schools, at the elementary school level the secular academic program is serious business. Much is accomplished in the space of the several hours that is allotted for secular instruction. This is true, as well, of secular education at the high school level in the modern day schools and in most of the girls' schools. In the boys' yeshivas, the high school years bring an intensification of the religious studies program, with students who want to shine tending to devote nearly all of their creativity and spare time to this effort. Inevitably, there is a relaxing of the commitment to secular education. Yet, most of the yeshiva high schools make serious demands on their students and the New York Regents' standards and examinations are maintained.

For all of their emphasis on scholastic excellence, Jewish schools cannot escape the impact of what seems to be the explosion in the number of special students who need a level of attention that cannot be provided in a crowded classroom. Many schools attempt to address this problem, although the meager resources at their disposal inevitably result in a limited range of activities. The typical approach is a resource room for this purpose, usually staffed by one or two teachers. Some schools have more developed remediation programs.

Despite their strong religious orientation, there is a distinct separation between the religious and secular components of the program, with the latter being taught without any effort to introduce religious elements. While school officials are careful not to let the secular program counter the religious mission, they do not regard it as a tool for religious training.

Administration and Faculty

When we speak of Jewish day school educators, except in the most modern institutions the reference is always to the religious educators. Their role is an integral aspect of the predominantly religious curriculum. Whatever their secular educational attainments, these administrators and the Judaic faculty are not regarded as outside staff members who have been hired to teach or to direct programs. They are of the community that is being served by the schools, people who themselves are quite Orthodox and who share the mission that the institution professes to pursue. Their service as Jewish educators is at once a religious and professional commitment. If the educational head of a yeshiva or Orthodox day school is a man, as most often is the case, he is likely to be an ordained rabbi, someone whose career has veered toward religious education rather than service as a pulpit rabbi. There are Orthodox girls' schools that prefer to have an Orthodox woman as principal, not out of any feminist concern but because they believe it to be more appropriate.

As is true almost everywhere in elementary and secondary education, principals have risen in the ranks, having started out as classroom teachers.[9] There are several programs, mainly of recent origin, which train Jewish school principals, both those on the job and aspirants. This is an outgrowth of the widespread view that the talent pool is limited and too many of the occupants of these positions do not have the requisite skills or knowledge for effective leadership. While modern day schools require that their top educational leaders be university educated, there is no licensing arrangement for Jewish school principals. Rabbinical ordination and usually some background as an educator are generally regarded as sufficient credentials in Orthodox schools, although there are principals who voluntarily seek advanced degrees in education. Salaries paid to Jewish principals have risen rapidly in recent years, not infrequently surpassing what is being paid to the principals of the invariably much larger public schools in the same communities. However, other benefits—pensions, for example—lag behind the public sector.

Except in some loose or informal sense, Jewish principals do not have tenure. Unless they have a proprietary stake in the institution, as some do, their jobs are always on the line. The smallness of the schools, the intensive scrutiny of tuition-paying parents who tend to see the school through the prism of their children's success and happiness, and, at times, the interference of lay officers and directors—all can combine to create a difficult atmosphere for the principal.

As noted, the religious faculty of yeshivas and most day schools are rabbis, men who were trained in rabbinical seminaries in advanced Talmudic subjects and not directly for teaching careers. This training ensures subject matter mastery, but too often leaves these teachers, at least early in their careers, with shortcomings as educators. To an extent, what they lack is compensated for by their remarkable enthusiasm and commitment and increasingly by the expanding array of courses available to religious faculty who want to upgrade their skills. Because of the attractiveness of the New York area as the center of Orthodox life, schools seeking to recruit faculty do not have to worry about a scarcity of applicants, although the lower grades are usually problematic, since graduates of rabbinical seminaries almost invariably aspire to teach at a higher level.

Salaries, even at the higher-paying schools, are low by public school standards, generally not above $40,000 a year. There is also an old, if not honorable, yeshiva practice of not paying on time. And the benefits package is not generous.[10] In a word, the life of these educators is one of constant financial stress, as their teaching income does not provide for even a subsistence existence. The younger, American-born educators in particular have large families and they also encounter the additional costs entailed by an Orthodox lifestyle. As a consequence, many have second or even third jobs and/or depend on parental support, perhaps also on governmental benefits.

As with the principals, tenure for Jewish faculty is not formalized, although in yeshivas it is generally accepted that a rabbi or religious studies teacher who has been retained for three years has rights akin to tenure and can be dismissed only for cause and with severance pay. There is no retirement policy or common retirement age, such as prevails in New York City's public schools. The tendency in yeshivas is for the religious teachers to stay on as long as they can, an inclination that can result in painful conflict as school officials seek to compel the retirement of an educator whom they believe is no longer effective.

Religious educators in women's schools fare even worse financially. Since Orthodox schools tend to charge relatively low tuition and have generous scholarship policies, they must rely on contributions to meet their obligations. For historic and social reasons, the girls' schools are far less able to attract philanthropic support than the yeshivas. In girls' schools the pay scale can dip below $10,000 a year. Many of these teachers are young women who are recent seminary graduates and are unlikely to make teaching a permanent career. As yet, they do not have family responsibilities, and though this does not justify how little they earn, it provides a context for understanding their situation. In fact, despite the very low salaries, each opening attracts a swarm of applicants.

Whatever these teachers may lack in training or perhaps in subject matter skill is often compensated for by their dedication and by the extraordinary effort they make and the extra hours that they throw into their work. The girls' schools also have cadres of more veteran, better-paid teachers. Especially at the high school level, there is a reliance on adjuncts who are expert in particular subjects and teach at a number of schools. The pattern is quite varied in the coeducational day schools. Some hire rabbis to teach religious subjects, others rely on young women seminary graduates, and still others—usually the most affluent and/or most modern institutions—seek teachers who are trained and expert in the subjects they teach. They want faculty with licenses and standard credentials, beginning with the preschool faculty.

While day school salaries invariably lag behind what is paid in the public sector and stronger private schools, there are notable exceptions, such as Ramaz and the Heschel School in Manhattan and the Yeshiva of Flatbush in Brooklyn. These schools charge far above the standard yeshiva and day school tuition and offer salaries that are in the range of what is paid at the stronger private schools. In the financially stronger day schools, the secular studies faculty members are paid on a par with the religious faculty.

Elsewhere in yeshivas and day schools, the secular studies faculty comes from any of a number of sources. These include retired or moonlighting public school teachers, Jewish studies teachers who have some competency in general subjects, young women who are seminary graduates, and, on occasion, whomever the school can get to fill in. The salaries for these teachers are usually below what the religious faculty earns. But schools are under pressure from parents to do a credible job in educating students in the key secular education areas and this at times forces them to pay more to recruit teachers who have the requisite knowledge and skill. Unlike their Catholic school counterparts, teachers in Jewish schools are not unionized, nor have there been any serious efforts to form a union for them. In some schools, faculty committees negotiate with the administration and lay leaders on behalf of the faculty.

School Governance and Lay Leadership

In contemporary religious life, particularly in what may be loosely termed fundamentalist groups, key institutions such as the church and school are at times considered to be the property of the persons who established or who now lead them. However, inasmuch as such institutions are also entrepreneurial in nature, lay officers and directors are not the ultimate authority with respect to corporate matters or academic programs. In Jewish schools, entrepreneurship is most pronounced in the most Orthodox sector, where lay leaders may be no more than figureheads or people who are expected to help raise money and ensure that the bills are paid, without in any way being involved in the ongoing life of the institution.

In less orthodox schools, lay involvement is far more significant. In nearly all day schools and in a fair number of yeshivas, voluntary officials have the authority to hire and fire, set tuition and scholarship policy, decide on corporate matters, and make financial decisions that directly affect the academic program. As is well known, voluntarism has declined sharply in the nonprofit world, and Jewish schools are no exception. Where there are functioning lay boards and officers, the tendency is for these people to come from the parents, a development that can result in a more intensive and giving commitment to the school. But it also inevitably results in authority being vested in people whose view of the school is formed by how it serves them and their families, not the larger community. Lay interference in educational policy and administration is not unknown to Jewish day schools.

There are schools with education committees that advise the principal and have some authority to shape the educational program. Where there is a cooperative spirit between principal and committee, the arrangement often results in educational improvements. Otherwise, it is apt to be the catalyst for ongoing conflict.

Each Jewish school is a separate entity, corporately and educationally, and there is no outside body that has the authority to determine how any of the schools operate, in the way that Catholic dioceses exercise authority over the schools in their catchment areas. Overwhelmingly, Jewish schools in New York are affiliated in some fashion with the National Society of Hebrew Day Schools (Torah Umesorah), an agency that provides an array of services, including publications and curriculum material, in-service training, and staff recruitment.

Because almost all of the schools are Orthodox, whatever ideological or educational elements may distinguish them, their educational and lay leaders share a fundamental commitment to Halacha, the comprehensive system of Jewish law that impacts constantly on the lives of religious Jews. The major issues that arise in Jewish schools often involve the application of religious law. The usual practice is to seek the guidance or ruling of respected religious figures who are not directly involved in the institution.

Finances

There is scarcely a school anywhere, public or private, for which finances are not a constant concern. Public schools whose budgets are met through governmental outlays fret over unanticipated expenses, cutbacks, rising costs, capital needs, and a good deal else with a dollar sign attached to it. For all of the real pressure public schools face, their lot is easier than what confronts most nonpublic schools. These schools often operate at a more fundamental level of economic stress as they attempt to meet payroll and other pressing obligations and wonder whether they will be able to survive.

This is the situation of a great number of Jewish schools in New York. There are relatively affluent institutions, but for the large majority of schools urgent financial pressure is a permanent condition. The dual academic program and the small size of the schools combine to create a sharp imbalance between tuition income and expenditures. There are piles of unpaid bills and, far too often, late payment of salaries, cutbacks, and a hand-to-mouth existence that can dominate the attention and energy of the school leadership, educational and lay, and undermine their ability to fulfill their mission.

It needs to be underscored that this bleak description pertains to the basic educational obligations, rather than to budgeting for extras beyond the reach of the school, even if from an educational standpoint they are sorely needed. With some exceptions, Jewish schools are badly underfunded. In staff, auxiliary and supplementary educational programs, supplies, facilities, extracurricular activities, and anything else pertinent to the operations of an educational institution, they anticipate financial shortfalls by not doing what other schools often take for granted.[11]

While school officials have a good intuitive sense of what it costs to operate, in most instances the budget is an ad hoc arrangement rather than a carefully crafted document prepared in advance of the school year. Adjustments are made as the year progresses and officials get a sense of how they are faring with tuition collection and fundraising. On the income side, the bulk comes from tuition—which seems to be an obvious point to make with respect to private institutions. In fact, this was not always the case. For much of this century, when there were fewer Jewish schools and most parents could not afford to pay for their children's religious schooling, contributions played a more significant role than they now do. As budgets have risen, so have tuition charges, not only in absolute dollar terms, but perhaps more importantly, as a percentage of the budget. This reflects, to an extent, the relatively greater affluence of parents and, even more, the commonly held view that there is no other reliable source of income and that without parents' carrying the lion's share of the burden, it is impossible to remain open. In a typical yeshiva or day school, tuition accounts for about two-thirds of the budget, with the figure rising to 90 percent or more in the most affluent schools and in those that are not Orthodox.

It is difficult to generalize about the range of tuition charges, since at one end of the spectrum—in certain outreach schools or those for immigrant students—it is not much above zero and in some schools the per capita charge is above $10,000 a year. In most institutions, the range is roughly $4,000 to $6,000, with most schools tacking on additional mandatory fees and charges that can add $1,000 to the tuition bill. What is charged and what is paid often are two separate matters, depending on the orientation of the institution. The most Orthodox schools continue to abide by the old religious Jewish tradition that schooling for the young is a communal responsibility and that special concern must be shown toward needy families. This consideration is especially acute in view of the increased size of Orthodox families—six or more children are common—and with the obvious pressure faced by parents who cannot afford the posted charges.

The instinct to be solicitous has been challenged by financial reality, as schools and their officials recognize or believe that unless they are tougher, some parents will take advantage and, more importantly, sufficient funds will not be available to continue to operate. As a result, there is a constant struggle between the school and many parents and a good deal of anguish, to boot, with institutions imposing a minimum tuition—at times $3,000 per student—irrespective of the parents' financial situation. Just the same, yeshivas continue to be relatively liberal in their scholarship policy, deciding each family's need without reference to how much scholarship money is being allocated to other families. On the other hand, scholarship policy in day schools is more in line with what occurs at other private educational institutions, with a specified sum being set aside for financial aid. Parents who apply for aid are in competition against each other. Obviously, in day schools financial aid is far harder to come by.[12]

Like other parochial schools in New York, Jewish schools receive no more than a trickle of government funding, although Chassidic schools in particular may participate in public programs that benefit economically disadvantaged families.[13] Endowments are also a negligible source of income for most schools, since their penurious existence scarcely allows them to indulge in long-term financial planning. This leaves voluntary contributions as a necessary source of funds to close the budgetary gap. Fundraising in Jewish schools is not a discrete activity conducted apart from the academic program. As an inescapable consequence of their small size and staff, Jewish schools bring fundraising onto center stage, involv-

ing the key personnel and occupying a good deal of the attention and resources of school officials, lay and educational. In some fashion, fundraising, at times in combination with personal loans from parents or friends of
the institution, closes the gap, allowing schools to continue to operate at an
underfunded, nearly subsistence level.

Fundraising for Jewish schools is not philanthropy writ large, involving gifts from large foundations and respected communal figures. It is an
intimate process that encompasses in the main a school's community—
parents, alumni, neighbors, and others who have an association with the
institution. While efforts are made at times to attract outside support,
fundraising success is essentially dependent on the giving of those who already are involved. With rare exceptions, New York schools do not receive
meaningful financial support from the Jewish philanthropic sector. This
has to do in part with the antipathy toward day school education evinced
for decades by wealthy, assimilated Jews. Yet even with the greater receptivity in secular Jewish circles toward day schools, New York poses a special challenge because of the exceptionally large number of elementary and
secondary schools. Whatever the reasons, Jewish schools are the stepchil-
dren of Jewish philanthropy.

On the expense side, not surprisingly, salaries—for educators, not auxiliary staff—constitute nearly the entire budget, in some schools accounting for as much as 90 percent. Other needs and services are stinted, as is
evident in building maintenance and improvement, books and supplies,
and the small, often besieged, office staffs.

Facilities

While schools everywhere are pinched in their operating budgets, their
subsistence existence is not necessarily evident in the facilities that are
available for their use. Catholic schools, for example, operate on little more
than a shoestring as compared with the per student cost in public schools,
but their facilities are usually well maintained and attractive.

Jewish schools—and here New York is worse than elsewhere—have
the distinction of being badly underfunded and of being housed in facilities that too often range from the inadequate to the disgraceful, providing
depressing testimony about the priorities of Jewish philanthropy. Of the
approximately 250 schools in the New York City area, it can be safely estimated that half are not properly housed and some are in spaces that
scarcely resemble what ordinarily would be regarded as a school. The near
squalor of too many of New York's Jewish schools is a stain on the record
of the Jewish community.

Apart from this doleful situation, the city's Jewish schools—notably in
Brooklyn where far more than half of the students are enrolled—are fac-

ing a space squeeze that is approaching crisis proportions, and it is certain to get worse, at least in the near term. Most of the schools are operating at or near capacity, capacity being defined as how many students can be squeezed in and not how many seats the school should fill under optimum educational conditions. In the lower grades, starting with preschool, applicants are being turned away in droves, and it is not uncommon for new admissions to be limited to young children who have siblings in the school.

The city itself is a prime factor in this situation, since in most neighborhoods—and certainly where the Orthodox live in concentrated numbers—there is a space shortage, with little vacant land for development and few buildings that can readily be converted into school use. Jewish schools may be housed in makeshift facilities, including congregational buildings. Also pressed into service are former public school buildings, walk-up tenements, storefronts, loft buildings, private homes, and whatever else might be available and can hold classrooms and an office or two, these being the basic and, at times, only facilities needed to open the doors and admit students.

There are bright spots in this gloomy profile. Curiously, they occur at the poles of the religious spectrum. Non-Orthodox and Modern Orthodox schools tend to invest in the development of attractive facilities. Since their budgetary shortfalls are small, as almost all of the necessary income is raised through tuition payments, their fundraising efforts generally focus on building campaigns. They must pay careful attention to the quality of their facilities because they are under pressure to meet the expectations of parents who are comparison shoppers. Parents know what is available at the nearby public and private schools and do not believe that it is their inescapable religious obligation to send their children to schools housed in what they regard as inadequate facilities.

At the other end of the spectrum, Chassidic schools have shown a flair for creativity, at times aesthetic creativity, in developing facilities for their ever-expanding school-age population. Necessity is, of course, the mother of their invention, yet it is to their credit that they have risen to the challenge and established, at times, attractive facilities. While other yeshivas and most day schools have lagged behind, there is evidence of a greater alertness about the negative consequences of relying on buildings that are terribly overcrowded and do not have either the ambience or the attributes of a school. Expansion plans have been announced by a number of institutions and others are considering how best to proceed.

An Assessment

In view of their core religious mission, the accomplishment of the goal of promoting enduring Judaic commitment is for the schools and the communities that sponsor them the primary determinant of success. While the accomplishment of this mission cannot be downplayed, it remains true that these are all educational institutions in which students spend long hours studying Jewish and secular subjects. How well they do in this regard must be part of the accounting. Elementary and secondary schools are also society's instruments for preparing young people for productive lives, for the ability to respect civic virtues and to advance the general welfare through their careers and personal lives. This dimension is also part of the reckoning.

What we know, impressionistically and indirectly from survey research, about the fulfillment of their religious mission is that for much of this century, yeshivas and day schools were more successful in inculcating an enduring sense of Jewish identity and commitment than any other mode of Jewish education. Yet, they were not able to guarantee protection against the strong forces of assimilation that impelled so many American Jews away from even identifying as Jews. The 1990 National Jewish Population Survey points to a strong movement away from Orthodoxy, including among day school attendees, in the Jewish population.

But this data essentially reflects developments that occurred much earlier in this century when Orthodoxy was generally feeble and certainly not as confident as it now is. Even in the earlier period, day school graduates were far more faithful to Jewish tradition than other American Jews. In the recent period, the degree of Judaic retention among those who have attended yeshiva and day school has risen sharply, although because of the newness of many non-Orthodox schools and their small number of graduates, it is difficult to reach as yet any conclusion regarding their alumni.

It is also true that while yeshivas and day schools seem to be succeeding in their religious mission, other factors are clearly at work as well, since nearly all of the associations experienced by yeshiva and day school students conform to the expected religious pattern. Accordingly, it might be the case that Jewish schools are most effective in their reinforcement role, rather than in any widespread ability to inculcate Jewish commitment in families in which there is a less religious lifestyle. It is important to note, however, that factor analysis based on the 1990 data indicate that as an independent variable, yeshiva and day school education has been effective.[14]

As for religious educational outcomes, schools have succeeded in creating a new generation of knowledgeable Jewish youth and in providing talented cadres of graduates who enter community service, often as educators. This is a critical achievement that surpasses what most other parochial schools are able to accomplish. However, this record is tarnished somewhat by the inability of Jewish schools, notably those for boys, to create an educational alternative for students who are not adept in the ordinary subjects taught in the religious program. The drop-out rate for older boys is worrisome, even though it does not approach what has been reported for non-Jewish schools.

Secular instruction is inevitably impacted by the curtailment of hours and educational options, including electives and supplementary programs for special and gifted students, and, more broadly, by the severe financial pressures that constantly confront most Jewish schools. The result often is an academic program that looks primitive when it is compared to what is available elsewhere. But there is also evidence that students do well academically. New York State has an abundance of statistics on how nonpublic school students perform on standard tests, but the reliability of the data is brought into question because the criteria under which they are derived may, for some tests, be more lax in private and religious schools than they are in public schools. This issue has generated controversy. The *New York Times* has reported that "now that New York has enacted new standards intended to improve learning in public school classrooms, the Education Department and the Board of Regents are increasing their resolve to have private and public schools follow suit." Carl Hayden, the chancellor of the Board of Regents, was quoted as saying, "One of the things that discussions can expose is the myth of high performance among some of the private schools."[15]

Under New York's Pupil Evaluation Program, which was in operation until the 1997–98 school year, elementary school students in all schools were required to take a series of standard tests. Reading and mathematics were tested in grades three and six, writing in grade five, science in grade four, and social studies in grades six and eight. Table 11.1 presents results for 1996–97, the most recent year for which statistics are available, for the tests in reading, writing, and mathematics given in grades three, five, and six. These have long been regarded as the core subjects—they are the legendary three R's—which students are expected to master in their formative elementary school years.

In constructing this table, Jewish schools were grouped into six categories, ranging from the non-Orthodox to the Chassidic. In broad terms, the expectation was that there would be a falling off in achievement along the continuum, as the most Orthodox schools devote only a relatively small proportion of their resources and the school day to secular subjects. Within each group, four to six schools were randomly selected, for a total of thirty schools. About 3,500 students were tested, constituting nearly the entire enrollment in the three grades in these schools.

These results must be interpreted with some caution. The SRP (Standard Reference Point) is best viewed as a minimum passing grade, below which students must be provided with remedial instruction. All that is being reported is how many of the students who were enrolled in these grades took the required examinations and how many scored above what is referred to as the Standard Reference Point for each test. In fact, about 99 percent of the enrollees took the test, so that the results include the performance of weaker students. From the statistics made available by the New York State Education Department, it is not possible to know what the range was for the large majority of the students who performed above the SRP.

TABLE 11.1 Performance of Jewish Elementary School Students on New York Standard Achievement Tests, 1996–1997

Type of School	Non-Orthodox	Modern Orthodox	Centrist Orthodox	Immigrant	Yeshiva World	Chassidic
No. of schools	4	6	5	4	5	6
Grade 3. Reading						
No. of students	133	227	174	136	217	302
No. above SRP[a]	126	196	154	92	168	196
% above SRP	95	86	89	68	77	65
Grade 3. Math						
No. of students	132	231	172	133	219	311
No. above SRP	132	225	164	130	212	239
% above SRP	100	97	95	98	97	77
Grade 5. Writing						
No. of students	146	193	142	143	216	330
No. above SRP	132	176	117	108	198	280
% above SRP	90	91	82	76	92	85
Grade 6. Reading						
No. of students	101	194	163	146	209	255
No. above SRP	91	176	147	99	169	154
% above SRP	90	91	90	68	81	60
Grade 6. Math						
No. of students	101	194	161	148	207	255
No. above SRP	100	193	156	135	196	213
% above SRP	99	99	97	91	95	84

Source: New York State Education Department.
[a]SRP refers to the Standard Reference Point, below which students are required to receive remediation.

We do not know how many just got by and how many students did considerably better.

In the aggregate, the Jewish students did quite well. As was expected, those in the non-Orthodox and modern and centrist sectors of Orthodoxy did considerably better than those in the other three groups. Overall, the math results are extremely impressive. The same cannot be said about how students in the three weaker categories performed on the reading and writing tests.

Several factors need to be taken into account in considering academic performance in the immigrant, yeshiva world and Chassidic schools. As a rule, they are not selective in their admission policies, the inevitable result being that they accept weaker students. Also, many of their students come from homes in which English is not the primary language. As has been underscored, these schools operate in a constant state of financial distress and, among much else, they do not have funds for tutors, science labs, and other educational accoutrements that are routine in most schools. Finally, the dual education program means that relatively few hours are devoted to secular instruction.

Under the totality of circumstances, yeshiva and day school students do well on mandatory standard tests, including for those who take them, on the Regents examinations given to high school students. The strong performance of students in Jewish schools, at times in the face of powerful negative factors, may be attributed to the intellectual and study skills that are developed in the course of a rigorous academic career. When we evaluate these schools in the context of the resources at their disposal, it is fair to conclude that they have compiled an impressive record.

NOTES

1. Marvin Schick, "A Census of Jewish Day Schools in the United States," Avi Chai Foundation, January 2000. The scholarly literature on yeshivas and day schools is extremely sparse and there are huge information gaps. Perhaps the best study is William C. Helmreich's *The World of Yeshivas* (New Haven: Yale University Press, 1986) which is already dated and focuses, in the main, on advanced yeshivas, beyond the secondary school level.

2. Many of the non-Orthodox who believed that some form of religious instruction was necessary opted for after-school programs that were originally called Talmud Torahs. Typically, these were three-times-a-week experiences—two afternoons and Sunday morning—although the prevalent mode in Reform circles was the once-a-week Sunday school. While a considerable number of these programs continue to operate, their enrollment has declined, in large measure because of the consequences of advanced assimilation and also because of the growing receptivity toward day schools.

3. The question of whether Jewish schools are succeeding in their religious mission is considered at the end of this chapter. It is also rather tricky, because yeshiva students overwhelmingly come from homes that are quite observant and their primary and secondary associations outside of the school conform with this religious outlook. It is difficult to say how much the school contributes to the commitment to a religious lifestyle. Overall, however, yeshivas are now succeeding in attaining their religious goals, certainly to a considerably greater extent than was true of the first two-thirds of the century. As for day schools, much depends on their particular orientation. The evidence suggests that students who are enrolled through the elementary school years, and certainly into high school, are far more likely to maintain their religious commitment.

4. There is a sharp debate among Jews of different religiosity as to "who is a

Jew," with the non-Orthodox—and especially the Reform—accepting a far more lenient definition. This has an obvious bearing on the admission policy of certain day schools, but it is hardly a factor in New York.

5. While preschool programs offered by day schools vary, few have nursery programs and many, perhaps most, utilize the terminology preferred by public schools, so that kindergarten is the year immediately before the first grade.

6. As a boy, I traveled six days a week by subway from my home in Borough Park in Brooklyn to the Rabbi Jacob Joseph School on the Lower East Side. Except for Fridays, the school day extended until 6 P.M., including on Sundays. Early in the school's history, the school day had extended until 7 P.M.

7. I am not aware of any studies of this interesting subject.

8. This reflects, as well, a change in the teaching pool away from European-born and educated faculty. These were the main Talmud teachers in yeshivas for a generation after the Holocaust. Many have been succeeded by American-born Orthodox men whose primary language is English.

9. In large yeshivas with comprehensive programs ranging from preschool through high school and perhaps beyond, the highest education administrator may be called "dean." In the modern day schools where there is a proclivity to borrow from upscale private schools, "headmaster" or just "head of school" is the preferred title.

10. For yeshiva and day school educators in the New York metropolitan area, the Gruss Foundation provides a creative array of benefits, including life insurance, disability, some medical coverage, and pension contributions.

11. "The Financing of Jewish Day Schools" by Marvin Schick and Jeremy Dauber (Rabbi Jacob Joseph School, 1997) is the most comprehensive survey of the subject.

12. While few Orthodox families forgo sending their children to a yeshiva or day school because of financial constraints, it is widely believed that tuition charges are an important consideration for the marginally Orthodox and certainly for the non-Orthodox.

13. For more than a generation, Orthodox Jews have supported government aid for parochial schools, a position that is not shared by the great majority of American Jews. Major Jewish organizations have long been in the forefront of the battle against governmental aid, including any voucher arrangement. The posture of organized American Jewry has changed very little despite the growing number of non-Orthodox who are inclined toward a day school education.

14. See, for example, the monograph "Jewish Involvement of the Baby Boom Generation" by Mordechai Rimor and Elihu Katz (Louis Guttman Israel Institute of Applied Social Research, 1993).

15. *New York Times*, December 26, 1998, p. B1.

12   Historically Black Independent Schools

GAIL FOSTER

African Americans have always believed that education is the key to gaining a foothold in the American mainstream. Consequently, they want their children taught by teachers who expect them to graduate, go to college, and get good jobs. Like most other Americans, African American parents, regardless of income level, want schools that will provide their children with high academic standards, high expectations, discipline, and an affirmation of their identity. The story of historically black independent (HBI) schools is the story of parents who were denied good schools by the public system and who joined with black educators and churches to create the schools they desired.

As the school desegregation and civil rights movement of the fifties moved north in the sixties and early seventies, blacks in New York City had expectations that their children would finally be able to attend the better (and predominantly white) public schools in the city. They even hoped that they would finally control the school boards that governed the low-quality, segregated schools in their own neighborhoods. Frustration with the continuing circumstances led some African American educators and churches to open their own schools, and rekindle an independent school movement that had begun during the early 1800s. While educators today debate ways to make the current system work, African American parents have been voting with their feet, enrolling their children in a range of black-financed and black-operated independent schools, both nationally and in New York City.

Today there are close to four hundred schools nationally that were created by African Americans, enrolling some fifty-two thousand African American students.[1] The Toussaint Institute Fund, which for the last eleven years has been collecting data on HBI schools in New York and New Jersey and on boarding schools around the country, has documented seventy HBI schools in New York City serving approximately twelve thousand students, almost all at the elementary level, though most also have intermediate school programs. While HBI schools still enroll only a small number of African American students, their long presence suggests both the vitality of the tradition of educational entrepreneurship among African Americans and a widespread and deeply felt distress over the quality of the public school system. Further, many view HBI schools as models of the type of curriculum and pedagogy—infused with community values, culture, and expectations for children—that should be a fundamental part of any school reform effort.

Though they operate on limited budgets and often survive without the materials and facilities they need, the great strength of the HBI schools is that they are small, intimate environments—families, which parents believe have the capacity to nurture African American youngsters, academically, culturally, and—whether they are secular or sectarian—spiritually. My research suggests that HBI students outperform students in public schools on standardized tests.

This chapter serves as an introduction to historically black independent schools and their current role in educating African American students. It is based on data collected over the past eleven years from many sources, including site visits, in-depth interviews with HBI teachers and administrators, and reports about children enrolled in HBI schools through the Toussaint Institute Fund. For this essay I have drawn extensively on my experience as president of the Toussaint Institute and my interviews with many of these parents over the years. Toussaint is an organization that helps parents find good schools in the public and private sector. Since 1988 it has had contact with thousands of black parents each year as they turn to it in search of school referrals. The goal of this chapter is to expand the knowledge base on HBI schools, generate further interest in these unique American institutions, and further the longstanding mission of HBI schools to give African American children the best possible education.

HBI School Origins

African Americans have never been satisfied with a second-rate education. Whenever possible, at cost of life or scarce financial resources, blacks have sought to circumvent the established order of the day which set limits on what their children could learn. Historically, Africans in America (and later, after citizenship was granted, African Americans) opened independent schools in response to unsuccessful attempts to either integrate segregated schools, or gain influence over the policy, curriculum, and instruction at schools operated for them by European Americans.[2] In many ways the same is true today, as growing numbers of African American parents, educators, and churches search urgently for options. This is especially true for those living in America's inner cities.

Academic expectations have long been an issue. In his *Black Education in New York State*, Carleton Mabee notes that in the early nineteenth century black parents complained that white teachers did not expect enough of black students in the private schools operated by white religious and benevolent societies.[3] Many parents waged boycotts to protest the lack of black teachers in the public schools.[4] Others responded by starting their own schools. In 1815, Peter Cruger, a free African, opened the African School in his home in Brooklyn; it was the earliest weekday HBI school on record in New York State.[5]

In the 1830s and 1840s, frustrated by their inability to gain seats on segregated school boards run by white benevolent societies, Africans established charitable societies of their own for the purposes of setting up private schools. Among these were the African Woolman Benevolent Society, the Phoenix Society (founded with the assistance of whites), and the Society for the Promotion of Education among Colored Children.[6] Founding mainly elementary schools, these groups also created some private high schools, since their white counterparts would fund only elementary schools for blacks.[7]

Others, however, attempted to secure quality educations for their children by challenging the system to change. By the early 1800s the school system began to respond to black protests by hiring more black teachers. Between the first and last decades of the nineteenth century, the proportion of black teachers in black schools in New York State rose from 33 percent to 76 percent.[8] Still, as Carter G. Woodson's *Mis-education of the Negro* indicates, the textbooks and attitudes at white-run schools for blacks reinforced the perception of African Americans as second-class citizens.[9] By the 1850s, African Americans attended a mix of white-run and black-run segregated private schools. The Brooklyn superintendent of schools stated that the children in black schools compared favorably with children in corresponding classes in the other schools.[10]

The spread of public schools and later desegregation in the United States was a mixed blessing for African Americans throughout the country. While increasing educational opportunities, it often placed black students in hostile environments, eliminated black educators from the lives of black students, and challenged HBI schools for enrollments.

In the 1960s and early 1970s there was a renaissance in HBI schools, fueled by the Ocean Hill–Brownsville struggle for community control of local school boards, a movement led by African American educators and parents in Brooklyn with collaborative efforts in Lower Manhattan and

Harlem.[11] Frustrated with their efforts to improve public schools, participants formed an independent school in 1969 called Uhura Sasa Shule
(Kiswahili for "Freedom Now School"). Direct control allowed the educators and parents to create what many felt was a model school, with committed teachers, African American role models, high expectations, and an
emphasis on culture and community values. At one point, it enrolled as
many as five hundred students. Another seven or eight schools were
founded as offspring of Uhura Sasa. During the mid-1970s, these schools
collectively became known as the Brooklyn Family Schools. Founded on
what would later become known as the seven principles of Kwanzaa, they
had a common philosophy and heritage. The schools were a direct outgrowth of the efforts of the New York African American Teachers Association's initiative for improvement of public schools through community
control. Uhura Sasa closed in 1985, but this wave of "Brooklyn Family"
schools was only the beginning. A recent survey by the Toussaint Institute
indicates that nineteen of the seventy existing schools in New York City
were founded in the 1970s and another twenty-seven in the 1980s.

Today, African American students make up 35.9 percent of the city's
public school population and Latinos comprise 37.5 percent.[12] Most black
students find themselves at public schools with mostly black and Latino
populations. Citywide scores on reading and math tests show gains and
losses from year to year, but in the districts serving the bulk of the city's
African American students, the results are consistently abysmal. The city's
lowest-performing schools, called Schools under Registration Review, are
concentrated in fourteen districts, all of which have black and Latino students in the majority.[13] Against this backdrop, and in the long-standing
black tradition of self-help, black ministers and educators continue to open
and operate HBI schools.

HBI Schools Today

HBI schools are small neighborhood schools. Most families struggle to pay
tuition, and most schools barely survive. A state-of-the-art computer system is rare. Nevertheless, the schools are clean, well tended, and cheerfully
decorated. A tour of a typical school finds the children sitting well postured
at their desks, with uniforms of blue, gray, or green, often made distinctive
with materials from Africa. They usually stand when an adult enters the
room and may greet the person with a unison "good morning"—or in a
few schools its Kiswahili translation "Habara Za Leo."

Some of the seventy HBI schools in New York City are small operations
with little money and only a few students, while others are full-scale academies. HBI school enrollments range from 10 to 485 students. The average
enrollment is 160, with about half having more than 125 students, and of

these, twenty-two having more than 200. Only eight schools have under 50 students. Of the seventy schools, there is only one dedicated high school; all of the others have elementary school programs. Thirty-seven of these have K–8 programs, while another thirteen have K–12 programs. HBI schools are located in every one of the city's boroughs, except Staten Island. Most are in Brooklyn and Queens. Since the early 1800s, Brooklyn has bustled with African American entrepreneurship and leadership in education.[14] HBI schools tend to cluster in those school districts where less than 60 percent of the public school students score on grade level, including seven of the city's eight lowest-performing districts.[15]

Parents indicate class size as a compelling factor in choosing an HBI school. Classes average eighteen students per class, with a reported low of ten students and a high of twenty-eight. Parents with children who have been assigned to special education in the public schools sometimes opt for an HBI school to secure the small class and the needed individual attention without the special education stigma or dead-end prognosis.

HBI schools are tuition-based institutions. Whereas tuition at New York City's elite prep schools averages $15,000 per year,[16] HBI tuitions averaged about $3,000 for the 1997–98 academic year—double that of Catholic schools, but well below the elite schools. (This figure, however, marks a significant increase from the $2,500 average we found in 1992.)[17] City Catholic school tuition ranges from $1,300 to $1,500 per year.[18] In the 1997–98 academic year, HBI tuition ranged from a low of $1,650 to a high of $6,430. Inner city Catholic schools, with their lower tuition, better facilities, and similar emphasis on morality, discipline, and academics, provide stiff competition for the HBI schools. Yet, many low-income parents pool the resources of family members to afford HBI schools. Even for low-middle-income parents, it is a sacrifice to send their children to HBI schools.

Unlike many parochial schools, HBI schools, regardless of affiliation, are not subsidized in any significant way by larger sectarian or even nonsectarian organizations. However, schools affiliated with churches gener-

TABLE 12.1 HBI Schools in New York City

Grades Served		Distribution by Borough	
Grades	Number of Schools Serving	Borough	Number of Schools
K–3	5	Bronx	7
K–5/6	15	Brooklyn	37
K–8	37	Manhattan	11
K–12	12	Queens	15
9–12	1	Staten Island	0

Source: Toussaint Institute Fund.

TABLE 12.2 NYC Historically Black Independent Schools Overview

	High	Low	Mean	Median	Sample Size
Class size	28	10	18	18	69
Enrollment	485	10	163	129	70
Tuition ($)	6,430	1,650	3,000	3,000	68
Years in operation	64	2	23	19	70

Source: Toussaint Institute Fund.

ally have received some subsidy by virtue of using space owned by a church, or even a facility built for it by the church. Beyond this, or an occasional emergency collection taken up for the school, the churches generally expect the schools to fund themselves. Nevertheless, church support is reflected in the lower tuition found among church-affiliated schools compared to secular schools that have leases or mortgages. HBI schools, religious or secular, have virtually no alumni support or estate giving to complement their fundraising initiatives. Unfortunately, the tradition of alumni and estate giving is woefully underdeveloped in the African American community, which otherwise gives generously to the church and its social projects. The schools have no endowment funds, and despite strenuous efforts, virtually no corporate or philanthropic support. As a result, they place most of their emphasis on small school-based fundraising activities. Most HBI schools have no formal financial aid programs. Nevertheless, every year, schools make adjustments for parents who become unemployed, for families in crisis, and for children whom they simply can't bear to return to public school.

Half of the schools sampled stated that their facility was inadequate.[19] Many have outgrown their space, and while they have long waiting lists and a desperate need for additional income, they have nowhere to expand. The difficulty black entrepreneurs have gaining financing holds true for those in the field of education.[20] This initial underfinancing has haunted HBI schools for decades. Yet, since the average HBI school has been in operation for twenty-three years, HBI schools are indeed survivors.

Almost all HBI schools offer after-school and summer tutorial programs. After-school programs frequently offer music lessons, martial arts, and homework help. Summer programs often begin with a few hours of academics in the morning, followed by recreational activities and trips to local parks or museums in the afternoon. Both after-school and summer programs enroll neighborhood children who attend other private and public schools.

New York City public school teachers' salaries start at $29,611 per year.[21] Teachers at HBI schools start as low as $13,000 with no benefits, and they seldom exceed $21,000, although a few schools pay close to $30,000 plus benefits for teachers who have been with them many years. In the more financially insecure schools, teachers are sometimes asked to be patient when the school fails to make payroll. One compensation is that teachers have the advantage of tuition waivers for their own children, and this is the reason that many of them can afford to work for struggling schools.

Principals, who are often the schools' founders, may double as teachers, and stay late discharging administrative tasks with little or no support staff. Since commitment to the school's mission is both a motivating force and a practical necessity, principals look for teachers committed to working long hours, extending through the after-school activities. Moreover, though some schools screen students, many practice open enrollment. Staff commitment is all the more essential considering that these schools are not elitist institutions. In the same classroom may be found gifted, average, and underperforming students who may also have had a history of behavior problems in the public schools. Such a mixture demands a depth of pedagogical skill, compassion, and perseverance.

Parents hold HBI schools accountable. They will not tolerate a teacher who does not have classroom control, or a school that allows bullying among students. This is one of the reasons they left the public schools. They expect the children to be challenged by their teachers and the curriculum, and will organize themselves into assertive pressure groups to challenge the school administration if they feel the students are underperforming on standardized tests, or not being prepared for a rigorous curriculum in their next school. Nevertheless, while it is difficult for schools to attract and keep teachers in some subject areas, such as math and science, many schools report a core group of teachers who have served the schools for years and often view their work as a mission. Schools report that all of their teachers are state certified or working toward it.

Most of the HBI—forty out of seventy—are affiliated with various Christian churches or sects, though a significant number—twenty-four—are secular. "Secular," however, does not mean the absence of spirituality or the mention of God, as it generally does in the mainstream. Prayer and spirituality are found in most secular schools, as is true throughout most aspects of black secular life. The remaining eight religious schools represent the faiths of Islam and indigenous African traditions like Yoruba and Kemet.

Academic Efficacy

Academic performance in both public and private schools should be measured across a range of assessments, including student grades, standardized tests, high school graduation rates, and even student portfolios. Although there are no comprehensive studies measuring academic achievement among HBI students, the Toussaint Institute's research suggests that they outperform their public school peers on standardized tests.

In 1991 I was part of a study team organized by the Institute for Independent Education in Washington, D.C., which gave the first indication of student performance. The team collected the standardized test data for 1989 and 1990 for almost three thousand students in the first through the eighth grade, enrolled in what were termed "independent neighborhood schools." Eighty-nine percent of the student bodies of the eighty-two schools sampled were African American, and the remaining were Latino, Asian, and Native American. The study found that "students in independent neighborhood schools generally scored above national norms on the five nationally standardized tests: CTBS, CAT, Iowa, MAT, and the Stanford."[22] Approximately 88 percent of sampled schools, serving 89 percent of the students tested, were at or above the norm.

To get a more up-to-date reading of HBI schools on a single test that would allow comparison with public schools, Toussaint looked at the New York State Pupil Evaluation Program (PEP) test, which has been required of all public schools and optional for private schools. Scores on this test indicate the percentage of students scoring above the State Reference Point (SRP) in key subject areas. Students scoring below the SRP have failed to meet the state's minimum performance requirements in a subject area, a rough equivalent of about one year below grade level.[23]

When considering these findings one should keep in mind the limitations of the study. The twenty-eight HBI schools examined are not a random sample, but represent all of the HBI schools whose students took the test, and for which the state provided complete data for the academic year ending in 1996. Not all private schools take this test. Most HBI schools, like other private schools, consider the PEP test to be merely a minimum skills test and prefer to take the more rigorous Stanford, Iowa, or California Achievement tests. Also, there is little demographic data available on HBI school families. We can infer from tuition levels and school administrator reports that HBI schools enroll mostly low-middle-income and higher-low-income families. Of course, whenever public and private school students are compared there is the possibility that differences in family background have influenced student achievement.[24] Yet research shows that some inner city private schools have a mitigating effect on family background characteristics which shows up in test scores.[25]

We found that students in the twenty-eight HBI schools sampled outperformed students in the public school districts in which their schools are located on the 1996 PEP test in reading and math for third graders.[26] (See table 12.3.) This finding is consistent with the findings of the prior national study cited above.

TABLE 12.3 Percent of Students Scoring above the
State Reference Point on *Pupil Evaluation Program*
(PEP) Test, 1996

Grade 3	Public Schools in 17 HBI Districts	HBI Schools	Number of HBI Schools Sampled
Reading	58.3	76.8	28
Math	88.5	94.1	28

Source: Toussaint Institute Fund.

"At-Risk" Children and HBI Schools

The Toussaint Institute Fund's experiences suggest that HBI schools are particularly effective with students considered to be "at-risk." The institute has a scholarship program that was founded in 1988 to place "at-risk" boys from public schools into HBI schools in an effort to save them from special education. A disproportionate number of African American students, particularly boys, are assigned to special education programs for problems related more to behavior and low achievement than to a learning disability. In 1998, a two-year federal investigation found that the city's special education programs had become warehouses for black and Latino children, something African American parents had known for at least a decade.[27] Parents are told that the only way to get their child the smaller class size and extra attention he or she needs is by signing the child over to special education, as a temporary measure. Though many of these students have only minor, if any, impairments, and parents are encouraged to believe that children will eventually return to the mainstream, very few special education children are ever "decertified" into general education.[28] Most eventually drop out of school.

To date, the Toussaint Institute Fund has paid for eighty-five students to attend sixteen HBI schools around the city; currently thirteen scholars are placed in ten HBI schools. The program targets poor performing students, often with multiple risk factors, as they enter the second or third grades.

The bureaucratic school model does not work for children with chronic behavior problems, nor does placement in segregated classes with other children with behavior problems. Such students need a more nurturing model, one that surrounds them with peers who display the best behavior—and adults who expect it. The HBI schools of New York City provide this kind of environment for Toussaint Scholars, as they are called. Part of the effectiveness of HBI schools comes from mainstreaming children with weak skills, though not necessarily in their public school grade. Low-achieving students from public schools are often placed back a grade—or even two or three in certain subject areas. (Special remediation classes are almost never found in HBI schools.) Another part of the effectiveness seems to emerge from the attitude HBI schools take toward African American males in trouble. "We *must* find a way to save this child" is a common attitude. Despite the trouble a boy may cause, HBI schools rarely expel the student. Instead, the school becomes the child's surrogate family and provides love, discipline, nurturing, and belonging.

The most dramatic improvements in behavior of former special education students takes place in the first few months as they begin adopting the social and academic behavior and attitudes expected of all students at the school. Peer influence is very powerful. Students feel embarrassed when they behave in ways that are considered extreme by their new private school peers or are the only ones in the class without completed homework. The schools report that by the end of the academic year, the student becomes fully acclimated to the school culture. Students report a safer environment and even former bullies express feelings of greater security.

In the virtual absence of HBI high schools with full programs, most Toussaint Scholars find themselves back at public school for their high school years. They have consistently been placed in mainstream, and even honors, programs. Typically, they find the schoolwork undemanding and "easy." But, sadly, by the end of the first semester, study habits, attendance, and grades deteriorate rapidly for most of these students. Initially they are shocked at the nonacademic attitude of their new peers and their disrespectful behavior toward adults, as well as the lower expectations of teachers and administrators who tolerate this. Over time they tend to "join the crowd" and revert to previous school-dysfunctional behavior.

While Toussaint Scholars do well in HBI elementary and intermediate schools, most of the institute's early scholars are now in their teens, attending public high schools, and have fallen into this pattern. In response, the institute has recently modified its program. It now works hard to encourage parents to send their children to HBI boarding schools once they graduate from HBI day schools in the city. Most parents have been uncomfortable with the idea of sending their children away, but Toussaint believes that the pull of New York City streets and the school culture of New York's public secondary schools make HBI boarding schools an important, even critical alternative.

Finally, Toussaint has turned with hope to Rice High School in Harlem. Rice, founded in 1938, is a Christian Brothers Catholic school that distinguished itself in 1998 by hiring the city's first African American principal of a Catholic high school in the Archdiocese of New York. Orlando Gober, also the school's first lay principal, is known among HBI educators for developing St. Mark's Lutheran School into a model HBI elementary school during his tenure. He has brought to Rice much of what made St. Mark's a model HBI school.[29] Although Toussaint's scholarship program has worked exclusively with HBI schools, Rice might well serve HBI graduates.

Mission, Expectations, Identity, and Culture

Like most private schools, HBI schools are not burdened with the bureaucratic regulations that often distract public schools from their core educational mission. This allows them to develop into self-contained communities, resembling the private institutions that James Coleman described in his important work,[30] and the Catholic schools I came across in New York when collaborating on a study for the Rand Corporation.[31] Like Catholic schools, HBI schools are communities in which parents, teachers, and administrators are brought together by a shared set of values. They cultivate a safe, orderly, and caring environment. They have high expectations for all pupils, because they believe that their students can perform at a high level and they strive to ensure that students can reach the high standards. HBI schools also pay a great deal of attention to molding the character of their students, and often these efforts are related to the religious orientation of the schools.

HBI schools are culture driven as well. In a recent site visit to a Solomon Schechter School in Queens, part of a nationwide network of seventy Conservative Jewish schools, in which students come from a range of observant families, I had the opportunity to visit classes and later to interview the principal. In many ways, HBI schools are similar to Conservative Jewish schools, which emphasize culture, Jewish heritage, and the Israeli homeland.

In similar fashion, HBI schools provide a sense of identity by affirming African American, Caribbean, and African culture. Most schools teach from the intellectual traditions and perspectives of Europe and Africa, some more Afrocentric than others. Included in a science or literature lesson may be the contributions of scholars or authors of African descent. Some schools have "Black Studies" courses, others include the perspectives and contributions of people of African ancestry throughout the curriculum. One school prefers to refer to what it teaches as "Whole History" and tries to correct what it sees as the partial view presented in most textbooks. Often, HBI schools convey African American culture by transmitting the values of the peoples across the African diaspora. These values are summed up in the Nguzo Saba, or seven principles upon which Kwanzaa is based.[32] They are memorized and recited (with full explanations) regularly by students in a few schools, and communicated more subtly in most.

African American parents are frequently spurred to choose black independent elementary schools over other private schools out of concern for the psychological well-being of their children. African American parents are frightened by the "crisis of self-hatred"[33] so prevalent among African American youth, especially at neighborhood public schools and even some private schools where the "n" word is commonplace in student peer discourse. On the other hand, parents worry about their children's ability to relate to their own culture if they attend other private schools with predominantly white student bodies, with few African American role models, and where cultural affirmation is rarely an integral part of the school's curriculum.[34]

The curriculum and instruction of HBI schools reflect the fact that the schools assume a sense of responsibility to provide students with the skills and attitudes they will need to uplift not only themselves but their communities. They have high aspirations for their students, viewing them as a critical, even precious part of the solution to the problems that plague their communities—rather than part of the problem. This is why expulsion of students is so rare in HBI schools, perhaps more rare than in any other kind of school. Mainstreaming is not simply a result of limited resources; it is an expression of the schools' underlying reverence for their students, even the difficult and the slow.

School Profiles

The Cambria Center for the Gifted

While Cambria's name suggests that it is an academically elite institution, the school was founded on the idea of discovering the gift in all children. The job of the educator is to uncover and nurture inborn talent. Cambria Heights is a low- to middle-income black neighborhood consisting of homeowners, civil service workers, and professionals. About half the population is of Caribbean origin. There are several other HBI schools nearby, including Allen Christian School, which was founded by the Reverend Dr. Floyd H. Flake, the former six-term congressman. The school is located in District 29, where 50 percent of the students are at grade level in reading and 65 percent in math; the district performs slightly above the HBI citywide average in both subjects.[35]

At Cambria, as at most HBI schools, the principal is also its founder. In 1980, after teaching only one year at a public junior high school in the city, Sheree Palmer became so disenchanted with the low expectations and the abysmal level of student performance that she founded her own school. Without backers, but with twenty-one eager children, Ms. Palmer opened the Cambria Center for the Gifted in her home in Cambria Heights, Queens. Cambria grew quickly as Ms. Palmer converted her garage into a classroom. Ms. Palmer next moved the school into a building on Linden Boulevard in Cambria Heights, and eventually took over most of the block. The buildings were renovated and now house a library, two music rooms, and classrooms, all of which receive a fresh coat of paint every year. Throughout the inside of the building are security cameras, and outside there is a padded playground.

Cambria offers grades pre-K–5 and charges $3,300 in tuition. The school has grown to capacity at 250 students and, remarkably, another 250 children are on the waiting list. Academically, Cambria supplements the New York State curriculum with music, foreign language, computer training, multiculturalism, and black history classes. Cambria students typically complete the state curriculum by April and then start on a preview of the next year's work. Study habits are ingrained from an early age. Even third graders are expected to do an hour and a half of homework a night. Yet there are rewards for hard work. Every month, the teachers take their classes on trips to local museums, parks, and cultural events.

Cambria offers an extensive music program with classes in violin, piano, woodwinds, and voice. Many parents pay to continue the lessons at the school's after-school program. The music program is designed to help students build self-confidence and discover new talents. "Some part of the program," said Ms. Palmer, "touches on every aspect of giftedness—if not academics, something." Especially with slower students, finding an area in which they excel spills over positively into their studies and classroom behavior.

Ms. Palmer says many parents choose her school because they want to give their children a "good foundation." Sometimes, Ms. Palmer admits, parental expectations are excessive. Some want their three-year-olds to be accomplished writers. "I am not paying for them to play," parents say, making it clear that they want the best education they can afford to ready their children for a college-prep high school. Many Caribbean parents, appalled at the city's public schools in their neighborhoods, choose Cambria so their children will be exposed to a rigorous curriculum, core values, and character development similar to what they would receive in Caribbean schools.

Integral to character formation is Cambria's black studies curriculum, which proceeds primarily through storytelling. "We try not to get into, 'Oh, this is a black person.' We try to let the story and pictures convey that this is a person of color," Ms. Palmer explained. "I don't like kids to feel they are being indoctrinated. We don't get into 'these people did this to us.' We start before slavery so they can see the positive first. We talk about people and heroes throughout the year in terms of what Kwanzaa principles they used, so it's not just at Kwanzaa time."

Though Cambria is a secular school, morning assembly begins with a prayer. "We've been working on developing the moral base of the child, especially since we're not affiliated with a church," Ms. Palmer said. "How do you develop your values, how do you know what's right from wrong for yourself? Becoming humane. The school also works to develop a sense of responsibility for the group among students. We try to get them to understand that morally they are a group, supporting each other and defending each other. That's what I didn't see in public school."

Even though Cambria has a long waiting list, last year the school took in ten public school holdovers, several special education students, and another student with a history of behavioral problems. "This year we ended up adding a reading specialist to work with two of them twice a week," said the principal. "It really hurt our budget, but even if you're not sure you can keep them, you don't want the child to leave without some growth."

During Cambria's first nine years, Ms. Palmer doubled as both principal and teacher. Since then, she has been able to devote herself full-time to administration. Her support staff consists of an assistant principal, a bookkeeper who also takes care of secretarial duties, and a part-time receptionist. Though Ms. Palmer can pay teachers only between $15,000 and $21,000 for the ten-month school year, she insists they become involved in school programs outside the classroom. "[I'm concerned about] whether they see it as a job or a profession. If they see it as a job, they're gone at 3 P.M., and they're trying to do lesson plans during class time." Thirteen teachers have enrolled sixteen of their children in the school, taking full advantage of tuition waivers. Several teachers want to start schools of their own. For financial reasons, some teachers plan to teach in the public school system after they earn state certification.

Cambria expects parental involvement and even requires ten hours a year spent helping out at school activities. Once a month, the parents sponsor a family event, such as game night or a movie, and most families attend. The school has developed a program to educate parents in family and community responsibility. Seminars are given on health issues and finances, and, to encourage attendance, babysitters are available at the school. Almost all the parents join one of the Parent Organization's committees and help raise the 10 percent of the budget that tuition does not cover.

In the future, Ms. Palmer hopes to install a science laboratory, an art studio, and additional classroom space so she can admit more students. She also hopes one day to be able to pay her teachers more.

St. Paul's Community Christian School

St. Paul's Community Christian School was founded in 1984 by the Reverend Dr. Johnny Ray Youngblood of St. Paul's Community Baptist Church in East New York, Brooklyn. At the beginning of his tenure in 1974, Rev. Youngblood found irony in the church's name. "St. Paul Community Baptist Church could call nothing in the surrounding community its own. If anything, the congregation was held hostage and its religious values mocked by what happened along Stanley Avenue. Purses were snatched, chains ripped from necks, car batteries stolen."[36] Violent crime was so bad in the area, police officers wore T-shirts printed with "The Killing Fields." Sponsoring community development and helping neighborhood youngsters aspire to more than life on the streets became cornerstones of the new pastor's ministry. Opening a school became a natural part of that calling.

In the midst of a troubled neighborhood, Rev. Youngblood and his congregation organized a funding drive and raised enough money to build a school that is attached to the church. The school has fourteen classrooms, a large recreation area it shares with the church, and, unlike most HBI schools, a science laboratory and a dedicated library. St. Paul's school opened with fifty-five students. The enrollment has grown to 237 students with twenty-six full-time teachers. The school offers pre-K through the eighth grade, and the lower grades have a waiting list that has lengthened as the school's reputation has grown. About half the students come from families in the congregation. The self-empowerment of African American males through the church's men's program has become so successful that it may be the reason most students now come from intact families.

Rev. Youngblood modeled St. Paul's after St. Mark's Lutheran, another Brooklyn HBI school, which at the time was known for its strong fathers' involvement program and Afrocentric Christian curriculum. St. Paul's requires its students to wear uniforms, partly to counter the values expressed in clothing styles popular with youngsters and teens in their neighborhood and partly to set a professional and orderly tone. Further, they "may not wear jewelry, gold teeth, designer haircuts, earrings for boys, and sheer stockings for girls."[37] St. Paul's has developed an extensive academic program that combines both Christian and African-centered approaches. In addition to core classes that fulfill the state curriculum requirements, the school offers courses including honors math, honors writing, computer, black history, CPR and first aid, geography, conversational Spanish, Christian living, Bible, and communication arts skills.

Parents are expected to review and sign their children's homework every day. Most sacrifice and struggle, some even work second jobs to pay the $3,210 yearly tuition in this low-income area. Some families live in nearby housing projects. Rev. Youngblood makes a point of reading the report cards of the children in his congregation out loud during Sunday service, whether or not they attend St. Paul's school. To further encourage parental involvement, the school serves meals at parent meetings. St. Paul's has been particularly successful in getting fathers to take part in their children's education. The men often chaperone school trips, and many serve in the PTA.

Although St. Paul's does not screen applicants on an academic basis, diagnostic tests for basic-skills proficiency are given in September, followed by achievement tests in the spring. Individual tutoring is available for students with academic problems. In addition, the church runs a tutoring program for both children and adults, open to anyone in the community who lacks basic academic skills. The surrounding school district (District 19) has been cited as having a "concentration of failing schools."[38] "Only 30 percent of the students district-wide are reading at grade level and only 47 percent are performing math at grade level."[39] Saint Paul's scored 83 on the reading and 100 on the math in the 1996 PEP tests. This was six points above the HBI citywide average on both tests.

Rev. Youngblood shares the widespread concern in the black community about the disproportionate representation of African American children in special education programs for reasons related more to behavior than disability. The pastor even addresses parents from the pulpit, encouraging them to take their children out of special education if the placement was not due to a serious disability. St. Paul's has a history of willingness to take in students who had behavioral problems in the public schools. Adele Toussaint, the recently retired founding principal, says she expelled only two children during her fifteen-year tenure. "I'd rather keep children and try to work with them," she says.

St. Paul's hires teachers who see their profession as a "ministry to children" and who have talents to contribute to the school's extracurricular programs. Teacher salaries range from $21,000 to $29,000 and include health benefits. Recently, a pension plan was put in place. Teacher turnover is rare since St. Paul's compensation package is much better than most other HBI schools. The obvious enthusiasm teachers bring to the classroom makes it clear that they share St. Paul's mission. No doubt Rev. Youngblood's leadership is a motivating factor. All the teachers have bachelor's degrees and several have completed graduate programs. Most are state certified, but none has a New York City teaching license. Several Caribbean teachers were certified in their home countries and are working toward certification here.

Conclusion and Recommendations

Historically black independent schools have existed in this country since at least 1798.[40] Though individual schools come and go, the tradition persists, often against all odds. Unfortunately very little research has been done on this subject, past or present. There may be lessons for the public schools about working with mainstream as well as "at-risk" students, particularly as it relates to the power of academic and behavioral expectations. As many African American educators have urged, perhaps rather than try to create new models, we can find ways to support existing models that work for children in urban areas.

Further study is needed to examine the academic performance of students in HBI schools across a range of measures. Of particular importance is the question of whether these schools also have the "common school effect" discovered in inner city Catholic schools, from which students from disadvantaged backgrounds were found to benefit.[41] There are also lessons that public and other private schools could learn about incorporating the history and values of people of African ancestry. Africa can serve as part of the educational foundation for all students.

Future issues for HBI schools include developing a better network of funding sources, including corporate as well as alumni development. If more HBI schools are to be founded to meet this unsatisfied demand, it will be critical for HBIs to secure a strong financial base for start-up schools, the absence of which keeps schools perennially focused on day-to-day survival, unable to plan adequately for their long-range future, or even take advantage of opportunities that come along.

As the recent charter school legislation emphasizes, the current debate on school reform is principally about the question of options. But for African Americans, school choice is more than a discussion. For families who live in school districts that for decades have earned the dubious accolade "dead zones," school choice is the most important decision they must make for their children's sake.

NOTES

1. *School Directory* (Washington, D.C.: Institute for Independent Education, 1995), p. ii.

2. See Charles Wesley, *Prentice Hall: Life and Legacy,* 2nd ed. (Chicago: Drew Sales Lodge Regalia, 1983).

3. Carleton Mabee, *Black Education in New York State from Colonial to Modern Times* (Syracuse: Syracuse University Press, 1979), pp. 23, 25.

4. In an address to black youth in 1827, William Hamilton, a successful education activist, complained that white teachers did not expect enough of black students in the private schools then operated by white benevolent societies for blacks. Ibid., pp. 98–99, 157–58.

5. Ibid., pp. 51–52.

6. Over the five years of its existence, the Society for the Promotion of Education among Colored Children won the respect of black parents, the New York City Board of Education, and the Public School Society. The African-founded society was issued a charter that allowed it to operate elementary schools under the Board of Education's supervision. It could charge tuition, but was required to allow children unable to pay to attend for free. Ibid., pp. 63–66.

7. Ibid., pp. 30, 57–58.

8. Ibid., pp. 102.

9. Carter G. Woodson, *Mis-education of the Negro* (Washington, D.C.: Associated Publishers, 1933).

10. Mabee, *Black Education in New York State from Colonial to Modern Times*, p. 279. Yet there was a general belief that, while blacks students made progress, it was not equal to that of white students.

11. This fight over community control led to the creation of the city's thirty-two community school districts. However, according to Kenneth B. Clark, "whatever community control may have yielded in favor of black students remains unknown, because actual control was never realized. Control over the quality of education for black students was viewed [by blacks] to be in the hands of the United Federation of Teachers" (Kenneth B. Clark, "Issues in Urban Education," in *Black Manifesto for Education*, ed. Jim Haskins [New York: William Morrow, 1973], p. 82).

12. *Annual Pupil Ethnic Census* (New York: Office of User Support Services, Board of Education, October 31, 1997).

13. "The State of City Schools '98" (Public Education Association, 1998).

14. Mabee, *Black Education in New York State from Colonial to Modern Times*, pp. 51–56.

15. Districts 5, 7, 9, 10, 16, 19, and 23 are identified among the lowest performers in the city in "State of the City Schools, 98" (Public Education Association, 1998).

16. This figure is the one given by the Parents League of New York.

17. Gail E. Foster, "New York City's Wealth of Historically Black Independent Schools," *Journal of Negro Education* 61 (1992).

18. See chapter 10.

19. Thirty-two HBI schools were sampled on this question.

20. Earl Graves, *How to Succeed in Business without Being White* (New York: Harper Collins, 1997).

21. See chapter 6.

22. *On the Road to Success* (Washington, D.C.: Institute for Independent Education, 1991), pp. 41–42. Comprehensive Test of Basic Skills, California Achievement Test, Iowa Test of Basic Skills, Metropolitan Achievement Test, and the Stanford Achievement Test.

23. Office of Assessment and Accountability, New York City Board of Education.

24. See James S. Coleman et al., *Equality of Educational Opportunity Report* (Washington, D.C.: United States Government Printing Office, 1966).

25. See Andrew M. Greeley, *Catholic High Schools and Minority Students* (New Brunswick, N.J.: Transition Books, 1982).

26. *1996/97 Annual School Reports* (Division of Assessment and Accountability, New York City Board of Education) and *Comprehensive Assessment Report* (State Education Department of New York, December 1997). Data was available from the Board of Education for all seventeen public school districts for the third grade tests, and only for nine public school districts for the sixth grade tests.

27. Anemona Hartocollis, "U.S. Questions the Placement of City Pupils, Its Study Suggests Bias in Special Education," *New York Times*, November 21, 1998.

28. Kay S. Hymowitz, "Special Education: Kids Go in But They Don't Come Out," *City Journal* 6 (1996): 28.

29. St. Mark's Lutheran School had a program that emphasized involvement of

fathers and a Christian Afrocentric curriculum. Rev. Johnny Ray Youngblood, founder of St. Paul's Community Christian School, profiled here, used St. Mark's as the model for building his own school.

30. James S. Coleman and Thomas Hoffer, *Public and Private High Schools* (New York: Basic Books, 1987).

31. Paul T. Hill, Gail Foster, and Tamar Gendler, *High Schools with Character* (Santa Monica, Calif.: Rand, 1990).

32. The elements of Nguzo Saba are: *Umoja* (unity), *Kujichagulia* (self-determination), *Ujima* (collective work and responsibility), *Ujamaa* (cooperative economics), *Nia* (purpose), *Kuumba* (creativity), *Imani* (faith).

33. See Cathy Royal, "Support Systems for Students of Color in Independent Schools," and Deborah Johnson, "Racial Socialization Strategies of Parents in Three Black Private Schools," in *Visible Now: Blacks in Private Schools,* ed. Diane T. Slaughter and Deborah J. Johnson (New York: Greenwood Press, 1988).

34. Ibid.

35. *1995/96 Annual District Reports* (Division of Assessment and Accountability, New York City Board of Education).

36. Samuel G. Freedman, *Upon This Rock: The Miracle of the Black Church* (New York: Harper Collins, 1993), p. 49.

37. *Student Handbook*, St. Paul's Community Christian School.

38. *Futures Denied: Concentrated Failure in the New York City Public School System* (New York: Parents Organized to Win Reform: Industrial Areas Foundation of Metropolitan New York and Public Education Association, March 1997).

39. *1995/96 Annual District Reports* (Division of Assessment and Accountability, New York City Board of Education).

40. Horace Mann Bond, *Education for Freedom* (Oxford, Pa.: Lincoln University Press, 1976).

41. Anthony S. Bryk, Valerie E. Lee, and Peter B. Holland, *Catholic Schools and the Common Good* (Cambridge, Mass: Harvard University Press, 1993), p. 57.

PART V

Choice

13 Public School Choice: A Status Report

PAUL TESKE, MARK SCHNEIDER,
CHRISTINE ROCH, AND MELISSA MARSCHALL

In 1992, the New York City Board of Education approved a system of interdistrict public school choice, making it possible for parents to choose a school for their children outside of the community school district in which they live. This choice plan eliminated the need for parents to get a waiver from their zoned district (an "exit visa") in order to apply to a school in another district. This effectively allowed the thirty-two community school districts that operate the elementary and middle schools in New York City the opportunity to promote choice for students within their areas, which some have done more actively than others.

Choice is not a new concept in New York City. At the high school level the city has long had a tradition of a large number of public schools of choice. These range from elite schools for academically talented students, such as Stuyvesant and Bronx Science, to schools for students with particular talents, such as Performing Arts, and career-oriented magnet schools.[1] In addition to this formal choice mechanism, many parents, as is well known, have "scammed" the system by using false addresses to get their children into schools or districts they prefer. Also, the alternative schools sponsored by New York Networks and the Annenberg program in the 1990s,[2] which now serve nearly 5 percent of the more than one million students in New York, are mainly schools that parents choose for their children. Finally, rounding out the list of choice programs found in the city's school system, a few of the thirty-two districts adopted intradistrict choice plans before 1992. Thus, although New York State is one of about twenty states that did not have a charter school law until 1998, there were several forms of public school choice technically available to a considerable number of parents and students prior to then.

Despite these mechanisms, the city Board of Education has mostly paid lip service to interdistrict choice since 1992. As a result, even though interdistrict choice is stated policy, parents trying to select a school usually find it extremely difficult to exercise choice. Most of the desirable schools are already oversubscribed with students from within the district, and procedures for entry from outside the "home" district vary widely across the city. According to Hill et al., open enrollment in New York City is "rendered virtually meaningless by the fact that the nonselective magnet schools to which all students may apply get 10 to 30 applicants for every seat. The majority of students who try to choose a school other than the one in their neighborhood end up back in the school they tried to flee."[3]

Just getting accurate information about the schools and about how to exercise choice is difficult. Clara Hemphill, who recently wrote an advice book about choosing New York schools, notes that getting information from districts and schools "can be like nailing Jell-O to the wall."[4] In theory, schools cannot discriminate based on race, gender, or special needs, and are supposed to utilize random lotteries when applicants exceed seats. However, bureaucratic obstacles and lack of information can make it extremely difficult for parents, unless they are extremely energetic, to find a spot in a school outside their district.

We were unable to locate anyone or any office at the Board of Education that tracks interdistrict choice programs and no one could supply us with comprehensive figures on the number of students or the number of schools involved in interdistrict choice. This alone suggests that the Board of Education is not strongly committed to that form of choice. Instead, each community school district can keep track of its own student figures, but they do not do so in a consistent format. Willen found that District 2 in Manhattan, a district with considerable intradistrict choice, had 1,422 students apply from outside the district in 1997, with 1,027 accepted for admission.[5] One of the top-rated districts, District 26 in Bayside, Queens, had 767 students seek entry in 1997, and accepted less than half. District 4 historically has had more than one thousand students come into the district from outside. These three districts represent some of the most desirable districts. If we assume, liberally (as the true number is probably smaller) that another five hundred students have been accepted into schools outside of their home districts in thirteen more districts, then about nine thousand students from grades K-8 are now utilizing interdistrict choice. While this number may put some pressure on unattractive schools and districts to improve their performance, it represents a mere 1 percent of the 1.1 million students across the city. (Including the choices made at the high school level would, of course, increase this percentage.) In contrast, the Annenberg-sponsored alternative schools now represent a far larger number of students, at nearly 5 percent.

Thus interdistrict choice in New York City does exist, but we do not believe it is yet a major factor in stimulating much educational change. We now turn our attention to choice at the intradistrict level.

As noted above, intradistrict choice is allowed throughout New York City. However, some districts had adopted such choice plans on their own prior to the 1992 citywide legislation. Indeed, District 4 has a history of choice tracing back nearly twenty-five years. Most of this chapter is devoted to analyzing performance issues associated with choice in District 4. Existing studies of school choice are limited by the simple fact that reforms such as vouchers and charter schools have been in place for relatively short periods of time, making the assessment of the effects of choice difficult. In contrast, we believe that looking at the effects of choice in District 4 over the more than two decades it has been in place can give us analytic insight on how broader programs of choice in New York might affect school performance.

If imitation is the sincerest form of flattery, District 4 should consider itself highly flattered. In recent years, partly in direct imitation of District 4's successes, a few other districts have developed and/or expanded choice within their boundaries. District 2 has gone the furthest in this effort. These changes took place in the eleven years in which Anthony Alvarado, who not coincidentally led the efforts to implement choice in District 4, was District 2 superintendent (1988–98). District 1 in Manhattan established five alternative schools of choice in the 1990s, and some other districts have made similar but limited forays into choice programs.[6] After we explore the relationship of choice to performance in District 4, we will present a more limited examination of District 2's experience with choice. This provides a useful contrast, as District 4 has a student body that is of lower than average income for the city, while District 2 has a student body with higher than average levels of income.

Our goal is to try to identify the effects of choice on performance. While our data and analysis focus on intradistrict choice, we believe that some of the lessons we draw from this study can apply to other forms of choice that are being implemented in New York.

Choice in District 4

There is considerable anecdotal evidence that choice in District 4 has increased the performance of the schools in the district. However, the argument that choice in District 4 has been a success has been based on relatively little quantitative evidence. In turn, some scholars have argued that the data used to show District 4's successes are flawed. Beyond the question of whether or not District 4 has been successful, others have argued that any successes may be attributable to such factors as administrative

leadership and innovation, small school size, and "extra" resources generated from external federal magnet programs and from District 4's over-
spending its budget. If these points are accurate, then we might not expect
any improvements from choice in District 4 to be replicable in other districts. To the extent possible with the existing data, we try to isolate the effects of choice from the effects of other factors on changing performance in
District 4 schools.

In presenting our results, we address two critical dimensions of this
question: (1) Has student performance in District 4 really improved since
the implementation of choice, and if so, has choice contributed to this improvement? (2) Has choice expanded the range of educational opportunities for all parents and students in District 4, or only for a select group?

Student Performance in District 4

Supporters of choice point to considerable evidence that academic performance improved after the implementation of choice in District 4. A few
studies illustrated an improvement in raw reading and math test scores in
District 4 over time.[7] These studies also showed that more District 4 students were accepted into prestigious selective high schools than in the
past.[8] For example, in 1973, only ten District 4 students were accepted into
Bronx Science, Stuyvesant, Brooklyn Tech, or the LaGuardia School of Music, but by the mid-1980s, District 4 was placing three hundred students annually in these schools.[9] The rate of acceptance gradually but steadily increased throughout the 1970s and 1980s, and by 1987 the rate of acceptance
from District 4 was twice that of the rest of the city.

Several schools in District 4 are truly excellent. For example, today over
90 percent of graduates from Central Park East Elementary School go on
to earn high school diplomas, and 90 percent of Central Park East Secondary School students go on to college (a rate that is nearly double that
for the city as a whole).[10] In 1996, the New York City Board of Education
reported that the elementary school with the highest reading scores of the
city's 670 schools was District 4's TAG school. The schools have so dramatically improved that many parents from outside the district have tried
to send their children to District 4 schools. This demand is in marked contrast to a past pattern of flight from the district and a continuing pattern of
flight from most other New York City districts with similar demographic
characteristics. However, some analysts have questioned whether District
4's purported successes are "real" and whether choice was the actual cause
of any such improvements. They often note that, at a minimum, the existing analysis of District 4 performance is incomplete. As Boyer notes more
generally, "In states and districts where choice has been adopted, little effort has been made to record the process carefully or to document results."[11]

The arguments questioning the success of school choice in District 4 are based on several interrelated issues. One major set of concerns is based on the instability of test scores over time. The New York City Board of Education has changed its test several times over the past twenty-two years. Kirp argues that the largest improvement in test scores (a gain of 13 percentage points) occurred in 1973 when choice was first getting started, and in 1986 (10 percentage points) when New York City switched to a different test.[12] He notes that in both years reading levels improved dramatically for the city as a whole, and thus he questions whether District 4's gains were independent of citywide gains. Furthermore, he reports that after new norms were established in 1989, the proportion of District 4 students doing grade-level work dropped to 42 percent (vs. 48 percent citywide). Cookson argues that the more detailed study prepared by Domanico just recycled Fliegel's data and "does not attempt to expand upon these data somewhat by comparing District 4 reading scores to citywide reading scores."[13] Given these problems, in this chapter we control the extent to which test instruments affect performance by standardizing District 4's test results relative to the citywide average for the tests administered by the city in that year, creating a common baseline for a reliable over-time analysis.

Some scholars argue that while District 4 test scores may have improved over time, the improvement was the result of bringing in better prepared students from other districts.[14] They argue that these students came from higher socioeconomic status backgrounds and were more motivated than students living in the district. According to Henig, several different articles reported that between eight hundred and two thousand students came into District 4 from outside the district.[15] Kirp states: "It is largely because of this hidden selection process—which screens for both levels of skills and traits of character—that some very good schools have been created in East Harlem."[16]

Fliegel argues that staff in District 4 analyzed these data and found that the profile of incoming students was virtually the same as the District 4 resident students in terms of test score performances.[17] In our analysis in this chapter, to address this issue, we control for the demographic characteristics of students enrolled in the district schools, including race and poverty levels.

Some scholars have also argued that any improvements in District 4 were driven more by extra money from federal magnet programs and from the district's running over budget during the 1980s.[18] Indeed, at one point District 4 received more per capita federal aid than any other district in the United States.[19] Thus we model the effects of resources using proxies for expenditures (such as pupil/teacher ratios, since expenditure data are not available over the years by district). We note at this point that this criticism also reflects a belief in an extraordinary sensitivity of test score performance to enhanced resources, a belief that has not been documented in the literature (see below).

Some of those who are skeptical of District 4's success argue that, rather than choice, the key factor in District 4's success has been the creation of smaller schools. (Note that this concern involves not the creation of smaller *classes*, which requires greater resources, but the creation of smaller *schools* through the establishment of many minischools). Harrington and Cookson argue that "probably the most important ingredient was school size. Every one of the alternative schools was small. . . . Size alone made these alternative schools nontraditional in New York City, where public schools are about as large and impersonal as you can get, even at the elementary level."[20] In our analysis we control for the possible effects of school size on student test score performance.

Another perspective on District 4's choice program is that any increase in test scores was driven by a small number of elite alternative schools of choice. Many scholars are concerned about stratification and its effect on those "left behind" in an education system in which there are already significant educational inequities.[21] According to Young and Clinchy, "East Harlem's practice of allowing individual schools to set admissions criteria and select students aggravates, rather than reduces, such inequities."[22] Thus we examine the performance of students in the non-choice elementary schools, to see if they were indeed "left behind."

Some scholars believe that the attention focused on District 4 created a "Hawthorne effect" in which teachers, administrators, students, and parents responded to an experimental setting by changing their behavior in the short run, and that such an effect is unsustainable over time.[23] Cookson argues: "Clearly there is something of a Hawthorne effect going on in District 4. . . . It is little wonder that this positive feeling is reflected in student's attitudes. . . . Change preceded choice in East Harlem, not the other way around."[24] To address this concern, we examine school performance in District 4 today, when any Hawthorne effect would now be nearly twenty-five years old.

A final concern often expressed is that leadership was more important than choice.[25] Some argue that District 4 benefited from outstanding leadership, from Alvarado, Fliegel, Meier, and others, who have become symbols and practitioners of successful education, and that their leadership produced more positive benefits than did choice. It is very difficult to separate the emergence of strong leaders from the opening up of opportunities that choice allowed. It is also reasonable to ask why outstanding leaders have not emerged in such numbers in districts without choice. By examining performance today, when none of the above leaders has been active in District 4 for many years, we can partially distinguish the two causes.

Thus those who are critical of the simple arguments about success in District 4 suggest that choice did not drive improvements, but instead that any actual improvements were driven by leadership, innovation, stratification, Hawthorne effects, and/or extra resources. Cookson argues: "In fact, one could say that there is almost no convincing evidence that there is a relationship between school choice policies and student achievement."[26] Fortunately many of these issues now can be addressed with data we gathered and with data reported by the New York City Board of Education. Before we present these analyses, we examine briefly the large and often very contentious literature on whether any school reforms have been shown to improve student performance.

Can Schools Do Anything to Improve Student Performance?

In recent years, scholars in economics, political science, and education policy have developed a large and often contentious literature exploring whether and how school resources or institutional arrangements affect student performance. We review briefly the empirical research focusing on student performance on standardized tests. We do this to help establish reasonable expectations for the size of the effects we might expect of any reform, including the intradistrict choice programs we study.

Coleman et al. initiated much of this research by examining student test score performance as a function of three sets of variables: (1) those related to the family background of students, (2) those related to peer groups, and (3) those related to school resources.[27] The "Coleman Report" and other studies found little evidence that school resource policy variables had any significant impact on test scores, and instead found that family background had the strongest effects. In perhaps the most widely cited study on school effects after Coleman's work, Hanushek examined 187 different equations of educational "production functions" from thirty-eight publications and found inconclusive evidence that school resources, such as pupil/teacher ratio, teacher education, teacher salary, total expenditure per pupil, administrative expenditures, and quality of facilities, affect test score performance.[28]

Recently, a few researchers have challenged Hanushek's findings. Hedges et al. argue that in contrast to Hanushek's simple "vote count" methodology, a more sophisticated meta-analysis that combines different results shows that resources do affect test scores.[29] Card and Krueger argue that test scores are not necessarily the best measure of school performance, and instead analyze future earnings of individuals as a function of the educational resources devoted to them, controlling for a range of other factors.[30] They find evidence of the effects of school resources, such as teachers' salaries, on future earnings, as well as on higher educational attainment.[31] Sander finds that in Illinois, high school graduation rates by school district, controlling for average family background, are significantly higher for districts with lower pupil/teacher ratios.[32] Other recent studies find that school resources affect test scores.[33] Ferguson and Ladd studied both student- and district-level data in Alabama and found that teacher education and class size affect student learning.[34] They also argue that test scores are a reasonable proxy for future success and earnings. Perhaps most convincing, Mosteller illustrates how experimental data from Indiana and Tennessee show that smaller class sizes produce better test scores and other outcomes.[35]

The random experiments with different class sizes might seem to be enough to establish definitive results. But Hanushek points out that the effect takes place only in kindergarten and perhaps first grade, and there is no evidence that reduced class sizes in later grades further improve test scores.[36] Not convinced by this recent research showing that smaller classes and better-trained teachers can lead to higher performance, Hanushek summarizes nicely: "The existing work does not suggest that resources never matter, nor does it suggest that resources could not matter. It only indicates that the current organization and incentives of schools do little to ensure that any added resources will be used effectively."[37]

The literature on school choice has been directly aimed at those questions of organization, incentives, and effectiveness. Chubb and Moe argue that school choice provides more autonomy for school-level decision making, which they find to be associated with better performance.[38] They suggest that marketlike settings, rather than local politics, are more likely to create the incentives for effective schools. Only a few studies have addressed the question of whether choice actually leads to improved outcomes. A heated debate has emerged in the study of Milwaukee's limited experiment with private school vouchers for some low-income children. Witte found no significant improvements in tests scores over time for the children utilizing vouchers, compared to others, but Peterson et al., using a different comparison and methodology, have found positive effects on test scores after three years.[39] By the fourth year, Peterson finds significant math score increases of eleven points and reading score increases of five points. A recent reanalysis by Rouse finds a result in between Witte and Peterson, in which math scores are shown to have improved for voucher students in Milwaukee (though not to the extent that Peterson reports), but not reading scores.[40]

Without entering this debate directly, we surmise, for our purposes here, that these studies suggest that any test score improvements from resource or institutional changes should be expected to be moderate, rather than overwhelming, in scale. They also clearly indicate that analyses must try to control for student backgrounds as much as possible, while testing school or district-level effects.

Analyzing District 4 Performance over Time

To study the effects of choice, it is imperative to look at performance indicators in District 4 over time. To do this, we gathered historical data on the reading and math scores in the district and in the city as a whole. We quickly discovered why no one else has taken on this task—it was extremely difficult to gather these data going back to the late 1960s, when decentralization first created community school districts. By combining data from the Board of Education archives at Teachers College of Columbia with more recent data held at the Board of Education's headquarters, we were able to put together this time-series, which includes the years 1974–96.

Using the data from tests administered by the New York City Board of Education, we examine the percentage of district students reading (or performing math) at or above grade level in each year, averaged for all grades 3–8.[41] One concern noted by critics is that the actual test administered has changed over time. For example, for reading tests, from 1974–77 the test used was the 1970 version of the Comprehensive Test of Basic Skills, from 1978–85 it was the 1977 version of the California Achievement Test; from 1986–88 it was the 1982 version of the Degrees of Reading Power Test; from 1989–92 the 1988 version of the Degrees of Reading Power Test. Thus students in District 4 might have performed differently over time simply because of taking different tests, with different nationally normed baselines.

To address concerns that the baseline of tests administered in New York City has changed over time, we divided the average District 4 performance by the citywide average figure for grades 3–8. Thus we have a "standardized" measure of performance, reflecting how well District 4 is doing relative to other districts in the city. This is a consistent measure over time that can be used to evaluate changes in District 4.

The over-time patterns are presented graphically in figure 13.1. The graph shows a significant increase over time in both reading and math scores in District 4 relative to the city average. While we were not able to get data tracing all the way back to 1969, figure 13.1 shows that when choice started in District 4 in 1974, the district was one of the worst in the city, performing only about half as well as districts in the city as a whole. After the implementation of choice, the relative scores in District 4 climbed, and by the early- to mid-1980s, District 4's performance nearly reached the city average for reading. Note that there has been a recent decline, but that today District 4 schools are still working at a level higher than 80 percent of the citywide average—almost twice as high as in 1974. District 4 math

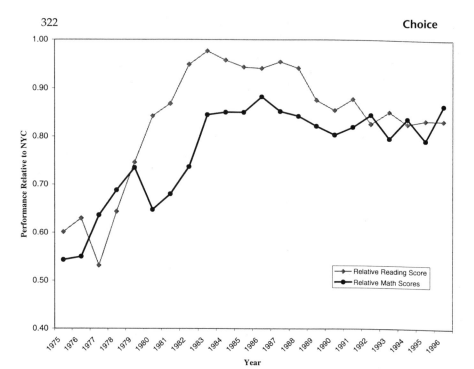

Figure 13.1. District 4 Performance over Time: Relative Math and Reading Scores

scores also climbed, though not as high, and they also showed a leveling off after the late 1980s.[42]

To see if the overall positive trend remained after controlling for other factors that might affect performance, we created a pooled data set, combining data from all thirty-two New York districts over the years 1974–96. While this does not cover the entire period since choice was instituted, these were the only years for which data are available—and even then, not all the data we wanted were available for every year. Fortunately, our major indicator, test scores, was available over the full range of years. For those variables that were missing for certain years, we interpolated values to fill in the observations in our time-series. In the case of demographics, which change very slowly over time, these interpolations are quite reliable. However, we also interpolated values for the teacher variables, which do change more rapidly. This greater fluctuation leaves us less confident in the reliability of the estimates for those independent variables.

We examined time trends employing the following control variables: the percentage of students in the district eligible for free lunches (a poverty measure); the percentage of black and Hispanic students in the district; the average pupil/teacher ratio in the district; and the percentage of teachers in the district with more than five years teaching experience.

The most important independent variable in our model is the measure of the expansion of choice in District 4 over time. We measure the prevalence of school choice as the percentage of choice schools out of the total number of operating schools in the district each year. In District 4, this measure increases from 0 percent in 1973 to 55 percent by 1996, and is set to zero for all other districts in all other years.[43] With these controls in the model, we can assess the extent to which basic underlying factors are responsible for the improvement in scores. We rely on Ordinary Least Squares to estimate our model and report panel-corrected standard errors.[44]

The results in table 13.1 show a statistically significant relationship between the expansion of choice in District 4 and both reading and math test score performance. As we estimated a linear model, the coefficient on the percentage of choice schools is easy to interpret: on average, each ten-percentage-point increase in the proportion of choice schools in District 4 in-

TABLE 13.1   District 4 Test Score Performance over Time Compared to Other Districts in New York City, 1974–1996[a]

Independent Variable	Reading Scores Coefficient[b]	Math Scores Coefficient[b]
% of schools in District 4 that are choice schools	0.59** (0.11)	0.36** (0.13)
Pupil/teacher ratio	0.07 (0.16)	−0.02 (0.20)
% of teachers with more than 5 years experience	−0.04 (0.04)	−0.09 (0.05)
% of students eligible for free lunches	−0.70** (0.28)	−0.69** (0.10)
% of black students	−.71** (0.10)	−0.86** (0.12)
% of Hispanic students	−0.64** (0.08)	−0.79** (0.10)
Constant	203.26** (8.06)	222.28** (10.04)
	N = 715; Adjusted R^2 = 0.91 Significance $p < .000$	N = 683; Adjusted R^2 = 0.87 Significance $p < .000$

[a]Pooled district-level fixed effects model of relative test scores as a function of district characteristics and District 4 location. We also included, but do not report, dummy variables for 31 of the 32 districts and 22 of the 23 time points.
[b]Panel-corrected standard errors.
**Significant at 99% level of confidence.

creased the reading scores six percentage points and the math scores four percentage points, relative to the citywide average. For example, if the percentage of District 4 students reading at grade level, relative to the city average, was 60 percent, and during the time period we studied four new choice schools were opened, out of forty currently operating schools, District 4 reading scores would rise to 66 percent of the city average.[45] These are not trivial improvements. For example, recall that studies have found mixed results for the use of vouchers to send low-income children to private schools; the most positive such findings show gains of about five points for math scores and eleven points for reading scores after four years.[46]

Our findings also show that districts with higher percentages of students in poverty (for reading only) and districts with higher percentages of black and Hispanic students are likely to have lower test scores.[47] Our results also address some of the concerns of critics by identifying the effects of resources (teacher/pupil ratio) and teacher quality (percent of teachers with more than five years experience) on student performance. Neither of these variables has a statistically significant effect on relative performance. Partly, this lack of effect may result from a measurement problem—recall that because of missing data we had to interpolate some of the data. But note, too, that in New York City budgets are allocated such that low-income and low-performance districts receive more resources— thus reducing the possible effects of resources on performance. Despite these issues, our analysis shows that a higher proportion of higher SES students, possibly coming into the district from other locations, does not explain District 4's improved performance, since demographic characteristics are controlled in our model.

Performance in District 4 Schools Today

From the time of the decentralization decision in 1969, which created the thirty-two local school districts now responsible for K-8 education in their areas, the New York City Board of Education has been required to prepare a district-by-district ranking of reading scores. For 1996, the board prepared a more detailed study of reading scores, by school, and also conducted its own study of school performance.[48] Because this study adjusted for the characteristics of schools that may affect performance, it allows for a meaningful comparison of student performance across individual schools. In particular, this analysis controlled for: (1) the percentage of students eligible for free lunches in the school, a measure of poverty; (2) the percentage of students with limited English proficiency, a measure of academic disadvantage; and (3) the percentage of the students who were in that school for the full year, a measure of population stability.

Controlling for these factors, the board generated "predicted" average performance scores for each school. The board then developed an "honor roll" of high-achieving schools, which included those schools in which students scored at least fifteen points above the predicted value. With seven such high-performing schools, District 4 currently has more such schools than any other district in the city. However, with its emphasis on many small schools of choice, District 4 has more individual schools than most other districts. To address this difference, we examine the percentage of schools in a district that the Board of Education finds to have high-performing schools. In this calculation District 4 ranks fourth of the thirty-two districts, with 15 percent of its schools noted on this honor roll. Taking this calculation to its logical conclusion, since school sizes vary, we examine how many of the students who took the reading tests in each district are enrolled at schools on this honor roll. Here District 4 regains its top position in New York City, with 20 percent of tested students in high-performing schools. Thus, by whatever measure of high-performing schools, District 4 is the top, or nearly the top, district in New York City.

In analyzing the current performance of District 4, we are able to go one step further, thanks to the availability of more complete data. Having obtained data on school performance for the last three years for each school in the city, we are able to analyze how schools in District 4 today are performing compared to schools across the rest of the city. And, because this analysis is done at the school level, we are able to create more refined models than was possible for the district-level analysis over time. As we are analyzing data at the school level, we utilize the New York State performance tests.

The results of our analysis for grade six test scores are presented in table 13.2. Our data show that, for both math and reading scores in 1996, on average schools in District 4 performed significantly better than schools in the rest of the city. This analysis is more refined because it controls for many variables, including race (percent black, percent Hispanic, and percent Asian students in each school), school size, poverty (percent eligible for free lunch), turnover of students (percent in the same school all year), immigration status (percent in the United States less than three years), and percent of students with limited English proficiency. This is a robust test of today's performance, and our analysis shows a strong District 4 performance.

The coefficient on the District 4 variable shows that, with other variables held equal, schools in District 4 score nearly eight points higher on sixth grade reading tests than other schools: increasing from a base rate of 45 percent of students performing at or above grade level to 53 percent at or above grade level. Schools in District 4 again show significantly better performance, with an increase of over four points in math scores, compared to equivalent schools in other districts.

TABLE 13.2   Test Score Performance (1996) at the School Level[a]

Independent Variable	Reading Scores Coefficient[b]	Math Scores Coefficient[b]
District 4	8.00**	4.64**
	(3.03)	(2.39)
Size of school	0.001	0.0009
population	(.002)	(0.001)
Limited English %	−0.54**	−0.28**
	(0.10)	(0.08)
Free lunch %	−0.009	0.004
	(0.01)	(0.01)
Less than 3 years	−0.11	0.08
in USA %	(0.16)	(0.13)
% in school all year	0.55**	0.26*
	(0.18)	(0.14)
% Black	−0.38**	−0.19**
	(0.04)	(0.03)
% Hispanic	−0.32**	−0.12**
	(0.05)	(0.04)
% Asian	0.09	0.08
	(0.07)	(0.06)
Constant	45.2**	75.1**
	(17.43)	(14.53)
	N = 467;	N = 453;
	Adjusted R^2 = 0.49	Adjusted R^2 = 0.26
	Significance $p < .001$	Significance $p < .001$

[a]Sixth grade test scores as a function of school factors and district 4 location.
[b]Standard errors.
**Significant at 99% level of confidence.
*Significant at 95% level.

These results also address some of the concerns expressed by scholars skeptical about the independent effect of District 4: our results show that it is not smaller schools that drive District 4 test performance nor is it higher SES students "imported" into the district. Moreover, any "Hawthorne effect" must be incredibly powerful to still be in place in 1996, after twenty-two years of experience with choice.

We also ran these same models using test scores from 1995 and 1994, to test whether 1996 was a year of exceptional performance in District 4. Except for math scores in 1994, the District 4 effect is significant and positive in all of these cases. New York City students are also given New York State performance tests in the third and eighth grades. We ran these same models, and for third grade scores, the District 4 variable is significant and positive in half of the six cases (reading and math, over 1994, 1995, and 1996). Students are only tested for reading in eighth grade and here we do not find a District 4 effect. We believe that studies that show that minority adolescent students are less likely to be influenced by any school-related activities at this age may explain this finding for eighth grade test scores.[49]

Thus we have documented significant district-level improvements in math and reading scores, with the fastest growth happening during the greatest expansion of choice programs. Using more detailed, school-level data, we have shown a large and significant district-level effect for sixth grade reading and math scores, in a model with strong controls for student and school characteristics. The size of these improvements in test scores is not trivial. For example, in the literature we reviewed on other school reforms and their effects on test scores, even when researchers can document positive effects, and this happens in less than half of the studies, the percentage improvements are rarely larger than those documented here.

We note that, even with these improvements, District 4 is far from the top district in New York City. For example, in 1996 on average 35 percent of District 4 children in grades 3–8 read at or above their grade level, while the percentage performing math at or above grade level was 51 percent (citywide averages in 1996 were 42 percent and 59 percent, respectively). It would be impressive indeed if we could argue that a reform like choice, or any reform, could break the relationship between test scores and parent socioeconomic status. There is still room for schools and students in District 4 to do better, and 80 percent of the district's students are enrolled in schools that did not make the "honor roll." But it is impossible to dispute that test scores have improved and that they are better today than in schools in New York City districts with comparable levels of poverty and disadvantage.

How Has Choice in District 4 Improved School Performance?

Many analysts who are skeptical of school choice programs wonder how choice alone can lead to better schools. For schools to improve, there must be pressure from the "demand" side of the marketlike setting that choice encourages, as well as improvements on the "supply" side by the schools themselves. District 4 encouraged both types of responses. By providing choice and information to parents, District 4 encouraged important changes on the "demand" side.[50] Here we address briefly the supply side of choice in District 4.

Starting in 1974, District 4 encouraged smaller schools that would experiment with new teaching ideas and approaches. Administrators hoped that parents would discover the schools that were improving and "vote with their feet," enrolling their children in these schools. District officials also hoped that competition would stimulate improvements in the non-choice schools as well, a point we address in the next section.

But the creation of alternative schools responsive to parent interest and scrutinized for quality inevitably raises the problem of what to do about schools that are not successful. Many advocates of choice argue that, for choice to work, unsuccessful schools must be closed or face some other negative consequences. While everyone recognizes that closing a school is painful, and nearly impossible during the school year, advocates of choice argue that the occasional closing of schools should not be viewed as a failure but instead as a necessary step for improving schools. Choice advocates also point out that few unsuccessful schools are actually ever closed in non-choice districts.

We interviewed current officials in District 4 to identify the conditions they view as indicators of problems. Among the most important is declining enrollment, a concrete form of "exit" through which parents are clearly signaling unhappiness with a school. The use of "voice" or complaints from parents also can help draw attention to a problem school, but parents who have children who attend poorly performing schools do not complain as often as other parents.

While parental actions are the most important indicators of school problems, other signs of a school's decline monitored by District 4 officials include significant decreases in test scores and problems with the staff—high turnover, low morale, and weak leadership. None of this requires outstanding leadership: all these indicators—"consumer" dissatisfaction through exit and voice, declining performance, and poor staff morale—are typically used by private sector organizations to monitor performance. What is important is that choice has expanded the incentives and the opportunities for district administrators to monitor the quality of school performance.

If a school is performing poorly, administrators can attempt to change the school's approach or close it down. Closure, while not simple, is often more successful for a basic reason: Once a school has a negative reputation, it is very difficult to change. However, not all schools with low test scores, low enrollment, and staff problems are closed—only the worst schools have actually been shut down. District 4 schools that have been closed in the past include the School of Communications and Health Services, which was closed because of difficulties with student discipline, structure, and leadership. The Sports School was also closed, because its students were not meeting academic standards.[51] After its closure, the Sports School was remade into New York Prep, which is still open today. The School of Communications and Health Services was remade into Creative Learning Community, which has also recently been closed. Other recent closures include the Key School, Bridge School, East Harlem Maritime School, and the East Harlem Performing Arts School.

As the earlier examples illustrate, when District 4 closes schools they are often replaced by schools with new themes and new leadership. This provides some dynamism to the supply side of choice in District 4. As choice has matured and as the role of parents in the district has solidified, the source of inspiration for new schools has changed. Whereas in the 1970s and 1980s ideas for schools were mainly provided by individual teachers, ideas today are often provided by community-based organizations. Three new schools have been created in District 4 in the last five years. One of these new schools, the Young Woman's Leadership School, has attracted considerable attention in the national media because of its status as a publicly funded single-sex institution.

Has Choice in District 4 Affected the Distribution of Educational Opportunity?

Our second, and related, research question focuses on whether or not choice has left students in non-choice neighborhood schools worse off than they otherwise would have been had the schools of choice not been created. This is important because the majority of K–6 students in District 4 are still in neighborhood schools. We address this issue by investigating how neighborhood elementary schools have performed over time. By gauging the performance of these schools, we can assess the degree to which District 4 test score performance has been driven only by a top tier of elite schools.

We analyzed performance on the city-administered tests in the ten neighborhood elementary schools (of sixteen) in District 4 that had the lowest reading scores in 1996.[52] Earlier we analyzed the performance of these schools relative to the citywide average twenty years ago and today. If choice in District 4 has led to skimming and stratification, then, as better students choose to enroll in alternative schools of choice, these neighborhood schools should be particularly hard hit.

The evidence suggests that the neighborhood schools have *not* been adversely affected by the creation of alternative schools. We examined reading scores at grades three and six and math scores at grades three and five (there are no time trends for grade six math). Again, we compared the actual scores to citywide averages to address the problem of changing tests over time. For all ten schools taken as a whole, reading and math scores were actually *higher* relative to citywide averages in the period 1994–96 than they were in 1974–76. Third grade reading scores improved from 57 percent to 69 percent of the citywide average over this period, while sixth grade reading scores improved from 59 percent to 84 percent. For these ten schools, math scores improved even more; third grade scores went from 55 percent to 87 percent of the citywide average, while fifth grade math scores improved from 49 percent to 95 percent.

One possibility is that by combining all ten schools, we might be over-looking the fact that a few may have fallen substantially over the past two decades. But this is not the case. Combining four separate sets of scores (two different grades for reading and two for math) across the ten schools, we have forty comparisons. Of these forty comparisons, thirty show improvements over time, six show no change, but only four show decline over time.[53]

Thus there is no evidence that neighborhood schools have been left behind; indeed, the data show quite clearly that choice in District 4 has not produced any "loser" school. To the contrary: our data show most of these schools have improved over time, relative to the citywide averages, suggesting that choice has put competitive pressure on all schools to improve. Even if neighborhood elementary schools are not "choice" schools, parents can still opt out of them for alternative school programs, giving them the "exit" option. In turn, neighborhood schools are competing to retain, if not to attract, students and this has put pressure on them to maintain, if not improve, their academic performance. These patterns suggest that choice in District 4 has expanded the range of educational alternatives for parents and students of various types.

We believe that our results present strong evidence that intradistrict choice "works"—that at least in District 4, it has unleashed strong forces in the community and in the local school system that have led to significant improvements in academic performance. However, if we can "replicate" these results in another district that has implemented choice, then our confidence in these results should increase.

Choice in District 2

Community School District 2 covers much of midtown Manhattan, including a wide range of neighborhoods. Geographically, it is a large district, in part because it includes many office buildings without residences. With 22,000 students, it is nearly twice as large as District 4. Many of the residents in more affluent neighborhoods in District 2 had sent their children to private schools, as only a few of the district public schools were considered to be high quality. In contrast to District 4, which has higher percentages of low-income and Hispanic students than the citywide averages, students in District 2 are above city averages for income and are more likely to be white.

In 1988, Anthony Alvarado became superintendent of District 2, after he briefly had been chancellor of the New York City Board of Education, but lost that position due to a financial scandal. He quickly began to do in District 2 much of what he had done in District 4 some fifteen years earlier. Especially at the middle school level, he encouraged the creation of new, smaller schools of choice. As in District 4, this idea expanded, until the number of middle school programs reached twenty-five in 1998. In addition, there are four option schools at the elementary school level, and parents are allowed and encouraged to send their children to zoned, neighborhood schools other than their own, if they find the approach of that school more appropriate.

Associated with this expansion of choice, in recent years there has been considerable anecdotal evidence of test score improvements and exciting school environments, resulting in parents' clamoring to get their children into District 2 schools. For example, one author wrote that District 2 "has been a powerful magnet for many of the middle-class parents who have quietly been returning to public schools in droves."[54] This improvement was apparent to many observers and parents. Hemphill writes: "Anthony Alvarado . . . over the course of a decade, transformed the schools of midtown, downtown and the East Side of Manhattan from old-fashioned, lackluster institutions, avoided by anyone who had a choice, into exciting, creative places much in demand. . . . So popular are the schools in District 2 . . . that several students have been caught sneaking into them from the suburbs."[55]

While this analysis risks providing fuel for those who would argue that it isn't choice that improves performance but rather the magic leadership of Alvarado, again we suggest that the two factors are related, and that choice can continue to work without a particular leader. To see the effects of choice in District 2, we replicated the over-time analysis we performed for District 4. Here, we utilized a measure of the expansion of District 2 schools of choice, starting in 1988 and building through 1996. This variable equals zero for the period 1974–88, before District 2 began choice, and increases from zero in 1988 to forty by 1996 to capture the percentage of District 2 schools that are now choice schools.

The results, reported in table 13.3, show that District 2 reading scores, again relative to the citywide average, went up over this period, associated with the increase in the district choice variable. Math scores, however, do not show any statistically significant change. Thus, while we can be very confident that District 2 reading scores have improved over this period relative to the citywide averages on these tests, we can not say that for math scores. The other variables in the empirical model are mostly significant, all in the expected direction and all quite comparable to the results in table 13.1.

The coefficient for the District 2 choice variable means that, on average, reading scores improved by three percentage points, relative to the city average, for every ten-percentage-point increase in choice schools provided from 1988 to 1996. This is about half the size of the same increase in District 4 reported above, but the improvement took place in less than half the

TABLE 13.3 District 2 Test Score Performance over Time Compared to Other NYC Districts[a]

Independent Variable	Reading Scores Coefficient[b]	Math Scores Coefficient[b]
% of schools in District 2 that are choice schools	.25* (.13)	−.14 (.15)
Pupil/teacher ratio	.04 (.16)	−.05 (.20)
% of teachers with more than 5 years experience	−.06 (.04)	−.10* (.05)
% of students eligible for free lunches	−.69** (.09)	−.74** (.10)
% of black students	−.73** (.10)	−.84** (.13)
% of Hispanic students	−.68** (.09)	−.78** (.11)
Constant	208.04**	227.66**
	N = 746; Chi²(59) = 8898 Significance $p < .000$	N = 730; Chi²(59) = 6178 Significance $p < .000$

[a]Pooled district-level fixed effects model of relative test scores as a function of district characteristics and district 2 location, 1974–96. We also included, but do not report, dummy variables for 31 of the 32 districts and 22 of the 23 time points.
[b]Panel-corrected standard errors.
**Significant at 99% level of confidence.
*Significant at 95% level of confidence.

time. This supports the statement by Goldstein that "in eight years under Alvarado's tutelage, District 2 has moved from eleventh to second out of 32 districts in student test scores."[56]

We also ran a parallel cross-sectional analysis for 1996 test scores at the school level, comparable to the analysis reported in table 13.2 for District 4. Here, we did not find a significant effect for District 2 schools, although the coefficient is positive. This suggests that, contrary to the case for District 4, we cannot say that reading and math test score performance in District 2 today is significantly better than the demographics of the student body would "predict" that it should be.

Together, these results suggest that prior to the implementation of choice by Alvarado, students in District 2 were performing below expectations, given their socioeconomic status. Anecdotal evidence confirms this pattern. Choice has helped to raise performance, in eight years, to the "predicted" level for such a group of students. In contrast, District 4 was performing only a little below its "predicted" level twenty-five years ago, when choice was started, and it has now improved to be above "predicted" levels.

Conclusions

Since 1992, parents of New York City public school children have theoretically had the opportunity to send their children to any school in the city system. In reality, the opportunities for interdistrict choice are extremely limited by space constraints and by procedural hurdles. While the central board keeps no comprehensive figures, perhaps 1 percent of public school K–8 students are now enrolled in districts outside of their own. A larger number of students are involved in the Annenberg alternative schools. And a larger number are participating in choice within their own community school districts. The district with the longest history of choice in New York is District 4, and District 2 has the second longest experience. We studied the effects of choice in these districts.

Previous studies have provided some evidence that choice in District 4 was successful in improving performance. Scholars have attacked this evidence as insufficient and open to multiple interpretations. In this chapter we provide stronger evidence about the success of District 4 students. Where possible, we have shown how these successes are linked to the expansion of school choice in District 4. Moving to a more detailed, school-level analysis, we have shown that reading and math scores in District 4 are significantly higher today than in comparable schools in other districts.

By incorporating relevant control variables into our statistical models, we are able to address directly some of the concerns that thoughtful skeptics have expressed about the analysis of District 4 as a choice experiment. We find that smaller schools alone do not predict higher test score performance. We find that, to the extent that the pupil/teacher ratio is a reasonable measure of resources, these ratios do not influence academic performance in schools in New York City, and they do not explain the rising academic performance of schools in District 4 in the 1970s and 1980s. By controlling for student demographics, we show that the rise in District 4 test scores is not a function of bringing in more well-prepared students from outside the district. By showing that District 4's scores remain significantly higher today than in comparable schools, we show that if District 4 benefited from the "Hawthorne effect" of getting considerable attention and resources showered upon it in the 1980s, it has been a very long-lasting effect. Given that the original District 4 leaders have left the system, the continued higher performance of District 4 schools suggests that leadership is not the only factor in their improvement.

On the "supply side" of choice, we discuss several ways in which District 4 officials have responded to failing and under-enrolled schools—for example, by closing them or by reorienting their approach. We also address the concern that District 4 has stratified its students into "winners and losers," by illustrating that students in the non-choice schools also have shown improvements in their test scores over time.

We supplement the evidence from District 4 with an analysis of test scores in District 2, which implemented choice fifteen years after District 4. We show that a similar expansion of choice schools in the more affluent District 2 also led to improvements in test scores. This evidence of District 2 test score improvement is important because it shows that the District 4 experience was not a "fluke" related to some unmeasured conditions within that district. It also shows that the District 4 improvement was not a function of the specific time period or the specific tests administered at certain times.

While the data do not allow us to establish absolutely that choice itself caused all of these improvements, we have partially ruled out several alternative explanations. We believe that a complete explanation requires that choice be recognized as a catalyst of these improvements.

Performance in District 4 and in District 2 today is still not at the level that educators and parents want. But performance has improved markedly over time in both districts, and it is significantly better in District 4 than performance in comparable urban districts. District 4 used choice to achieve positive results without causing a higher level of stratification than we see in other American school districts.

The broader literature on educational policy changes, including increasing school resources and altering institutional structures, does not provide clear evidence of improved performance. Given that students with perfect attendance are only in school about 15 percent of the time from age 5–18, this should not be completely surprising. As Coleman found more than thirty years ago, student performance is heavily affected by family, home, and neighborhood characteristics. In this context, the finding that choice policies in District 4 are associated with significantly higher levels of performance is impressive.

Not all policy changes are easy to replicate, and the concept of "scaling up" success stories to a larger context is a major concern in educational policy circles. In part because of the success of District 4, the New York City Board of Education implemented choice across districts. But without adequate space in desirable schools and districts, without a centralized mechanism to make the choice process more accessible for all parents, and without even a "tracking system" to determine where students are going to and leaving from, the board's commitment can hardly be described as "strong." Given the now documented successes of New York districts that have embraced choice as part of a reform philosophy, this is unfortunate.

NOTES

1. Robert Crain, "New York City's Career Magnet High Schools," in *School Choice: Examining the Evidence*, ed. Edith Rasell and Richard Rothstein (Washington, D.C.: Economic Policy Institute, 1993).

2. See chapter 3 of this book for details.

3. Paul Hill, Lawrence Pierce, and James Guthrie, *Reinventing Public Education: How Contracting Can Transform America's Schools* (Chicago: University of Chicago Press, 1997), p. 97.

4. Liz Willen, "School Choice: Parents' Primer," *Newsday*, June 7, 1998, p. A7.

5. Ibid.

6. William Ubinas, "Introducing Choice in an Urban District," in *Privatizing Education and Educational Choice*, ed. Simon Hakim, Paul Seidenstat, and Gary Bowman (Westport, Conn.: Praeger, 1994).

7. Seymour Fliegel, with James McGuire, *Miracle in East Harlem* (New York: Times Books, 1993); Raymond Domanico, *Model for Choice: A Report on Manhattan's District 4*, Center for Educational Innovation, Education Policy Paper No. 1 (New York: Manhattan Institute for Policy Research, 1989).

8. Fliegel, with McGuire, *Miracle in East Harlem*; Domanico, *Model for Choice*; David Kirp, "What School Choice Really Means," *Atlantic Monthly*, November 1992, p. 127.

9. Seymour Fliegel, "Creative Non-Compliance," in *Choice and Control in American Education*, vol. 2: *The Practice of Choice, Decentralization, and School Restructuring*, ed. William Clune and John Witte (New York: Falmer, 1990).

10. Deborah Meier, *The Power of Their Ideas: Lessons for America from a Small School in Harlem* (Boston: Beacon Press, 1995).

11. Ernest Boyer, *School Choice* (Princeton, N.J.: Carnegie Foundation, 1992), p. 9.

12. Kirp, "What School Choice Really Means."

13. Peter W. Cookson Jr., *School Choice: The Struggle for the Soul of American Education* (New Haven: Yale University Press, 1994), p. 78.

14. This argument has been made by several authors, including Howard Hurwitz, *The Last Angry Principal* (Portland, Oreg.: Halcyon House, 1988); Peter W. Cookson Jr., *The Choice Controversy* (Newbury Park, Calif.: Corwin Press, 1992); Jeffrey Henig, "The Local Dynamics of Choice: Ethnic Preferences and Institutional Responses," in *Who Chooses? Who Loses?: Culture, Institutions, and the Unequal Effects of School Choice*, ed. Bruce Fuller, Richard F. Elmore, and Gary Orfield (New York: Teachers College Press, 1996); and Kirp, "What School Choice Really Means."

15. Henig, "The Local Dynamics of Choice," p. 131.

16. Kirp, "What School Choice Really Means."

17. Fliegel, *Miracle in East Harlem*.

18. Kirp, "What School Choice Really Means"; Diane Harrington and Peter W. Cookson Jr., "School Reform in East Harlem: Alternative Schools versus Schools of Choice," in *Empowering Teachers and Parents*, ed. G. Alfred Hess (Westport, Conn.: Bergin and Garvey, 1992).

19. See also Amy Stuart Wells, *Time to Choose: America at the Crossroads of School Choice Policy* (New York: Hill and Wang, 1993), p. 56.

20. Harrington and Cookson, "School Reform in East Harlem," p. 181.

21. Jeffrey Henig, *Rethinking School Choice: Limits of the Market Metaphor* (Princeton: Princeton University Press, 1994); Valerie Lee, "Educational Choice: The Stratifying Effects of Selecting Schools and Courses," *Educational Policy* 7, no. 2 (1993).

22. Timothy Young and Evans Clinchy, *Choice in Public Education* (New York: Teachers College Press, 1992), p. 25.

23. Henig, "Local Dynamics of Choice"; Myron Lieberman, *Privatization and Educational Choice* (New York: St. Martins, 1989).

24. Cookson, *School Choice*, p. 55.

25. See, for example, Kevin Smith and Kenneth Meier, *The Case against School Choice: Politics, Markets, and Fools* (Armonk, N.Y.: M. E. Sharpe, 1995).

26. Cookson, *The Choice Controversy*, p. 91; see also Richard Elmore, "Public School Choice as a Policy Issue," in *Privatization and Its Alternatives*, ed. William Gormley (Madison: University of Wisconsin Press, 1991).

27. James Coleman et al., *Equality of Educational Opportunity* (Washington, D.C.: U.S. Government Printing Office, 1966).

28. Eric Hanushek, "The Economics of Schooling: Production and Efficiency in Public Schools," *Journal of Economic Literature* 24 (1986).

29. Larry Hedges, R. Lane, and R. Greenwald, "Does Money Matter? A Meta-Analysis of Studies of the Effects of Differential School Inputs on Student Outcomes," *Educational Researcher* (April 1994).

30. David Card and Alan Krueger, "Does School Quality Matter? Returns to Education and the Characteristics of Public Schools in the United States," *Journal of Political Economy* 100, no. 1 (1992).

31. But see Robert Speakman and Finis Welsh, "Does School Quality Matter? A Reassessment," Texas A&M University, Department of Economics paper, 1995; Jeff Grogger, "Does School Quality Explain the Recent Black / White Wage Trend?" *Journal of Labor Economics* 14, no. 2 (1996).

32. William Sander, "Expenditures and Student Achievement in Illinois," *Journal of Public Economics* 52 (1993).

33. Ronald Ferguson, "Paying for Public Education: New Evidence on How and Why Money Matters," *Harvard Journal on Legislation* 28, no. 2 (1991); J. Folger, "Project STAR and Class Size Policy," *Peabody Journal of Education* 67, no. 1 (1992).

34. Ronald Ferguson, "How and Why Money Matters: An Analysis of Alabama Schools," in *Holding Schools Accountable*, ed. Helen Ladd (Washington, D.C.: Brookings Institution, 1996).

35. Frederick Mosteller, "How Does Class Size Relate to Achievement in Schools?" in *Earning and Learning*, ed. Paul Peterson and Susan Mayer (Washington, D.C.: Brookings Institution, 1999).

36. Eric Hanushek, "The Evidence on Class Size," in ibid.

37. Eric Hanushek, "School Resources and Outcomes," *Journal of Educational Research and Analysis*, 1997.

38. John Chubb and Terry Moe, *Politics, Markets, and America's Schools* (Washington, D.C.: Brookings Institution, 1990).

39. John Witte, "Evaluation of Choice in Milwaukee," in *Who Chooses? Who Loses?: Culture, Institutions, and the Unequal Effects of School Choice*, ed. Bruce Fuller, Richard F. Elmore, and Gary Orfield (New York: Teachers College Press, 1996); Paul

Peterson, Jay Greene, and Chad Noyes, "School Choice in Milwaukee," *The Public Interest* 125 (1996).

40. Cecilia Rouse, "Private School Vouchers and Student Achievement: An Evaluation of the Milwaukee Parental Choice Program," *Quarterly Journal of Economics* 113 (1998).

41. Because of limited data, we could average only grades three, six, and eight in the years 1974–81. However, this three-grade average is highly correlated with the full 3–8 grade average in years when both averages can be computed.

42. Note that sometimes when the tests were changed the variance of the thirty-two community school districts around the city average also changed. Without detailed figures on the national variances of these tests, it is not clear how to handle this issue. It is clear that in the 1980s the variance of the thirty-two districts for math got much smaller, meaning that lower-performing districts generally moved closer to the mean, as did higher-performing districts. This may imply that the improvement in District 4 math scores relative to the city average overstates the "real" improvement, or it may have to do with the variance of the tests generally. In general, "regression to the mean" is a phenomenon in which districts tend to converge over time toward an average level—that is, over time, the worst districts should do better, while the best districts are expected to do worse. We tested for this problem by examining District 4's performance in the early days of choice in the mid-1970s. We found that, controlling for race and poverty, District 4 was performing about as "predicted" at that time.

43. We believe that this percentage is a reasonable measure of the extent of competition involved in District 4 choice. A better measure would be the percentage of students enrolled in choice schools, but we were unable to get the information going back twenty years. Note that we could also create a simple model with a "counter" that grows by one each year. Since math and reading scores in District 4 increase over time, any variable that reflects the temporal expansion of choice will correlate with this increase in scores. But we have theoretical reasons to expect that choice was associated with improved performance, as well as empirical data.

44. When estimating a pooled model, researchers must address a complex set of problems that includes those normally arising in a cross-sectional analysis, as well as additional problems due to the spatial and temporal nature of the data. In this chapter, we follow Beck and Katz in relying on OLS when estimating our models (Nathaniel Beck and Jonathon Katz, "Nuisance vs. Substance: Specifying and Estimating Time-Series-Cross-Section Models," *Political Analysis* 6 [1995]). Since different districts are likely to perform at different levels, we follow a fixed-effects approach and correct for different levels of the dependent variable across districts by including a dummy variable for each district in both models. We also include a dummy variable for each year but one, to deal with time effects. And finally, in both models, we report the panel-corrected standard errors.

45. Of course, as with any linear regression model, one must be careful about projecting these results beyond the range for which they were estimated. That is, there is clearly some limit to the payoffs that can be expected to be achieved by creating additional choice schools, and we should not expect improvements to be unbounded.

46. Peterson et al., "School Choice in Milwaukee."

47. Note that we include the racial variables as statistical controls for different student body characteristics across districts and schools. That black and Hispanic students score lower on these tests is a function of the data reported by the Board of Education. We do not in any way suggest that school officials or parents do or should have lower expectations for minority student performance. But if we do not include racial variables in these equations, we will not be comparing properly different student bodies and may mistakenly attribute or not attribute changes to choice or other policy variables.

48. This is the Board of Education's "Ranking of Schools by Reading Achievement: Overall Comparison of Reading Achievement in Similar Schools," prepared by the board's Division of Assessment and Accountability.

49. See, for example, Ronald Ferguson, "How Professionals in Community-based Programs Perceive and Respond to the Needs of Black Male Youth," in *Nurturing Young Black Males*, ed. Ronald Miney (Washington, D.C.: Urban Institute Press, 1991).

50. See, for example, Mark Schneider, Paul Teske, Melissa Marschall, and Christine Roch, "Shopping for Schools: In the Land of the Blind, the One-Eyed Parent May Be Enough," *American Journal of Political Science* 92 (1998).

51. Fliegel, *Miracle in East Harlem*, pp. 120–26.

52. These schools are PS 7, 50, 52, 72, 96, 101, 102, 108, 121, and 155.

53. Of these four negative trends, two are from PS 155, where reading scores in grades three and six declined; however, over the same time period, math scores in the school improved. Scores for grade three reading in PS 57 declined, but performance in two other tests remained steady and the school improved on one test. The final decline occurred in PS 96, where performance on grade five math dropped, but the three other comparisons showed improvement over time.

54. Michael Goldstein, "The Trials of Anthony Alvarado," *New York Magazine*, October 13, 1997, p. 82.

55. Clara Hemphill, *The Parents' Guide to New York City's Best Public Elementary Schools* (New York: Soho Press, 1997), p. 39.

56. Goldstein, "The Trials of Anthony Alvarado."

14 When Low-Income Students Move from Public to Private Schools

PAUL E. PETERSON AND WILLIAM G. HOWELL

Over the past few years, the school choice movement has taken off. Congress and many state legislatures have considered school voucher proposals that enable families, particularly low-income families, to choose among a wide range of schools, public and private, religious and secular. In 1990 the Wisconsin legislature enacted a pilot program that gave public students access to secular private schools in Milwaukee; then in 1996 the legislature expanded this program to include religious schools. After surviving a constitutional challenge, the program went into effect in the fall of 1998. A similar program in Cleveland, enacted by the Ohio legislature, began its fourth year of operation in the fall of 1999, but at the time of this writing its future was uncertain due to a court challenge. Also in 1999, a potentially large state-wide voucher program was initiated in Florida.

Interest groups, political leaders, and policy analysts on all sides of the ideological spectrum have debated the merits of school-choice programs. The conversation is charged, and the country remains far from any kind of consensus. Supporters of school choice assert that low-income, inner-city children learn more in private schools; critics retort that any perceived learning gains in private schools are due to the more advantaged student body typically found in private schools. Proponents insist that families develop closer communications with schools they themselves choose; critics reply that when choices are available, mismatches often occur and private schools expel problem students, adding to the educational instability of children from low-income, inner-city families. Champions of choice suggest that a more orderly educational climate in private schools enhances learning opportunities, while opponents submit that private schools select out the "best and the brightest," leaving behind the most disadvantaged.

Voucher advocates argue that choice fosters racial and ethnic integration;[1] critics, meanwhile, insist that private schools balkanize the population into racially and ethnically homogenous educational sectors.[2]

Few of these disputes have been resolved, in part because high-quality information about school-choice programs is in short supply. Although many published studies compare public and private schools, they consistently have been criticized for comparing dissimilar populations. Even when statistical adjustments are made for background characteristics, it remains unclear whether findings describe actual differences between public and private schools or simply differences in the kinds of students and families attending them.[3]

Though the problem of selection bias has plagued education research for years, it is not insurmountable. The best solution is to randomly assign individuals to treatment and control groups, thus creating two populations that are by and large identical to one another. This procedure is standard in medical research, and recently it has found its way into education studies, such as the Tennessee Star experiment that found that smaller classes positively affect the achievement of those in kindergarten and first grade.[4] Until now, however, this type of research design has not been carefully used to study the validity of competing claims about school choice.

In this chapter we report outcomes from a randomized experiment conducted in New York City that was made possible by the School Choice Scholarships Foundation (SCSF), a privately funded school choice program. The program represents the first opportunity to evaluate a school-choice pilot program that has the following characteristics:

1. A lottery that allocates scholarships randomly to applicants and that has been administered by an independent evaluation team that can guarantee its integrity.
2. Baseline data on student test performance and family background characteristics are collected from students and their families prior to the lottery.
3. Data on a broad range of characteristics are collected from a high proportion of the test group and the control group one year later.

Because it has these qualities, the SCSF is an ideal laboratory for studying the effects of school choice on such things as parental satisfaction, parental involvement, school mobility, racial integration, and student achievement.

The School Choice Scholarships Foundation Program

In February 1997 SCSF announced that it would provide 1,300 scholarships to low-income families currently attending public schools. These scholarships were worth up to $1,400 annually, and could be used for up to three years to help pay the costs of attending a private school, either religious or secular. SCSF received initial applications from over twenty thousand students between February and late April 1997.

In order to become eligible for a scholarship, children had to be entering grades one through five, live in New York City, attend a public school at the time of application, and come from families with incomes low enough to qualify for the federal government's free school lunch program. Students and an adult member of each family had to attend verification sessions at which SCSF administrators documented family income and children's public-school attendance. Because of the large number of initial applications, it was not feasible to invite everyone to these verification sessions. Therefore, to give all families an equal chance of participating, a preliminary lottery determined whose income and public school attendance SCSF would verify. Only these families were then included in the final lottery that determined the allocation of scholarships among applicants.

The final lottery, held in mid-May 1997, was administered by Mathematica Policy Research (MPR); SCSF announced the winners. SCSF decided in advance to allocate 85 percent of the scholarships to applicants from public schools whose average test scores were less than the citywide median. Consequently, applicants from these schools, who represented about 70 percent of all applicants, were assigned a higher probability of winning a scholarship. The results presented in this chapter have been adjusted, by weighting cases differentially, so that they can be generalized to all eligible applicants.

Subsequent to the lottery, SCSF helped families find placements in private schools. By mid-September 1997, SCSF reported that 1,168 scholarship recipients, or 75 percent of all those offered a scholarship, had successfully gained admission to some 225 private schools.

Evaluation Procedures

In order to evaluate the voucher program, SCSF collected baseline data on student test scores, family demographics, and parents' opinions on matters relating to their child's education; one of the conditions for participating in the program was agreement to provide confidential baseline and follow-up information.

Collection of Baseline Data

During the initial verification sessions, students entering grades two through five took the Iowa Test in Basic Skills (ITBS) in reading and mathematics. Each student's performance was given a national percentile ranking that varies between one and one hundred. The national average is fifty. While children completed the hour-long test, adults answered questionnaires in a separate room. Although grandmothers and other relatives and guardians also accompanied children to verification sessions, in over 90 percent of the cases a parent completed the questionnaire. Because scholarships were allocated by a lottery, there were few differences between scholarship recipients and nonrecipients, though baseline test scores of nonrecipients were somewhat higher.

First-Year Follow-up

To evaluate the effects of the scholarship on students and their families, MPR selected at random students from 1,000 families who had been offered a scholarship and from 960 families who had attended a verification session but had not been offered a scholarship. Procedures used to select the control group are described elsewhere.[5] In April, May, and June of 1998, these families were invited to attend sessions during which students again took the ITBS in mathematics and reading. Parents completed follow-up surveys that asked a wide range of questions about the educational experiences of their oldest child within the age range eligible for a scholarship. Students in grades three, four, and five also completed short questionnaires.

Among recipients and nonrecipients, 83 percent of those selected for participation agreed to attend the testing and questionnaire sessions held in April and May 1998. This high response rate was achieved in part because SCSF conditioned the renewal of scholarships on participation in the evaluation; nonrecipients selected to become members of the control group were financially compensated and told that they could automatically enter a new lottery if they participated in these follow-up sessions.[6]

Validity of the Randomized Experiment

When randomized experiments are conducted, it is important to consider their internal and external validity. The internal validity of an experiment depends on whether or not the test and control groups are in fact similar in all respects, save for the experimental condition. Its external validity depends on the extent to which one can generalize from the experimental group to a larger population. We consider each in turn.

Internal Validity

As mentioned previously, three conditions allowed the evaluation team to execute an experiment that had a high degree of internal validity. First, since the evaluation team itself performed the lottery assigning students to test and control groups, one can be confident that the comparison groups were similar, on average, except that the members of one group were offered a scholarship. Second, response rates were high, reducing the chances that results would be dependent upon the characteristics of those applicants who proved willing to remain in the evaluation after one year.[7] Third, 75 percent of those receiving the scholarship made use of the scholarship. As compared to those who did not use their scholarships, users had similar incomes but were more likely to be college educated and were advantaged in a number of other respects; on the other hand, they were also more likely to be African American.[8] Because of these differences, comparisons between scholarship users and the appropriate control group were estimated by means of a statistical technique commonly used in medical evaluations to adjust for differential patient use of the medical procedure under investigation.[9]

External Validity: Small Groups and Large Groups

Although a randomized experiment can achieve a high degree of internal validity by securing high response rates and adjusting for noncompliance (in this case, scholarship recipients who stayed in the public schools and nonrecipients who attended private schools), questions of external validity remain. In medical research, it may be unclear whether one will obtain the same results when one expands treatment beyond a small group. The difficulties of generalization are no less significant in the field of education. Vouchers and scholarships may have positive effects when used on a small scale, but the consequences may be quite different when writ large. Because the SCSF program only reached a small percentage of eligible New York City students, for example, it probably had little impact on the composition of public and private student bodies: larger programs may have a more substantial effect on the two educational sectors and thereby generate a different set of findings. The only way to find out is to expand the scale of the experiment to include ever larger populations.

External Validity: Differences between Applicant and Eligible Population

Questions about the external validity of a school choice experiment arise , however, even before any student has been awarded a scholarship. As with any intervention, only a certain percentage of the eligible population will be interested in and have the means of taking advantage of it. If the applicant population is very unusual, it becomes difficult to generalize from this group to one that a larger voucher program might reach.

It is quite possible that many families who met SCFS's requirements, and who were interested in sending their child to a private school, never heard of the program in the first place. And of those who were informed and who considered applying, many others may have decided not to participate in the lengthy eligibility verification sessions. Given these barriers to entry, it is possible that the application process attracted a population substantially different from a cross-section of all those eligible.

To estimate the distinctiveness of the voucher applicants, Rachel Deyette at Harvard's Kennedy School of Government obtained demographic information on the general New York City population that would have been eligible had scholarships been offered in 1990, the last year in which a U.S. census was taken.[10] Her estimate is based on data collected at a time when New York's economic and social conditions differed from those prevailing when applicants were surveyed. For one thing, in 1990 the economy was in a recession, whereas in 1997, the year SCSF first accepted applications, it was in the midst of a boom. In addition, education levels of the adult population rose during the interceding seven years. Nonetheless, Deyette's data provide a useful, albeit rough, estimate of the extent to which the SCSF applicants differ from those eligible within the larger New York population.

Deyette found no significant difference between these two groups' incomes, having adjusted for inflation between 1990 and 1997. Father employment rates were similar. Also, the residential mobility of the applicant population was about the same as that of the eligible population. And applicant mothers were only slightly more likely to be foreign-born than were the eligible population. Applicants were also more likely to be dependent on various forms of government assistance, less likely to be non-Hispanic white and more likely to be African American. If this suggests that the applicant population was particularly disadvantaged, other findings point in the opposite direction. Mothers and fathers were considerably more likely to have some college education, English was more likely to be the language spoken in the household, and mothers were more likely to be employed either full or part-time.

While SCSF applicants were somewhat different from the eligible population within New York City, these differences do not indicate that the applicant pool was a particularly advantaged group. Indeed, along most dimensions scholarship applicants appeared less advantaged than the large population from which they were drawn. While not definitive, these finding ought to allay some of voucher critics' concern that only "white and higher-SES families will . . . be in a position to take greater advantage of the educational market."[11]

Parental Reports on Public and Private Schools

In this section of the paper we discuss the effects of the choice program on student experiences in school, as perceived by their parents. Significant differences were observed in the school facilities available to students, the degree of ethnic integration, parental satisfaction, discipline problems in school, and school-parental communications.

School Facilities

Most observers believe that the facilities in central-city public schools are generally larger and more sophisticated than are those in central-city private schools. With a few exceptions, reports from applicant parents in New York City are consistent with this conventional wisdom. First of all, public schools are larger. As estimated by parents, the effect of taking a scholarship was to reduce the size of the school a child attended by 141 students, or about 30 percent. Private school parents also reported that their children were in smaller classes. With a scholarship, the size of a child's class dropped, on average, by 2.7 students, or about 10 percent.

But while public schools may be larger, they also have more varied and extensive programs and facilities to serve their students. (See figure 14.1.) Public schools were more likely to have a library, a cafeteria, a nurse's office, child counselors, and special programs for non–English speakers and students with learning problems. The biggest difference was for programs for non–English speaking students. Forty-eight percent of the scholarship parents reported such a program in their schools, as compared to three-quarters of the control group. Most other differences, however, were substantially smaller; for example, 80 percent of the scholarship families reported their school had a nurse's office, as compared to 94 percent of the parents in the control group. In a couple of instances, private school parents reported more extensive facilities and programs. For example, private school parents were somewhat more likely to say their schools had a computer laboratory and a music program. In other cases, such as arts programs, after-school programs, and programs for advanced learners, no differences between the two groups could be detected.

Ethnic Composition of School

Using a scholarship in New York City slightly reduced the racial isolation of minority students (figure 14.2). When asked, "What percentage of the students in this child's classroom are minority?" 18 percent of the scholarship users replied that less than half of the students in the classroom were of minority background. Only 11 percent of the parents in the control group gave this response. At the other end of the spectrum, 37 percent of the control-group parents said their child's classroom was all-minority, as compared to just 28 percent of the parents of scholarship users.

Parental Satisfaction

Most studies of voucher programs for low-income minority families have found that families receiving the scholarships are much more satisfied with

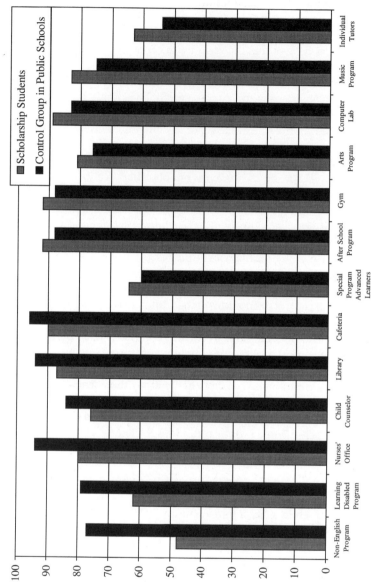

Figure 14.1. Facilities for Students in Public Schools

their child's schooling than are families who remain in public schools.[12] The results from New York confirm these earlier findings. When asked to assess the school's overall performance, private school parents give significantly higher grades than do public school parents. Half of the scholarship users gave their school an "A," as compared to one-eighth of the control group.

We also examined particular dimensions of parental satisfaction (figure 14.3). On every aspect of a school about which parents were questioned, scholarship parents were substantially more satisfied than parents in the control group. The percentage of "very satisfied" parents within the private school sector was significantly higher for all of the following: location of the school, school safety, parental involvement, class size, school facility, student respect for teachers, teacher communication with parents, freedom to observe religious traditions, parental support for the school, discipline, clarity of school goals, staff teamwork, teaching and academic quality.[13]

The scholarship program had the smallest impact on parents' satisfaction with school location. One-half of the scholarship parents were very satisfied with the school's location, but over a third of the control group was also very satisfied. In every other domain, however, differences between the two groups were considerably larger. For example, more than half of the scholarship parents were very satisfied with the academic quality of the school, while just one-sixth of the control group were. Similarly, 58 percent of the scholarship parents expressed the highest satisfaction with "what's taught in school," as compared to 18 percent of the control group.

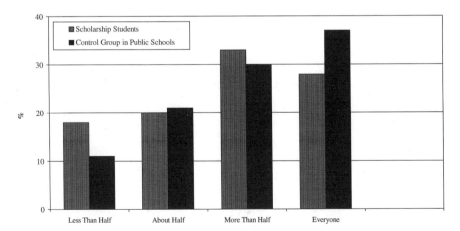

Figure 14.2. Racial Composition of Classroom (Percentage of students in child's class who are minority)

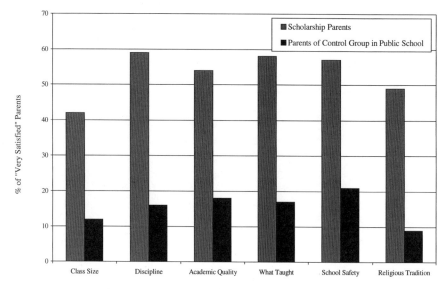

Figure 14.3. Parent Satisfaction with Child's School

The consistency of these findings reveals strong enthusiasm for the private schools participating in the voucher program, as compared with the level of satisfaction with public schools. Less emphasis, however, should be placed on the reports parents provide for specific items. Other evaluations of school voucher programs suggest that scholarship parents become increasingly discerning about the quality of their children's schools the more time that passes. Overarching excitement often gives way to a more considered assessment of the merits of public and private education. In Cleveland, for example, parents after two years in the program remained equally satisfied with the academic program, safety and school discipline at their school, but their satisfaction with school facilities, and parental involvement declined significantly.[14]

Discipline Problems in School

If parental reports are accurate, the scholarship program had a major impact on the quality and safety of students' lives at school. Take a look at figure 14.4. Scholarship parents were more likely to report that the following were *not* a serious problem at their school: students destroying property, being late for school, missing classes, fighting, cheating, and causing racial conflict. For example, 39 percent of the parents with students in private schools thought fighting was a serious problem at their school, versus nearly two-thirds of the control group. Thirty-eight percent of scholarship users perceived tardiness as a problem, as compared to 57 percent of parents within the control group. Nearly 30 percent of scholarship users and 49 percent of the control group said destruction of property was a serious problem.

Although student reports are not as sharply differentiated, they are nonetheless consistent with parental assessments. Scholarship students were more likely to report that "students got along with teachers" and "students are proud to go to this school." Scholarship students were also less likely to feel "put down" by teachers and to have friends who use bad language, though these differences are not statistically significant.

School Communications and Parental Involvement

Parents of scholarship users report much higher levels of communications from their children's schools. Figure 14.5 indicates that a higher percentage reported:

—being informed about student grades halfway through the grading period;
—being notified when their child is sent to the office the first time for disruptive behavior;
—parents speaking to classes about their jobs;
—parents participating in instruction;
—parent open-house or back-to-school night being held at the school;
—receiving notes about their child from the teacher;
—receiving a newsletter about what is going on in school;
—being informed by school administrators when the child is absent.

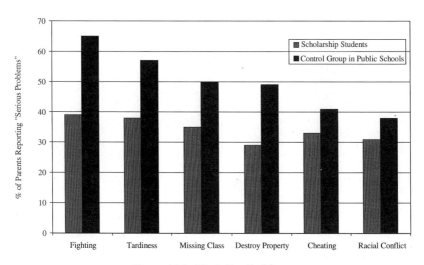

Figure 14.4. Discipline Problems

The largest differences involved parents receiving newsletters and notes from teachers and parents participating in instruction and speaking about their jobs. Over 90 percent of the scholarship users reported receiving notes from teachers as compared to just over three-fourths of the parents in the control group.

Critics of school choice often argue that perceived differences between voucher recipients and public school students have little to do with the schools themselves, but rather are a function of parental involvement. By virtue of applying for a voucher, parents distinguish themselves as more involved with their child's education. And from this basis, all subsequent differences in achievement and satisfaction derive. There is some reason to believe that the parents of voucher recipients differ somewhat from parents of public school students generally. Indeed, findings described earlier speak to this very issue. But it would be misleading to then conclude that parental involvement is a fixed characteristic. Again, because treatment and control groups were virtually identical at baseline, differences detected in New York can meaningfully be attributed to programmatic effects. The evidence presented here suggests that private schools may do a better job at communicating with parents about their children's progress and convincing them to participate in the classrooms.

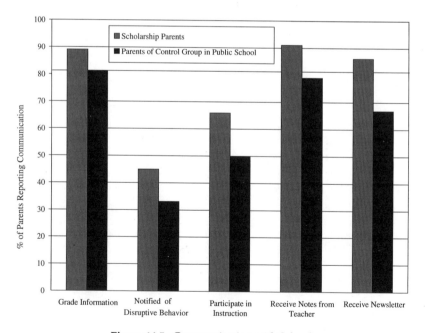

Figure 14.5. Communication with School

Continuing in the Program

All else being equal, students do better the less their education is disrupted. Does school choice destabilize a child's educational experience? In his evaluation of the Milwaukee school choice program, John Witte voiced concern about the high rate of attrition within private schools.[15] And a number of choice critics have raised questions about the readiness of private schools to expel students who do not "fit in."[16] But it is not entirely clear that a public school education is any more stable than a private one. Indeed, a number of studies of school choice have found that students from low-income families are more likely to remain in the same school, both within the school year and from one year to the next.[17]

Remaining in Same School during School Year

Most educators think that it is especially important that students remain within the same school for the entire school year. If school choice disrupted the education of many children within one school year, it would raise questions about the viability of voucher programs. In general, however, the findings from the SCSF pilot program indicate that this is not a serious concern: scholarship students were no more likely to move from one school to another than were the students in the control group.

Ninety-five percent of all students in the study were said to have remained in the same school the entire year, much higher than is typical of inner-city minority children in general.[18] No differences in school mobility rates are apparent between the scholarship parents and the control group. Similarly, suspension rates were much the same for both groups. Six percent of the parents in the control group and 4 percent of the scholarship users reported their child had been suspended.[19]

The few families who did change schools were asked why they changed. Among both groups, the reasons given were fairly evenly distributed across the variety of alternatives provided in the questionnaire. The most frequently mentioned reasons were that the school was too expensive or that the family had moved away from the school.[20] School expulsion or suspension was a trivial factor, affecting less than 1 percent of each group. In short, school mobility was very low and virtually identical for both scholarship users and members of the control group.

Plans for Next Year

Scholarship recipients said they were more likely to attend the same school next year than were members of the control group. Things look much the same when examining mobility rates across school years. Once again, differences between public and private schools are minimal. As one might expect, a larger percentage of families in both groups plan on switching schools over the summer than during the school-year itself. Eighty-four percent of the families using a scholarship said they expected their child to be back at the same school, as compared to 69 percent of the control group. Approximately 5 percent of scholarship parents said they planned to change schools because they did not find the quality of their school acceptable, and another 5 percent said they were preparing to move away from the school. The next most frequently mentioned reasons, given by less than 2 percent of scholarship parents, were expense and an inconvenient location. Less than one percent of all scholarship users said their school had asked them "not to return."

Nearly a third of the families in the control group were planning to change schools after the program's first year. However, 12 percent of those changing schools said it was because their child was graduating—presumably from elementary to middle school, a division found in New York public schools but not in most New York private schools. If these families are put to one side, there remains 19 percent of the control group that planned to change schools, about the same rate as among scholarship parents. Seven percent of the control group said the quality of their school was not acceptable. Less than 1 percent of all control group members said they were changing schools because their child had been asked not to return.

Test Performance

Most school choice experiments conducted thus far have not conformed to a classic randomized experiment. Privately funded programs in Indianapolis, San Antonio, and Milwaukee admitted students on a first-come, first-served basis. In the state-funded program in Cleveland, scholarship winners were initially selected by means of a lottery, but eventually all applicants were offered a scholarship, thereby precluding the conduct of a randomized experiment. The public Milwaukee program did award vouchers by a lottery, but data collection was incomplete.[21] Given the limitations on prior research, this evaluation provides a much improved opportunity to estimate the impact of attending a private school on scholarship recipients' test scores.

Figure 14.6 reports test score differences after one year between private school students and students in the control group. Results are provided on reading and mathematics for students in grades two, three, four, and five, and, finally, in order to increase the number of observations, for the combined group of fourth and fifth graders. Because baseline test scores were not collected from applicants then in kindergarten, no first grade results are reported.

Results varied somewhat from one grade to the next. After one year, second grade scholarship recipients scored, on average, five percentile points higher in math than students in the control group; the difference was seven percentile points for those in fourth grade and five points for those in fifth. The impacts of school choice are much the same for reading. Second grade reading scores increased by four points; fourth grade scores increased just one point; fifth grade scores jumped by six points. The effects among third graders are −2.0 points in math and −3.0 in reading; these results are not statistically significant. We do not know why gains are not observed in grade three.

Because they are based on a larger number of observations and thus are more robust, the results for fourth and fifth grade students combined are worthy of special attention. For these students, the impact of a scholarship student's attendance in a private school is five percentile points in math and three points in reading.

Equal Opportunity

Some critics of school choice concede that test scores may improve, but they suggest that gains will be concentrated among the most advan-

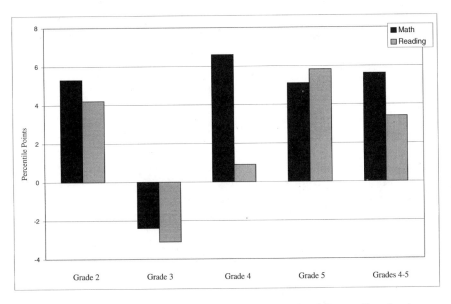

Figure 14.6. Test Score Gains from Attending a Private School (Percentile points by which private school students outperform control group in public schools)

taged, thereby increasing differences between higher-scoring and lower-scoring students.[22] Better students may win access to higher-quality schools, the argument goes, while lower-scoring students are relegated to less effective schools. The net result may constitute aggregate gains, but these come at the cost of greater variations in student performance.

Some defenders of school choice, by contrast, have argued that the opposite will occur.[23] They point to the fact that public schools need only report summary test score statistics, and it is on this basis that they are judged; to maximize these aggregate scores, public schools focus on the more talented students, then place the less talented in special education classes and exclude them from high-stakes tests. Private schools, by contrast, need to keep all of their paying customers happy, or else they will leave. Students in private schools, thus, ought to receive roughly the same amount of attention, regardless of their ability level.

To test these competing hypotheses, we calculated the coefficient of variation, a measure of test score dispersion for student test scores at baseline and again at the end of the first year. By identifying the direction and amount of change in the coefficient of variation between test scores at baseline and at the end of the first year, it is possible to determine the extent to which test score gains are becoming more or less dispersed. A negative sign suggests that achievement differences among students are diminishing, a positive sign, obviously, suggests that differences are increasing. As can be seen in table 14.1, the coefficients declined—that is, scores were becoming more similar over time, in both public and private schools. In other words, neither public nor private schools are contributing directly toward greater inequality in ability levels. In five of the six observations, the drop is not statistically significant for the students who remain in public schools (the control group). The size of the decline varied beween 0.00 and −0.05 in these cases, except for the reading scores of students in second and third grade, where the drop was a statistically significant −0.19. Among choice students, however, the decline in the coefficient was statistically significant in every case for math; the coefficients of variation then ranged between−0.14 and −0.39. The coefficients also declined in reading, but the differences were not statistically significant.

These findings suggest that school choice does not increase disparities among student performances, as critics have suggested; on the contrary, it appears to reduce them. Reformers sometimes disagree as to which is more important: raising test scores or reducing test score differences among students. If the results from New York can be generalized, school choice seems to do both.

TABLE 14.1 Distribution of Test Scores, New York

	Grades 2–5		Grades 2–3		Grades 4–5	
Math						
Offered scholarship						
Baseline	1.18		1.12		1.21	
Year 1	0.91		0.98		0.82	
Change	−0.27**	[781]	−0.14*	[421]	−0.39***	[360]
Control group						
Baseline	1.05		1.10		0.98	
Year 1	0.98		1.04		0.92	
Change	−0.05	[670]	−0.05	[346]	−0.04	[329]
Reading						
Offered scholarship						
Baseline	0.99		1.04		0.89	
Year 1	0.86		0.93		0.79	
Change	−0.13*	[781]	−0.11*	[421]	−0.10	[360]
Control group						
Baseline	0.85		1.04		0.87	
Year 1	0.85		0.85		0.85	
Change	−0.00	[675]	−0.19*	[346]	−0.02	[329]

Note: Figures represent coefficients of variation (standard deviation divided by the mean) using weighted data. Unweighted number of observations reported in brackets. Only those observations which have test scores at *both* baseline and after one year are included. *Signifies difference between baseline and year 1 is statistically significant at the .1 level, 2-tail f-test conducted.
**Significant at the .05 level.
***Significant at the .01 level.

Interpretation

When reporting the effects of school choice on student achievement, *Education Week* labeled them "modest"; the *New York Times* found them "slight."[24] Whether or not the gains after one year amount to much depends in part on what happens in the years ahead. Nonetheless, there is reason to believe that these choice effects are already sufficiently large to be worthy of careful consideration.

Scholars typically calculate effect sizes in standard deviations. Although the concept can be confusing, one can grasp its essential quality by keeping in mind that one standard deviation approximates the current difference between the average test scores of blacks and whites nationwide. The effects of school choice on students in fourth and fifth grade are roughly one-fifth of a standard deviation. If similar effects occur in subsequent years, and to the extent that voucher programs are targeted toward inner-city populations with a high concentration of minorities, this may provide an important step toward achieving equal educational gains across ethnic groups, which would clearly represent a major accomplishment.

IMPACT OF TEST SCORES ON EARNINGS. Nor are test scores a trivial matter, the hobgoblin of academic researchers. Studies show that students who score higher on standardized tests are more likely to remain in school, more likely to achieve a college degree, more likely to remain married and avoid welfare dependency, and more likely to enjoy a higher family income. According to the best available estimates, a gain of one standard deviation in test scores later in life will translate into a 20 percent increase in that person's future earnings.[25] By this measure, if students in the choice program in New York City simply hold the gains they have already achieved, their family incomes, on average, ought to rise 4 percent—or $1,200 a year, if one assumes they would ordinarily have a modest annual income of $30,000. If these estimates are reasonably accurate, the philanthropists in New York will realize an ample return on their dollar once these students enter the labor force.

COMPARISON TO TENNESSEE STUDY OF CLASS SIZE. Another way of thinking about the size of the effects of the SCSF program is to compare them to those of another intervention. Very few other educational innovations of interest have been subjected to a randomized experiment, but one, which examined the effects of class size reductions, has been subject to rigorous evaluation. It is worth comparing the results from the school choice experiment with the results from a class size reduction, because both innovations can be introduced rather straightforwardly by legislative action. (Other reforms, such as requiring students to do more homework, are obviously much more difficult to mandate by legislative fiat.)

The class size field trial was conducted in Tennessee, where students were randomly assigned to classes of different sizes. No incremental effects on student learning were observed for students after the first grade. Among first graders, effect sizes varied between .15 and .30 standard deviations (table 14.2). In his comment on these effects, Fred Mosteller, one of the experiment's evaluators, observed, "Although effect sizes of the magnitude of 0.1, 0.2, or 0.3 may not seem to be impressive gains for a single individual, for a population they can be quite substantial."[26]

The effect sizes observed in our evaluation of the New York scholarship program in grades four and five do not differ materially from those observed in Tennessee in grade one. As can be seen in table 14.2, the effects among fourth and fifth graders of attending a private school were, on average, .23 standard deviation in math and .15 standard deviation in reading, not much different from the .2 to .3 effects observed in the first grade of the Tennessee study—the only grade for which incremental class size effects were detected. Following Mosteller's guidelines, these effect sizes, observed after just one year in the program, clearly warrant public attention.

COMPARATIVE COST-BENEFIT ANALYSIS. An investment in school choice programs is especially attractive once costs are taken into account. From a cost-benefit perspective, increasing school choice would seem to be preferable to decreasing class size. To get effects of about .2 standard deviations, class sizes were reduced from approximately twenty-five to approximately fifteen. If this were introduced as a school reform more generally, it would increase the size of the teaching staff and classroom space by 40 percent. Per pupil costs could be expected to rise by approximately 20 percent (assuming classroom costs constitute about half the cost of public schooling). By comparison, the per pupil cost of school choice is minimal; the taxpayer may in fact enjoy savings, if competition among schools leads to more efficient distribution of educational resources.[27]

Moreover, the incremental benefits of reducing class sizes disappear after the first grade. If larger differences between the test scores of scholarship students and those in the control group appear in subsequent years in New York City, the benefits of school choice will clearly outstrip those obtained by large reductions in class size.

TABLE 14.2 A Comparison of School Choice and Class Size Reduction Effects on Student Test Scores

| | Effects of Being Offered Treatment | | Effects of Receiving Treatment | |
	Math	Reading	Math	Reading
New York Scholarship Program				
Grade 4	0.21	0.10	0.27	0.12
Grade 5	0.16	0.23	0.18	0.27
Grades 4 & 5 combined	0.18	0.14	0.23	0.18
Tennessee School Size Study[a]				
Grade 1[b]			0.32	0.30
Grade 1[c]			0.15	0.25

Note: Effect sizes measured in standard deviations.
[a]No significant incremental effects detected, positive or negative, beyond the first year.
[b]Stanford Achievement Test.
[c]Tennessee Basic Skills First Test.

EXPLANATIONS FOR EFFECTS. When our findings were initially announced, Sandra Feldman, president of the American Federation of Teachers, offered the interesting hypothesis that we had documented what teachers' unions had been arguing all along, that smaller classes and schools increase students' test scores. "I see it as a validation of the need for small class sizes, and for smaller schools that are orderly and disciplined," she proclaimed.[28] The implication is clear. Test score gains have little to do with public and private schooling per se, for given the resources they require to reduce school and class sizes, public schools too could improve the test scores of inner-city children.

To test this hypothesis, we conducted a multivariate analysis in order to ascertain whether any of the following characteristics alone could account for the higher test score gains achieved by scholarship students:[29] class size, school size, discipline problems, school-parent communications, and / or the number of school programs and resources.

Data on these potential explanatory factors were available from the 1998 parent questionnaires. As we have seen, parents reported that private schools were superior in most respects, except that they had fewer programs and resources. To see whether these factors explain why school choice succeeds, we regressed test scores on all of these mediating variables, together with the key indicator variable that distinguishes the students who received a scholarship offer. The results are reported in tables 14.3 and 14.4.

When interpreting the results reported in these tables, it is important to recognize that the mediating variables—school discipline, school-parent communication, and class size—should not be included in an equation that is simply trying to detect whether school choice makes a difference for student achievement. Since the offer of a scholarship may cause an increase or decrease in these factors, it makes no sense to control for them when testing the effects of choice. On the other hand, it is interesting to see whether any one of them is the key factor connecting school choice to student learning. These two tables explore their potential as mediating mechanisms.

The lay person may read these two tables simply by star gazing. The more stars after a number, the more confident one can be that the relationships observed in the sample also exist in the population from which the sample is drawn, namely all potential applicants to an SCSF-type scholarship program. If a number does not have a star following it, one cannot be very confident that the observed result might not have appeared by chance alone.

When one examines the results for students in grades four and five, certain mediating factors have statistically significant effects on either reading or math scores. For example, class size affects math test scores. However, the direction of the effect is the opposite of what Sandra Feldman

TABLE 14.3   Explaining Test Score Achievement, Grades 4 and 5 (Math)

	OLS Model	2SLS Model
Estimated effect of scholarship offer [a]	4.19*	
Estimated effect of attending private school		5.59***
Scholarship offer	4.13*	
Attend private school		6.19*
School characteristics		
School size	0.82	1.23
Class size	1.59**	1.56**
Parent communications	5.43	4.20
Problems at school	−4.62	−4.55
Resources	5.60	6.59
Baseline test scores		
Math	0.53***	0.53
Reading	0.32***	0.32
Constant	1.81	4.30
(N)	(397)	(397)
Adjusted R^2	.52	.51

[a]This is the effect of offering a scholarship calculated using a fixed effects model with the only controls being baseline test scores and lotteries. For complete results, see Peterson, Myers, and Howell 1998.
Weighted, fixed effects models conducted, controlling for the 30 different lotteries held for applicants to the scholarship program. Unweighted number of observations reported.
*Significant at .10 level, two-tailed test.
**Significant at .05 level.
***Significant at .01 level.

hypothesized—all other things being equal, students learned more math in *larger* classes. Class size is measured by increments of five. The results show that, all other factors being equal, when classes had five more students, math scores increased by 1.6 percentile points, a modest effect that should not be overinterpreted, especially since class size had no effect on reading scores.

The other factors included in the estimate of the older students' test scores—school resources, discipline problems at school, and school-parent communications—are indices constructed from the items listed in figures 14.1, 14.4, and 14.6. In each case the index has been standardized so as to vary between zero and one.

Discipline problems at school and school resources had the largest and most consistent effect on reading test scores. Lower rates of discipline problems are associated with significantly higher test scores. More material resources and programs also had a positive effect on reading scores. But other than class size, no factor significantly affected math scores. Based on these results, it appears that private schools create an improved learning environment is by creating a framework that generates fewer discipline problems. On the other hand, the public schools have the advantage of greater material resources and programs.

Most importantly, though, none of these mediating factors through which school choice may have been affecting test scores, nor all of them together, materially reduced the size of the effects of receiving a scholarship offer. As can be seen in tables 14.3 and 14.4, the sizes of the effects of a scholarship offer do not change significantly when these other mediating school characteristics are included in the analysis.

Perhaps the program's impact comes from the sheer fact of choice, the opportunity to better match older students with an appropriate school. Al-

TABLE 14.4 Explaining Test Score Achievement, Grades 4 and 5 (Reading)

	OLS Model	2SLS Model
Estimated effect of scholarship offer[a]	2.51*	
Estimated effect of attending private school		3.35***
Scholarship offer	2.95*	
Attend private school		4.43
School characteristics		
School size	−0.18	0.13
Class size	0.05	0.02**
Parent communications	5.58	4.70
Problems at school	−8.72***	−8.66***
Resources	12.06***	12.77***
Baseline test scores		
Math	0.20***	0.20***
Reading	0.68***	0.68***
Constant	−11.34	−4.14
(N)	(397)	(397)
Adjusted R^2	.60	.59

[a]This is the effect of offering a scholarship calculated using a fixed effects model with the only controls being baseline test scores and lotteries. For complete results, see Peterson, Myers, and Howell 1998.

Weighted, fixed effects models conducted, controlling for the 30 different lotteries held for applicants to the scholarship program. Unweighted number of observations reported.
*Significant at .10 level, two-tailed test.
**Significant at .05 level.
***Significant at .01 level.

ternatively, scholarship students may be learning more simply because they are surrounded by new peers with higher aptitudes. And perhaps there is some interaction of many factors that affects scores in ways not easily captured by a linear statistical model. What is immediately apparent is that the advantages of attending a private school are not readily reduced to any one or single set of factors. In the future we plan to further investigate the sources of test-score gains associated with a private education.

Conclusions: Implications for Education Reform

As we have pointed out, the advantages of attending a private school in New York City are not clearly evident until a student enters fourth or fifth grade. This finding is consistent with other indications that problems in American public education begin during the middle years of schooling. According to the National Assessment of Educational Progress (NAEP), students in fourth grade are performing at higher levels than their counterparts a generation ago. Gains over the past two decades have been particularly large for students from minority groups. But NAEP data also show that, after fourth grade, initial gains disappear. In fact, students nationwide learned less between fourth and eighth grade in the 1990s than they did in the seventies. The slippage seems even greater in high school.

Similarly, international comparisons reveal that U.S. fourth grade students keep up in science and math with most of their peers abroad (though not with the Japanese and Koreans). By eighth grade, however, U.S. students trail those in all other leading industrial nations, so much so that by twelfth grade they fall to around the bottom of all participating countries.[30] If the problems in American education develop in the middle years of schooling, perhaps it is at this point that the advantages that come with school choice are particularly evident.

Of course, this evaluation observes results after just one year. Our evaluation is scheduled to continue for two more years, and only time will tell whether the initial gains are maintained. And it remains to be seen whether school choice, if generalized to a larger population, will yield comparable gains. But the initial gains detected here make a strong case for the continued support of existing voucher programs and the initiation of larger ones, allowing us to deepen our understanding of the potential impact of school choice.

NOTES

David Myers and Paul E. Peterson were co-principal investigators for the evaluation. We wish to thank the School Choice Scholarships Foundation (SCSF) for cooperating fully with this effort. This evaluation has been supported by grants from the following foundations: Achelis Foundation, Bodman Foundation, Lynde and Harry Bradley Foundation, Donner Foundation, Milton and Rose D. Friedman Foundation, John M. Olin Foundation, David and Lucile Packard Foundation, Smith Richardson Foundation, and the Spencer Foundation. We are grateful to Kristin Kearns Jordan and other members of the SCSF staff for their cooperation and assistance with data collection. We received helpful advice from Paul Hill, Christopher Jencks, Donald Rock, and Donald Rubin. Daniel Mayer and Julia Kim, from Mathematica Policy Research, were instrumental in preparing the survey and test score data, and in implementing many of the analyses reported in this chapter. Additional research assistance was provided by David Campbell, Rachel Deyette, and Jennifer Hill; staff assistance was provided by Shelley Weiner. The methodology, analyses of data, reported findings, and interpretations of findings are the sole responsibility of the authors and have not been subject to the approval of SCSF or of any foundation providing support for this research.

1. Recent works making a case for school choice include John E. Brandl, *Money and Good Intentions Are Not Enough, or Why a Liberal Democrat Thinks States Need Both Competition and Community* (Washington, D.C.: Brookings Institution, 1998); Andrew J. Coulson, *Market Education: The Unknown History* (New Brunswick, N.J.: Transaction Press, forthcoming); Clifford W. Cobb, *Responsive Schools, Renewed Communities* (San Francisco, Calif.: Institute for Contemporary Studies, 1992); and Alan Bonsteel and Carlos A. Bonilla, *A Choice for Our Children: Curing the Crisis in America's Schools* (San Francisco, Calif.: Institute for Contemporary Studies, 1997). A collection of essays that report mainly positive school choice effects is to be found in Paul E. Peterson and Bryan C. Hassel, eds., *Learning from School Choice* (Washington, D.C.: Brookings Institution, 1998).

2. Recent works criticizing school vouchers include Carol Ascher, Norm Fruchter, and Robert Berne, *Hard Lessons: Public Schools and Privatization* (New York: Twentieth Century Fund Press, 1996); Carnegie Foundation for the Advancement of Teaching, *School Choice: A Special Report* (Princeton, N.J.: Carnegie Foundation for the Advancement of Teaching, 1992); Amy Gutmann, *Democratic Education* (Princeton, N.J.: Princeton University Press, 1987); Henry M. Levin, "Educational Vouchers: Effectiveness, Choice, and Costs," *Journal of Policy Analysis and Management* 17, no. 3 (1998); Bruce Fuller and Richard F. Elmore, with Gary Orfield, eds., *Who Chooses? Who Loses? Culture, Institutions, and the Unequal Effects of School Choice* (New York: Teachers College Press, 1996); E. Rasell and R. Rothstein, eds., *School Choice: Examining the Evidence* (Washington, D.C.: Economic Policy Institute, 1993); Peter W. Cookson, *School Choice: The Struggle for the Soul of American Education* (New Haven, Conn.: Yale University Press, 1994).

3. Major studies finding positive educational benefits from attending private schools include James S. Coleman, Thomas Hoffer, and Sally Kilgore, *High School Achievement* (New York: Basic Books, 1982); John E. Chubb and Terry M. Moe, *Politics, Markets, and America's Schools* (Washington, D.C.: Brookings Institution, 1990); Derek Neal, "The Effects of Catholic Secondary Schooling on Educational Achievement" (University of Chicago, Harris School of Public Policy and National Bureau for Economic Research, 1996). Critiques of these studies have been prepared by Arthur S. Goldberger and Glen G. Cain, in "The Causal Analysis of Cognitive Outcomes in the Coleman, Hoffer, and Kilgore Report," *Sociology of Education* 55 (1982);

Douglas J. Wilms, "Catholic School Effects on Academic Achievement: New Evidence from the High School and Beyond Follow-up Study," *Sociology of Education* 58 (1985).

4. Frederick Mosteller, "The Tennessee Study of Class Size in the Early School Grades," *The Future of Children* 5 (1995).

5. Jennifer Hill, Donald B. Rubin, and Neal Thomas, "The Design of the New York School Choice Scholarship Program Evaluation," paper presented before the American Political Science Association annual meeting in Boston, Mass., August 31, 1998.

6. Paul E. Peterson, David Myers, William G. Howell, and Daniel Mayer, "An Evaluation of the New York City School Choice Scholarships Program: The First Year," Occasional Paper 98–12, Program on Education Policy and Governance, Taubman Center for State and Local Government, Kennedy School of Government, Harvard University, 1998. This report is available at the website: data.fas.harvard.edu/pepg/.

7. The response rate for those offered scholarships was 85 percent; for the control group, it was 80 percent. The response rate for those who used the scholarship was 89 percent; for those who did not, 66 percent. To adjust for nonresponse, we used adjusted sample weights (see Peterson, Myers, and Howell, "An Evaluation of the New York City School Choice Scholarships Program," appendix). Since the number of missing cases is relatively small and the characteristics of the missing cases do not differ markedly from observed cases, the assumptions necessary for utilization of this procedure are not particularly restrictive. We have adjusted the weights given to individual cases in order to account for differential response rates.

8. Paul E. Peterson, David Myers, Josh Haimson, and William G. Howell, "Initial Findings from the Evaluation of the New York School Choice Scholarships Program," Occasional Paper, Harvard Program on Education Policy and Governance, November 1997. This report is available at the website: data.fas.harvard.edu/pepg/.

9. The effects are estimated by means of a two-stage least squares regression in which the lottery outcome is used as the first-stage estimator. The procedure is discussed in Peterson et al., "Initial Findings from the Evaluation of the New York School Choice Scholarships Program."

10. Rachel Deyette, "Selection into Voucher Programs: How do Applicants Differ from the Eligible Population?", paper prepared for Program on Education Policy and Governance, Harvard University, 1998. Information is drawn from the Integrated Public Use Microdata Series data set of the U.S. Census, which has been created at the University of Minnesota.

11. Amy Stuart Wells, "African-American Students' View of School Choice," in *Who Chooses? Who Loses?*, ed. Fuller and Elmore, p. 47.

12. A summary of findings from earlier studies is available in Paul E. Peterson, "School Choice: A Report Card," in Peterson and Hassel, *Learning from School Choice*, p. 18. Mark Schneider, Paul Teske, Melissa Marschall, and Christine Roch, "Tiebout, School Choice, Allocative and Productive Efficiency," a paper prepared for annual meetings of the American Political Science Association, 1998, finds higher levels of parental satisfaction within New York City public schools when parents are given a choice of school.

13. Not all satisfaction measures are shown in figure 14.3. Some have wondered

whether the higher level of satisfaction with private schools is an artificat of a characteristic of our research design, namely, the comparison of scholarship recipients with families who had applied for a scholarship but did not receive one, a group that might be thought to be a group of "sour grapes." In Cleveland we tested the sour grape hypothesis but found no support for it: there were no significant differences in satisfaction levels between parents who applied for but did not receive vouchers and a cross-section of parents of students in public school. Paul E. Peterson, William G. Howell, and Jay P. Greene, "An Evaluation of the Cleveland Voucher Program After Two Years," Report Number 99-02. Program on Education Policy and Governance, Kennedy School of Government, Harvard University, 1999, table 3a.

14. Peterson, Howell, and Greene, 1999, table 3b.

15. John F. Witte, "First Year Report: Milwaukee Parental Choice Program," University of Wisconsin—Madison, Department of Political Science, and Robert M. La Follette Institute of Public Affairs, November 1991.

16. Dan Murphy, F. Howard Nelson, and Bella Rosenberg, *The Cleveland Voucher Program: Who Chooses? Who Gets Chosen? Who Pays?* (New York: American Federation of Teachers, 1997).

17. Jay P. Greene, William G. Howell, and Paul E. Peterson, "Lessons from the Cleveland Scholarship Program," in *Learning from School Choice*, ed. Peterson and Hassel, pp. 376–80.

18. John F. Witte, Andrea B. Bailey, and Christopher A. Thorn, "Second Year Report: Milwaukee Parental Choice Program," University of Wisconsin—Madison, Department of Political Science, and the Robert M. La Follette Institute of Public Affairs, December 1992, pp. 19–20.

19. These percentages may underestimate the actual rate of school mobility for both scholarship students and those in the control group. The families that did not attend questionnaire administration sessions probably were more likely to have moved, making it more difficult for evaluation staff to locate them. If so, the children in those families that could not be located would be more likely to have changed schools. In this regard, it is important to note that the response rate was less for the control group than for scholarship users.

20. Next in importance was the quality of the school, a response given by just four scholarship parents and seven members of the control group. Seven scholarship parents and four members of the control group said expense was a factor. Only three scholarship users and two members of the control group said their child had been expelled or suspended.

21. Results from these evaluations are reported in *Learning from School Choice*, ed. Peterson and Hassel.

22. "What mechanisms ensure that those students who need extra time and attention to do well receive this more costly instruction?" ask Carol Ascher, Norm Fruchter, and Robert Berne, *Hard Lessons: Public Schools and Privatization* (New York: Twentieth Century Fund, 1996), p. 9.

23. John Chubb and Terry Moe, "Effective Schools and Equal Opportunity," in *Public Values, Private Schools*, ed. Neil Devins (London: Falmer Press, 1989).

24. Lynette Holloway, "Pupils Using Vouchers Had Better Scores, Study Finds,"

New York Times, October 28, 1998; Jeff Archer, "N.Y.C. Voucher Students Post Modest Gains," *Education Week,* November 3, 1998.

25. Christopher Winship and Sanders Korenman, "Economic Success and the Evolution of Schooling and Mental Ability," in *Earning and Learning: How Schools Matter,* ed. Susan Mayer and Paul E. Peterson (Washington, D.C.: Brookings Institution, 1999); Christopher Jencks and Meredith Philips, "Aptitude or Achievement: Why do Test Scores Predict Educational Attainment and Earnings?" in *Earning and Learning,* ed. Mayer and Peterson.

26. Frederick Mosteller, "The Tennessee Study of Class Size in the Early School Grades," *The Future of Children* 5 (1995); Eric A. Hanushek, "Evidence on Class Size," in *Earning and Learning,* ed. Mayer and Peterson; Frederick Mosteller, "How Does Class Size Relate to Achievement in Schools?" in *Earning and Learning,* ed. Mayer and Peterson.

27. Caroline Minter Hoxby, "The Effects of School Choice on Curriculum and Atmosphere," in Susan B. Mayer and Paul E. Peterson, eds., *Earning and Learning: How Schools Matter* (Brookings, 1999), p. 281–316; Caroline B. Hoxby, "Does Competition Among Schools Benefit Students and Taxpayers?" *American Economic Review,* forthcoming.

28. Jeff Archer, "N.Y.C. Voucher Students Post Modest Gains," *Education Week,* November 9, 1998.

29. The effects of being offered a scholarship were somewhat less than the effects of actually using the scholarship to attend a private school. See Peterson et al., "An Evaluation of the New York City School Choice Scholarships Program," for a discussion of the ways in which we estimated the effects of being offered a scholarship and, separately, the effects of receiving a scholarship reported in the figures in this essay. In this section, we look at the effects of the other variables, controlling for the effects of being offered a scholarship.

30. Though the fourth graders trailed students in Japan, Korea, the Netherlands, and the Czech Republic, they did better than students in England, Norway, and New Zealand ("U.S. 4th Graders Score Well in Math and Science Study," *Education Week,* June 18, 1997, p. 22). The U.S. eighth graders clearly outscored only seven countries—Lithuania, Cyprus, Portugal, Iran, Kuwait, Colombia, and South Africa—none of them usually thought to be U.S. peers ("U.S. Students Rank about Average in 41-Nation Math, Science Study," *Education Week,* November 27, 1996, p. 32). United States National Research Center, "TIMMS High School Results Released," Michigan State University, College of Education, Report 8, April 1998; Paul E. Barton and Richard J. Coley, "Growth in School Achievement Gains from the Fourth to the Eighth Grade," Policy Information Center, Research Division, Educational Testing Service, Princeton, N.J., May 1998.

15 School Finance Reform: Introducing the Choice Factor

THOMAS NECHYBA AND MICHAEL HEISE

Most judicial remedies in successful challenges to public school finance systems seek to make schools more equal or adequate by directing increased educational spending to underperforming school districts.[1] This remedy brings with it an array of practical and legal problems.[2] First, courts are perceived as seemingly "rewarding" underperforming schools and may therefore unintentionally create perverse incentives for public school bureaucracies as well as generate a serious threat to the much-needed political support for public education. Second, courts face a difficult problem regarding the timing of reforms in relation to the immediate need for action on behalf of plaintiffs. Specifically, it remains unclear how increased educational spending directed toward such a school offers adequate relief to its current students during the time in which a constitutionally inadequate school endeavors to improve. Finally, despite sustained, nationwide school finance litigation and a clear overall trend of steadily increasing educational spending, many of the problems that school finance litigation seeks to solve persist. The usual court remedy ignores much of the scholarly evidence suggesting that spending plays only a minor role in producing good schools and it does not consider the broader forces that have caused current inequities in public schools.

One viable but relatively unexplored legal remedy to constitutionally inadequate school systems is to target additional funding to the parents of schoolchildren assigned to underperforming schools rather than to the public schools or school systems that have failed to deliver adequate educational services. Eligible schoolchildren, through their parents, could redeem such vouchers at any eligible public or private, religious or secular school. In this way the legal remedy might be more precisely calibrated with the legal harm without undermining public support for education. Furthermore, such a remedy may get at the heart of factors that have given rise to existing public school quality differences.

The potential for this kind of reform as a legal remedy in school finance court decisions in general, and in New York in particular, stems from two recent developments. First, lawsuits challenging public school systems, including New York's, have shifted from emphasizing equality in per pupil spending across schools to focusing on a state's constitutional obligation to ensure access to adequate educational opportunities for all children. Thus, to the extent that any given legal remedy could address concerns over the adequacy of educational opportunities, such a remedy warrants consideration. Second, a growing body of literature suggests that thirty years of state efforts to equalize per pupil spending levels across the United States have generally not led to an expansion of adequate educational opportunities, particularly for children in poor districts. Thus it would seem natural that courts look toward new and innovative policy proposals to address their adequacy criterion.

Meaningful consideration of choice-based proposals, however, requires careful study of the possible effects of a relatively large-scale publicly funded school voucher program, an endeavor thus far hindered by a scarcity of data.[3] This represents a considerable challenge for policy makers, who disagree widely in what they consider to be important in education reforms. However, even among those who voice such disagreements,[4] consensus exists on at least some points. Families for whom private schools are not an option routinely choose among public schools through their choice of residence in school districts, and the data suggest that parental perception of public school quality is among the most important determinants of residential location. Parents' willingness to pay for schools can thus be observed both directly through the choices they make as well as indirectly through property values that reflect local public school quality.[5] Consequently, it is possible to combine existing data with insights from economic models to simulate how the same factors that currently govern public school district choices might inform an expanded array of choices created through private school vouchers.

Below, we outline a specific methodology that attempts to accomplish this. Quite apart from the issue of whether public schools operate efficiently and whether competition can raise overall public school productivity, such an approach must begin with a setting that recognizes existing equity problems. Put differently, the public school sector cannot be thought of as one entity that treats all children equally, but rather as consisting of many different schools and school districts with wide variations in quality. Therefore, a crucial distinction between our methodology and that found more commonly in the economics literature is that we will explicitly take the current public school system with all its equity problems as the starting point of our analysis of vouchers. Our approach will therefore begin by incorporating the forces that give rise to current inequalities across school districts and will then demonstrate that the mere inclusion of such forces tends to overcome the generally negative equity implications found for vouchers in the current literature.[6] Furthermore, a consideration of additional forces for which we have at least some empirical evidence suggests quite favorable equity and efficiency consequences.

Constitutional Implications of Public School Inequities

For decades education reformers have challenged the constitutionality of school finance systems on both equity and, more recently, adequacy grounds. Equity-based lawsuits focused on per pupil spending disparities. In contrast, the more recent adequacy lawsuits focus on whether schools or school districts meet constitutionally mandated education thresholds regardless of educational spending levels or per pupil disparities. More precisely, commentators note three distinct "waves" of school finance court decisions.[7] The first wave focused on the U.S. Constitution's Equal Protection Clause, beginning with the 1971 *Serrano v. Priest*[8] decision and ending three years later with the U.S. Supreme Court's *San Antonio Independent School District v. Rodriguez*[9] decision. The New Jersey court's *Robinson v. Cahill*[10] decision in 1973 marked the emergence of the second wave of school finance court decisions that focused on state rather than federal constitutional challenges while maintaining the first wave's focus on equity. Finally, the third and current wave of court decisions, again at the state level, began in 1989, and signaled a subtle yet dramatic shift in school finance litigation theory by replacing the traditional focus on equity with adequacy.[11] Despite this dramatic shift, however, the nature of judicial remedies in this area has remained largely unchanged. New York's school finance litigation experience reflects national trends. Furthermore, while New York judges grappled with school finance lawsuits, New York policy makers experimented with small school choice reforms, funded both publicly and privately.

A Constitutional Overview of Public Schooling in New York

New York's educational system resembles those found in other states, with the exceptions of Hawaii and Michigan (and the District of Columbia).[12] Although the state retains the ultimate responsibility for discharging its constitutional duty to educate, it delegates much of this authority to local school districts. Outside New York City, local school districts possess the power to tax (mainly through property taxes). Variations in educational spending between New York's public school districts pivot largely on variations in local property values and, to a lesser extent, nominal tax rate differentials. However, the New York City Board of Education is another line on the municipal budget, and an additional political process governs resource allocations.[13] In addition, substantial state subsidies generate a state education budget that recently surpassed eight billion dollars.[14]

New York's education clause,[15] which originated in the state's 1894 constitutional convention, is remarkably unremarkable and often ranks in the third or fourth tier in what it compels the state to provide.[16] Its precise meaning, however, has been the subject of fierce litigation for more than two decades. Frustrated with legislative inability to address educational spending disparities among school districts, New York school reformers turned to the courts in 1974 to see if they could achieve judicially what they had not achieved legislatively. In *Levittown v. Nyquist*,[17] twenty-seven school districts, the boards of education of four of New York's five largest cities (including New York City), and various student and parent groups joined a legal challenge arguing that variations in per pupil spending violated equal protection clauses in the state and the federal constitution. The trial court agreed with the plaintiffs,[18] and the appellate court concurred except as to the claim involving the federal equal protection clause. New York's highest court, however, essentially reversed the lower courts in a six-to-one decision by declaring New York's school finance system constitutional.[19] But, while the court concluded that spending discrepancies alone did not rise to a constitutional violation, it held open the possibility of such a violation if "gross and glaring" inadequacy could be shown.[20] A subsequent lawsuit, *Reform Educational Financing Inequities Today v. Cuomo (REFIT)*,[21] resurrected the equity-based theory that failed in the *Levittown* litigation, but despite ever increasing per pupil spending discrepancies, New York courts again rejected the equity-based challenge.[22]

Concurrent with the *REFIT* litigation, a separate lawsuit, *Campaign for Fiscal Equity v. State of New York*,[23] has been brought against New York State and advanced an *adequacy* theory. In this lawsuit the plaintiffs allege that the educational services provided within New York City fall below constitutional minimum standards regardless of how much funding the districts receive.[24] While the case has thus far reached New York's judiciary only on a procedural motion, two themes seem to have emerged. Judges appear to recognize a constitutional floor of educational adequacy as well as a corresponding duty for the state to ensure that this floor is not breached. However, how much this differs from merely ensuring minimal funding at this juncture remains unclear.

School Choice in New York

Concurrent with yet independent of these judicial battles over school finance reform, New York has experimented with some of the nation's largest public and private school choice programs. East Harlem's District 4 implemented a public choice program as early as 1974, and the New York City Board of Education implemented a citywide public choice program (unfortunately hindered by substantial waiting lists for desirable public schools) in 1991.[25] Furthermore, the state is home to some of the nation's largest and oldest private voucher programs, including the Student-Sponsor Partnership Program founded in 1986,[26] the School Choice Scholarship Program (which presently serves more than 2,500 students from the city's fourteen lowest performing public districts[27]), and numerous smaller programs (such as Operation Exodus and Hope through Education).[28] Despite these programs' successes, proposals to further expand school choice have failed politically.[29]

Merging School Finance and Choice Reforms

We propose that district-targeted vouchers constitute a viable court remedy in cases in which plaintiffs demonstrate inadequate public educational opportunities. Our proposed judicial remedy represents only a small departure from the typical judicial remedy that endeavors to direct increased educational spending to the very schools and districts that failed to perform in a constitutionally acceptable manner. By directing increased educational spending to eligible students rather than to underperforming schools, a judicial remedy that includes district-targeted education vouchers can alter the nature and structure of the relation among schools and students and their families in a fundamental manner. Such a remedy would be limited to only those students whose constitutional rights were infringed by inadequate public schools. Vouchers provide more immediate relief to aggrieved students by decoupling the immediate fate of students and underperforming schools than do remedies that seek to make inadequate schools less so over time with the benefit of additional resources. During the period of time it takes a school or district to begin performing at a constitutionally acceptable level, students would have access to schools already performing at such a level.

Underlying Assumptions of the Legal Case for Vouchers

Our argument differs from prior arguments[30] and rests on three basic assumptions: (1) judicial decisions are an acceptable vehicle to implement such a policy; (2) school choice can advance the broader goal of increasing equal educational opportunity; and (3) school choice can generate net social value, at least in the form of improved school quality.

The first of these assumptions is a matter of some controversy. While the courts' role in promoting equal educational opportunity enjoys a proud heritage (dating back to *Brown v. Board of Education*), an array of institutional, structural, and policy reasons certainly recommend that courts inclined to venture into such policy making areas do so with extreme caution.[31] However, insofar as courts continue to engage in legal efforts to change education policies, there exists no a priori reason as to why vouchers should be excluded from such consideration. Our second and third assumptions then become crucial for the question as to whether vouchers may constitute a possible court remedy. Put differently, once court involvement in these matters is taken as a given, we must ask to what extent vouchers would in fact advance the broader goal of increasing equal educational opportunity ("equity" and "adequacy") and generate net social value ("efficiency").

The Economic Roots of Inequities in Public School Quality

As has been observed and documented elsewhere,[32] interdistrict disparities in spending on public education can be traced to the combination of four factors: (1) a pronounced role for local funding and/or local politics, (2) the existence of profoundly unequal levels of household income and wealth, (3) the high willingness of households to move to districts that best meet their needs, and (4) the ability of districts to exclude fiscally undesirable residents through various explicit and implicit policies (such as zoning). Given the first factor that enables parents to fund and control public schools, the second provides incentives for higher-income households (who desire more spending and perhaps different types of schools) to segregate into separate school districts, and the third enables them to do so by moving. Finally, the fourth factor allows school quality differences across districts to persist as significantly higher house prices and the scarcity of low- and moderate-income housing there blocks residents of low-quality school districts from higher-quality districts.[33] As a result, publicly funded school districts in New York and other states can be ranked based on average local income and wealth, with wealthier districts tending to spend more (per pupil) on public schools and to contain fewer neighborhoods that are affordable to low-income households.

Even when per pupil spending is fully equalized across school districts (as in California), large interdistrict differences in educational quality persist. This provides strong evidence (confirmed elsewhere in the literature)[34] that educational quality depends on more than financial resources. More precisely, holding fixed the institutional structure of a school (i.e., the curriculum, the degree of competition, and unionization of teachers), households directly impact school quality first through parental involvement with schools (which provides valuable information to schools while at the same time monitoring their performance) and second by supplying children with abilities that positively impact other children's learning in a classroom. Thus educators often speak of "peer effects," by which they mean the positive or negative impact a household has on school quality through both of these channels.[35] Given strong evidence that parents from higher-income households monitor their schools more,[36] and given somewhat weaker evidence that their children have on average higher ability levels once they reach schools,[37] it is then not surprising that public school quality correlates highly with district wealth even after financial resources in schools are equalized. Furthermore, it strengthens the incentive for higher-income households to segregate into separate school districts.[38]

It then becomes important to recognize that courts are limited in their ability to fundamentally alter local political relationships, eliminate income differences across households, tamper with the freedom of mobility enjoyed by residents, or change the quality of housing in different urban neighborhoods and districts. They therefore cannot directly impact the fundamental economic causes of current public school inequities,[39] but rather must design remedies in full recognition of these limitations.

Our general strategy will therefore be to begin with a base model that contains most of the standard assumptions in previous economic models with the notable exception of explicitly including the economic forces leading to inequities in public education. We note at the outset, however, that the standard economic assumptions we adopt from previous models are likely to strongly bias results against finding positive equity or efficiency implications of vouchers. It is surprising, therefore, that the mere inclusion of the four economic forces responsible for current inequities yields results that are quite neutral with respect to both efficiency and equity, results starkly different from those often cited in the literature that does not explicitly model the causes of current inequities. In a later section, we then try to incorporate more plausible assumptions (which are admittedly difficult to quantify) regarding the efficiency impact of competition, and we find a large potential for favorable outcomes from vouchers for both equity and efficiency.

Constructing a Model of the Underlying Economic Realities

We begin our analysis by first defining a base model that explicitly takes into account the role of mobility, politics, household income inequalities, and housing markets. This is one appropriate starting point for analyzing vouchers. However, it incorporates none of the potentially positive forces cited by voucher proponents and, accordingly, reflects a "worst case scenario" model with respect to vouchers' efficacy. In a second scenario we then point out some of the additional aspects of public schools for which at least some limited empirical evidence exists and we include some of these in the analysis.

The Base Model

Space considerations unfortunately permit us only a brief overview of the various features of the framework we employ, and the more technically inclined reader is referred to other sources for the precise technical details of this approach.[40] There are five basic building blocks to the model:

1. Three "representative" school districts that differ in their overall housing quality but contain various neighborhoods (with different amenities and housing qualities).
2. Families that differ in socioeconomic status and child abilities, who choose where to live, where to send their children to school, and how to vote on local school funding issues.[41]
3. A school finance system that combines local property taxes with state taxes.[42]
4. District level public schools whose quality depends on per pupil spending, the average socioeconomic status of parents, and the average ability levels of school children in a way that is consistent with household choices and property values.[43]
5. A potential for private schools to emerge if they can persuade parents to leave public schools.

To avoid tilting the model artificially toward finding benefits from vouchers, we are consistent with the current economics literature and assume that private schools can set admission standards (i.e., they can choose to accept only "good students") in addition to setting a tuition rate.

Note that all four of the factors mentioned above as being important to understanding current public school inequities are included in this framework. Condition 1 incorporates a housing market that may exclude lower-income households from high-income public school districts, while condition 2 acknowledges socioeconomic differences between households and the reality of household mobility, and condition 3 provides for at least some degree of local political control. Furthermore, the model explicitly recognizes (as have previous economic models) that educational quality, while influenced to some extent by financial resources, is also dependent on other factors (condition 4). For any given set of model parameters, a computer algorithm can then calculate the equilibrium distribution of households across districts and schools, as well as other equilibrium variables of interest for policy. Before our model calculates an empirically meaningful equilibrium, however, it is necessary to match the model's various features to the available data. Again, we leave the technical details of this calibration exercise to be reported elsewhere[44] and only mention the main features.

The Relation of the Theoretical Model to the Empirical Data

We begin by dividing New York City jurisdictions into high-, middle-, and low-income categories and select randomly some in each category to be used as "representative" districts.[45] We then use housing price data from these districts to further divide each into neighborhoods of different quality, where both school quality in the districts as well as more local neighborhood qualities (such as crime rates, environmental quality, and public amenities) are recognized as important in determining local house prices. After replicating the household income distribution from the data, we observe where households of different socioeconomic status actually choose to live and how, on average, they vote on public school spending issues.[46] We infer from these data the value that households on average place on both the neighborhood characteristics of their place of residence and the level of per pupil spending in their public school. Furthermore, we use evidence that parents chose (mostly) public schools rather than available private alternatives to determine the likely value they place on the mix of parents and children who attend that school. Finally, we use estimates on the correlation between parental income and child ability to construct ability measures,[47] and we replicate the New York division between local and state financing.[48] This yields a rich model in which parental choices give rise to the stylized facts observed in the representative New York districts.

Important Caveats to the Base Model

Before considering the predictions offered by the computer-generated policy simulations, it is worthwhile to digress briefly to clarify two possible misconceptions that may have arisen in our discussion thus far.[49] First, some readers may have been left with the impression from our discussion above that we assume that higher-income parents "care more" about the education of their children than lower-income parents. This would be inconsistent with the empirical evidence,[50] and it is not the case in our model, in which all households are assumed to have the same underlying preferences for education and demands differ only due to different incomes. Second, neither do we assume that households care only about house prices and school quality when they choose where to live. Since we are using actual housing prices to calibrate the neighborhood qualities in our representative school districts, we are implicitly including the quality of neighborhood and house amenities in the model. Therefore, such factors as local crime rates, noise levels, proximity to job centers, and so forth are all implicitly captured (together with school quality) in the house prices that calibrate the neighborhood qualities in the model. Furthermore, house values are treated as annualized flows of housing services that closely resemble rental values. When the model is changed to explicitly include renters, none of the main results changes in any significant way.

Voucher Policy Simulations with the Base Model

In our analysis below, we primarily consider a judicial remedy that makes vouchers available only to residents of inadequately performing school districts. We call such vouchers "district-targeted vouchers," and we assume that they are funded at either the state or the city level. One can distinguish this type of voucher from a "nontargeted voucher" that does not restrict eligibility or an "income-targeted voucher" that restricts eligibility to poor households rather than residents of underperforming districts. Furthermore, we report in the tables simulation results for $2,500 vouchers and, in brackets and italics, $5,000 vouchers, where the face value of the voucher is the amount of tuition that is covered by the state or city for eligible households that choose to send their children to private schools.

It is crucial for our analysis to recall that, while school districts are far from homogeneous due to the presence of different kinds of neighborhoods within districts,[51] they can be ranked in terms of income, wealth, school quality, and school spending. As we noted previously, this underlying segregation across school districts exists in part because of public schools and is maintained as an equilibrium through property values and housing market conditions that exclude many low-income residents from high-quality school districts.[52] The main argument in this section is based on the intuition that vouchers, by decoupling the residential location choice from the school choice, can cause major changes in both these choices, assuming that households are willing to move (which a sizable fraction of metropolitan American households do in any given year).[53]

Migration, Residential Segregation, and Private Schools

The first two columns of tables 15.1 and 15.2 provide a comparison of some basic statistics from our policy simulation that introduces a district-targeted $2,500 [*and $5,000*] voucher (column 2) into the current no voucher environment (column 1) of our base model. Our simulations predict that the $2,500 [*$5,000*] voucher will cause roughly 14 percent [*26 percent*] of children to switch from public to private schools and that average public school spending will decline slightly, as will average household incomes, child ability levels, and school quality (as perceived by parents) within public schools. When measured across all students, average per pupil spending still declines (as private schools spend slightly less than the average for public schools), but average overall school quality remains relatively unchanged. In table 15.2, the variance in public school variables (perhaps surprisingly) declines, while the variance in school quality received by all students remains roughly constant, and the variance of incomes and property values across districts narrows.

What is not apparent without looking at more detailed results, however, is exactly what drives these numbers. In particular, given that the vouchers can be used only in the districts whose schools are deemed inadequate (district 1), it is not surprising that private schools arise only in those districts. What is surprising, however, is that for a voucher level of $2,500 this result is the same regardless of whether the voucher is targeted to district 1 or not targeted at all. In both cases, two groups of households choose to utilize the voucher: (1) those who live in the poor district and have high-ability children and moderate to moderately high income, and (2) former moderate- to high-income households of other districts who relocate to desirable neighborhoods within the poor district in order to send their children to private school. The latter group composes the majority of private school attendees.

Why would households move into district 1 when choosing to send their children to private school, even when the voucher can be used anywhere? The answer lies in precisely the factors we discussed earlier. When a household purchases (or rents) a house in a district with high-quality public schools, it is implicitly paying for school quality that is incorporated by the market into the house price. Therefore, once a voucher has induced a moderate- to high-middle-income family in a relatively good school district to choose private schools, this family is less willing to pay the high cost of housing that is due to a service it no longer benefits from.[54] Thus, even though a majority of private school attendees at low voucher levels are middle- to high-income children, the private schools themselves appear in low-income districts whether the voucher is targeted to residents of that district or not. The migrations then cause property values and average incomes in low-income districts to rise and those in high-income districts to fall. As voucher levels rise, these effects become stronger until private schools begin to emerge in the middle- and high-income districts (at voucher levels of around $3,000 and $4,500 respectively). At the voucher level of $5,000, district-targeted vouchers therefore have different effects than nontargeted vouchers. This is due primarily to the limited number of "good neighborhoods" within relatively poor school districts.

Because of political forces attributable to the emergence of private school parents, public school spending in the poor districts shows a tendency to decline slightly. Spending in other districts, however, also declines as former supporters of public schools leave for other districts (in order to send their children to private schools). The decline in public school spending reported in table 15.1 therefore does not occur mainly in the poorer districts where private schools arise, but migrations out of wealthier districts cause these variables to decline citywide, which then contributes to the declining variance in public school spending. Further, because of these migrations, residential diversity within school districts increases as the city becomes more integrated (along income lines).

The private schools that may limit the types of students they admit, however, are more differentiated in that a larger menu of different qualities becomes available. One might suspect, then, that this hypothesized private school "skimming" will cause the variance in educational oppor-

TABLE 15.1 School Averages under Different Assumptions. First Line—$2,500 Full or District-Targeted Voucher. [Second Line—$5,000 District-Targeted Voucher]

	Calibrated Base Model (4.2)		Curriculum Targeting (5.1)		Competition & Bureaucracy (5.2)	
	No Voucher	Base Model	Private Schools	All Schools	W/in Dist.	W/in & Across Dist.
% Switch to priv. sch.	—	14.2 [26.3]	18.9 [33.3]	13.8 [23.1]	13.1 [22.2]	10.5 [16.4]
Pub. school means						
Per pupil ($)	8,103	8,021 [8,010]	8,011 [8,120]	8,067 [8,078]	8,051 [8,055]	8,098 [8,039]
Household income ($)	34,321	29,723 [33,010]	28,948 [34,121]	29,735 [32,786]	29,892 [32,656]	30,871 [31,397]
Child ability[a]	6.20	5.86 [5.32]	5.74 [5.11]	5.89 [5.43]	5.91 [5.46]	6.01 [5.72]
School quality[b]	7.83	7.55 [7.29]	7.41 [7.20]	8.01 [8.43]	7.88 [7.90]	8.11 [8.76]

Across all students[c]

Per pupil ($)	8,103	7,822 [8,168]	7,901 [8,261]	7,872 [8,201]	7,891 [8,211]	7,932 [8,095]
Household income ($)	34,321	34,321 [34,321]	34,321 [34,321]	34,321 [34,321]	34,321 [34,321]	34,321 [34,321]
Child ability[a]	6.20	6.20 [6.20]	6.20 [6.20]	6.20 [6.20]	6.20 [6.20]	6.20 [6.20]
School quality[b]	7.83	7.84 [7.89]	8.17 [8.32]	8.42 [8.89]	8.02 [8.14]	8.39 [9.07]

[a]The child ability levels are arbitrarily calibrated to lie between 1 and 10.

[b]School quality arises endogenously from the combination of per pupil spending, per pupil household income, and average child ability in the school. For purposes of this calculation, all values are scaled to lie between 0 and 10. While there is thus no natural interpretation for the magnitude of a particular school quality level, we emphasize here the direction and magnitude of change in the variable as we move across the table.

[c]Notes that "all students" here refers to all students who are initially in the public school system before the introduction of vouchers. Therefore, the values in the first column are identical to those for public schools.

TABLE 15.2 Variances under Different Assumptions

	Calibrated Base Model (4.2)		Curriculum Targeting (5.1)		Competition & Bureaucracy (5.2)	
	No Voucher	Base Model	Private Schools	All Schools	Within Dist.	Within & Across Dist.
Across public school students						
Per pupil ($)	1.0	0.97	0.96	0.97	0.97	0.98
		[0.88]	[0.61]	[0.70]	[0.87]	[0.92]
Household income ($)	1.0	0.91	0.89	0.92	0.93	0.95
		[0.90]	[0.68]	[0.73]	[0.89]	[0.91]
Child ability	1.0	0.72	0.78	0.71	0.73	0.74
		[0.67]	[0.56]	[0.53]	[0.70]	[0.70]
School quality[a]	1.0	0.88	0.94	0.69	0.72	0.91
		[0.81]	[0.65]	[0.51]	[0.64]	[0.84]
Across all students[b]						
Per pupil ($)	1.0	0.94	0.93	0.94	0.94	0.95
		[0.90]	[0.81]	[0.83]	[0.88]	[0.89]
Household income ($)	1.0	1.32	1.43	1.31	1.33	1.24
		[1.49]	[1.53]	[1.47]	[1.47]	[1.35]
Child ability	1.0	1.18	1.24	1.19	1.17	1.15
		[1.23]	[1.41]	[1.31]	[1.20]	[1.17]
School quality[a]	1.0	0.99	1.05	0.87	0.82	0.91
		[0.96]	[1.06]	[0.86]	[0.78]	[0.85]
Across school districts						
Household income	1.0	0.71	0.67	0.70	0.71	0.74
		[0.65]	[0.60]	[0.62]	[0.64]	[0.69]
Property values	1.0	0.61	0.56	0.61	0.59	0.64
		[0.55]	[0.49]	[0.53]	[0.51]	[0.58]

Note: in order to ease interpretation, these variance values are scaled in various ways to all equal 1 for the base case of no vouchers. Our emphasis here is therefore not on absolute but rather on relative magnitudes across columns.

First Line: $2,500 full or district-targeted voucher; *Second line:* $5,000 district-targeted voucher.

[a]School quality arises endogenously from the combination of per pupil spending, per pupil household income, and average child ability in the school.

[b]Note that "all students" here refers to all students who are initially in the public school system before the introduction of vouchers.

tunities to increase with the level of vouchers. This does not, however, seem to be the case. In particular, the variance of school quality for those attending public schools decreases (as public school quality falls more in high-income districts than in low-income districts), and the overall variance in educational quality across all students (both public and private) does not change. This is due primarily to the large variance in quality in public schools that exists prior to the introduction of vouchers as well as a decline in the variance of per pupil spending across all students as students now consume quality levels in between those offered previously. The variance in average abilities as well as the variance in average socioeconomic status within schools, on the other hand, increases.

One could argue, then, that vouchers result in household choices that cause a decline in residential stratification and an increase in school stratification, and these facts combine to imply that the overall variance in school quality consumed by all students who currently (pre-vouchers) attend public schools does not change. From the perspective of a court that is attempting to decrease the variance in educational opportunities, this base model therefore suggests that vouchers at least do not contradict that policy goal.[55] Furthermore, access to quality schools for residents of school districts that are deemed inadequate is increased in two distinct ways. First, some households are able to choose private schools under a district-targeted voucher policy. Second, a large fraction of other households are able to access public schools in other districts due to more affordable housing.

Finally, we should note that the limited direct empirical evidence we have on private school formation resulting from school finance policy changes generally supports the predictions of this model. In particular, after rather dramatic changes in school finance in the late 1970s in California, changes that benefited (in spending terms) low-income districts and hurt high-income districts, the number of private schools doubled within a short period of time, with new schools emerging disproportionately in relatively poor districts.[56] Similarly, many of our current private schools can be found in depressed inner cities and are often instrumental in keeping some households in the city.

Voucher Targeting

Our results thus far have profound implications as to how courts concerned about adequacy may wish to design choice-based remedies. Since many of the newly emerging private schools under district-targeted vouchers cater to middle- and high-middle-income households willing to move to find better private schools, much of the impact of these vouchers vanishes when vouchers are targeted to low-income families rather than to underperforming districts. Under vouchers that are targeted only to low-income households, simulations (not reported here) indicate that private schools again only emerge in the poor districts, but now at much slower rates and only at higher levels of vouchers. Such income-based targeting schemes therefore protect wealthier school districts from migration-induced competition while limiting the positive impact of vouchers on poor districts. While enabling some residents of poor school districts to access private schools, they maintain high housing and rental prices in good public school districts and therefore continue to exclude lower-income families from accessing good public schools. Thus, as a remedy to inadequate public schools, district-targeted vouchers are preferable from an economic as well as a legal perspective.[57]

An Unconventional Case for District-Targeted Vouchers

Our results indicate that vouchers are attractive in that they implicitly address at least three of the underlying factors (discussed above) responsible for current inequities. By enabling parents to choose private schools, vouchers allow families to escape the political peculiarities of the system. By removing incentives for high-income individuals to segregate, vouchers introduce a desegregating force through mobility. Moreover, by reducing the premium of housing prices in quality-school districts and raising it in low-quality districts, low-income households are more able to afford to live in better public school districts.

While the results from our simulations may be viewed as desirable from many perspectives, we have thus far offered little direct evidence that vouchers significantly lessen the overall differences in school quality experienced by families or raise overall social value. Rather, we have only considered thus far a model that "stacks the deck" against vouchers by assuming no competitive efficiency effects, no returns to specialization, and no benefit from increased parental involvement, and by assuming a private school market that discriminates severely in terms of peer quality. Yet, even in this "worst case scenario" we find no overall adverse impact of vouchers on the current inequities in the system and some expansion of opportunities for some households trapped in inadequate schools. We now turn to an expansion of the framework.

Deviations from the Base Model

Thus far we have modeled those factors that are important given a fixed institutional setting, but a move toward parental choice through vouchers represents a change in the current institutions governing primary and secondary education. We therefore consider two additional features[58] that might be important in discussing private school competition, features that come closer to what voucher proponents base their argument on. (1) It may be important to understand that children have different strengths and weaknesses and may therefore not benefit in the same way from a particular school.[59] As public and private school populations become more homogeneous, school curricula may then become more specialized in both subject matter and pedagogical approach to better match specific abilities and needs of children. If institutions respond in this fashion, school quality would increase as the variance in abilities within classrooms narrows, contrary to what our base model assumes. (2) Public school bureaucracies, often dominated by various interests such as teachers' unions, may have agendas that are not perfectly aligned with the desires of parents. Thus it may be plausible to assume that the marginal product of educational spending within public schools will rise as competition increases.[60]

We excluded these factors from the base model in part because we wanted to establish a "worst case benchmark" under assumptions commonly used in the scholarly literature and also because it is more difficult to use current data or empirical evidence to effectively calibrate each of the alternative factors. Despite these difficulties, there exists at least some empirical support for each of these propositions, and we suggest it is worthwhile to investigate to what extent such additional factors are likely to influence the lower bound results we have reported previously. We therefore introduce what we consider to be "modest levels" of such effects, and we report them in tables 15.1 and 15.2, again for district-targeted vouchers of $2,500 [and $5,000].

Curriculum Design and Benefits from Specialization

Because we assume in the base model that average peer quality within schools is one determinant of quality, we similarly assume that school specialization, designed to serve narrow bands of abilities, will benefit higher-ability children at the expense of lower-ability children.[61] These assumptions hold in schools in which the curriculum is the same across all students. However, it is likely that schools, especially in the later grades, will compete by attempting to differentiate themselves as "science schools" or "foreign language schools," and that the curriculum in each school will target a school's mission as well as its students' ability levels. Furthermore, there may exist pedagogical advantages from being able to adjust teaching styles, especially in earlier grades, where current private schools have successfully pursued different teaching approaches (e.g., Catholic and Montessori schools). We therefore now consider the implications of school specialization on our simulation results, and we report these in the next columns of tables 15.1 and 15.2. First we assume that only private schools target their curriculum and take advantage of specialization, and then we proceed to assuming that similar targeting will emerge in public schools as they become more homogeneous.[62]

In each case, vouchers still give rise to migration effects similar to those reported in the base model, but implications for the improvement of educational opportunities now differ. If only private schools are assumed to be responsive in reforming their curriculum, the model predicts an increase in the fraction of households choosing private schools in the presence of vouchers (from 14 to 19 percent for a $2,500 voucher) and a further decline in average school quality within the public system (as more "high peer quality" children leave public schools). Since private schools are now more effective, however, overall school quality rises despite the decrease in the quality of the public system, as does the variance in school quality across all students. When public schools are assumed to also respond, greater homogeneity in the public school population (particularly in the poor district) allows resources to be directed more precisely to more sharply defined needs, causing public schools to become more competitive, private school attendance to rise less sharply, and the variance of school quality to decline. Greater homogeneity for both public and private schools under a voucher system therefore may have positive efficiency and equity implications.

Competitive Forces and Bureaucracy

The argument (explored above) that greater homogeneity may allow for better *matching* of resources with abilities is quite different, however, from the more traditional notion that private school competition may cause more efficient *utilization* of resources in public schools. While we lack conclusive evidence due to limited data, there does exist suggestive evidence on the inefficiency of public schools in general,[63] the likely impact of its bureaucratic and union- dominated governance structure,[64] and the positive correlation between competition and school performance in the absence of vouchers.[65] We therefore proceed to include in the base model (with the original model of ability effects) a parameter specifying the marginal productivity of a dollar in public schools as an increasing function of the fraction of children attending private schools. While we have little guidance from the empirical literature as to what value such a parameter should take, the mere inclusion of a modest competitive effect will indicate at least the qualitative change in the model's prediction such an effect would entail. Furthermore, it is unclear whether the competitive impact of private schools would be limited to the school district in which the private schools arise. Given the emphasis we have placed on the potential of voucher-induced mobility, it seems plausible that competitive effects spill over into other districts, although they are likely to be less pronounced in districts that do not actually lose student population but only acquire a different mix of students. In tables 15.1 and 15.2, we report results for both kinds of competitive effects.

If the effects are only local, public school quality continues to decline modestly in the wealthier districts of the model (as high-peer-quality households exit the system to move to good neighborhoods within poorer districts), but it rises in the poor district despite the exit of high-peer-quality households and despite the absence of the kinds of curriculum changes modeled in the previous section. This causes a slight decline in the speed with which public school attendees from the poor district exit the system, and thus causes a larger fraction of private school attendees to be composed of households that previously chose public schools in other districts. It furthermore causes the equity outlook for vouchers to improve as now the variance in quality among public school students as well as among all students declines. If, on the other hand, the competitive effect is assumed to spill over into other districts that do not have additional private schools, overall public school quality improves further (as public schools in middle- and high-wealth districts now also improve their marginal product of school resources) while the variance in school quality does not decline as much.

Conclusion

Until recently, school finance reform and school choice have been viewed quite separately, with the former arising primarily in the context of court challenges and the latter conducted in small public and private policy experiments. We acknowledge that, in a perfect world, court decisions may not be the appropriate vehicle for articulating or implementing either policy. However, given the already substantial involvement of the courts in the education reform policy debate, we argue that it may be helpful for courts to find ways to link school finance and school choice proposals in their judicial remedies. Specifically, we propose that judicial remedies flowing from successful challenges to the adequacy of school finance systems should direct any increased educational funding in the form of vouchers to the families of those schoolchildren who are served by inadequate schools rather than to the very schools that have failed to deliver adequate educational services. Our argument, of course, rests on the assumption that such choice proposals are likely to improve equity of educational opportunities and raise social net value.

To this end, we test these assumptions' efficacy and the likely equity and efficiency implications of vouchers in the context of an economic model consistent with current stylized facts on existing inequities and calibrated to available data. Our model suggests that our proposed district-targeted voucher initiatives would have only minor impacts on the overall level and distribution of educational opportunities in a system like that of New York City under the worst-case scenario (the base model) and potentially large positive impacts for both equity and efficiency of the entire educational system under the more optimistic assumptions. Note again, however, just how pessimistic the base model is: It includes none of the positive features generally predicted by proponents of vouchers, while incorporating a quite unflattering portrayal of private schools as skimming institutions aimed primarily at those with income or ability. With the modification of any one of these features, district-targeted voucher systems begin to have quite favorable implications for both efficiency and equity. We believe there is at least some credible evidence that such positive effects exist and hope that future research will be aimed at quantifying them more cleanly than we are able to do with current data. Overall, however, the case for expanding choice in places like New York appears quite favorable and consistent with emerging judicial standards.

NOTES

1. The landmark Kentucky decision, *Rose v. Council for a Better Education*, 790 S.W.2d 186 (Ky. 1989), which helped usher in the transition from equity- to adequacy-based school finance court decisions, is typical of adequacy-based court decisions in that it sought (successfully) to increase educational spending in Kentucky. See, for example, Kern Alexander, "The Common School Ideal and the Limits of Legislative Authority: The Kentucky Case," *Harvard Journal on Legislation* 28 (1991).

2. See Michael Heise, "Equal Educational Opportunity, Hollow Victories, and the Demise of School Finance Equity Theory: An Empirical Perspective and Alternative Explanation," *Georgia Law Review* 32 (1998), for a discussion and evidence on the efficacy of state supreme court decisions in the school finance area.

3. Other countries, like Chile, have more experience with vouchers, but the many other differences between Chile and the United States make direct inferences from this experience problematic. See, for example, Martin Carnoy and Patrick McEwan, "The Effects of Competition from Private Schools on Achievement: A Longitudinal Analysis of Chilean Schools," Stanford University working paper, 1997.

4. For one example of a collection of differing viewpoints on issues relating to school choice policy, see Edith Rasell and Richard Rothstein, eds., *School Choice: Examining the Evidence* (Washington, D.C.: Economic Policy Institute, 1993).

5. See, for example, Thomas Nechyba and Robert P. Strauss, "Community Choice and Local Public Services: A Discrete Choice Approach," *Regional Science and Urban Economics* 28 (1998), and references therein.

6. See, for example, Dennis Epple and Richard Romano, "Competition between Private and Public Schools, Vouchers, and Peer-Group Effects," *American Economic Review* 88 (1998), and Charles Manski, "Educational Choice (Vouchers) and Social Mobility," *Economics of Education Review* 11 (1992).

7. See, for example, William E. Thro, "Judicial Analysis during the Third Wave of School Finance Litigation: The Massachusetts Decision as a Model," *Boston College Law Review* 35 (1994); Michael Heise, "State Constitutions, School Finance Litigation, and the 'Third Wave': From Equity to Adequacy," *Temple Law Review* 68, no. 3 (1995).

8. 487 P.2d 1241 (Cal. 1971), *cert. denied*, 432 U.S. 907 (1977).

9. 411 U.S. 1 (1973).

10. 303 A.2d 273 (N.J. 1973), *cert. denied*, 414 U.S. 976 (1977).

11. *Rose v. Council for Better Education, Inc.*, 790 S.W.2d 186 (KY 1990) is frequently pointed to as the decision signaling the emergence of the third wave.

12. See Heise, "Equal Educational Opportunity, Hollow Victories, and the Demise of School Finance Equity Theory," for a brief description.

13. One result is the potential for what some commentators refer to as "municipal overburden." See Hon. Leon D. Lazer, "New York Public School Financing Litigation," *Touro Law Review* 14, no. 3 (1998): 677n.

14. Ibid., p. 678n.

15. N.Y. Const. art. 11, § 1. The clause reads, in pertinent part, "The legislature shall provide for the maintenance and support of a system of free common-schools, where-in all the children of this state may be educated." Ibid.

16. See, for example, Thro, "Judicial Analysis during the Third Wave of School Finance Litigation," pp. 605–8, for a description of the four categories (or tiers) of state education clauses.

17. *Levittown v. Nyquist*, 439 N.E.2d 359 (1982) began in 1974. Ibid., p. 361.

18. Lazer, "New York Public School Financing Litigation," p. 682.

19. *Levittown School District v. Nyquist*, 439 N.E.2d 359 (1982).

20. Ibid., p. 369.

21. *Reform Educational Financing Inequities Today v. Cuomo*, 655 N.E.2d 661 (1995)[hereinafter "*REFIT*"].

22. *REFIT*, 655 N.E.2d 647 (1995).

23. *Campaign for Fiscal Equity v. State of New York*, 655 N.E.2d 661 (1995)[hereinafter "*CFE*"].

24. Ibid.

25. See chapter 13.

26. For a description of one of New York City's largest privately funded school choice programs see Paul T. Hill, "Private Vouchers in New York City: The Student-Sponsor Partnership Program," in *Private Vouchers*, ed. Terry M. Moe (Stanford: Hoover Institution, 1995), pp. 120- 35.

27. See chapter 14.

28. See Nina H. Shokraii and Sarah E. Youssef, *School Choice Programs: What's Happening in the States* (Washington, D.C.: Heritage, 1998), pp. 106–11.

29. In 1989, for example, the state's education commissioner proposed a pilot program of publicly funded vouchers, but the proposal quickly died at the behest of Governor Cuomo and other public officials. See Sol Stern, "The School Reform That Dares Not Speak Its Name," *City Journal* 6 (1996). In 1998 Mayor Giuliani proposed an experimental plan for low-income children, but he was unable to garner legislative support for its enactment.

30. See Greg D. Andres, "Private School Voucher Remedies in Education Cases," *University of Chicago Law Review* 62, no. 2 (1995), for a brief discussion of two cases that advance a similar argument. See also Dominick Cirelli Jr., "Utilizing School Voucher Programs to Remedy School Financing Problems," *Akron Law Review* 30 (1997); Michael Heise, "Equal Educational Opportunity and Constitutional Theory: Preliminary Thoughts on the Role of School Choice and the Autonomy

Principle," *Journal of Law and Politics* 14 (1998). Also, see Carol Abrams, John E. Coons, and Stephen D. Sugarman, "School Integration through Carrots, Not Sticks," *Theory into Practice* 18 (1978).

31. For a general discussion, see Nathan Glazer, "Towards an Imperial Judiciary?" *Public Interest* 42 (1975); Michael Heise, "The Courts vs. Educational Standards," *Public Interest* 120 (1995).

32. See, for example, Robert Inman and Daniel Rubinfeld, "The Judicial Pursuit of Local Fiscal Equity," *Harvard Law Review* 92 (1979).

33. See Patrick Bayer, "The Role of Family Characteristics in Determining the Demand for School Quality," Stanford University working paper, 1998, for empirical evidence suggesting that low-income households are systematically priced out of districts with high-quality schools.

34. See Eric Hanushek, "The Economics of Schooling: Production and Efficiency in Public Schools," *Journal of Economic Literature* 24 (1986), who provides an extensive review of this literature. For a recent debate on the marginal product of additional school resources, see Eric Hanushek, "Conclusions and Controversies about the Effectiveness of School Resources," *Federal Reserve Board of NY Policy Review* 4 (1998), and Alan Krueger, "Reassessing the View that American Schools are Broken," *Federal Reserve Board of NY Policy Review* 4 (1998). Also, see Thomas Nechyba, "Public School Finance in a General Equilibrium Tiebout World: Equalization Programs, Peer Effects, and Private School Vouchers," NBER working paper, 1996, for illustrations of how state spending equalization is unlikely to produce equality in school quality. To acknowledge that this point is deeply disputed is to acknowledge the obvious. For other perspectives see Larry V. Hedges et al., "Does Money Matter? A Meta-Analysis of Studies of the Effects of Differential School Inputs on Student Outcomes," *Educational Researcher* 23, no. 3 (1994); Rob Greenwald et al., "The Effect of School Resources on Student Achievement," *Review of Educational Research* 66, no. 3 (1996).

35. There exists a long literature on peer effects within classrooms. For examples, further references, and problems with this literature, see Charles Manski, "Identification of Endogenous Social Effects," *Review of Economic Studies* 60 (1993); William Evans and Robert Schwab, "Measuring Peer Group Effects: A Study of Teenage Behavior," *Journal of Political Economy* 100 (1992); C. Link and J. Mulligan, "Classmates' Effects on Black Student Achievement in Public School Classrooms," *Economics of Education Review* 10 (1991); Richard Arnott and J. Rowse, "Peer Group Effects and Educational Attainment," *Journal of Public Economics* 32 (1987); Vernon Henderson, Peter Mieszkowski, and Y. Sauvageau, "Peer Group Effects and Educational Production Functions," *Journal of Public Economics* 10 (1978); A. Summers and B. Wolfe, "Do Schools Make a Difference?" *American Economic Review* 67 (1977).

36. See Robert McMillan, "Parental Involvement and Competition: An Empirical Analysis of the Determinants of Public School Quality," Stanford University working paper, 1998.

37. See Gary Solon, "Intergenerational Income Mobility in the United States," *American Economic Review* 82 (1992), and David Zimmerman, "Regression toward Mediocrity in Economic Stature," *American Economic Review* 82 (1992).

38. See table 4 in Thomas Nechyba, "School Finance Induced Migration and Stratification Patterns: The Impact of Private School Vouchers," *Journal of Public Eco-*

nomic Theory 1 (1999). In addition, the rise of a large "education establishment" dominated by teachers' unions may cause public schools to be inefficient overall. This, however, contributes less to differences across schools and more to overall inefficiency of the public school sector. See, for example, William Evers, *What's Gone Wrong in America's Classrooms* (Stanford: Hoover Institution Press, 1997). We will take up some related issues in a later section of the chapter.

39. Courts have attempted to force communities to provide low-income housing (see, for example, *Southern Burlington County NAACP v. Township of Mt. Laurel*, 67 N.J. 151,336 A.2d, appeal dismissed, 423 U.S. 808 [1975]), but these efforts are likely to meet with limited success, especially in well-developed areas in which housing stocks are difficult to alter (such as in New York City).

40. A detailed theoretical analysis of some of the properties of our model can be found in Thomas Nechyba, "Existence of Equilibrium and Stratification in Local and Hierarchical Public Goods Economies with Property Taxes and Voting," *Economic Theory* 10 (1997); Thomas Nechyba, "Local Property and State Income Taxes: The Role of Interjurisdictional Competition and Collusion," *Journal of Political Economy* 105 (1997); Thomas Nechyba, "A Computable General Equilibrium Model of Intergovernmental Aid," *Journal of Public Economics* 62 (1996); Thomas Nechyba, "Public School Finance and Vouchers in a General Equilibrium Tiebout World," *Proceedings of the 90th Annual Conference of the National Tax Association* (1999); Thomas Nechyba, "School Finance Induced Migration Patterns: The Impact of Private School Vouchers," *Journal of Public Economic Theory* 1 (1999); and Thomas Nechyba, "Mobility, Targeting, and Private School Vouchers," *American Economic Review* (2000, forthcoming).

41. We should note here that "districts" in the model are assumed to set their own funding levels through a political process by which the median voter's most preferred spending level is implemented within the district. While this is a good representation of how spending is often determined in many districts in New York State, it may not be representative of the process in New York City, where education funding across the city is determined by a central authority. However, there is a political process at work within the city government that allocates resources, and strong prior evidence suggests that actual per pupil funding within a school district in New York City is dependent on the political power of that district, which in turn depends on local constituent preferences (see, for example, Inman and Rubinfeld, "The Judicial Pursuit of Local Fiscal Equity," for a description of this process). Thus, in the absence of a model of how New York City government operates, we continue using the local median voter model as an approximation of that process.

42. Note that local taxes are assumed to be on property while New Yorkers also pay a city income tax. A replication of the simulations using income taxes in place of property taxes, however, yields qualitatively similar results.

43. Throughout this model we assume that parents have to send their children to the school in the jurisdiction (within the city) in which they reside. While this is nominally different from New York City's policy of allowing residents to send their children to public schools anywhere in the city, we have argued that it is in practice quite realistic, given that better public schools tend to claim capacity constraints that severely limit the ability of parents to actually choose good schools outside their jurisdiction.

44. See note 40 on the series of technical papers by Nechyba.

45. Data on local incomes and housing prices as well as public school features can be found in National Center for Education Statistics, *School District Data Book v. 1.0* (Washington, D.C.: U.S. Department of Education, 1995); and Bureau of the Census, *1990 Census of Population and Housing* (Washington, D.C.: Bureau of the Census, 1992). Information on specific spending levels within public schools in particular jurisdictions of New York City, however, is difficult to obtain because of the unified nature of New York City's school financing. Therefore, we have used data from other districts in New York State to approximate the likely levels of public spending within jurisdictions. These data are readily available in the sources cited above.

46. It is here that we use data on school districts outside New York City for which data on spending per pupil is more readily available. Thus the preference parameter for school spending is set using New York State data.

47. This empirical correlation has been shown to lie between 0 and 0.4. See Solon, "Intergenerational Income Mobility in the United States," and Zimmerman, "Regression toward Mediocrity in Economic Stature."

48. These data are somewhat difficult to obtain for the urban district of New York City, but we use data from districts elsewhere in the New York area to infer the spending relationships more precisely.

49. We are particularly grateful to Henry Olson for pointing out many of these possible misconceptions.

50. See Bayer, "The Role of Family Characteristics in Determining the Demand for School Quality."

51. See Dennis Epple and Holger Sieg, "Estimating Equilibrium Models of Local Jurisdictions," *Journal of Political Economy* 107 (1999).

52. Such equilibria often also require the presence of explicit or implicit exclusionary zoning. See Bruce Hamilton, "Zoning and Property Taxes in a System of Local Governments," *Urban Studies* 12 (1975); and William Fischel, "Property Taxation and the Tiebout Model: Evidence for the Benefit View from Zoning and Voting," *Journal of Economic Literature* 30 (1992).

53. See Eric Hanushek and John Quigley, "An Explicit Model of Intrametropolitan Mobility," *Land Economics* 54 (1978); and Yannis Ioannides, "Residential Mobility and Housing Tenure Choice," *Regional Science and Urban Economics* 17 (1987).

54. Given that most households (in New York) live close to different public school districts and not immediately next to their jobs, job locations are unlikely to play an important role in this decision. In fact, the urban economics literature (see, for example, Jan Brueckner, "Spatial Mismatch: An Equilibrium Analysis," *Regional Science and Urban Economics* 27 (1997), and references therein) has long been puzzled by the relative nonconformity of job and residential locations within urban areas, much of which can probably be explained by school district choices.

55. These results are in stark contrast to results our model gives in the absence of mobility by households. While such lack of mobility causes vouchers to give rise to significantly fewer private schools, these private schools again emerge in the poorest districts. Now, however, there is little benefit for the remaining residents of the poor districts. Ignoring general equilibrium mobility effects therefore

often causes many researchers to overstate adverse equity implications of voucher policies.

56. See Thomas Downes and Shane Greenstein, "Entry into the School Market: How Is the Behavior of Private Suppliers Influenced by Public Sector Decisions?" Tufts University working paper, 1997.

57. These issues are explored in detail in Nechyba, "Mobility, Targeting, and Private School Vouchers."

58. In a previous and lengthier version of this chapter, we also included a third effect that distinguished the impact of parental monitoring under different levels of competition and school size. Due to space considerations, we do not report these here, but the inclusion of such effects has impacts similar to those of the two effects we discuss here.

59. A recent illustration of this involves the confusing and confused debate over bilingual education in California. For a sense of the confusion in the current academic literature, see the references on peer effects cited previously. Also see Thomas Nechyba, "A New Look at Peer Effects: Implications for School Design and School Choice," Stanford University working paper in progress (1998), for a detailed analysis of the debate on peer effects.

60. See J. Chubb and Terry Moe, *Politics, Markets, and America's Schools* (Washington, D.C.: Brookings Institution, 1990), for a thorough discussion on this, and see Caroline Hoxby, "How Teachers' Unions Affect Education Production," *Quarterly Journal of Economics* 111 (1996), for empirical evidence on the impact of unionization.

61. As pointed out in note 35, much disagreement exists regarding the empirical nature of peer effects. Some of this disagreement may well be due to the fact that different studies utilize quite different data sets, and peer effects may well depend on the underlying institutional structure of the systems that are analyzed.

62. To be slightly more precise, we alter in these simulations the nature of the impact of peer quality by assuming that a combination of the average peer quality and the variance of peer quality within schools matters for school quality. Thus school quality in these simulations is assumed to be positively correlated with average peer quality (as before) *and* negatively correlated with the variance. We interpret the degree to which the variance enters school quality as the degree of targeting of curricula. In the simulations here, we assume that two-thirds of school quality is determined through the variance channel. Furthermore, for ease of comparison, we scale the school quality output function in such a way as to produce the same level of school quality in the public system before vouchers as we reported in the no-voucher column of the table.

63. See, for example, Hanushek, "The Economics of Schooling: Production and Efficiency in Public Schools."

64. See, for example, Chubb and Moe, *Politics, Markets, and America's Schools,* and Hoxby, "How Teachers' Unions Affect Education Production."

65. See Caroline Hoxby, "Do Private Schools Provide Competition for Public Schools?" NBER working paper 4978 (1994). Also, for different interpretations of the data regarding the relative performance of private schools and public schools, see Derek Neal, "The Effect of Catholic Secondary Schooling on Educational Achievement," *Journal of Labor Economics* 15 (1997); and David Figlio and Joe Stone,

"School Choice and Student Performance: Are Private Schools Really Better?," University of Oregon working paper, 1997. Finally, positive competitive effects are not without controversy, as some researchers have found a negative competitive effect (which may, however, be a skimming effect rather than a negative competitive effect)—see McMillan, "Parental Involvement and Competition."

Index